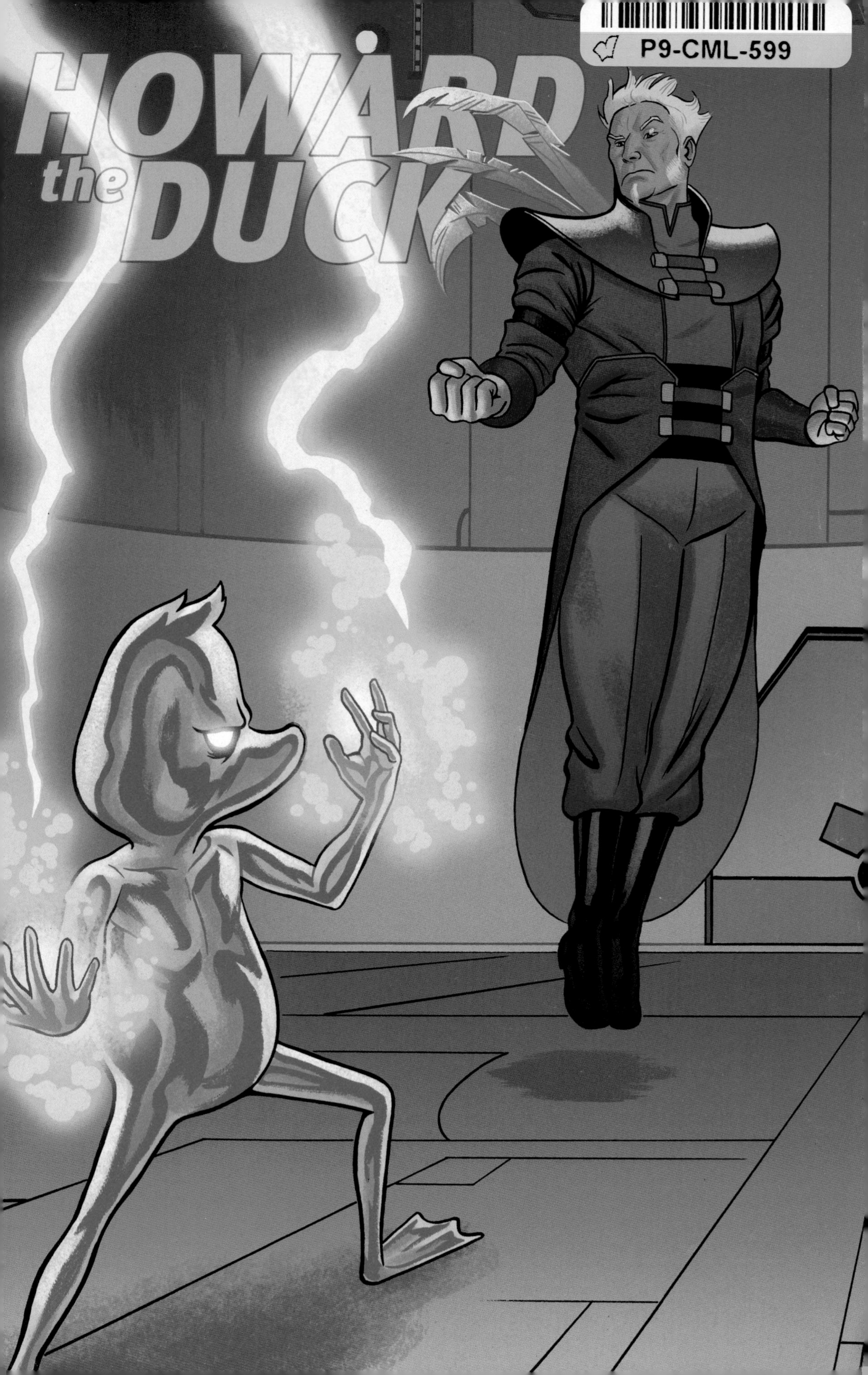
HOWARD
the DUCK

HOWARD the DUCK

DUCK HUNT

WRITER
CHIP ZDARSKY
WITH RYAN NORTH (#6)

PENCILER
JOE QUINONES
(#1 & #3-6)

INKERS
JOE RIVERA
(#1 & #3-6)
WITH RICK MAGYAR (#4),
GORAN SUDŽUKA (#5),
MARK DEERING (#6)
& JOE QUINONES (#6)

COLORISTS
JOE QUINONES
(#1 & #3-6)
WITH JORDAN GIBSON (#5-6)

ARTIST/COLORIST
VERONICA FISH
(#2)

COVER ART
JOE QUINONES
WITH KEVIN WADA (#4) &
ERICA HENDERSON (#6)

THE UNBEATABLE SQUIRREL GIRL #6

WRITER
RYAN NORTH
WITH CHIP ZDARSKY

ARTIST
ERICA HENDERSON

TRADING CARD ART
CHIP ZDARSKY

VAN ART
JOE QUINONES

COLOR ART
RICO RENZI

COVER ART
ERICA HENDERSON
WITH JOE QUINONES

LETTERER
VC'S TRAVIS LANHAM

ASSISTANT EDITORS
CHRIS ROBINSON
WITH CHARLES BEACHAM
(HOWARD THE DUCK #6)

EDITOR
WIL MOSS

HOWARD THE DUCK CREATED BY STEVE GERBER & VAL MAYERIK

COLLECTION EDITOR: JENNIFER GRÜNWALD
ASSOCIATE EDITOR: SARAH BRUNSTAD
ASSOCIATE MANAGING EDITOR: ALEX STARBUCK
EDITOR, SPECIAL PROJECTS: MARK D. BEAZLEY

VP, PRODUCTION & SPECIAL PROJECTS: JEFF YOUNGQUIST
SVP PRINT, SALES & MARKETING: DAVID GABRIEL
BOOK DESIGNER: JAY BOWEN

EDITOR IN CHIEF: AXEL ALONSO
CHIEF CREATIVE OFFICER: JOE QUESADA
PUBLISHER: DAN BUCKLEY
EXECUTIVE PRODUCER: ALAN FINE

HOWARD THE DUCK VOL. 1: DUCK HUNT. Contains material originally published in magazine form as HOWARD THE DUCK #1-6 and THE UNBEATABLE SQUIRREL GIRL #6. First printing 2016. ISBN# 978-0-7851-9938-0. Published by MARVEL WORLDWIDE, INC., a subsidiary of MARVEL ENTERTAINMENT, LLC. OFFICE OF PUBLICATION: 135 West 50th Street, New York, NY 10020. Copyright © 2016 MARVEL No similarity between any of t names, characters, persons, and/or institutions in this magazine with those of any living or dead person or institution is intended, and any such similarity which may exist is purely coincidental. **Printed in the U.S.A.** AL FINE, President, Marvel Entertainment; DAN BUCKLEY, President, TV, Publishing & Brand Management; JOE QUESADA, Chief Creative Officer; TOM BREVOORT, SVP of Publishing; DAVID BOGART, SVP of Business Affa & Operations, Publishing & Partnership; C.B. CEBULSKI, VP of Brand Management & Development, Asia; DAVID GABRIEL, SVP of Sales & Marketing, Publishing; JEFF YOUNGQUIST, VP of Production & Special Projec DAN CARR, Executive Director of Publishing Technology; ALEX MORALES, Director of Publishing Operations; SUSAN CRESPI, Production Manager; STAN LEE, Chairman Emeritus. For information regarding advertising Marvel Comics or on Marvel.com, please contact Vit DeBellis, Integrated Sales Manager, at vdebellis@marvel.com. For Marvel subscription inquiries, please call 888-511-5480. **Manufactured between 3/18/2016 a** 4/25/2016 by R.R. DONNELLEY, INC., SALEM, VA, USA.

10 9 8 7 6 5 4 3 2 1

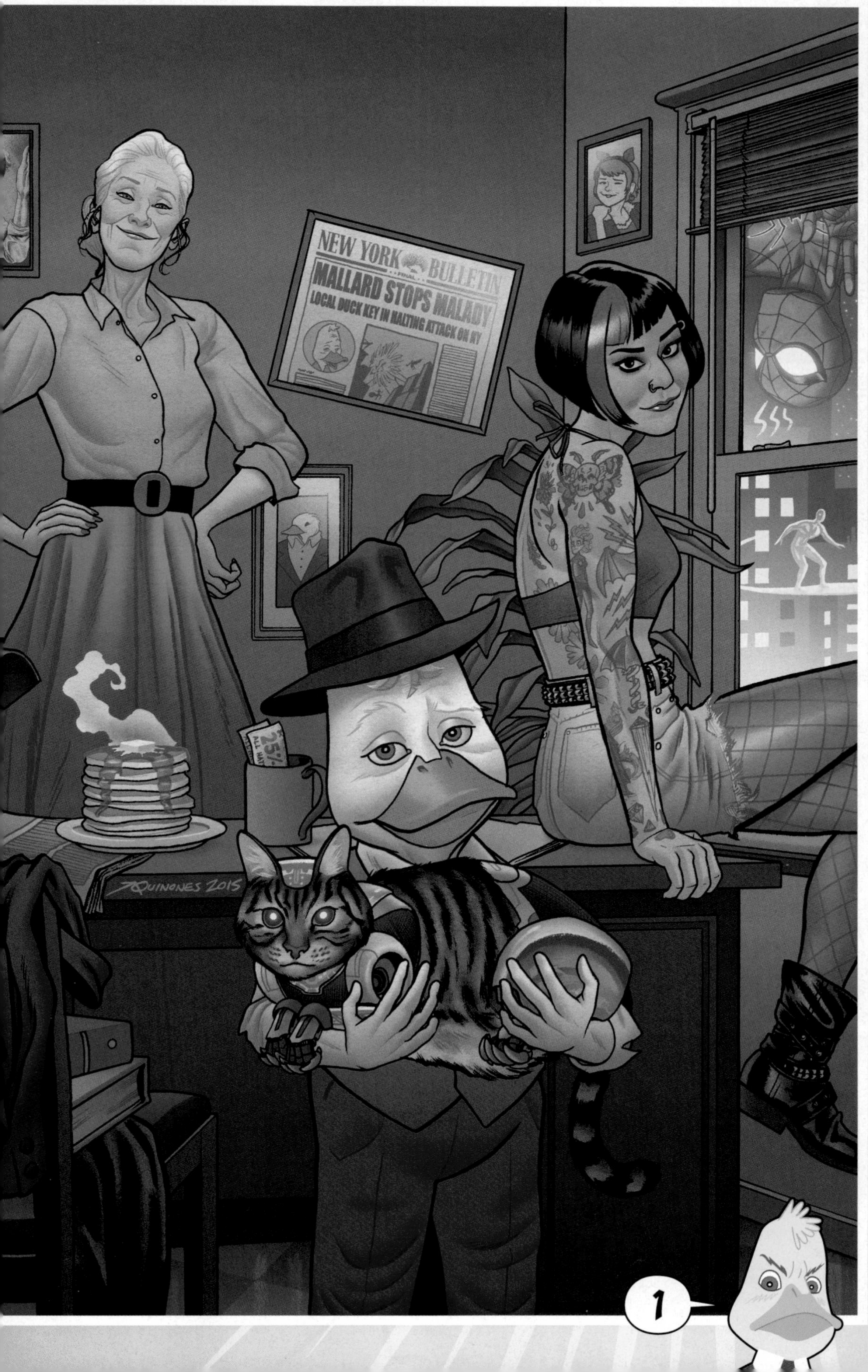
NEW YORK BULLETIN
FINAL
MALLARD STOPS MALADY
LOCAL DUCK KEY IN HALTING ATTACK ON NY
25¢
JQUINONES 2015
1

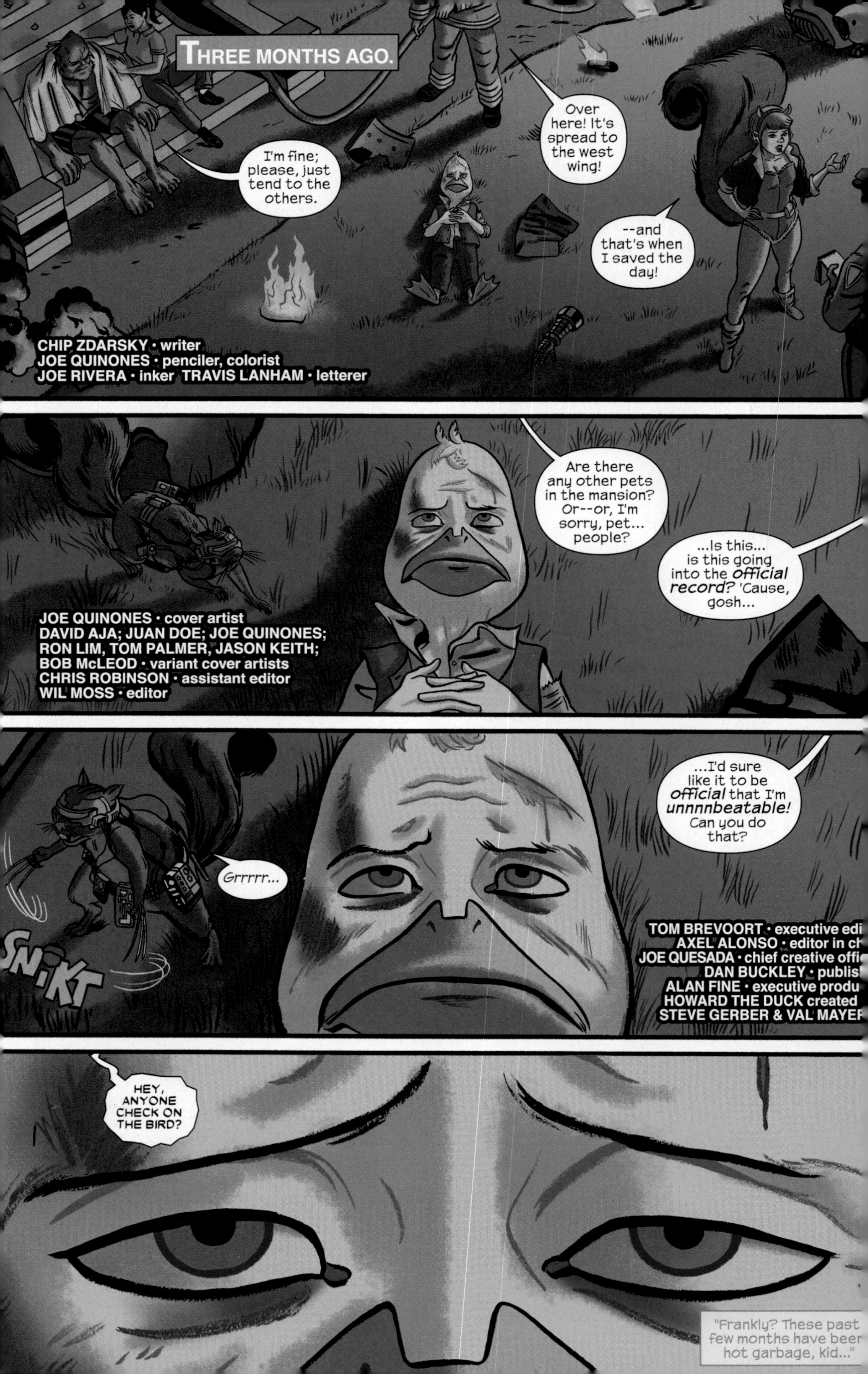
THREE MONTHS AGO.
I'm fine; please, just tend to the others.
Over here! It's spread to the west wing!
--and that's when I saved the day!
CHIP ZDARSKY • writer
JOE QUINONES • penciler, colorist
JOE RIVERA • inker TRAVIS LANHAM • letterer
Are there any other pets in the mansion? Or--or, I'm sorry, pet... people?
...Is this... is this going into the *official record?* 'Cause, gosh...
JOE QUINONES • cover artist
DAVID AJA; JUAN DOE; JOE QUINONES;
RON LIM, TOM PALMER, JASON KEITH;
BOB McLEOD • variant cover artists
CHRIS ROBINSON • assistant editor
WIL MOSS • editor
...I'd sure like it to be *official* that I'm *unnnnbeatable!* Can you do that?
Grrrrr...
SNIKT
TOM BREVOORT • executive edi
AXEL ALONSO • editor in ch
JOE QUESADA • chief creative offi
DAN BUCKLEY • publis
ALAN FINE • executive produ
HOWARD THE DUCK created
STEVE GERBER & VAL MAYER
HEY, ANYONE CHECK ON THE BIRD?
"Frankly? These past few months have been hot garbage, kid..."

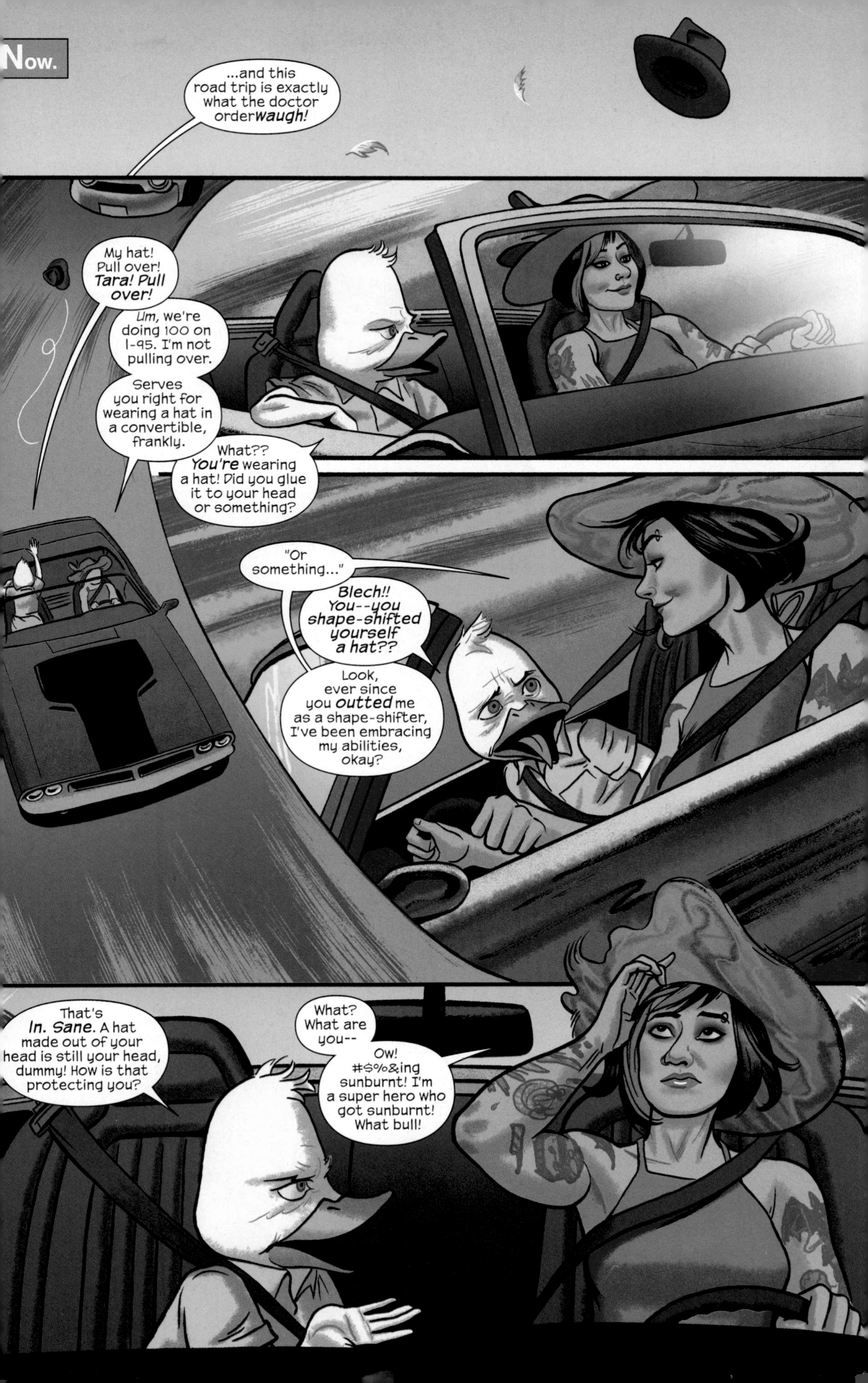
Now.
...and this road trip is exactly what the doctor orderwaugh!
My hat! Pull over! Tara! Pull over!
Um, we're doing 100 on I-95. I'm not pulling over.
Serves you right for wearing a hat in a convertible, frankly.
What?? You're wearing a hat! Did you glue it to your head or something?
"Or something..."
Blech!! You--you shape-shifted yourself a hat??
Look, ever since you outted me as a shape-shifter, I've been embracing my abilities, okay?
That's In. Sane. A hat made out of your head is still your head, dummy! How is that protecting you?
What? What are you--
Ow! #$%&ing sunburnt! I'm a super hero who got sunburnt! What bull!

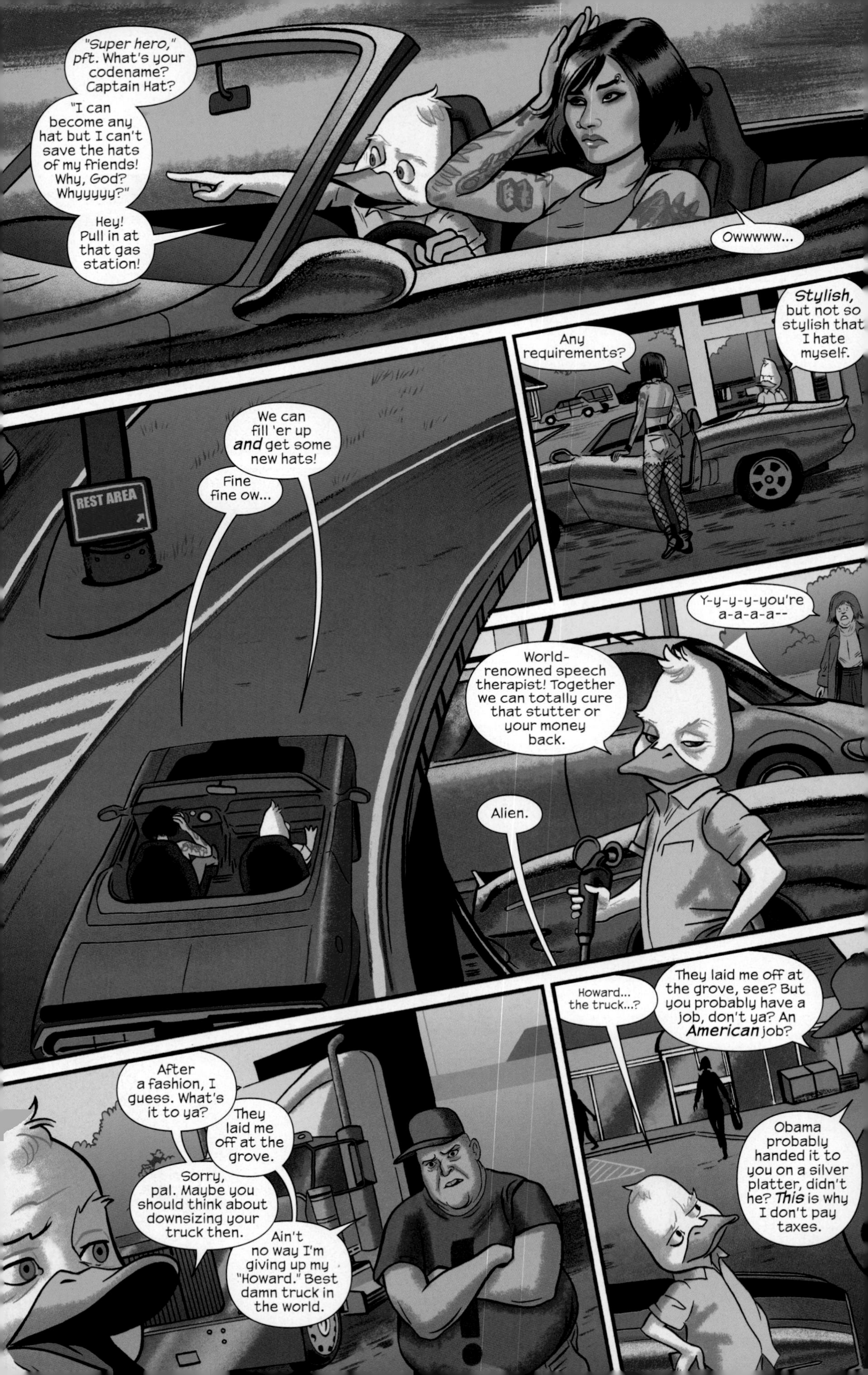

"Super hero," pft. What's your codename? Captain Hat?
"I can become any hat but I can't save the hats of my friends! Why, God? Whyyyyy?"
Hey! Pull in at that gas station!
Owwwww...
REST AREA
We can fill 'er up and get some new hats!
Fine fine ow...
Any requirements?
Stylish, but not so stylish that I hate myself.
Y-y-y-you're a-a-a-a--
World-renowned speech therapist! Together we can totally cure that stutter or your money back.
Alien.
Howard... the truck...?
They laid me off at the grove, see? But you probably have a job, don't ya? An American job?
After a fashion, I guess. What's it to ya?
They laid me off at the grove.
Sorry, pal. Maybe you should think about downsizing your truck then.
Ain't no way I'm giving up my "Howard." Best damn truck in the world.
Obama probably handed it to you on a silver platter, didn't he? This is why I don't pay taxes.

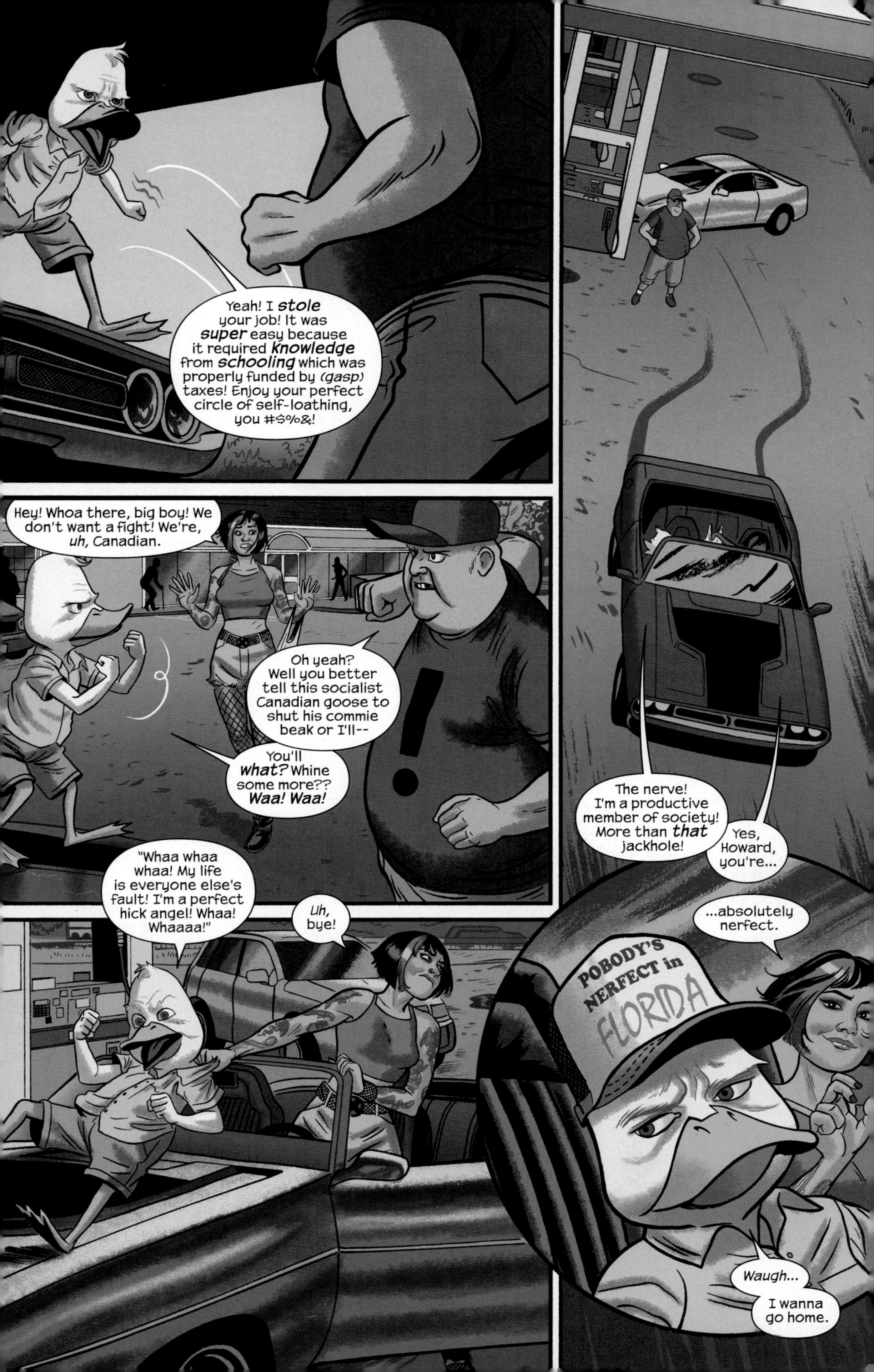
Yeah! I stole your job! It was super easy because it required knowledge from schooling which was properly funded by (gasp) taxes! Enjoy your perfect circle of self-loathing, you #$%&!
Hey! Whoa there, big boy! We don't want a fight! We're, uh, Canadian.
Oh yeah? Well you better tell this socialist Canadian goose to shut his commie beak or I'll--
You'll what? Whine some more?? Waa! Waa!
"Whaa whaa whaa! My life is everyone else's fault! I'm a perfect hick angel! Whaa! Whaaaa!"
Uh, bye!
The nerve! I'm a productive member of society! More than that jackhole!
Yes, Howard, you're...
...absolutely nerfect.
POBODY'S NERFECT in FLORIDA
Waugh...
I wanna go home.

I wanna go home.

Yes, I know, dear. But your afternoon *is* fairly full.

At one, you have Coach Reynolds, who insists his opposing basketball team contains mutants.

At two, you need to go to City Hall to determine if Central Park is an "eternal haven for vampires who steal pets."

And at three, you need to meet with The Centre For Radioactive Superhumans to see if complaints are--

Yeah, yeah...

...I know what I *have* to do. And you've been a great help around here, Aunt May, really. I don't know how I ran this private eye biz without you, but I'm just...tired.

Can't I pet Biggs all day instead?

PURR

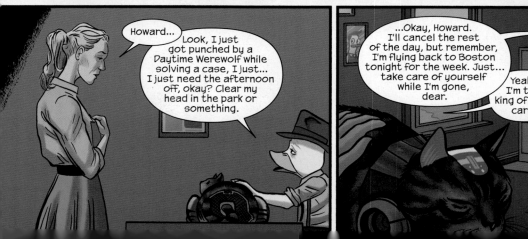

Howard...

Look, I just got punched by a Daytime Werewolf while solving a case, I just... I just need the afternoon off, okay? Clear my head in the park or something.

...Okay, Howard. I'll cancel the rest of the day, but remember, I'm flying back to Boston tonight for the week. Just... take care of yourself while I'm gone, dear.

Yeah, I'm the king of self-care.

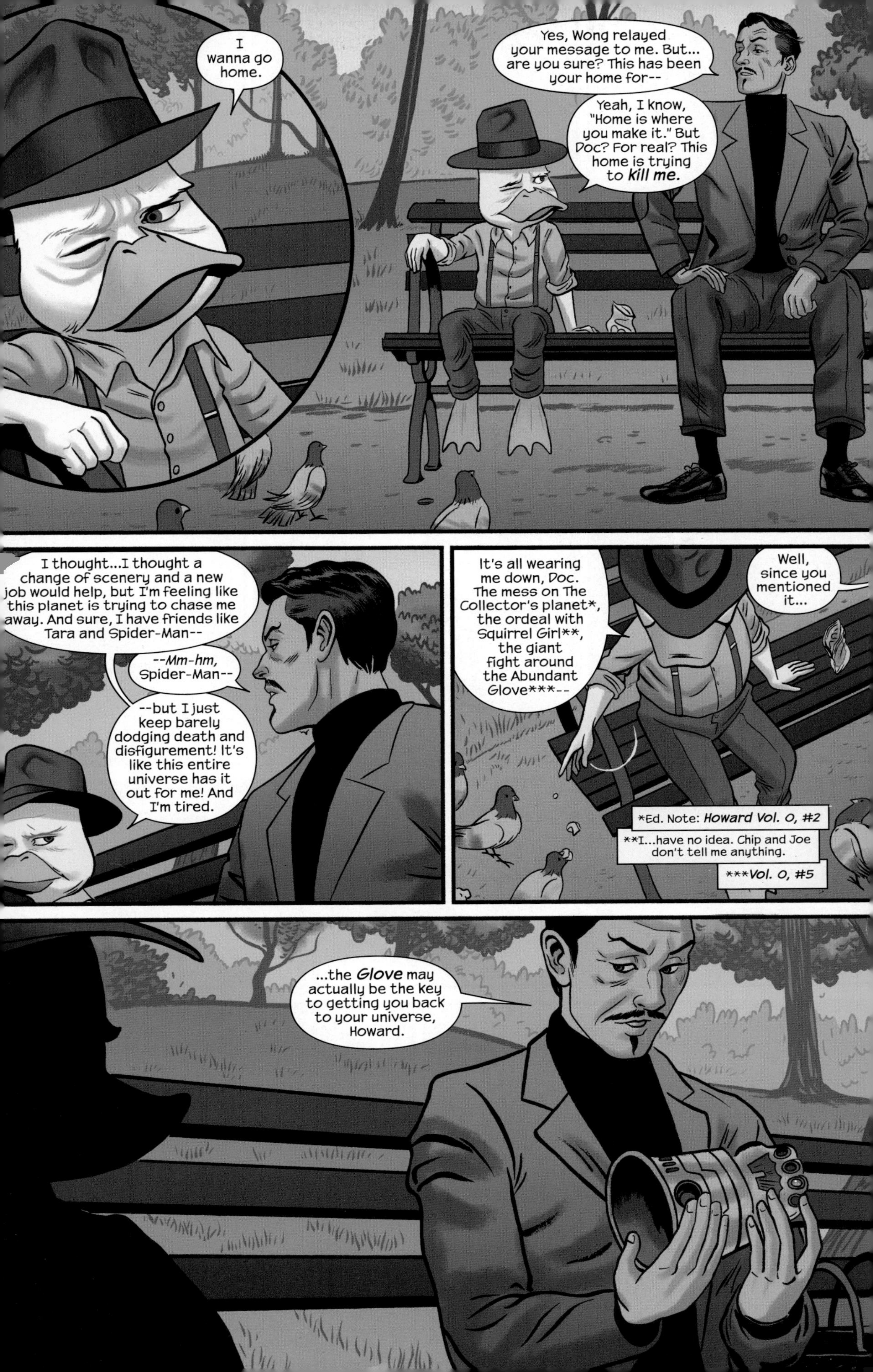
I wanna go home.
Yes, Wong relayed your message to me. But... are you sure? This has been your home for--
Yeah, I know, "Home is where you make it." But Doc? For real? This home is trying to *kill me.*
I thought...I thought a change of scenery and a new job would help, but I'm feeling like this planet is trying to chase me away. And sure, I have friends like Tara and Spider-Man--
--*Mm-hm,* Spider-Man--
--but I just keep barely dodging death and disfigurement! It's like this entire universe has it out for me! And I'm tired.
It's all wearing me down, Doc. The mess on The Collector's planet*, the ordeal with Squirrel Girl**, the giant fight around the Abundant Glove***--
Well, since you mentioned it...
*Ed. Note: *Howard Vol. 0, #2*
**I...have no idea. Chip and Joe don't tell me anything.
****Vol. 0, #5*
...the *Glove* may actually be the key to getting you back to your universe, Howard.

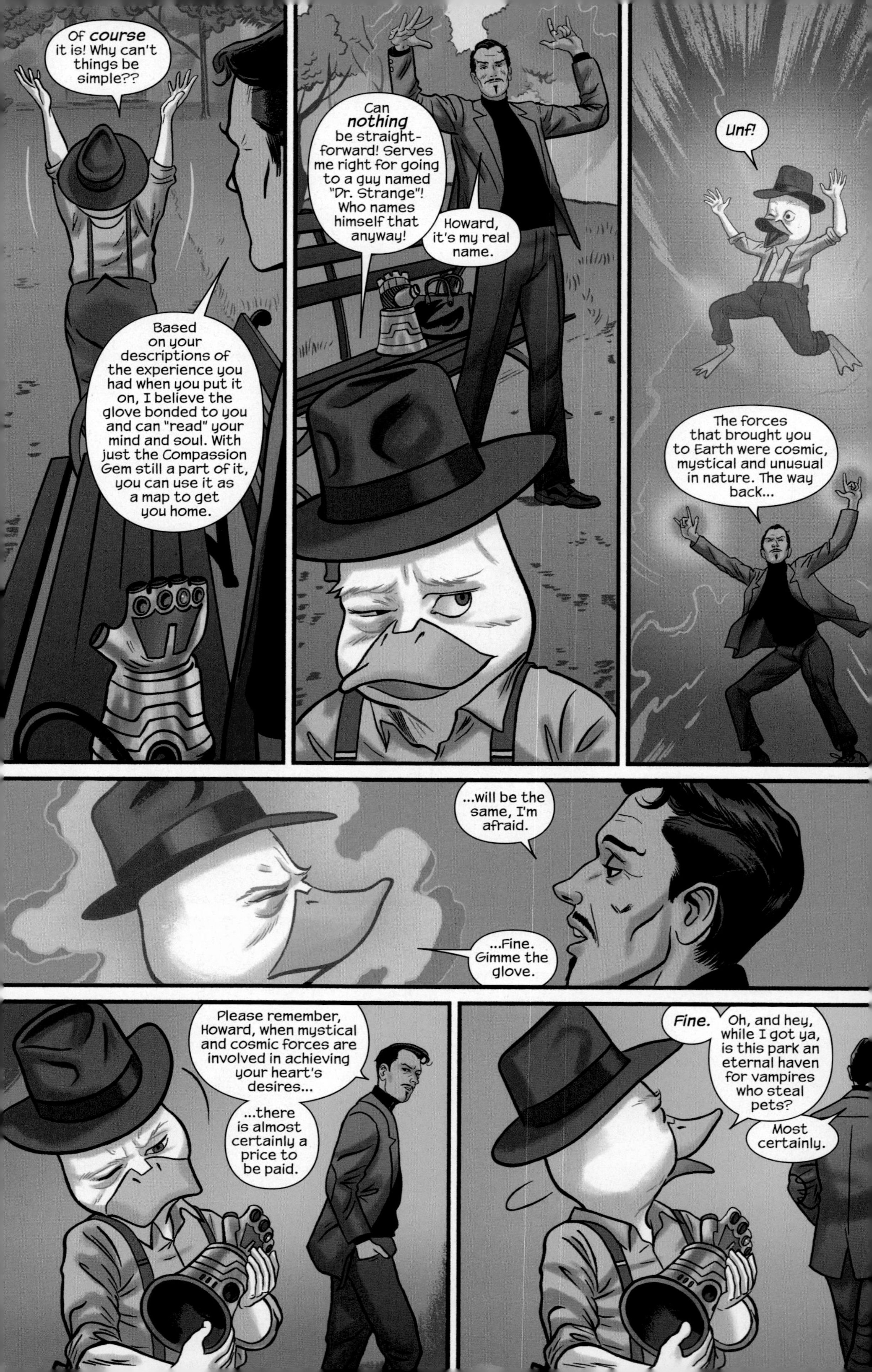

Of *course* it is! Why can't things be simple??
Based on your descriptions of the experience you had when you put it on, I believe the glove bonded to you and can "read" your mind and soul. With just the Compassion Gem still a part of it, you can use it as a map to get you home.
Can *nothing* be straight-forward! Serves me right for going to a guy named "Dr. Strange"! Who names himself that anyway!
Howard, it's my real name.
Unf!
The forces that brought you to Earth were cosmic, mystical and unusual in nature. The way back...
...will be the same, I'm afraid.
...Fine. Gimme the glove.
Please remember, Howard, when mystical and cosmic forces are involved in achieving your heart's desires...
...there is almost certainly a price to be paid.
Fine.
Oh, and hey, while I got ya, is this park an eternal haven for vampires who steal pets?
Most certainly.

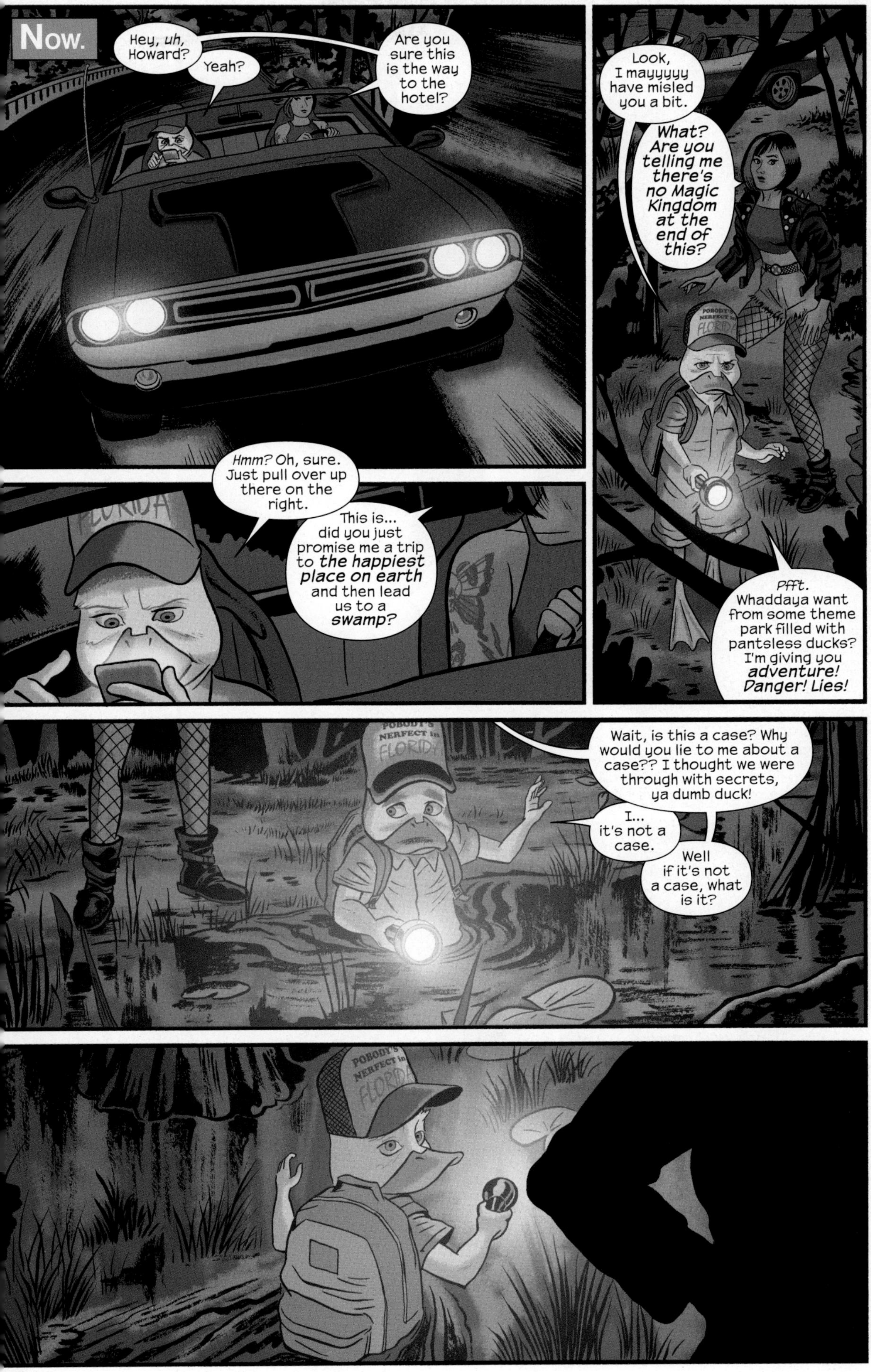
Now.
Hey, uh, Howard?
Yeah?
Are you sure this is the way to the hotel?
Look, I mayyyyy have misled you a bit.
What? Are you telling me there's no Magic Kingdom at the end of this?
Hmm? Oh, sure. Just pull over up there on the right.
This is... did you just promise me a trip to the happiest place on earth and then lead us to a swamp?
FLORIDA
Pfft. Whaddaya want from some theme park filled with pantsless ducks? I'm giving you adventure! Danger! Lies!
POBODY'S NERFECT in FLORIDA
Wait, is this a case? Why would you lie to me about a case?? I thought we were through with secrets, ya dumb duck!
I... it's not a case.
Well if it's not a case, what is it?

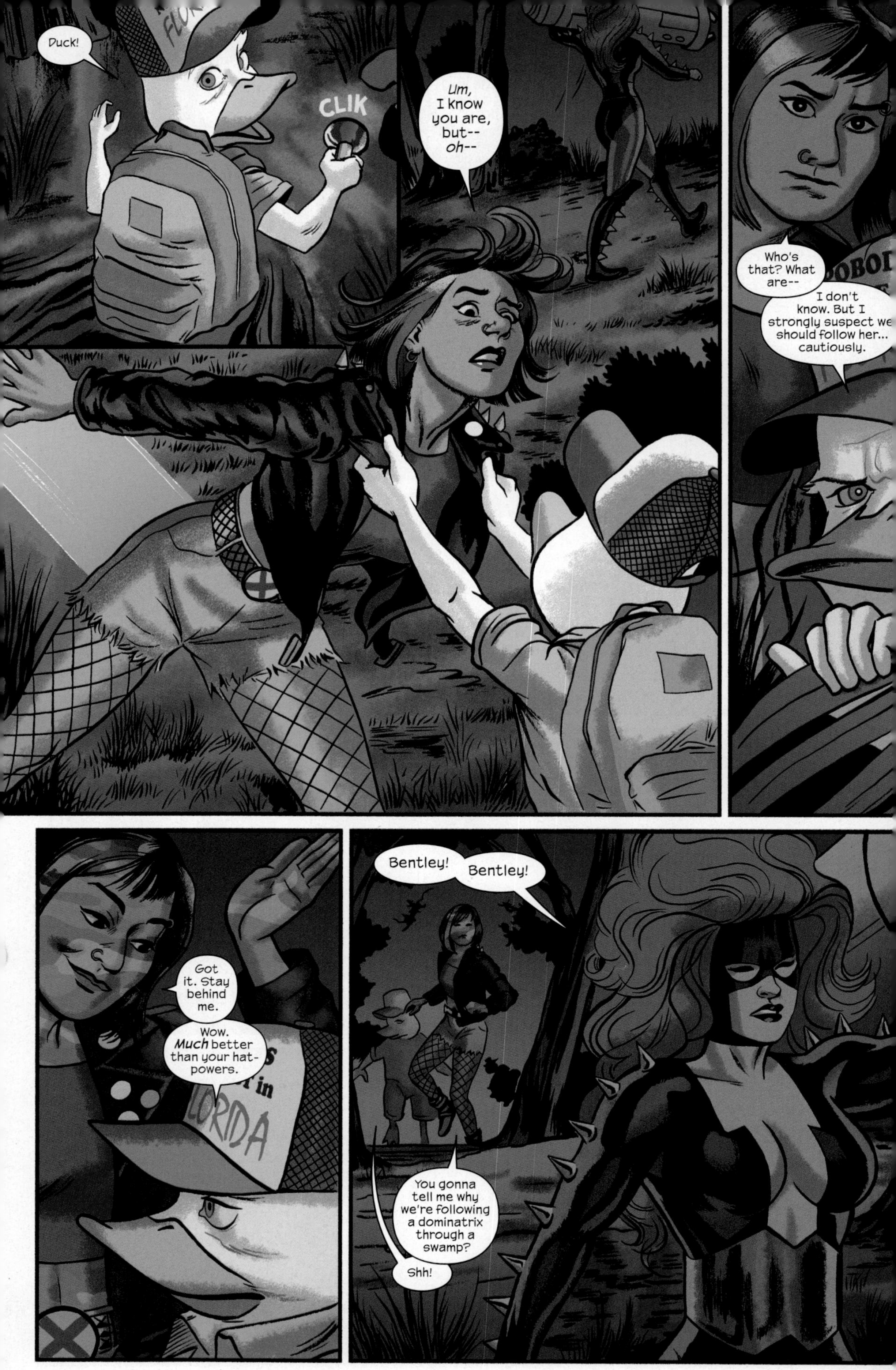
Duck!
CLIK
Um, I know you are, but-- oh--
Who's that? What are--
I don't know. But I strongly suspect we should follow her... cautiously.
Got it. Stay behind me.
Wow. Much better than your hat-powers.
Bentley!
Bentley!
You gonna tell me why we're following a dominatrix through a swamp?
Shh!

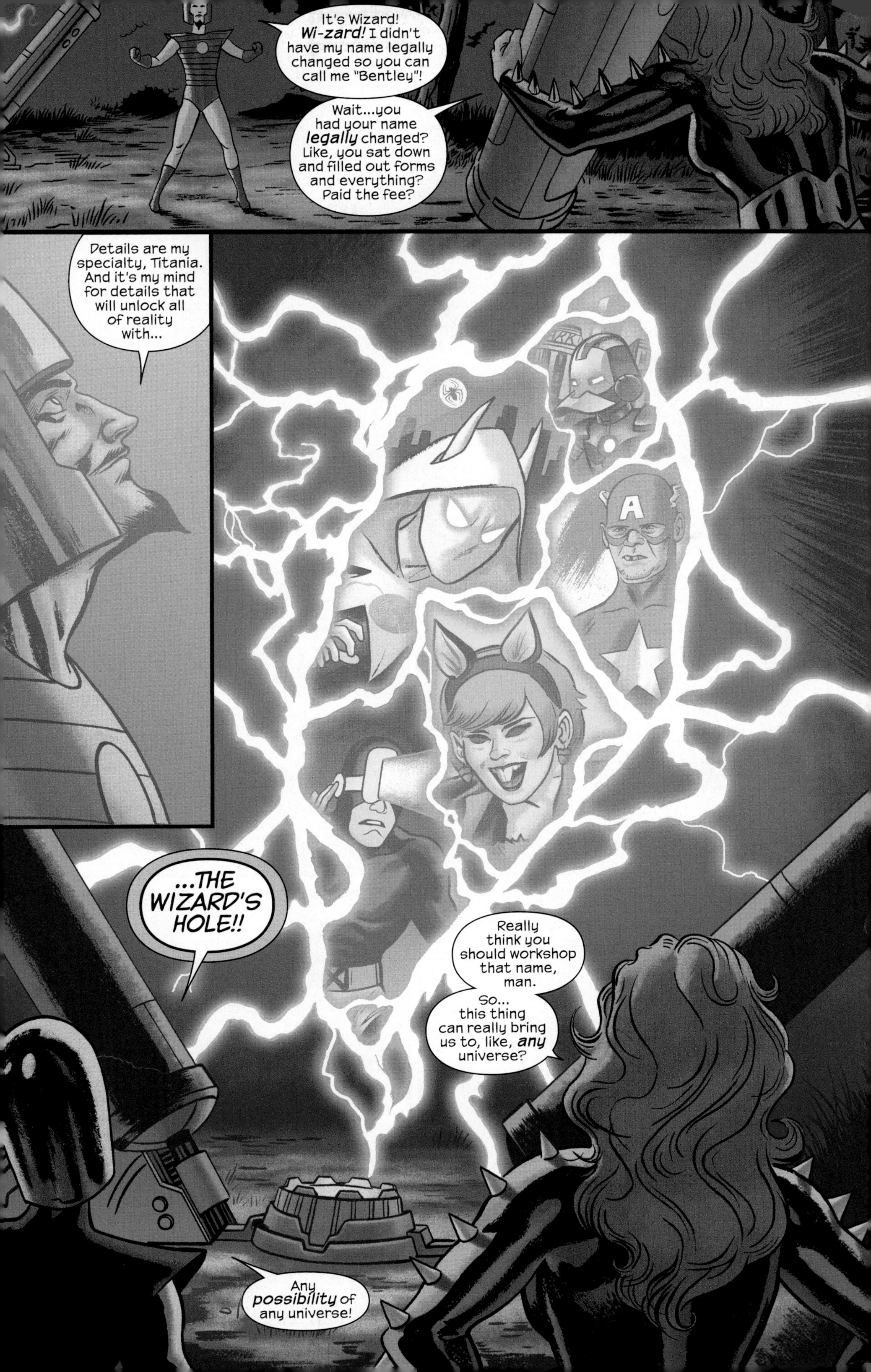
It's Wizard! *Wi-zard!* I didn't have my name legally changed so you can call me "Bentley"!
Wait...you had your name *legally* changed? Like, you sat down and filled out forms and everything? Paid the fee?
Details are my specialty, Titania. And it's my mind for details that will unlock all of reality with...
...THE WIZARD'S HOLE!!
Really think you should workshop that name, man.
So... this thing can really bring us to, like, *any* universe?
Any *possibility* of any universe!

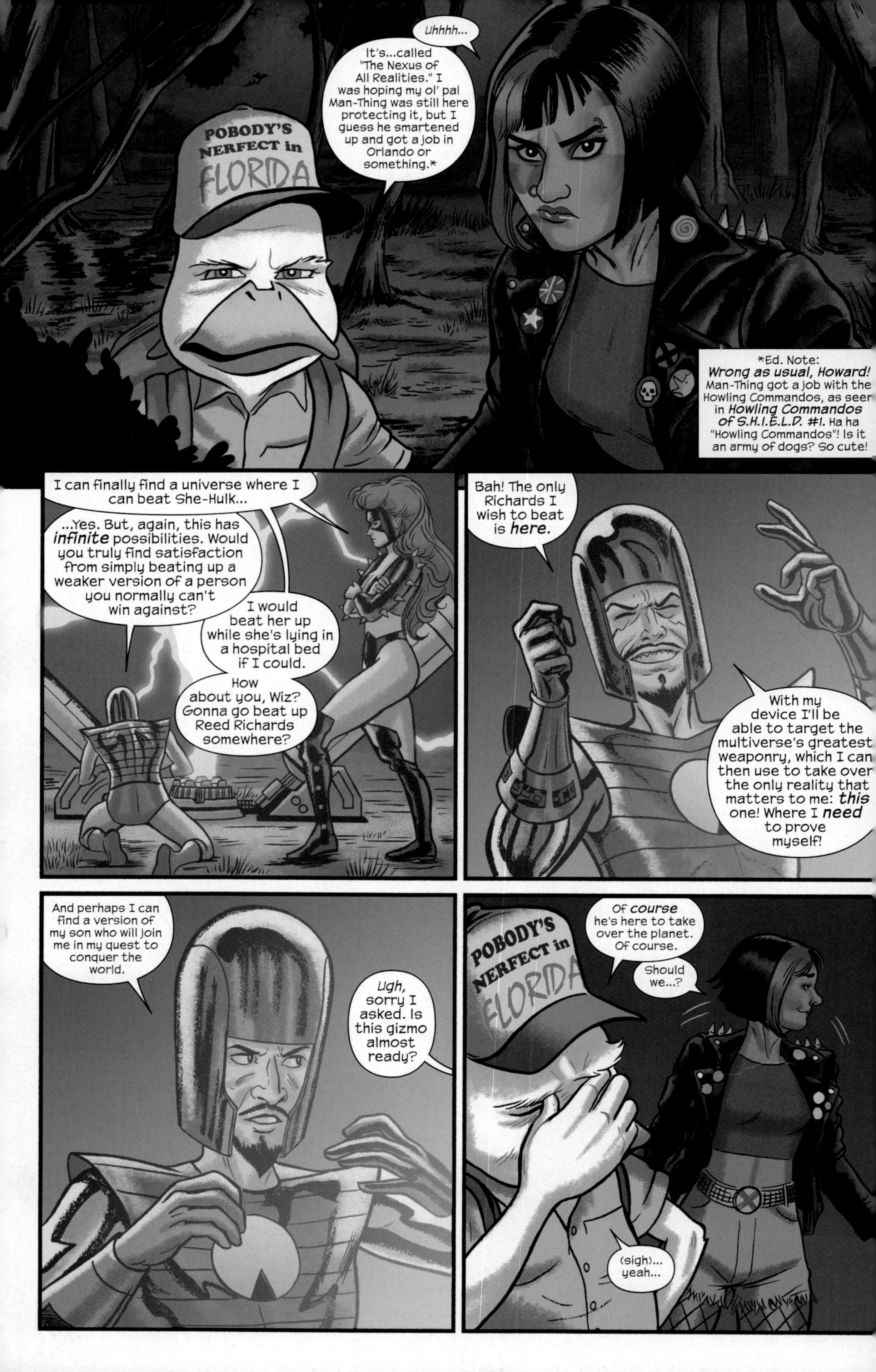
POBODY'S NERFECT in FLORIDA
Uhhhh...
It's...called "The Nexus of All Realities." I was hoping my ol' pal Man-Thing was still here protecting it, but I guess he smartened up and got a job in Orlando or something.*
*Ed. Note: *Wrong as usual, Howard!* Man-Thing got a job with the Howling Commandos, as seen in *Howling Commandos of S.H.I.E.L.D. #1.* Ha ha "Howling Commandos"! Is it an army of dogs? So cute!
I can finally find a universe where I can beat She-Hulk...
...Yes. But, again, this has *infinite* possibilities. Would you truly find satisfaction from simply beating up a weaker version of a person you normally can't win against?
I would beat her up while she's lying in a hospital bed if I could.
How about you, Wiz? Gonna go beat up Reed Richards somewhere?
Bah! The only Richards I wish to beat is *here.*
With my device I'll be able to target the multiverse's greatest weaponry, which I can then use to take over the only reality that matters to me: *this* one! Where I *need* to prove myself!
And perhaps I can find a version of my son who will join me in my quest to conquer the world.
Ugh, sorry I asked. Is this gizmo almost ready?
POBODY'S NERFECT in FLORIDA
Of *course* he's here to take over the planet. Of course.
Should we...?
(sigh)... yeah...

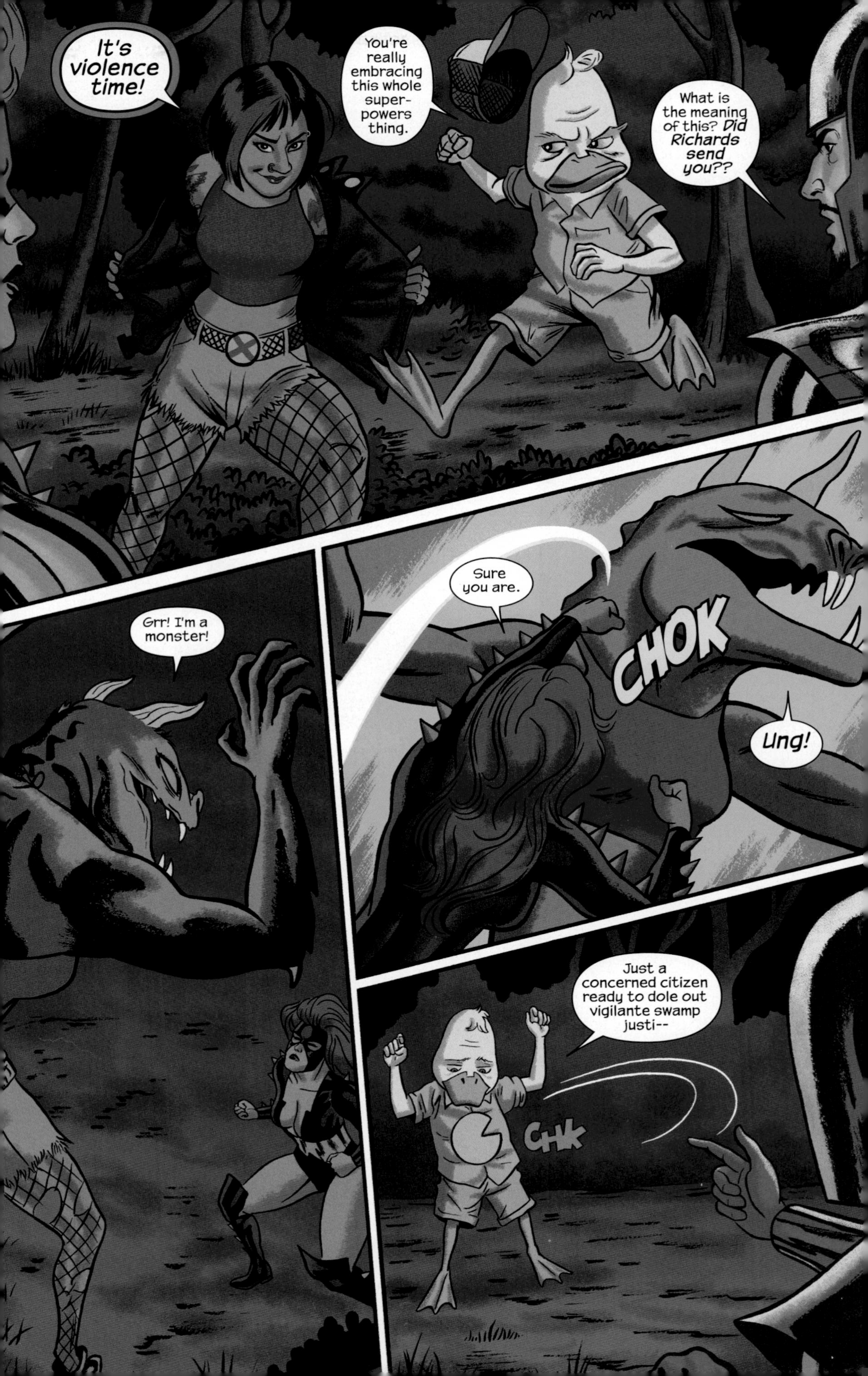
It's violence time!
You're really embracing this whole super-powers thing.
What is the meaning of this? Did Richards send you??
Grr! I'm a monster!
Sure you are.
CHOK
Ung!
Just a concerned citizen ready to dole out vigilante swamp justi--
CHK

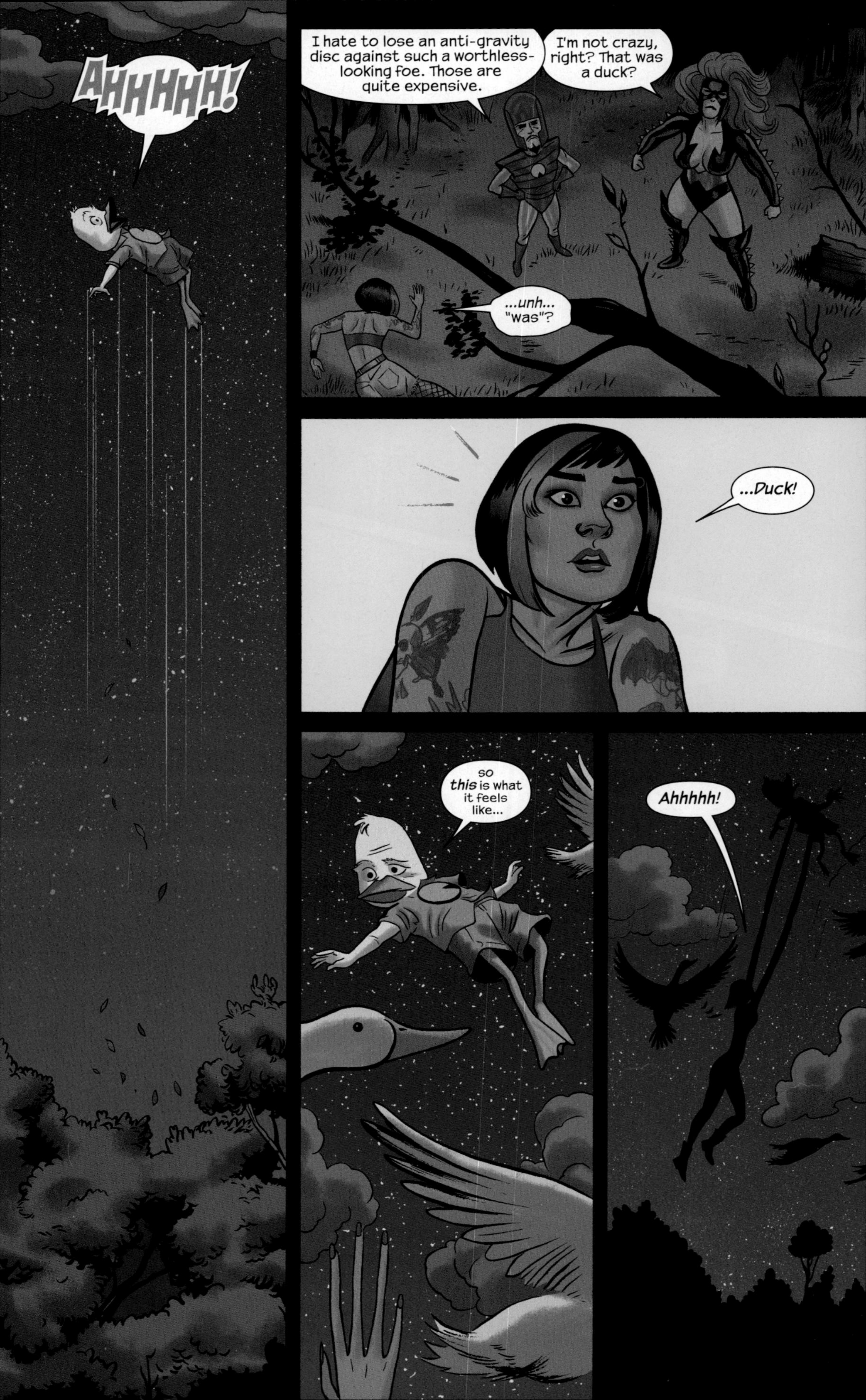
AHHHHH!
I hate to lose an anti-gravity disc against such a worthless-looking foe. Those are quite expensive.
I'm not crazy, right? That was a duck?
...unh... "was"?
...Duck!
so *this* is what it feels like...
Ahhhhh!

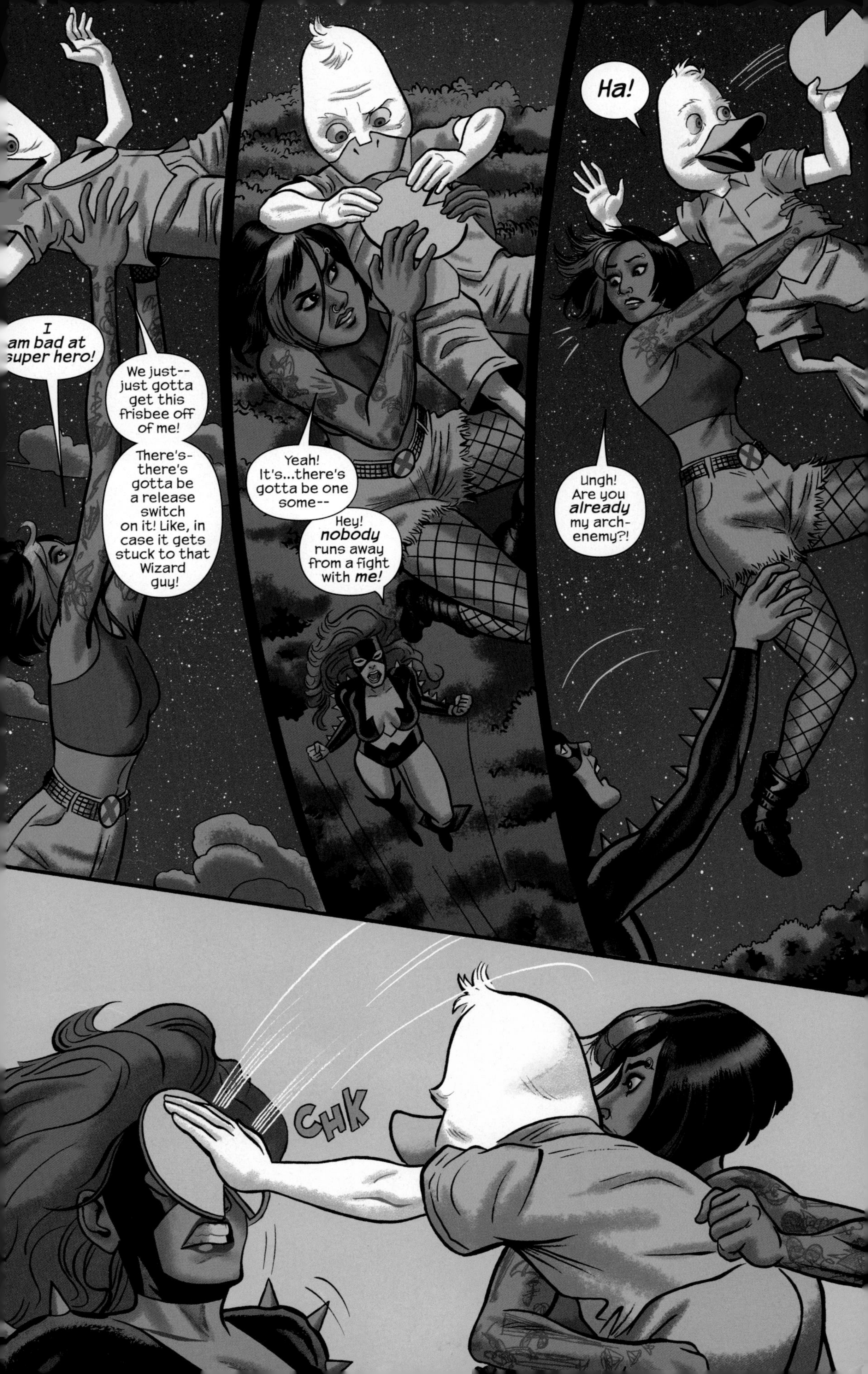
I am bad at super hero!
We just-- just gotta get this frisbee off of me!
There's- there's gotta be a release switch on it! Like, in case it gets stuck to that Wizard guy!
Yeah! It's...there's gotta be one some--
Hey! *nobody* runs away from a fight with *me!*
Ha!
Ungh! Are you *already* my arch-enemy?!
CHK

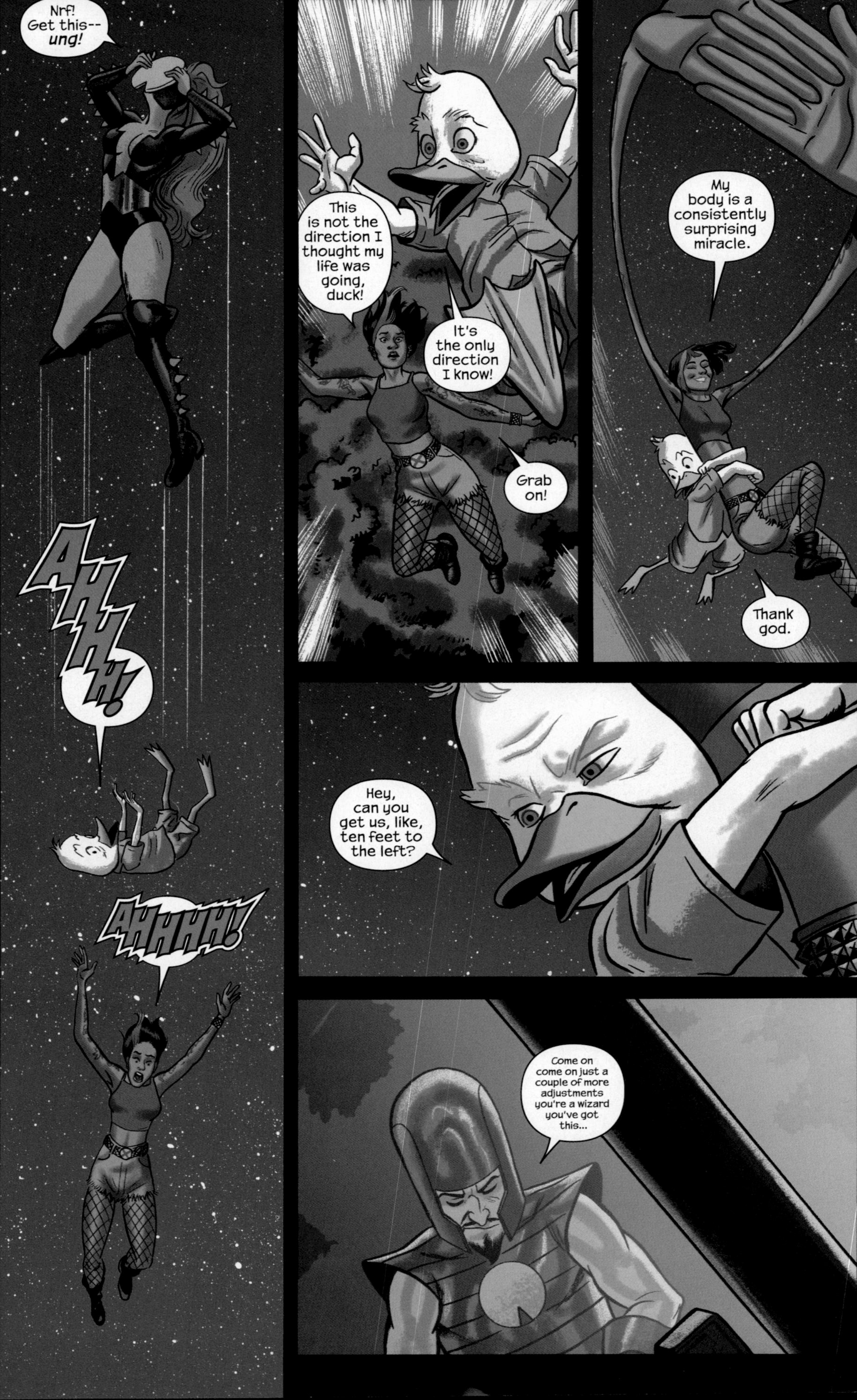
Nrf! Get this-- ung!
AHHHH!
AHHHH!
This is not the direction I thought my life was going, duck!
It's the only direction I know!
Grab on!
My body is a consistently surprising miracle.
Thank god.
Hey, can you get us, like, ten feet to the left?
Come on come on just a couple of more adjustments you're a wizard you've got this...

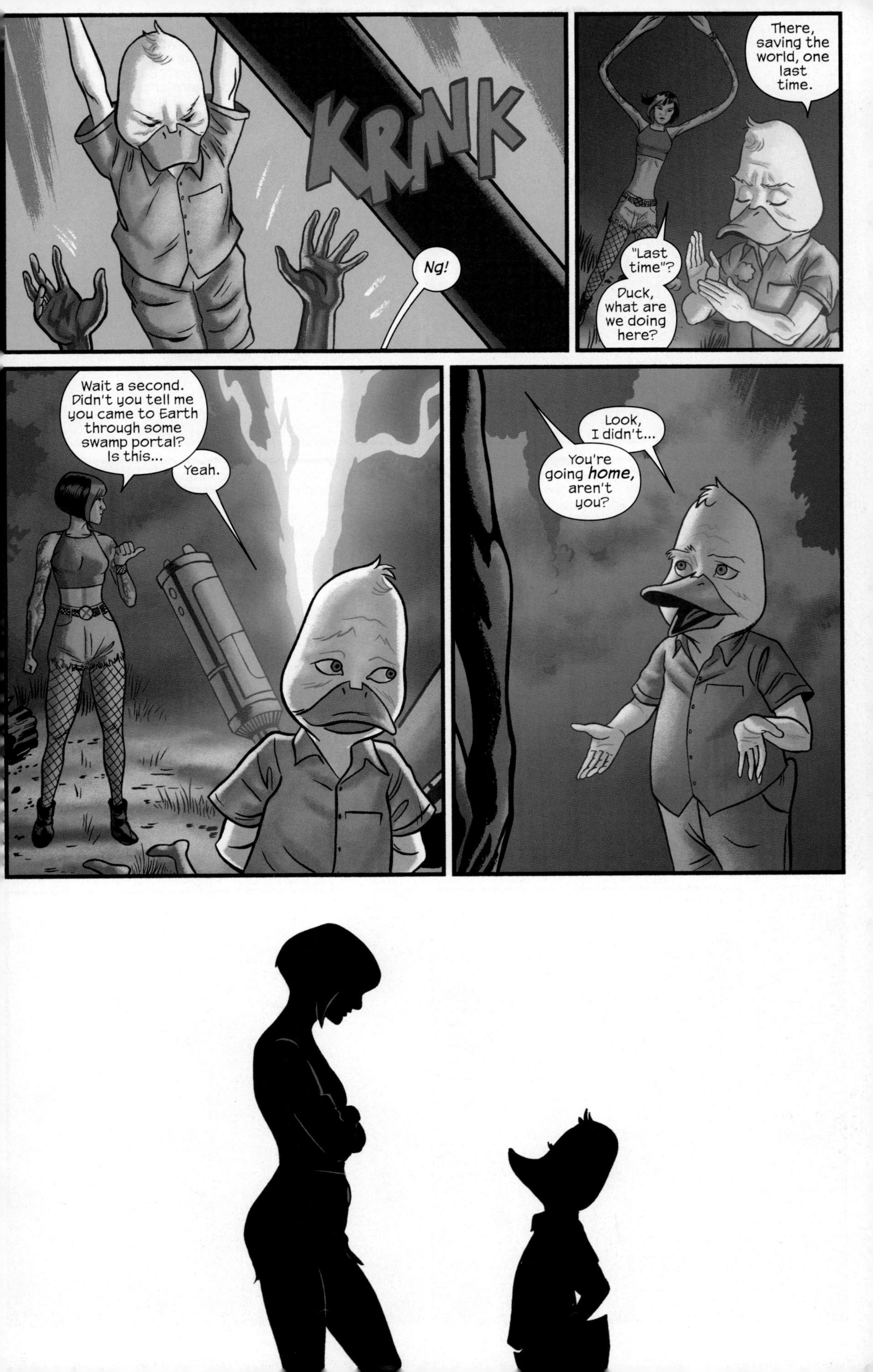
KRNK
Ng!
There, saving the world, one last time.
"Last time"?
Duck, what are we doing here?
Wait a second. Didn't you tell me you came to Earth through some swamp portal? Is this...
Yeah.
Look, I didn't...
You're going home, aren't you?

S#@% you, duck. I thought we were friends.

Wait! It's--it's not...this isn't my home!

Look, do you want to come with me? Live on a planet where you're a *freak?* Do you?

Yeah, I didn't think so. And it's fine.

You know how hard these past few months have been. *You've* been great. *Aunt May's* been great. But I feel like if I stay here any longer I'm gonna die. Either from some sort of super villain thug or a gas station hick.

I wanted to have you see me off, but I didn't want to make it so you wouldn't come...

Also, you can't drive without getting pulled over every ten minutes.

That too.

Aw, duck. You coulda told me. I would've still brought you.

I'm sorry. You're a peach, kid. It's been a short time, but a good one.

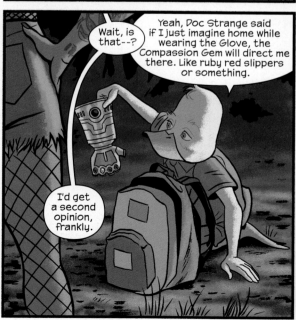

Wait, is that--?

Yeah, Doc Strange said if I just imagine home while wearing the Glove, the Compassion Gem will direct me there. Like ruby red slippers or something.

I'd get a second opinion, frankly.

Enh. Why be cautious now?

See ya later, kid.

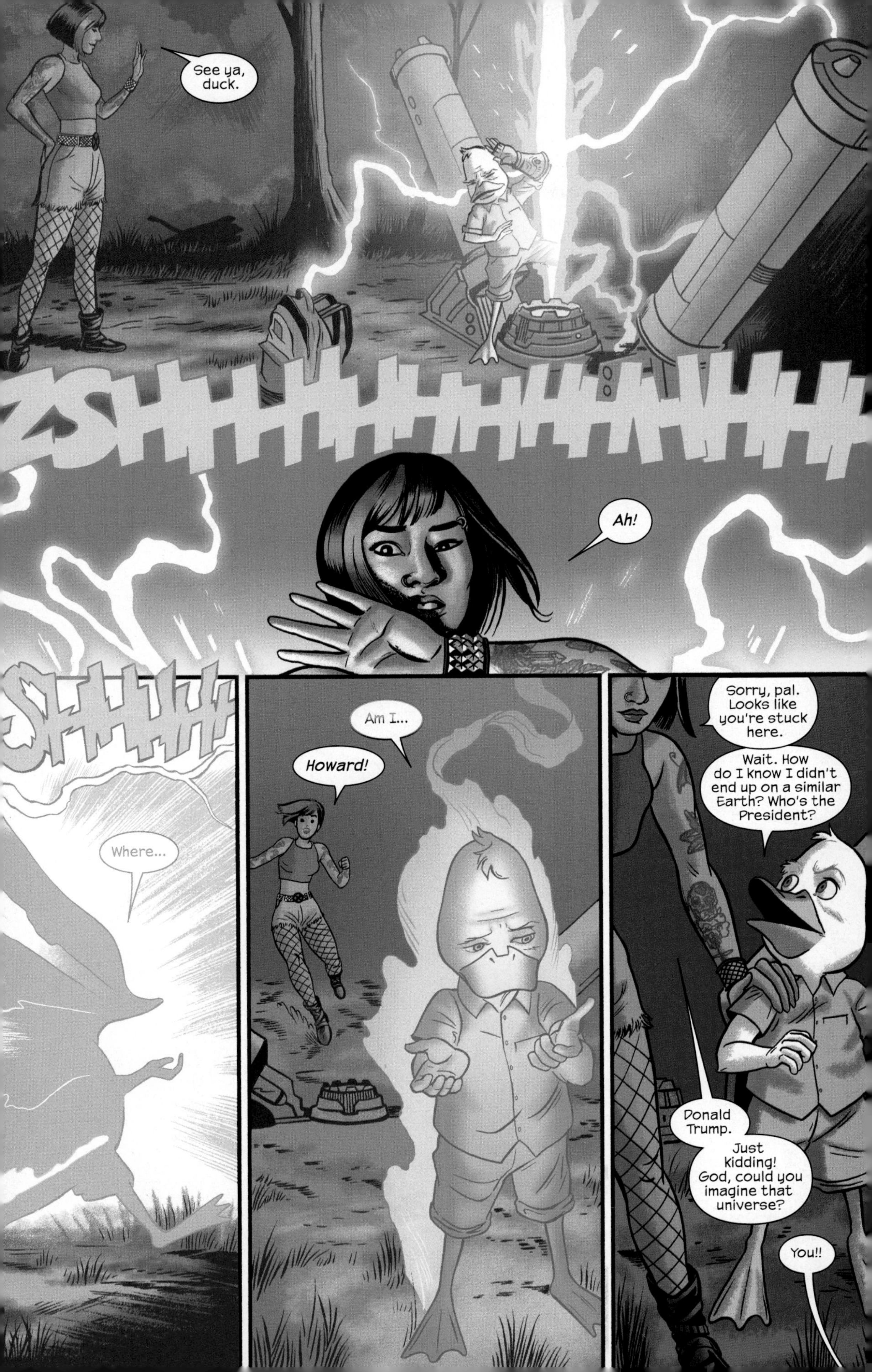
See ya, duck.
ZSHHHHHHHHHHHHHH
Ah!
SHHHH
Where...
Am I...
Howard!
Sorry, pal. Looks like you're stuck here.
Wait. How do I know I didn't end up on a similar Earth? Who's the President?
Donald Trump.
Just kidding! God, could you imagine that universe?
You!!

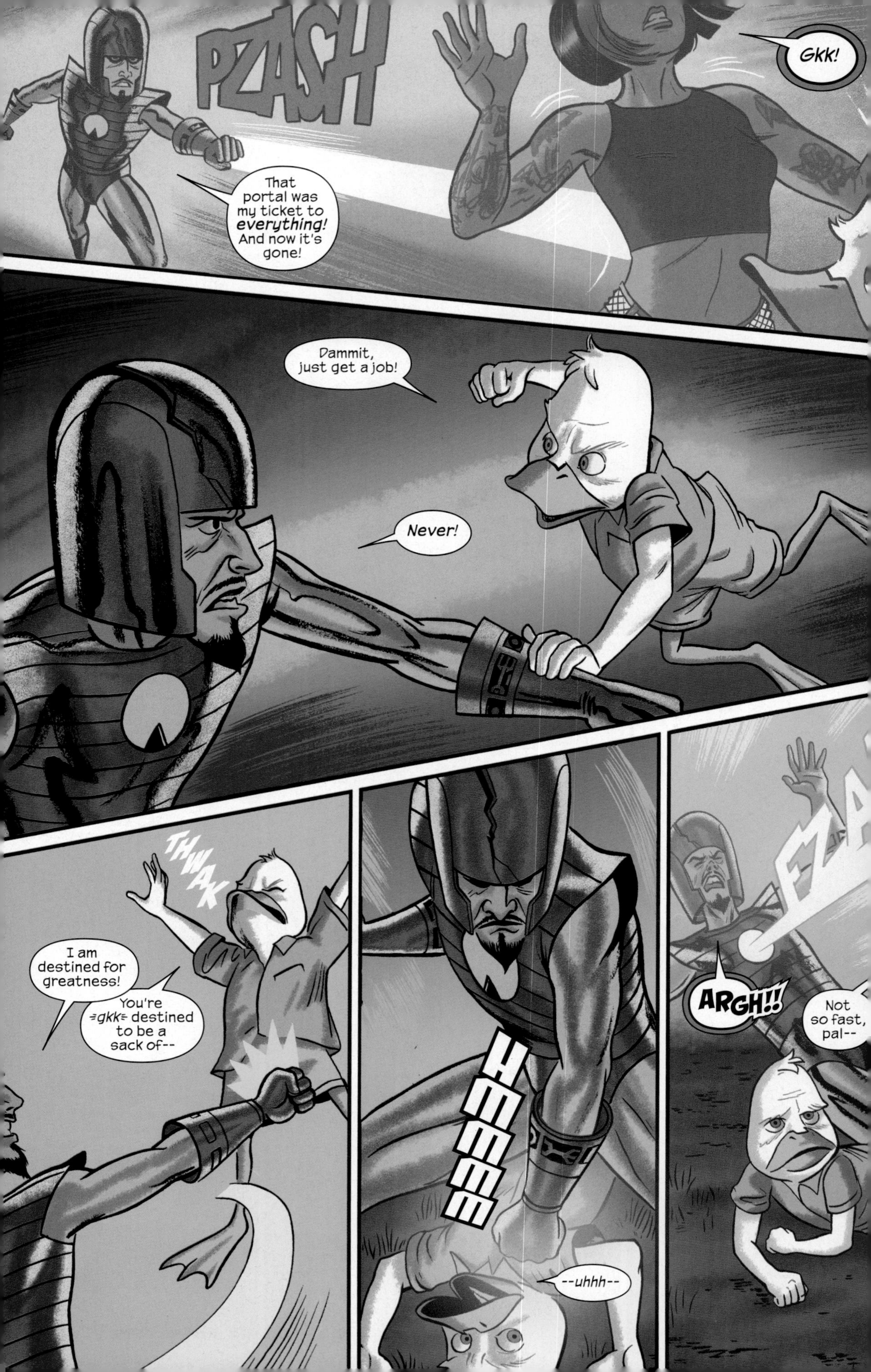
PZASH
Gkk!
That portal was my ticket to *everything!* And now it's gone!
Dammit, just get a job!
Never!
THWAK
I am destined for greatness!
You're =gkk= destined to be a sack of--
HEEEEE
--uhhh--
ARGH!!
Not so fast, pal--

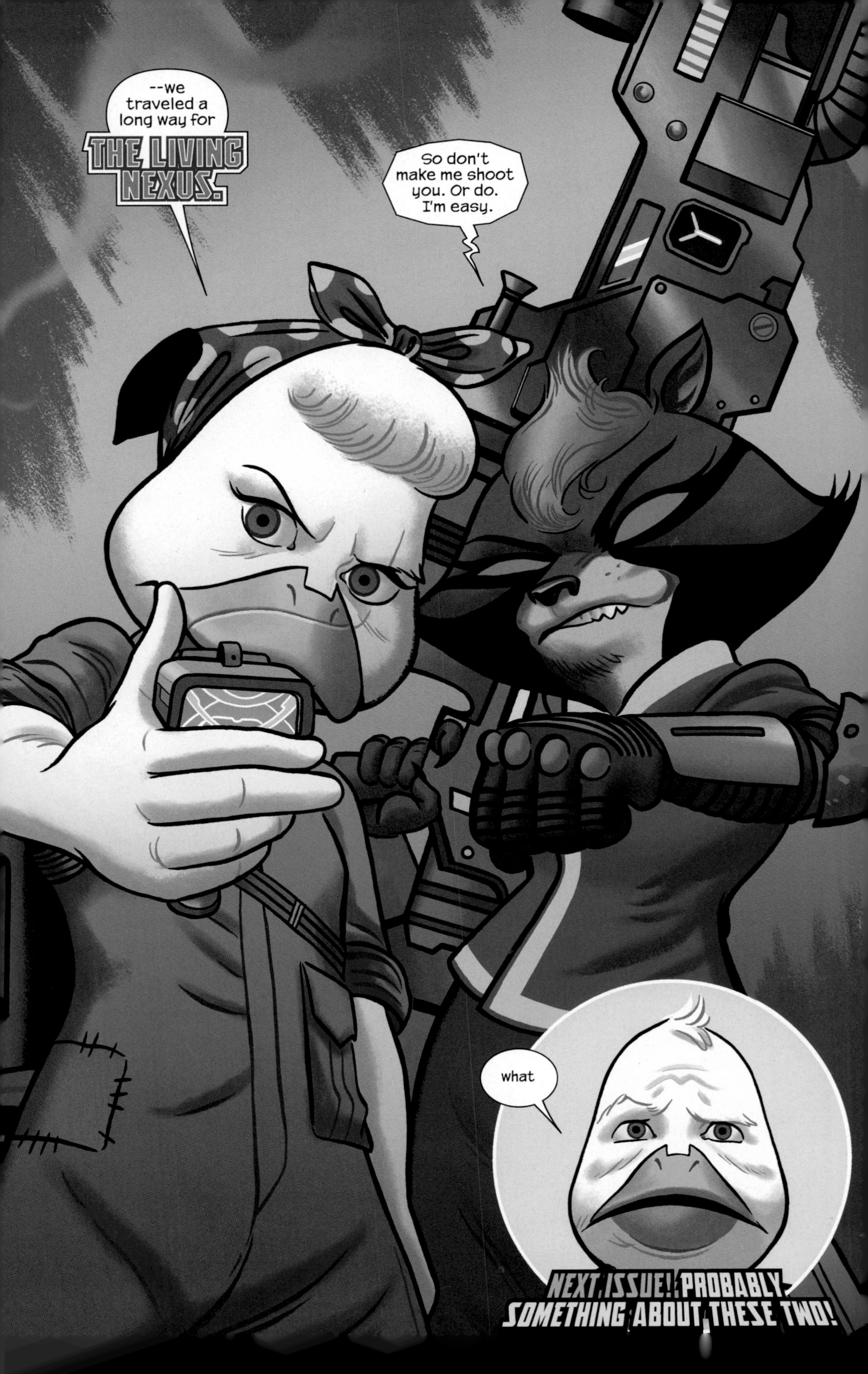

--we traveled a long way for
THE LIVING NEXUS.
So don't make me shoot you. Or do. I'm easy.
what
NEXT ISSUE! PROBABLY SOMETHING ABOUT THESE TWO!

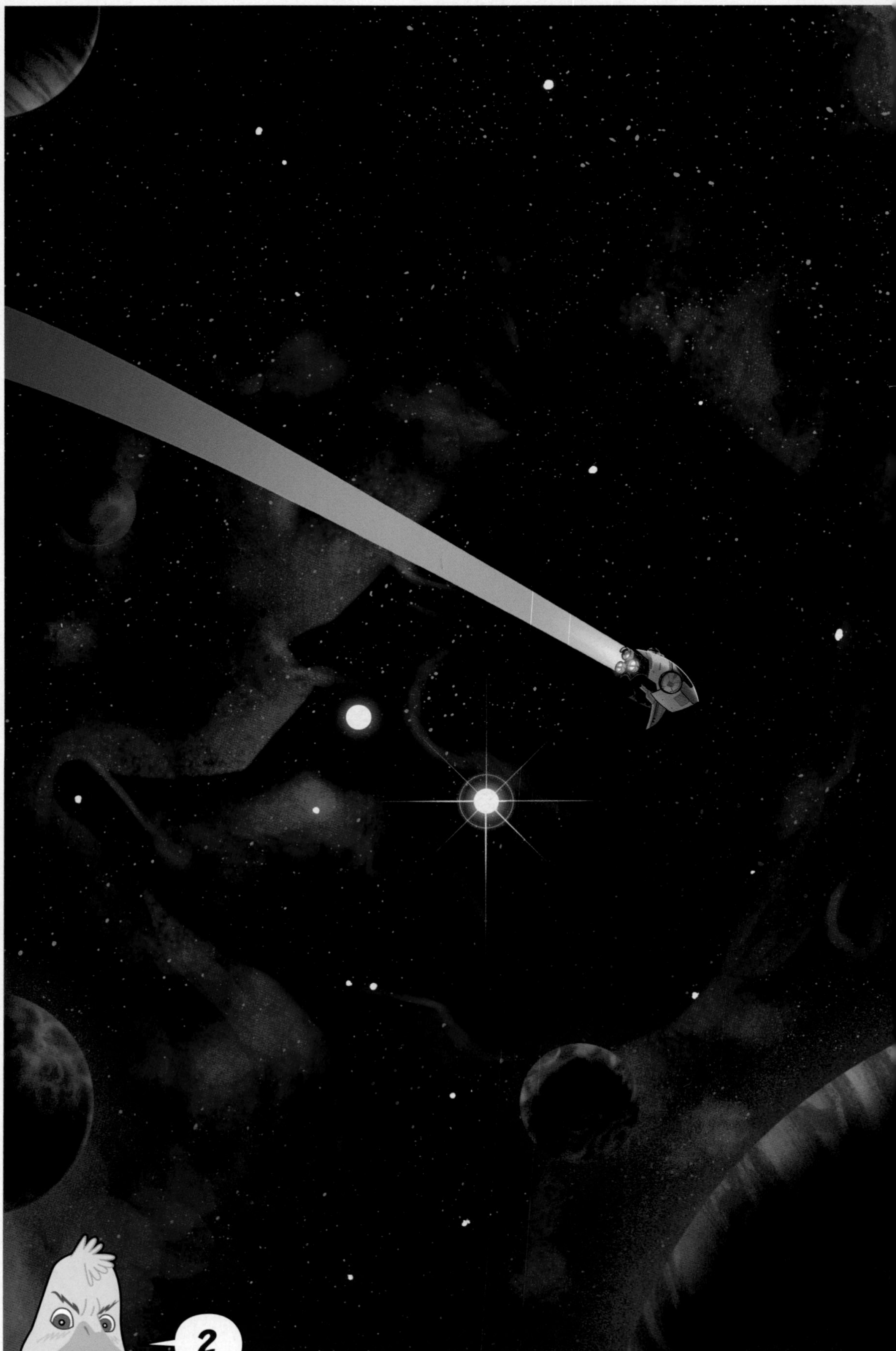

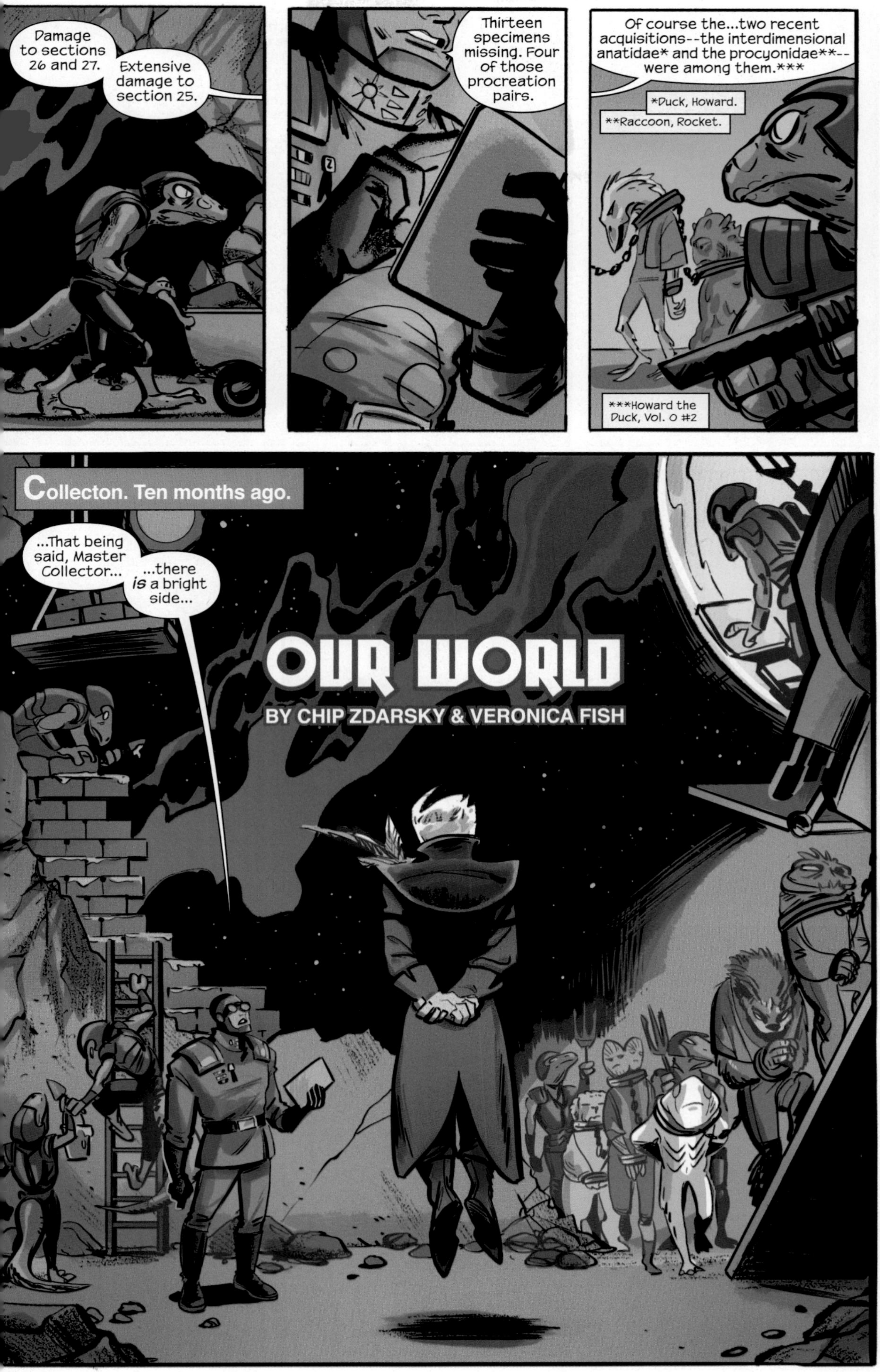
Damage to sections 26 and 27.
Extensive damage to section 25.
Thirteen specimens missing. Four of those procreation pairs.
Of course the...two recent acquisitions--the interdimensional anatidae* and the procyonidae**--were among them.***
*Duck, Howard.
**Raccoon, Rocket.
***Howard the Duck, Vol. 0 #2
Collecton. Ten months ago.
...That being said, Master Collector...
...there *is* a bright side...
OUR WORLD
BY CHIP ZDARSKY & VERONICA FISH

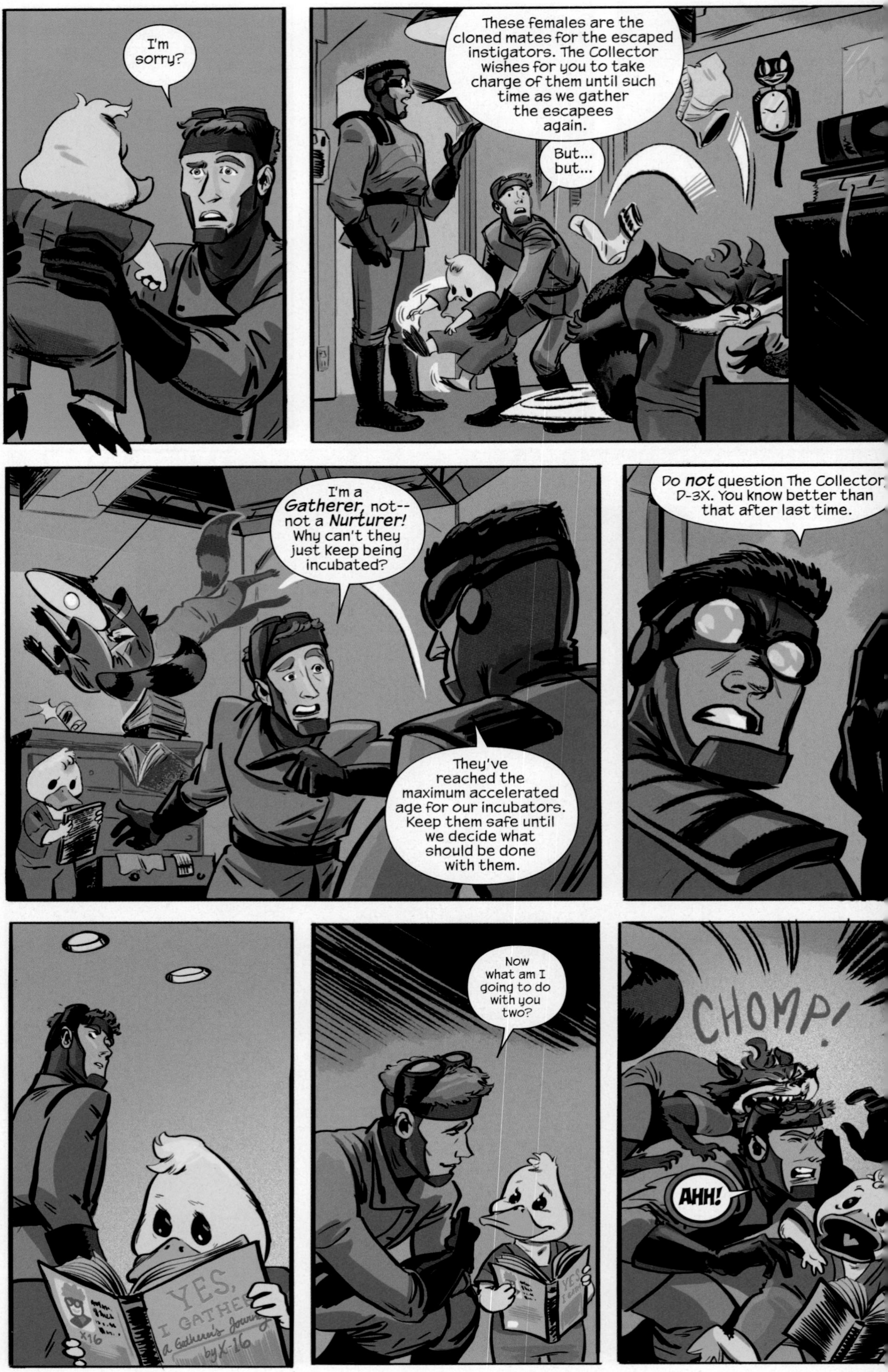
I'm sorry?
These females are the cloned mates for the escaped instigators. The Collector wishes for you to take charge of them until such time as we gather the escapees again.
But... but...
I'm a *Gatherer,* not--not a *Nurturer!* Why can't they just keep being incubated?
They've reached the maximum accelerated age for our incubators. Keep them safe until we decide what should be done with them.
Do **not** question The Collector, D-3X. You know better than that after last time.
YES, I GATHER
a Gatherer's Journey by X-16
X16
Now what am I going to do with you two?
CHOMP!
AHH!

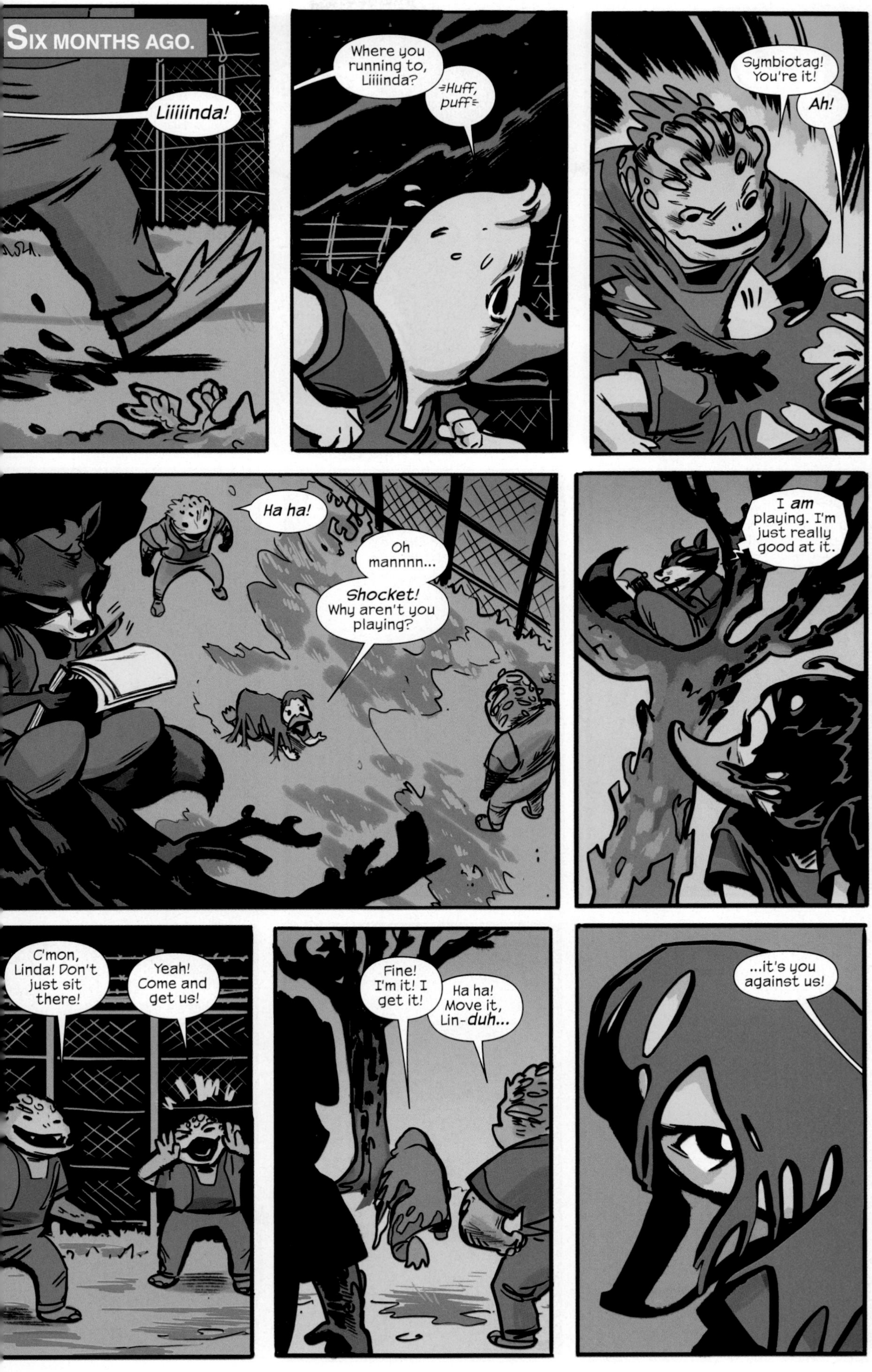
SIX MONTHS AGO.
Liiiiinda!
Where you running to, Liiiinda?
Huff, puff
Symbiotag! You're it!
Ah!
Ha ha!
Oh mannnn...
Shocket! Why aren't you playing?
I am playing. I'm just really good at it.
C'mon, Linda! Don't just sit there!
Yeah! Come and get us!
Fine! I'm it! I get it!
Ha ha! Move it, Lin-duh...
...it's you against us!

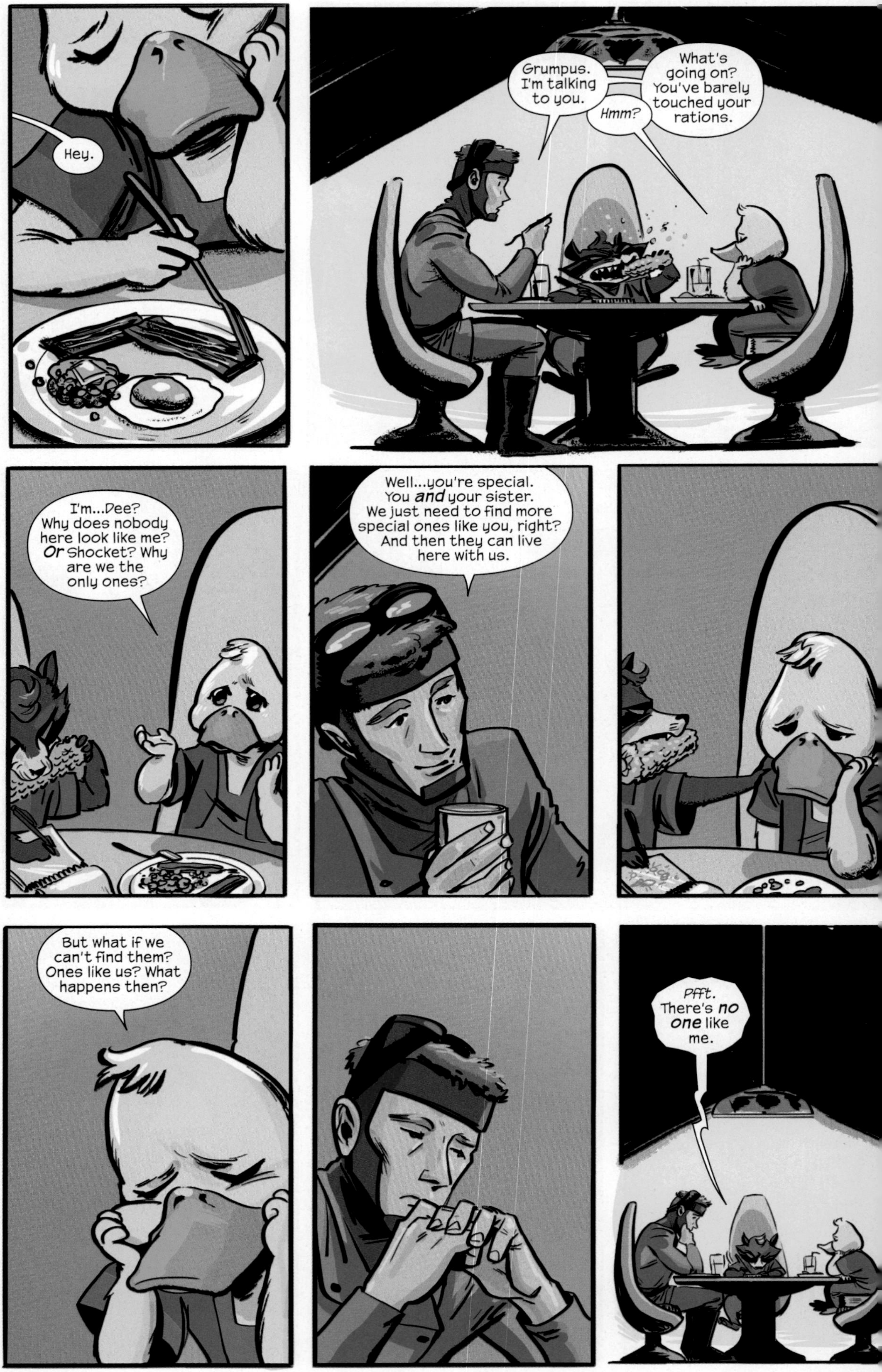
Hey.
Grumpus. I'm talking to you.
Hmm?
What's going on? You've barely touched your rations.
I'm...Dee? Why does nobody here look like me? *Or* Shocket? Why are we the only ones?
Well...you're special. You ***and*** your sister. We just need to find more special ones like you, right? And then they can live here with us.
But what if we can't find them? Ones like us? What happens then?
Pfft. There's ***no one*** like me.

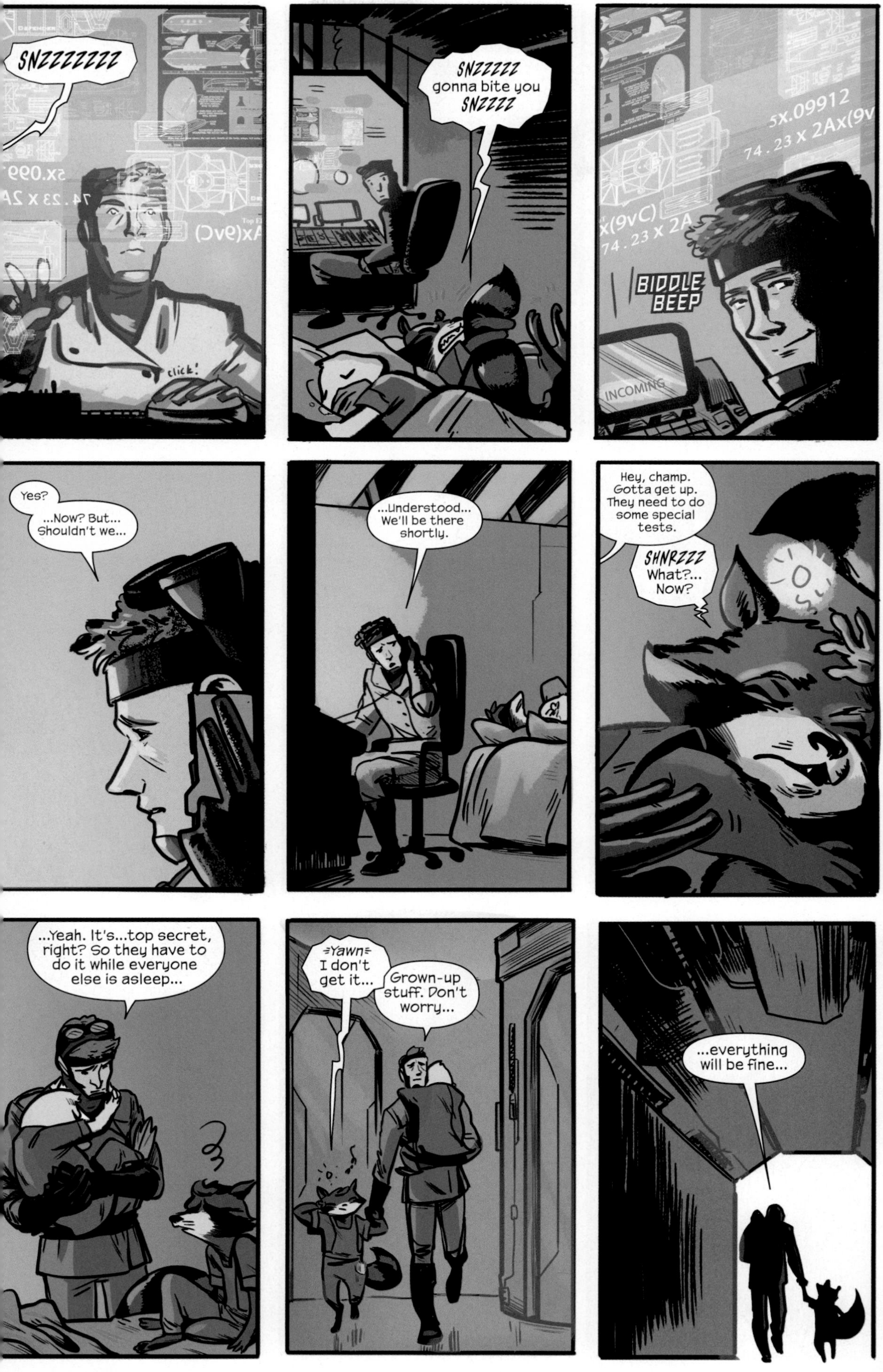

SNZZZZZZZZ
click!
SNZZZZZ gonna bite you SNZZZZ
5x.09912
74 . 23 x 2Ax(9v
x(9vC)
74 . 23 x 2A
BIDDLE BEEP
INCOMING
Yes? ...Now? But... Shouldn't we...
...Understood... We'll be there shortly.
Hey, champ. Gotta get up. They need to do some special tests.
SHNRZZZ What?... Now?
...Yeah. It's...top secret, right? So they have to do it while everyone else is asleep...
=Yawn= I don't get it...
Grown-up stuff. Don't worry...
...everything will be fine...

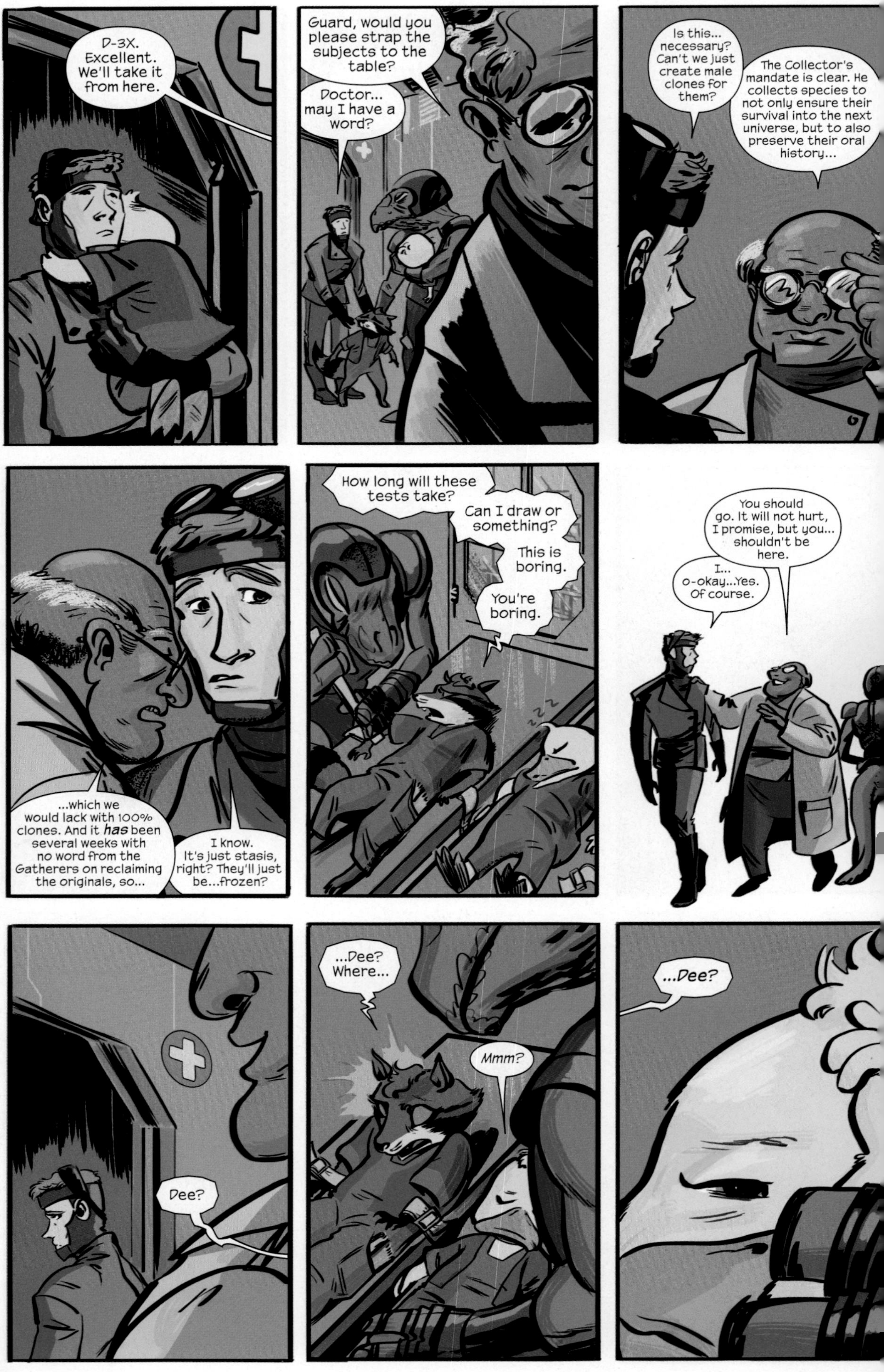
D-3X. Excellent. We'll take it from here.
Guard, would you please strap the subjects to the table?
Doctor... may I have a word?
Is this... necessary? Can't we just create male clones for them?
The Collector's mandate is clear. He collects species to not only ensure their survival into the next universe, but to also preserve their oral history...
...which we would lack with 100% clones. And it *has* been several weeks with no word from the Gatherers on reclaiming the originals, so...
I know. It's just stasis, right? They'll just be...frozen?
How long will these tests take?
Can I draw or something?
This is boring.
You're boring.
You should go. It will not hurt, I promise, but you... shouldn't be here.
I... o-okay...Yes. Of course.
Dee?
...Dee? Where...
Mmm?
...Dee?

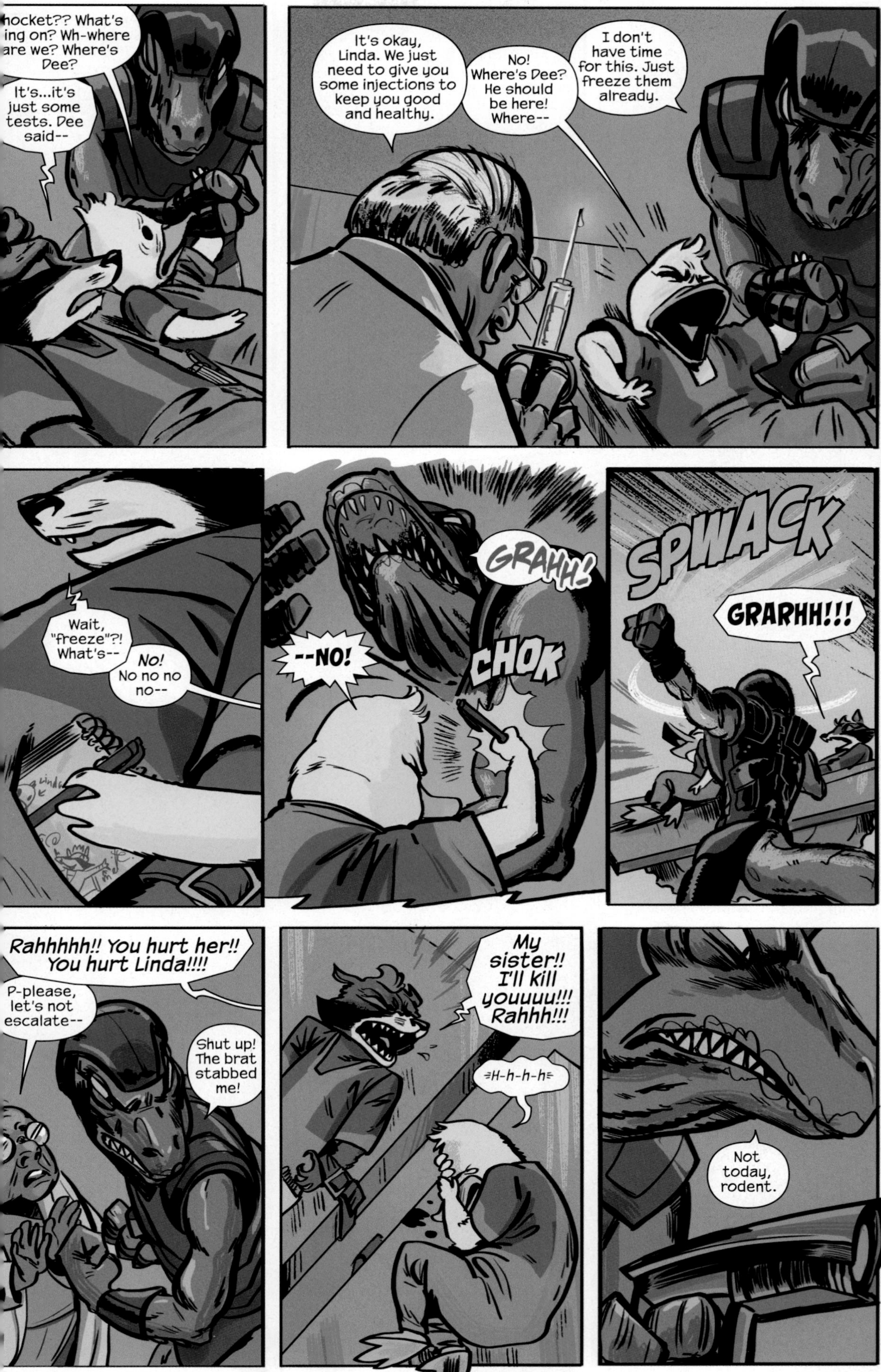

hocket?? What's ing on? Wh-where are we? Where's Dee?
It's...it's just some tests. Dee said--
It's okay, Linda. We just need to give you some injections to keep you good and healthy.
No! Where's Dee? He should be here! Where--
I don't have time for this. Just freeze them already.
Wait, "freeze"?! What's--
No! No no no no--
GRAHH!
--NO!
CHOK
SPWACK
GRARHH!!!
Rahhhhh!! You hurt her!! You hurt Linda!!!!
P-please, let's not escalate--
Shut up! The brat stabbed me!
My sister!! I'll kill youuuu!!! Rahhh!!!
H-h-h-h
Not today, rodent.

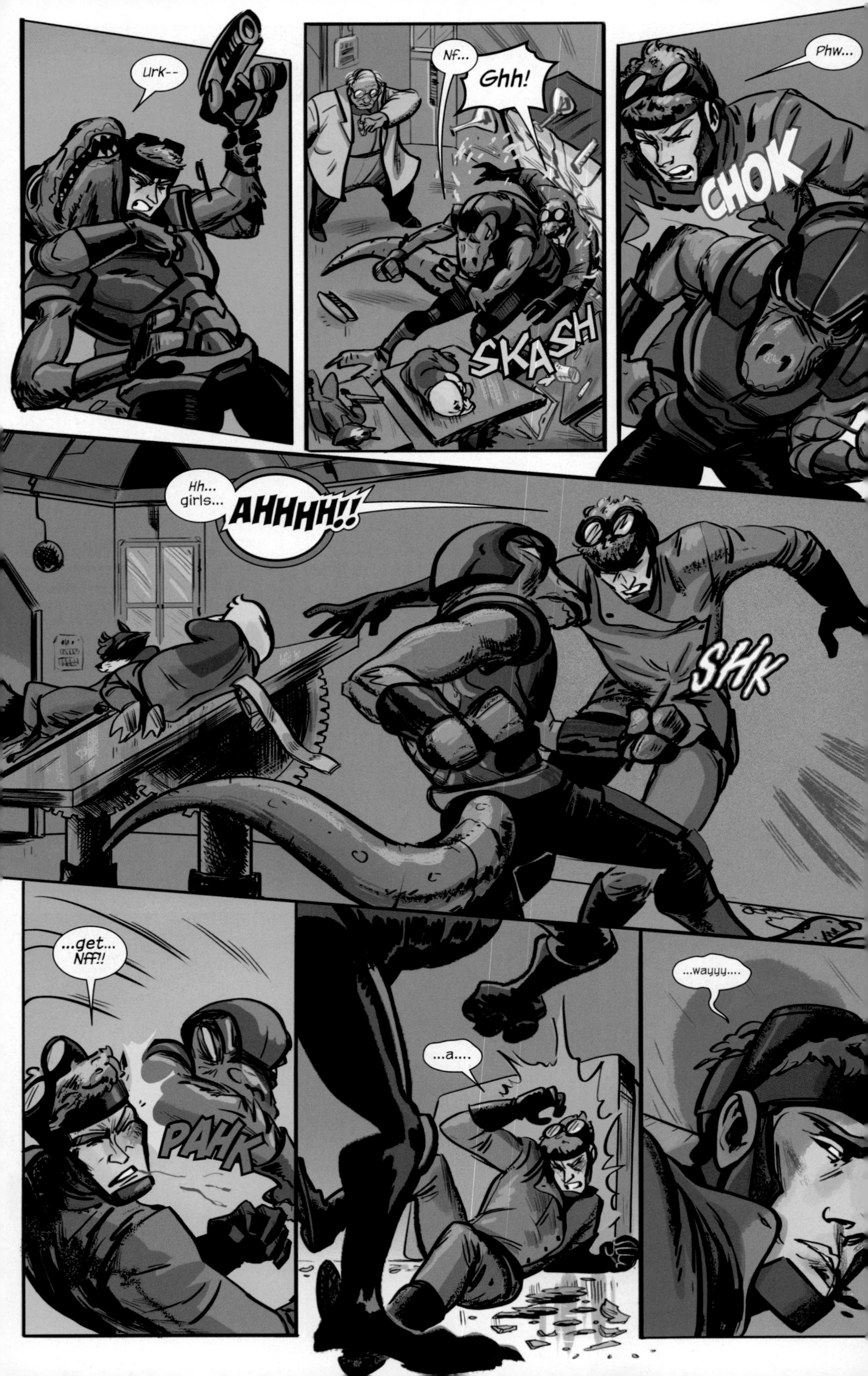
Urk--
Nf...
Ghh!
SKASH
Phw...
CHOK
Hh... girls...
AHHHH!!
SHK
...get... Nff!!
PAHK
...a....
...wayyy....

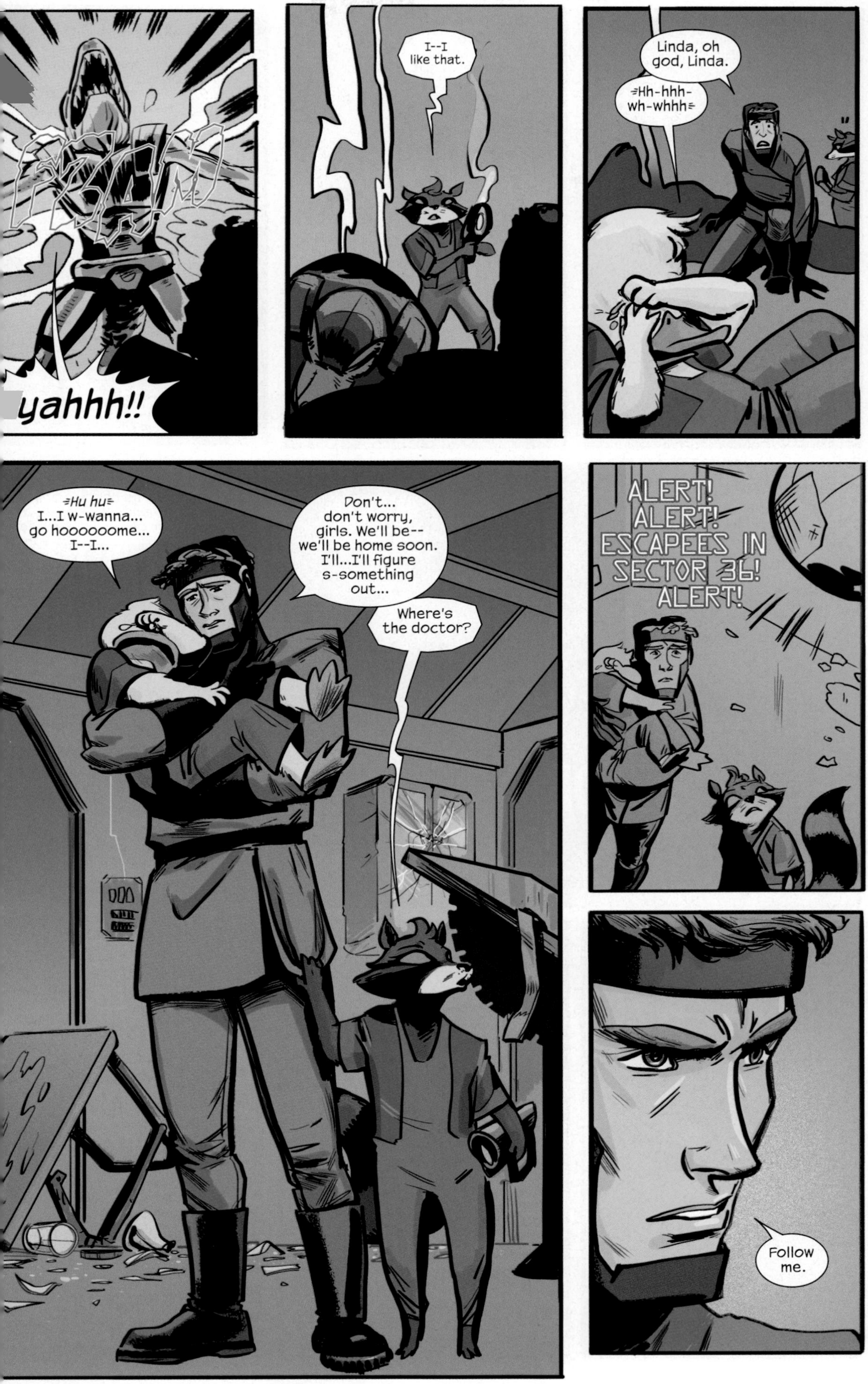
FZZAAM
yahhh!!
I--I like that.
Linda, oh god, Linda.
=Hh-hhh- wh-whhh=
=Hu hu=
I...I w-wanna... go hoooooome... I--I...
Don't... don't worry, girls. We'll be-- we'll be home soon. I'll...I'll figure s-something out...
Where's the doctor?
ALERT! ALERT! ESCAPEES IN SECTOR 36! ALERT!
Follow me.

Wait, are we going home? Dee?

Soon... just...right now we've got to get out of here, okay, champ?

Now...just help your sister while I pilot. Put this on her face to stop the bleeding, okay? Can you do that?

...Y-yeah.

Sh-Shocket?...

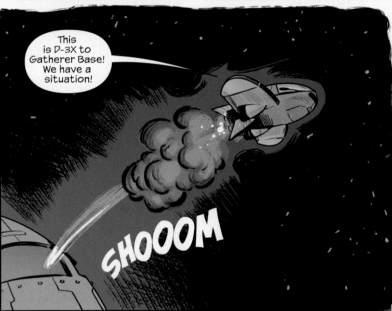

This is D-3X to Gatherer Base! We have a situation!

SHOOOM

There are seven escapees in four ships! Three heading towards zones 30, 36 and 63! Send ships to follow; I'm on the fourth one!

D-Dee?...

There, that should buy us some time...

Can...can I stop now? Where are we going?

SNIFF

...Dee?...

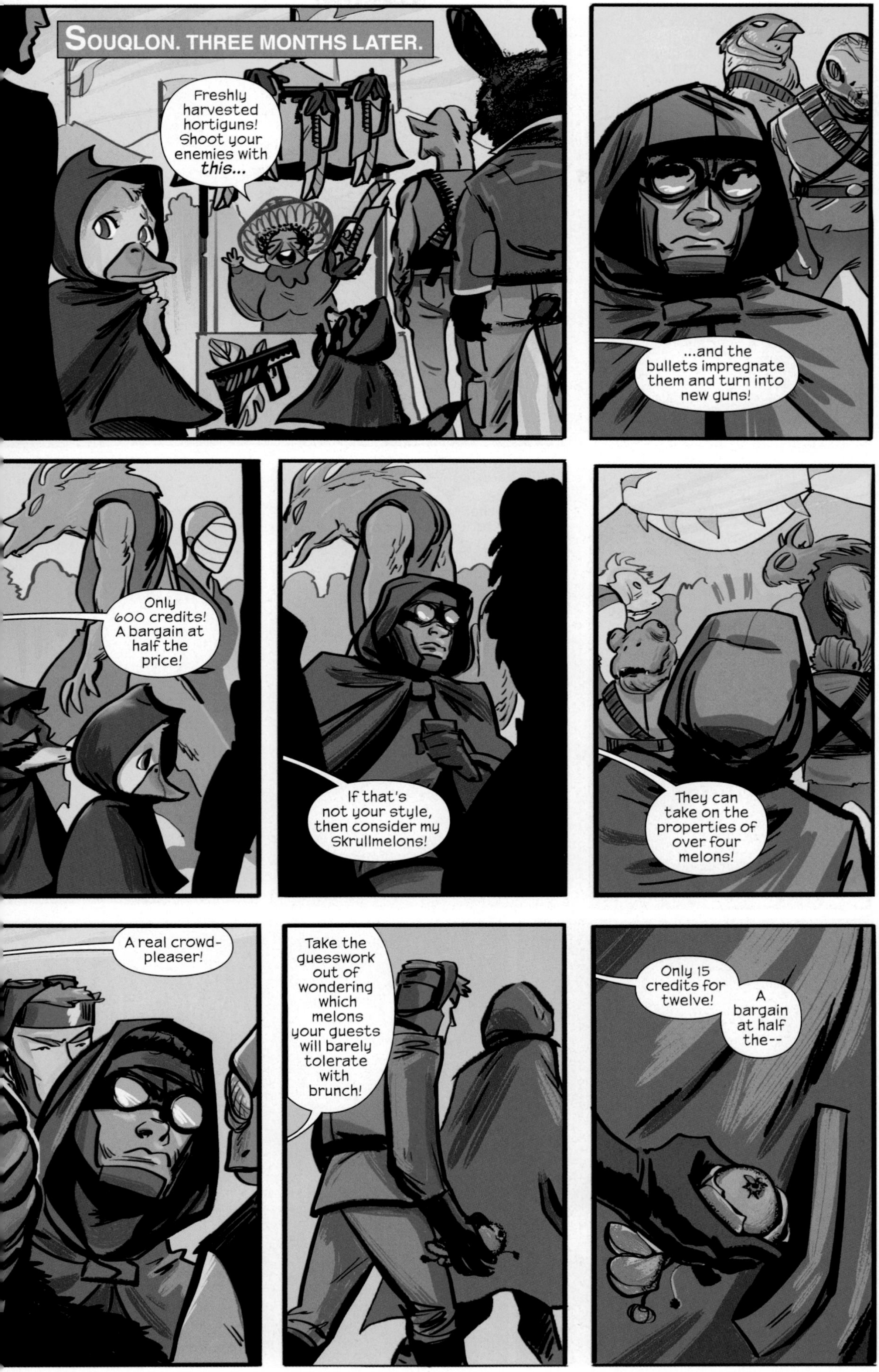

SOUQLON. THREE MONTHS LATER.
Freshly harvested hortiguns! Shoot your enemies with *this...*
...and the bullets impregnate them and turn into new guns!
Only 600 credits! A bargain at half the price!
If that's not your style, then consider my Skrullmelons!
They can take on the properties of over four melons!
A real crowd-pleaser!
Take the guesswork out of wondering which melons your guests will barely tolerate with brunch!
Only 15 credits for twelve!
A bargain at half the--

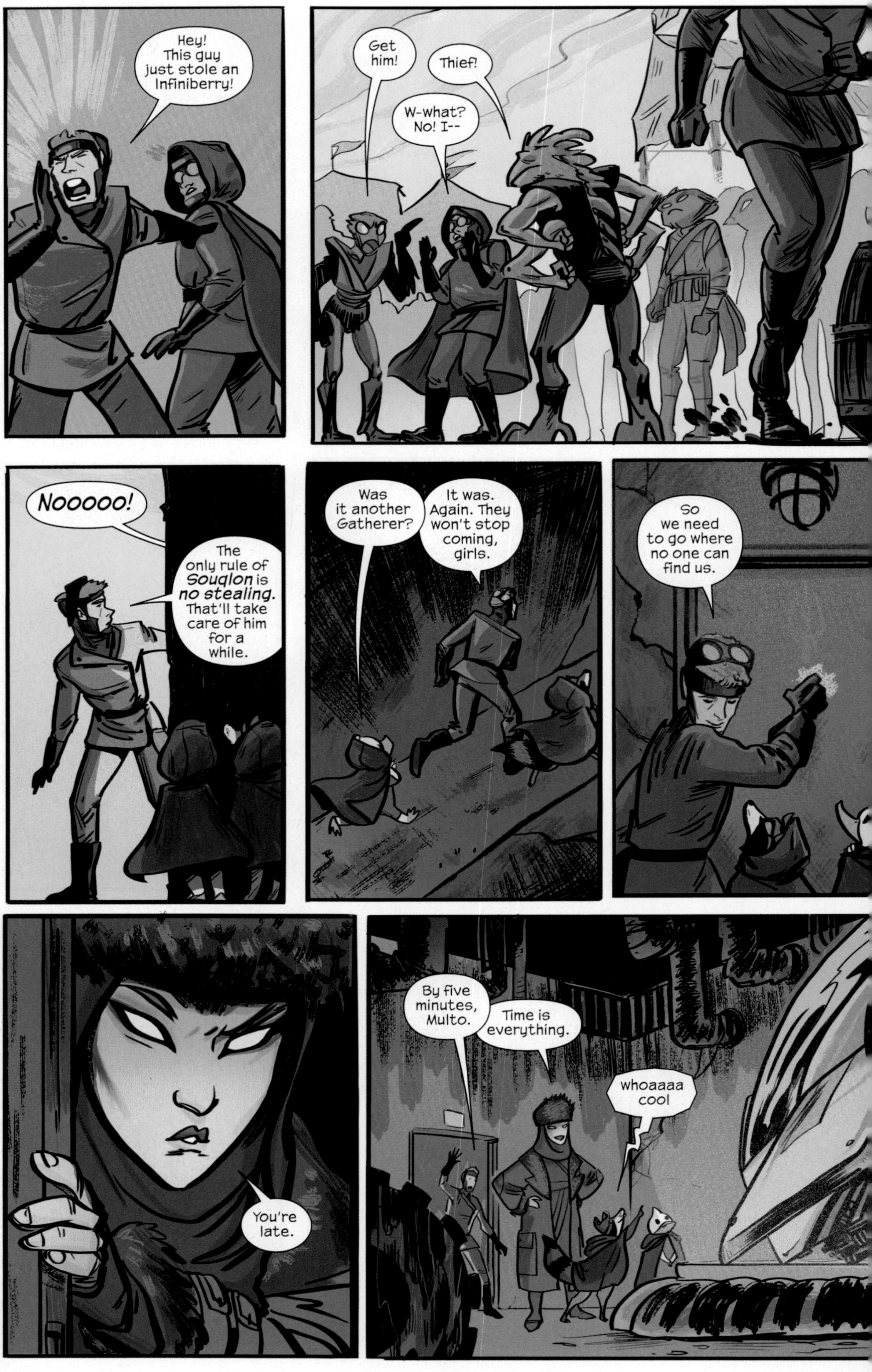
Hey! This guy just stole an Infiniberry!
Get him!
Thief!
W-what? No! I--
Nooooo!
The only rule of Souqlon is no stealing. That'll take care of him for a while.
Was it another Gatherer?
It was. Again. They won't stop coming, girls.
So we need to go where no one can find us.
You're late.
By five minutes, Multo.
Time is everything.
whoaaaa cool

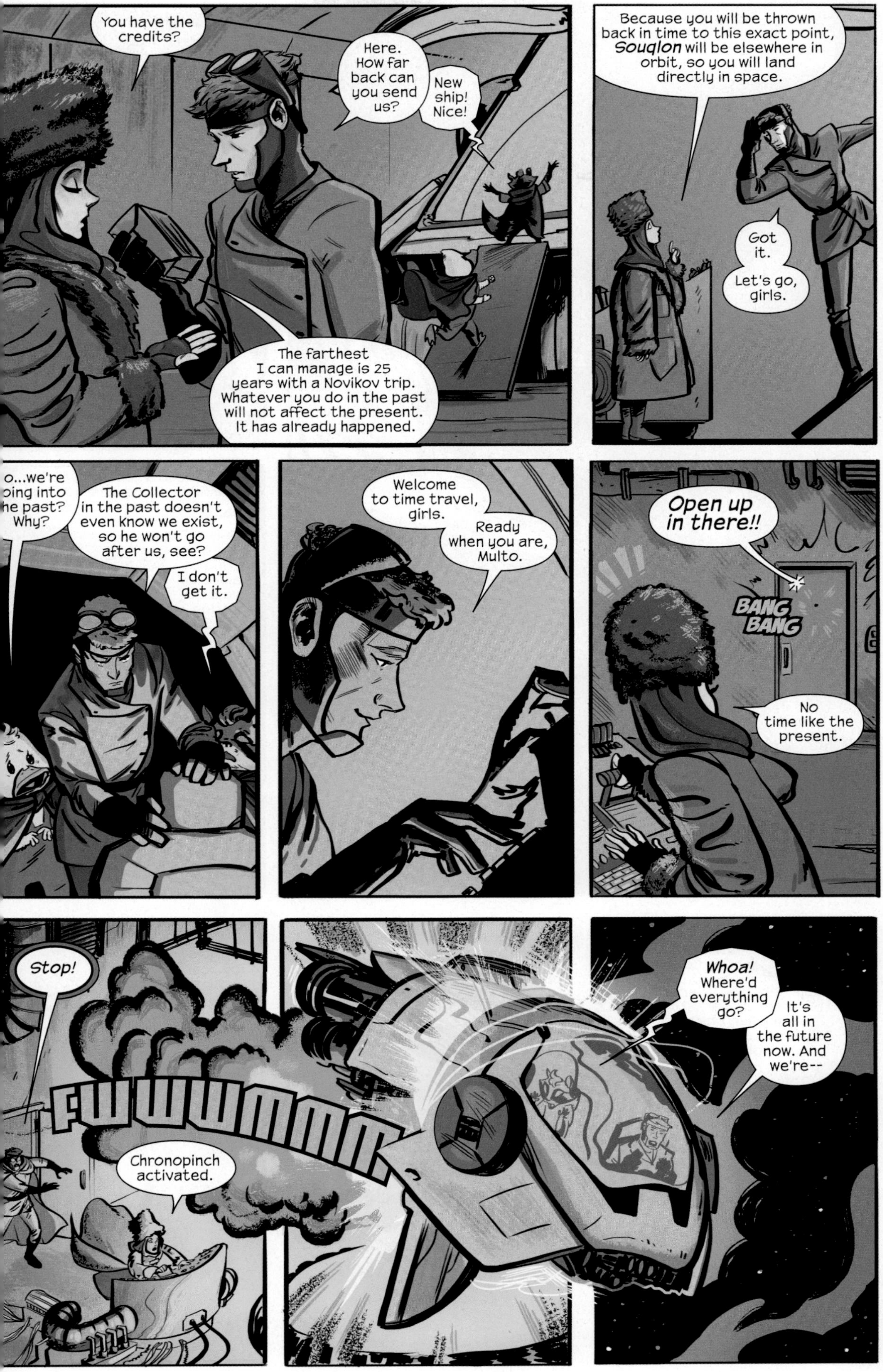
You have the credits?
Here. How far back can you send us?
New ship! Nice!
The farthest I can manage is 25 years with a Novikov trip. Whatever you do in the past will not affect the present. It has already happened.
Because you will be thrown back in time to this exact point, Souqlon will be elsewhere in orbit, so you will land directly in space.
Got it.
Let's go, girls.
o...we're oing into he past? Why?
The Collector in the past doesn't even know we exist, so he won't go after us, see?
I don't get it.
Welcome to time travel, girls.
Ready when you are, Multo.
Open up in there!!
BANG BANG
No time like the present.
Stop!
FWWWMMM
Chronopinch activated.
Whoa! Where'd everything go?
It's all in the future now. And we're--

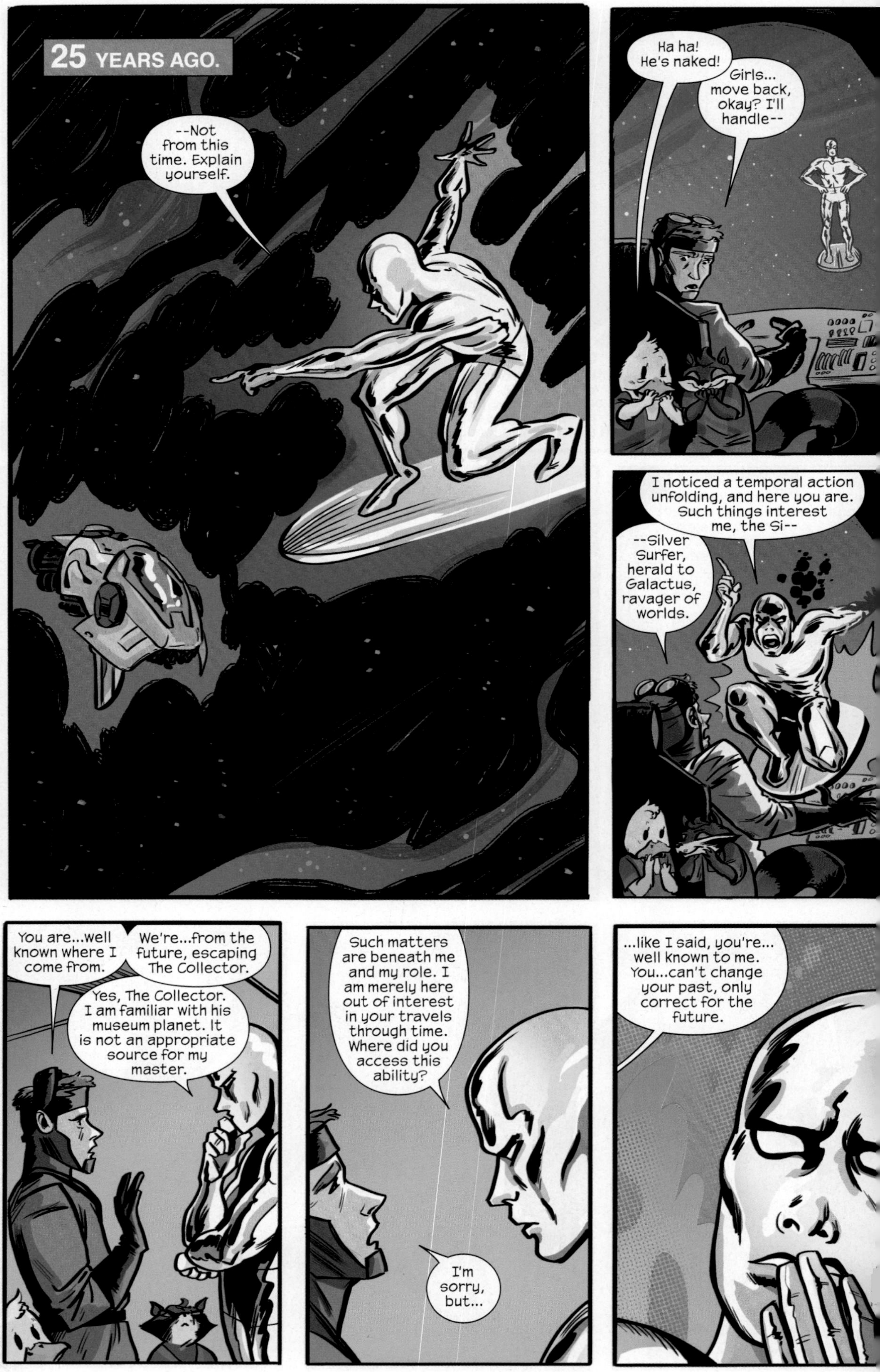
25 YEARS AGO.
--Not from this time. Explain yourself.
Ha ha! He's naked!
Girls... move back, okay? I'll handle--
I noticed a temporal action unfolding, and here you are. Such things interest me, the Si--
--Silver Surfer, herald to Galactus, ravager of worlds.
You are...well known where I come from.
We're...from the future, escaping The Collector.
Yes, The Collector. I am familiar with his museum planet. It is not an appropriate source for my master.
Such matters are beneath me and my role. I am merely here out of interest in your travels through time. Where did you access this ability?
I'm sorry, but...
...like I said, you're... well known to me. You...can't change your past, only correct for the future.

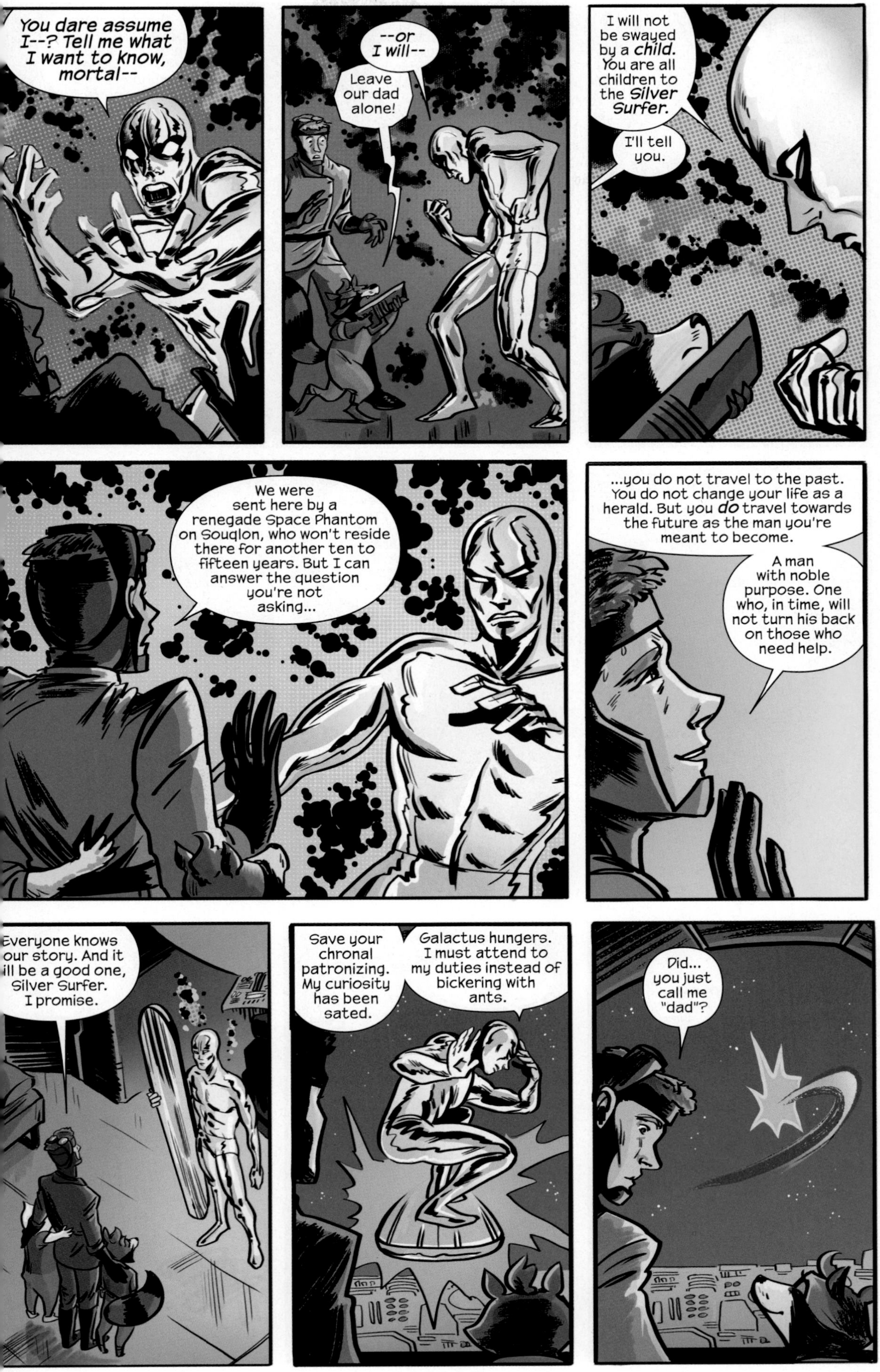

You dare assume I--? Tell me what I want to know, mortal--
--or I will--
Leave our dad alone!
I will not be swayed by a child. You are all children to the Silver Surfer.
I'll tell you.
We were sent here by a renegade Space Phantom on Souglon, who won't reside there for another ten to fifteen years. But I can answer the question you're not asking...
...you do not travel to the past. You do not change your life as a herald. But you do travel towards the future as the man you're meant to become.
A man with noble purpose. One who, in time, will not turn his back on those who need help.
Everyone knows our story. And it ill be a good one, Silver Surfer. I promise.
Save your chronal patronizing. My curiosity has been sated.
Galactus hungers. I must attend to my duties instead of bickering with ants.
Did... you just call me "dad"?

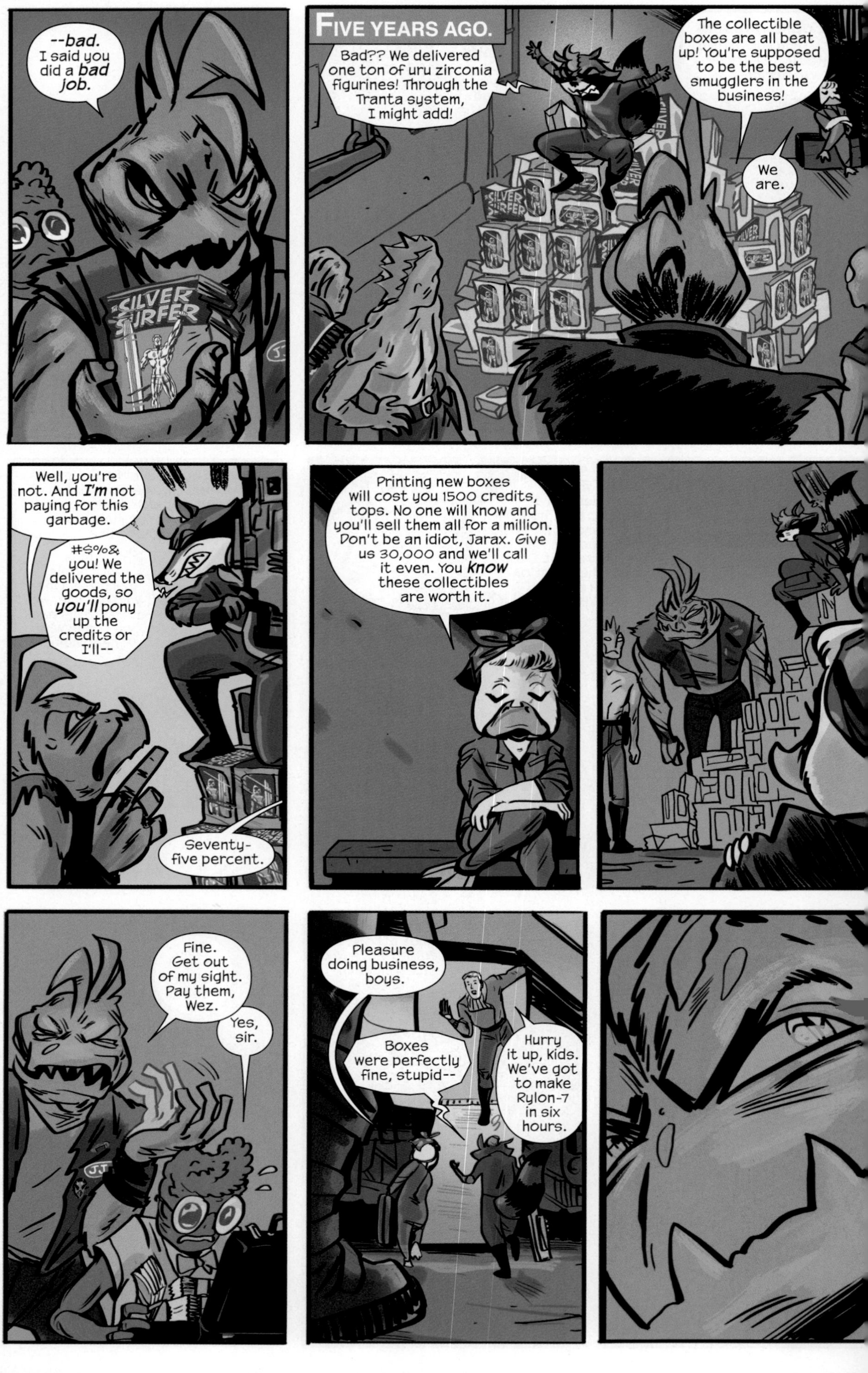

--*bad.* I said you did a ***bad job.***
FIVE YEARS AGO.
Bad?? We delivered one ton of uru zirconia figurines! Through the Tranta system, I might add!
The collectible boxes are all beat up! You're supposed to be the best smugglers in the business!
We are.
SILVER SURFER
Well, you're not. And ***I'm*** not paying for this garbage.
#$%& you! We delivered the goods, so ***you'll*** pony up the credits or I'll--
Seventy-five percent.
Printing new boxes will cost you 1500 credits, tops. No one will know and you'll sell them all for a million. Don't be an idiot, Jarax. Give us 30,000 and we'll call it even. You ***know*** these collectibles are worth it.
Fine. Get out of my sight. Pay them, Wez.
Yes, sir.
Pleasure doing business, boys.
Boxes were perfectly fine, stupid--
Hurry it up, kids. We've got to make Rylon-7 in six hours.

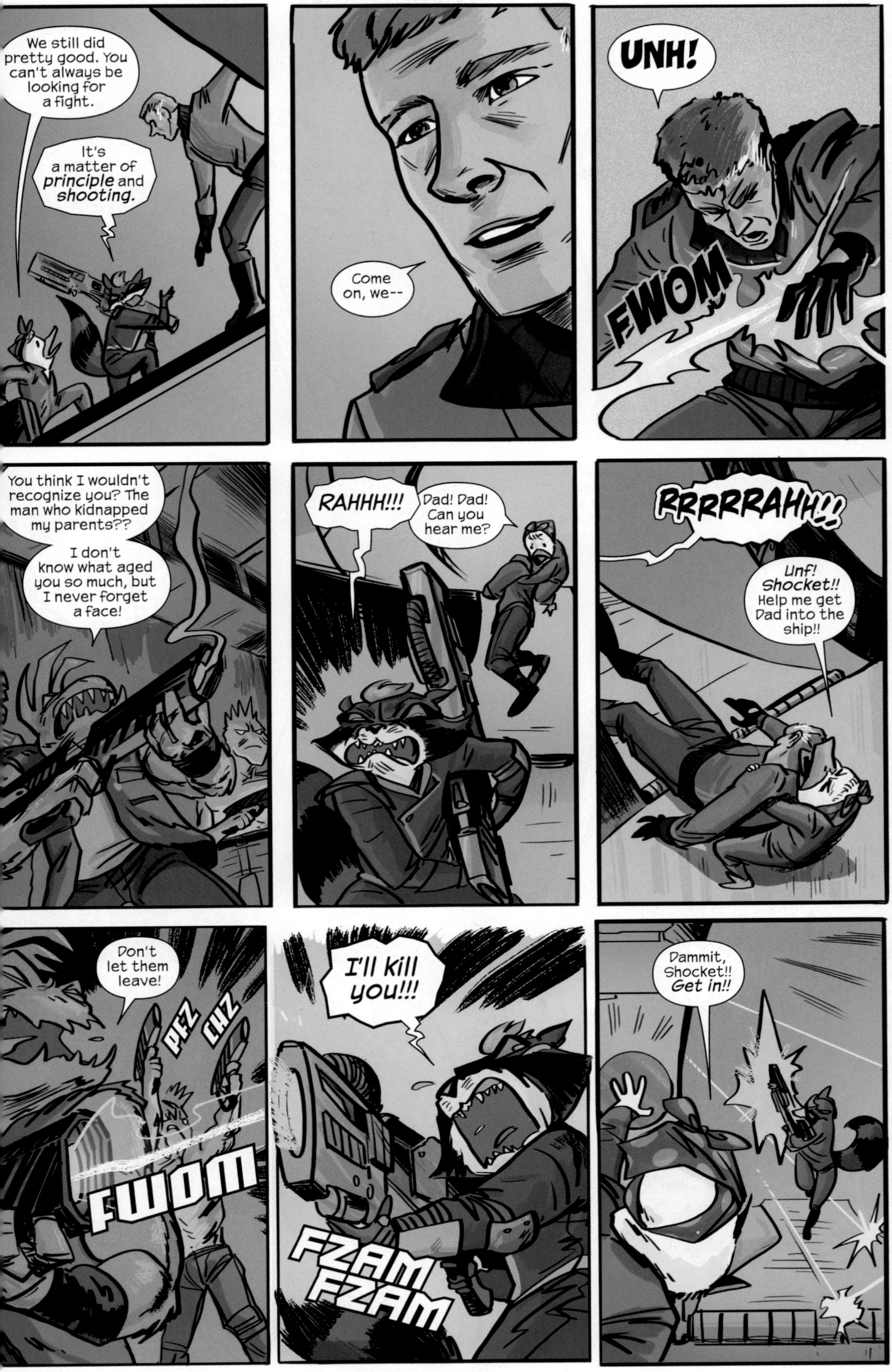
We still did pretty good. You can't always be looking for a fight.
It's a matter of *principle* and *shooting.*
Come on, we--
UNH!
FWOM
You think I wouldn't recognize you? The man who kidnapped my parents??
I don't know what aged you so much, but I never forget a face!
RAHHH!!!
Dad! Dad! Can you hear me?
RRRRRAHH!!!
Unf! *Shocket!!* Help me get Dad into the ship!!
Don't let them leave!
PFZ
CHZ
FWOM
I'll kill you!!!
FZAM FZAM
Dammit, Shocket!! *Get in!!*

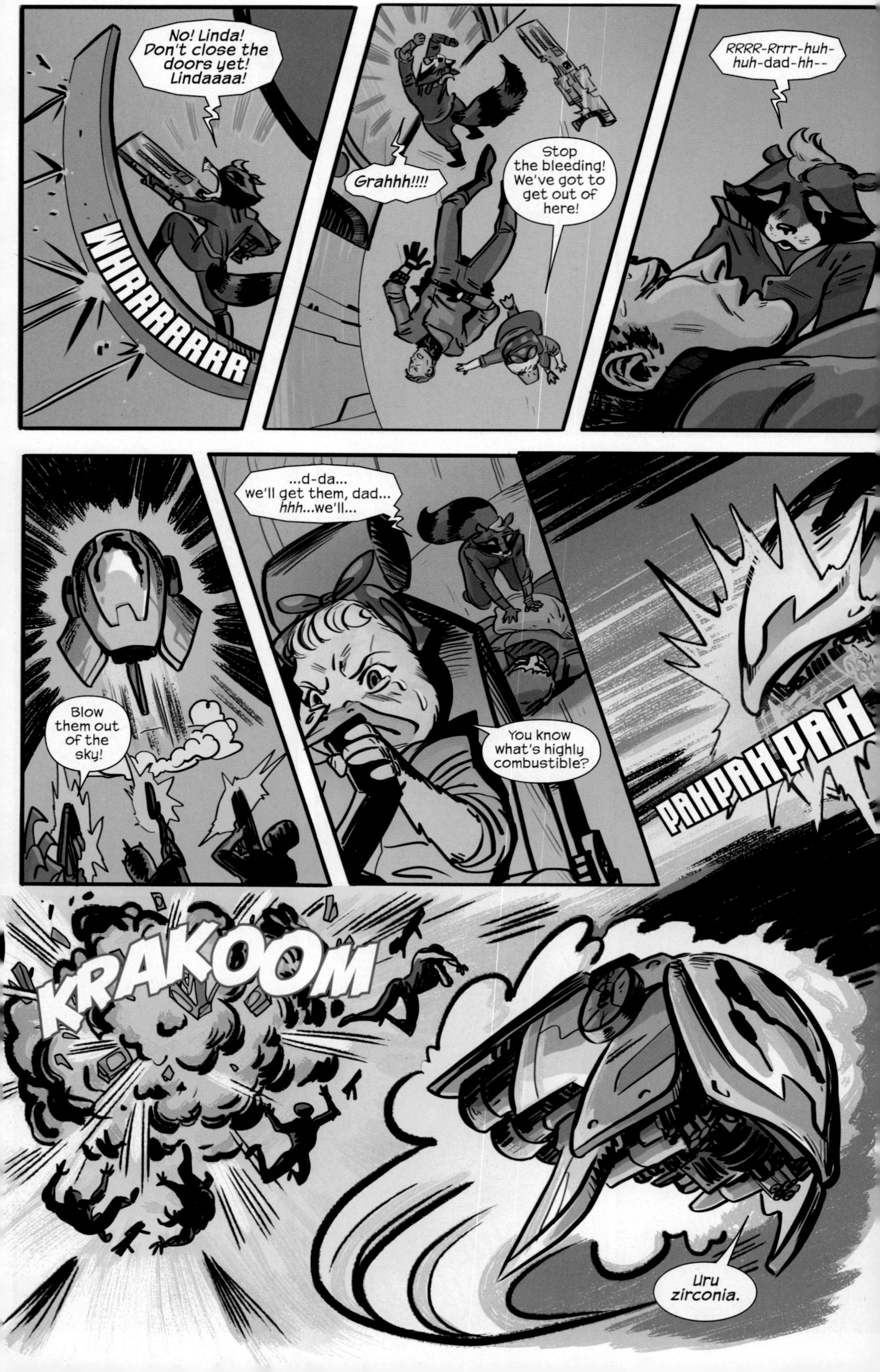
No! Linda! Don't close the doors yet! Lindaaaa!
WHRRRRRRRR
Grahhh!!!!
Stop the bleeding! We've got to get out of here!
RRRR-Rrrr-huh-huh-dad-hh--
Blow them out of the sky!
...d-da... we'll get them, dad... hhh...we'll...
You know what's highly combustible?
PAHPAHPAH
KRAKOOM
Uru zirconia.

Dad!

...heh...

Hold on! I punched in coordinates to Hornby-9! We'll get you help!

...Looks like... the past finally... caught up to us... ≠cough≠ or we caught up...to it... heh ≠cough cough≠...

≠snf≠... d-dad...

...I'm sorry, girls...≠cough≠ I promised you...I'd get you back ...to our world...≠cough≠

We don't care about that...

≠Hu hu hu≠ Nooooo no no no...

...you're our world!

Now what am I going to do with you two?

What am I going to...

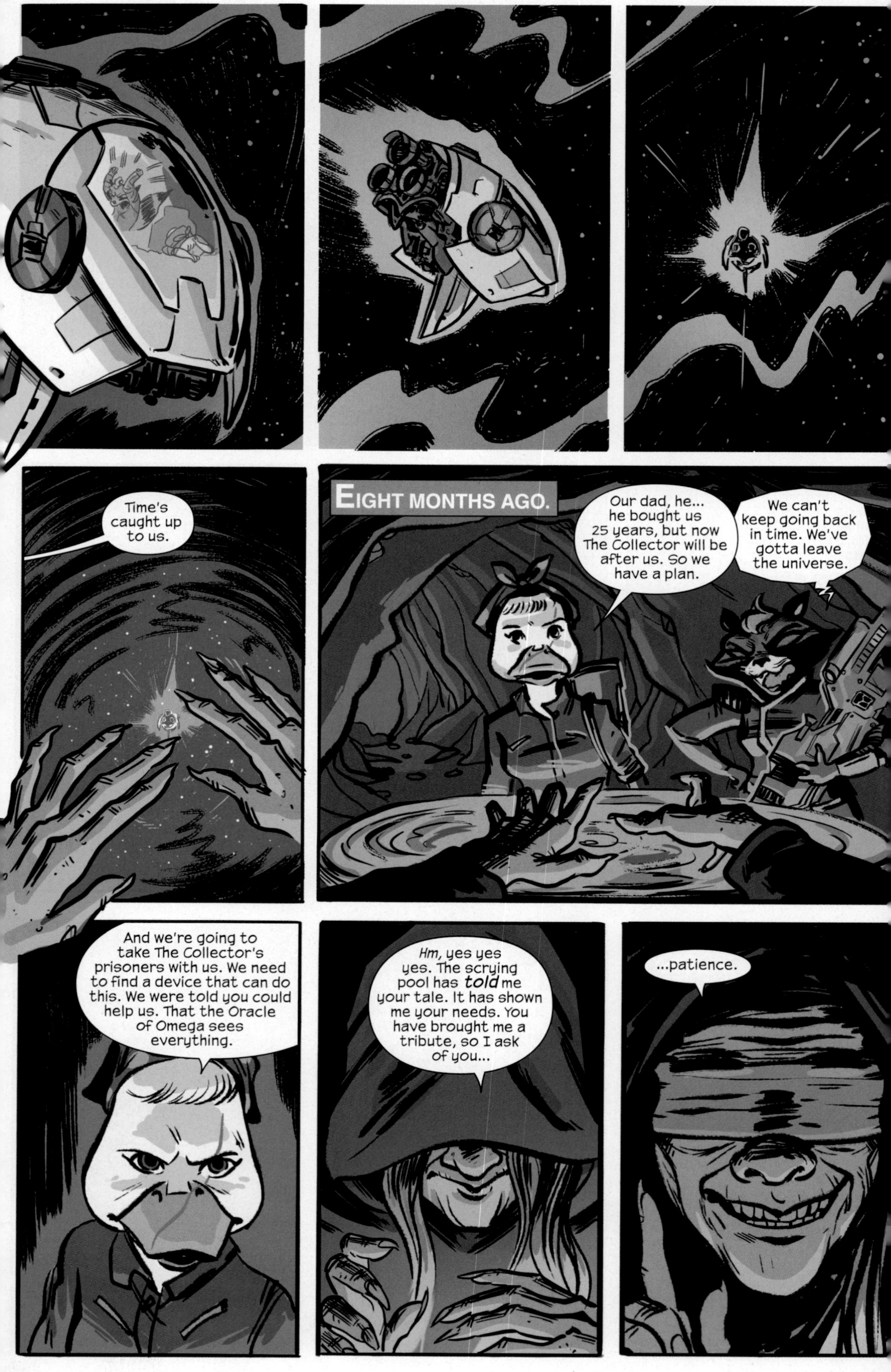
Time's caught up to us.
EIGHT MONTHS AGO.
Our dad, he... he bought us 25 years, but now The Collector will be after us. So we have a plan.
We can't keep going back in time. We've gotta leave the universe.
And we're going to take The Collector's prisoners with us. We need to find a device that can do this. We were told you could help us. That the Oracle of Omega sees everything.
Hm, yes yes yes. The scrying pool has told me your tale. It has shown me your needs. You have brought me a tribute, so I ask of you...
...patience.

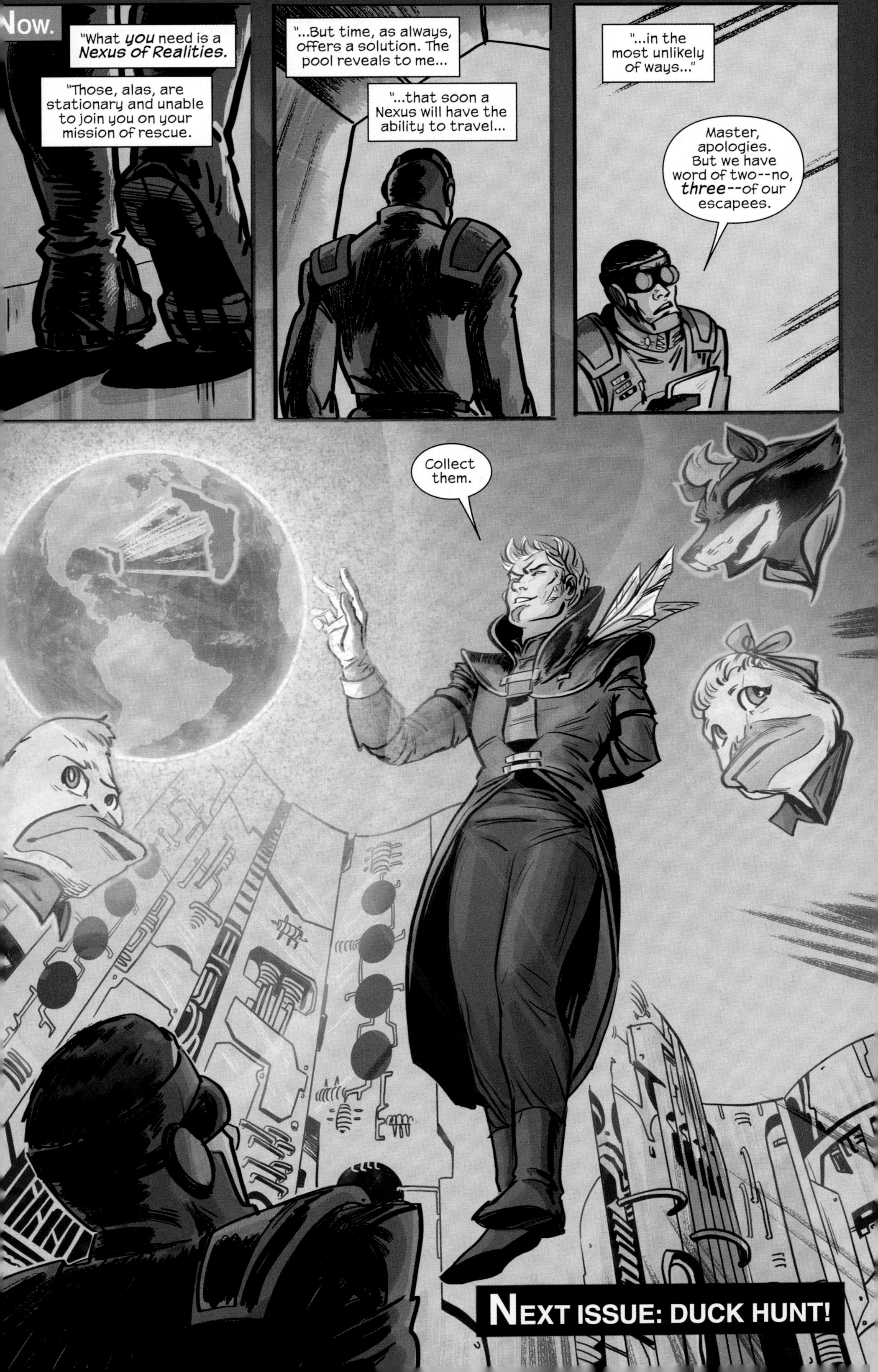

Now.
"What *you* need is a *Nexus of Realities.*
"Those, alas, are stationary and unable to join you on your mission of rescue.
"...But time, as always, offers a solution. The pool reveals to me...
"...that soon a Nexus will have the ability to travel...
"...in the most unlikely of ways..."
Master, apologies. But we have word of two--no, *three*--of our escapees.
Collect them.
NEXT ISSUE: DUCK HUNT!

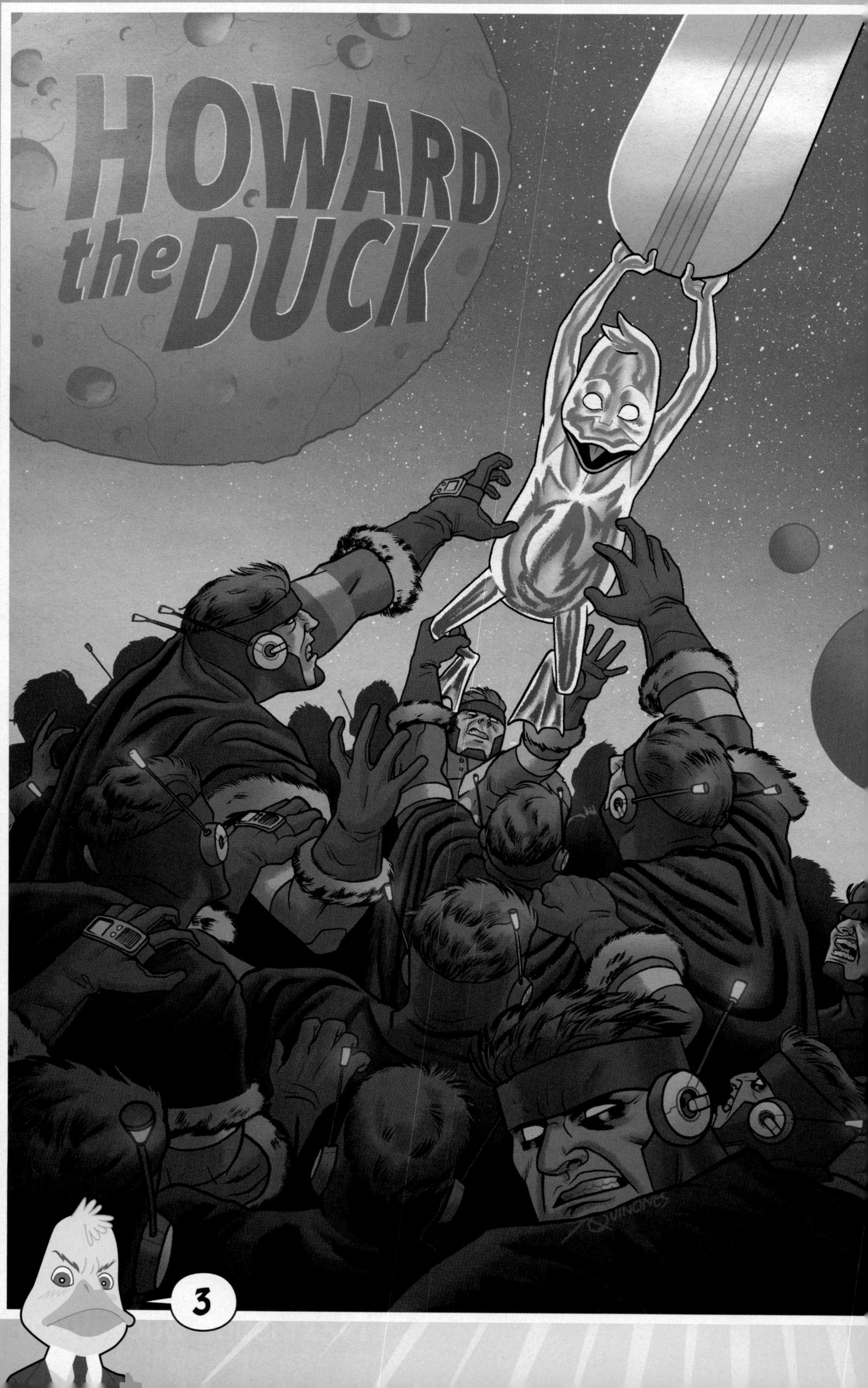
HOWARD
the DUCK

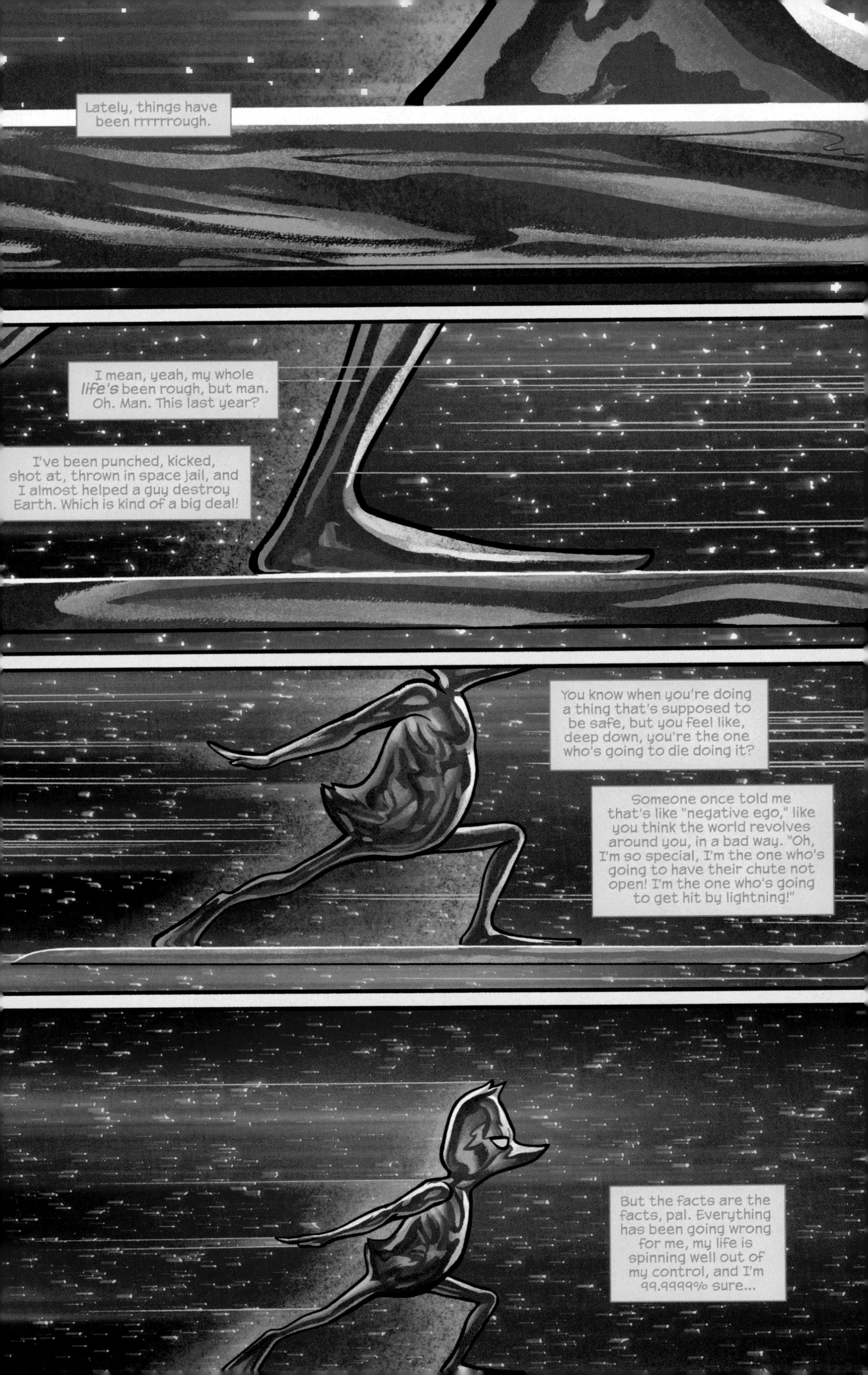
Lately, things have been rrrrrrough.
I mean, yeah, my whole *life's* been rough, but man. Oh. Man. This last year?
I've been punched, kicked, shot at, thrown in space jail, and I almost helped a guy destroy Earth. Which is kind of a big deal!
You know when you're doing a thing that's supposed to be safe, but you feel like, deep down, you're the one who's going to die doing it?
Someone once told me that's like "negative ego," like you think the world revolves around you, in a bad way. "Oh, I'm so special, I'm the one who's going to have their chute not open! I'm the one who's going to get hit by lightning!"
But the facts are the facts, pal. Everything has been going wrong for me, my life is spinning well out of my control, and I'm 99.9999% sure...

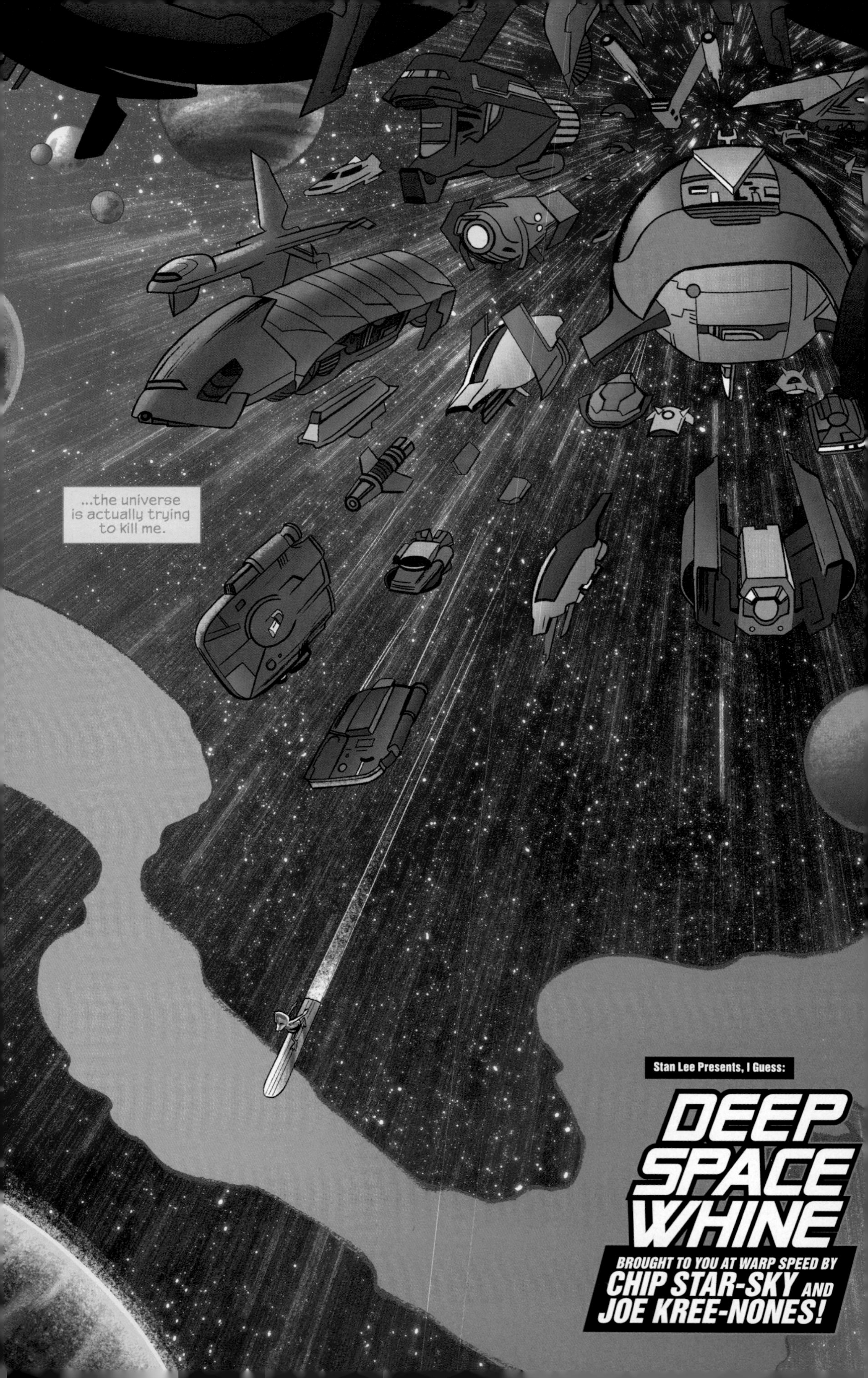
...the universe is actually trying to kill me.
Stan Lee Presents, I Guess:
DEEP SPACE WHINE
BROUGHT TO YOU AT WARP SPEED BY
CHIP STAR-SKY AND
JOE KREE-NONES!

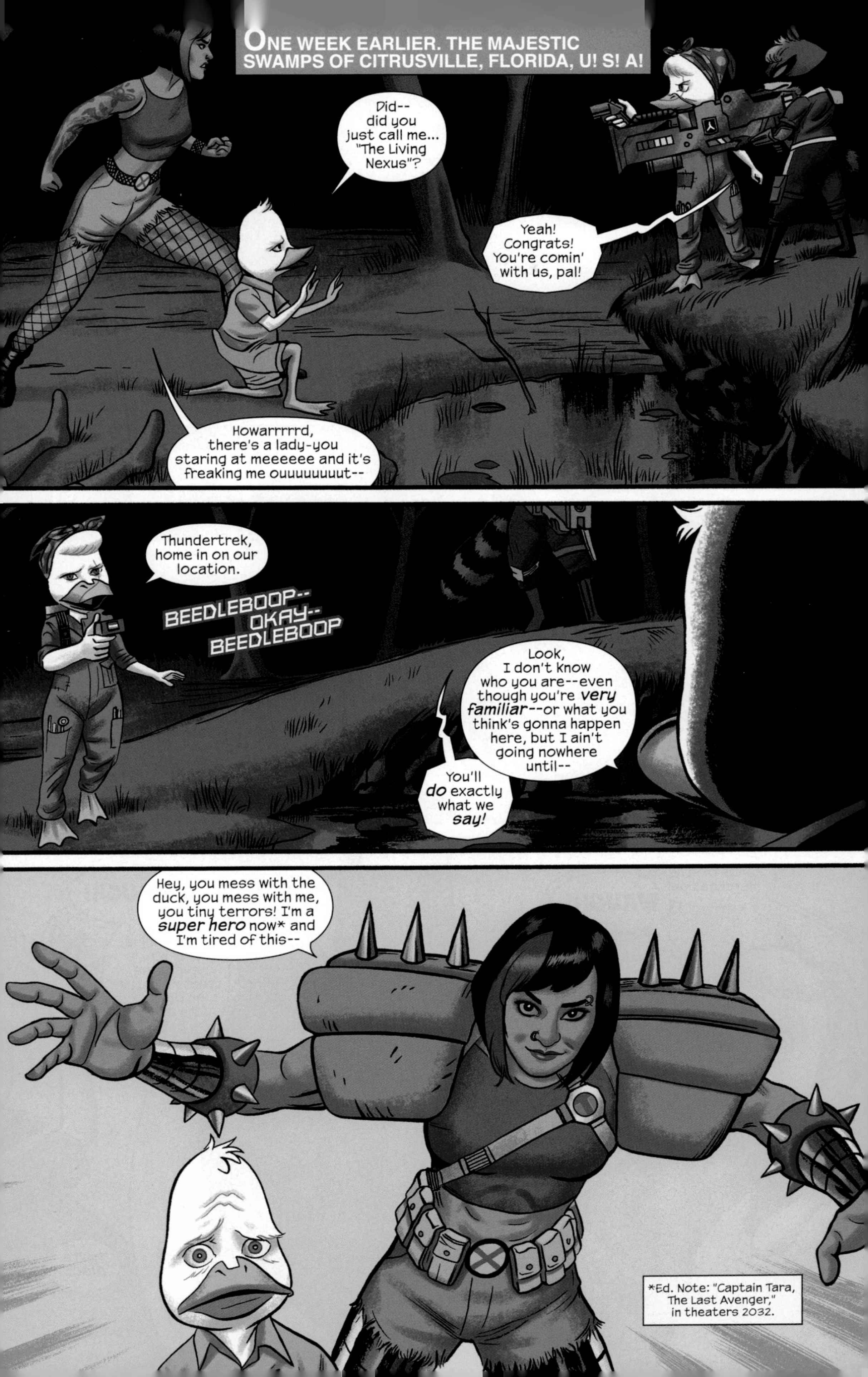
ONE WEEK EARLIER. THE MAJESTIC SWAMPS OF CITRUSVILLE, FLORIDA, U! S! A!
Did-- did you just call me... "The Living Nexus"?
Yeah! Congrats! You're comin' with us, pal!
Howarrrrrd, there's a lady-you staring at meeeeee and it's freaking me ouuuuuuuut--
Thundertrek, home in on our location.
BEEDLEBOOP-- OKAY-- BEEDLEBOOP
Look, I don't know who you are--even though you're very familiar--or what you think's gonna happen here, but I ain't going nowhere until--
You'll do exactly what we say!
Hey, you mess with the duck, you mess with me, you tiny terrors! I'm a super hero now* and I'm tired of this--
*Ed. Note: "Captain Tara, The Last Avenger," in theaters 2032.

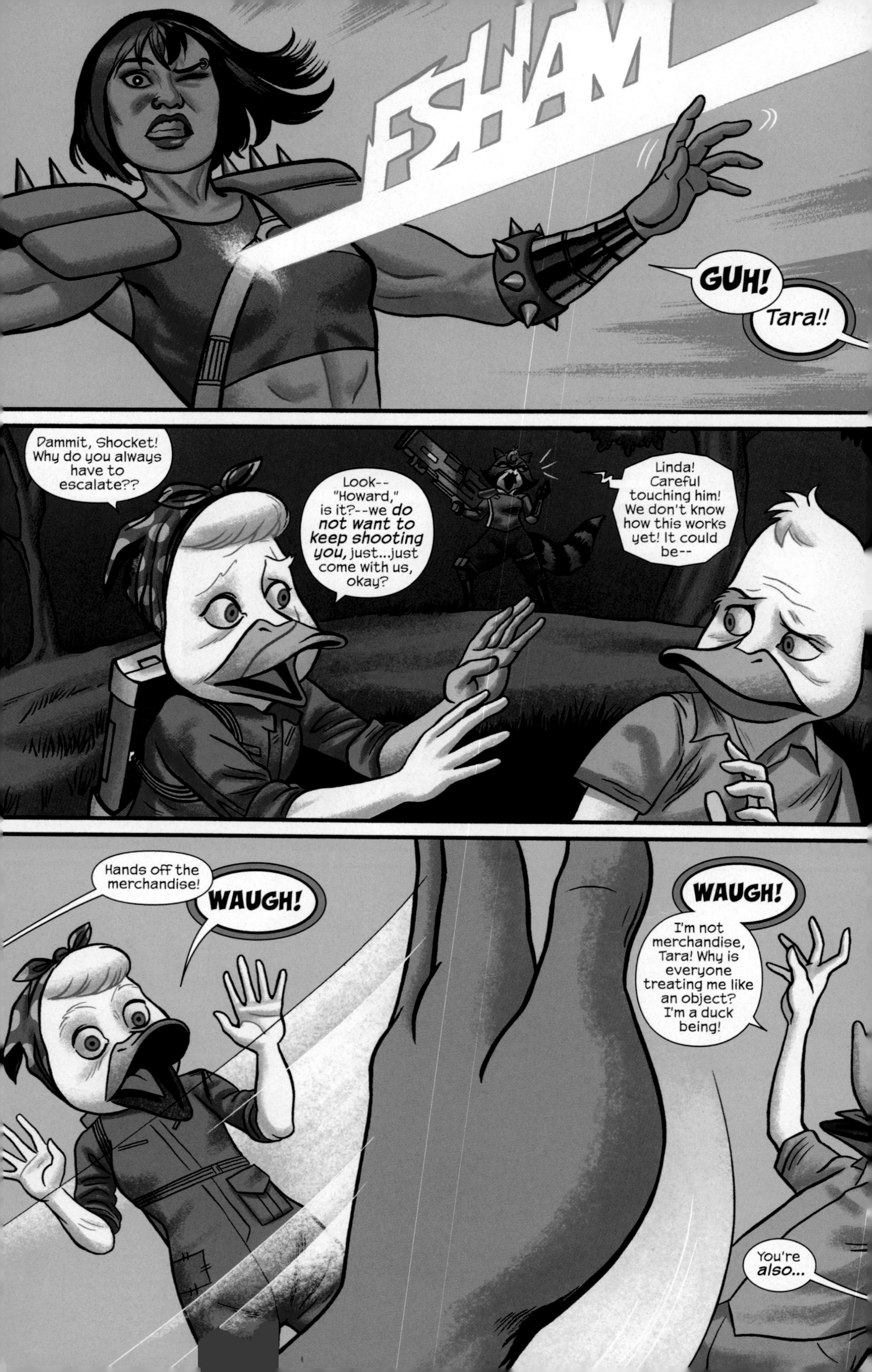
FSHAM
GUH!
Tara!!
Dammit, Shocket! Why do you always have to escalate??
Look-- "Howard," is it?--we do not want to keep shooting you, just...just come with us, okay?
Linda! Careful touching him! We don't know how this works yet! It could be--
Hands off the merchandise!
WAUGH!
WAUGH!
I'm not merchandise, Tara! Why is everyone treating me like an object? I'm a duck being!
You're also...

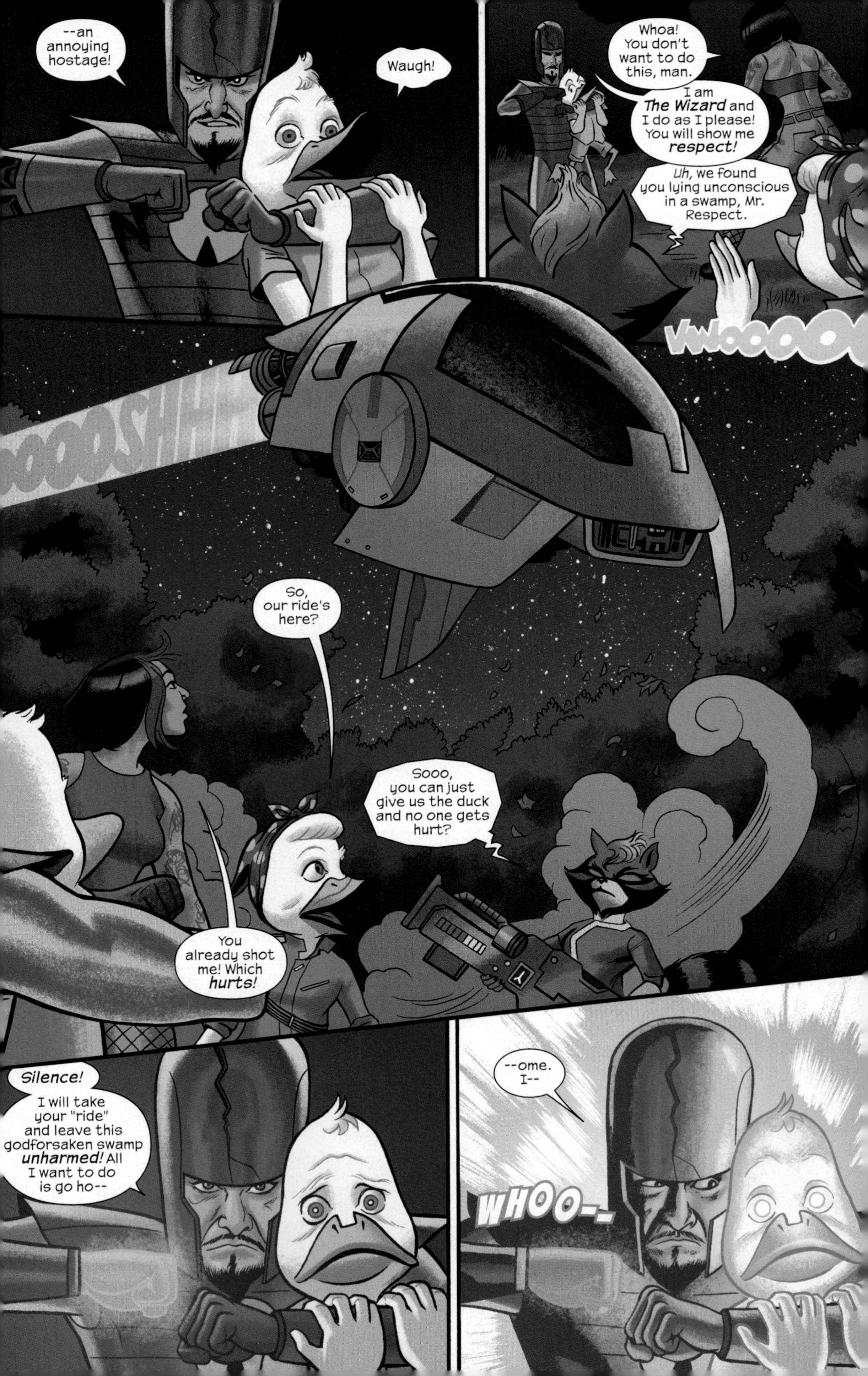
--an annoying hostage!
Waugh!
Whoa! You don't want to do this, man.
I am *The Wizard* and I do as I please! You will show me *respect!*
Uh, we found you lying unconscious in a swamp, Mr. Respect.
VWOOOOO
OOOOSHH
So, our ride's here?
Sooo, you can just give us the duck and no one gets hurt?
You already shot me! Which *hurts!*
Silence!
I will take your "ride" and leave this godforsaken swamp *unharmed!* All I want to do is go ho--
WHOO--
--ome. I--

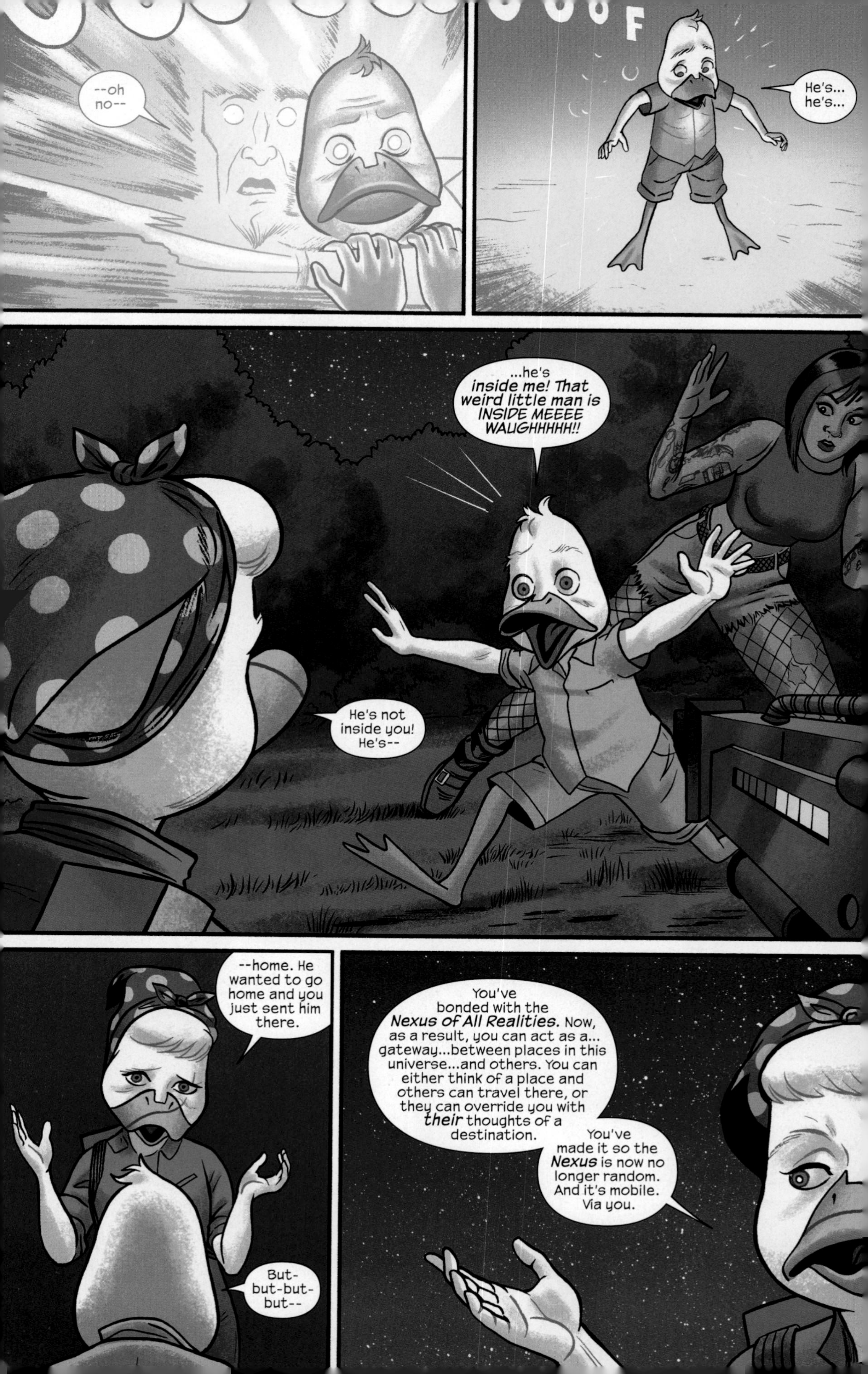

--oh no--
OOF
He's... he's...
...he's *inside me!* That weird little man is INSIDE MEEEE WAUGHHHHH!!
He's not inside you! He's--
--home. He wanted to go home and you just sent him there.
But- but-but-but--
You've bonded with the *Nexus of All Realities.* Now, as a result, you can act as a... gateway...between places in this universe...and others. You can either think of a place and others can travel there, or they can override you with *their* thoughts of a destination.
You've made it so the *Nexus* is now no longer random. And it's mobile. Via you.

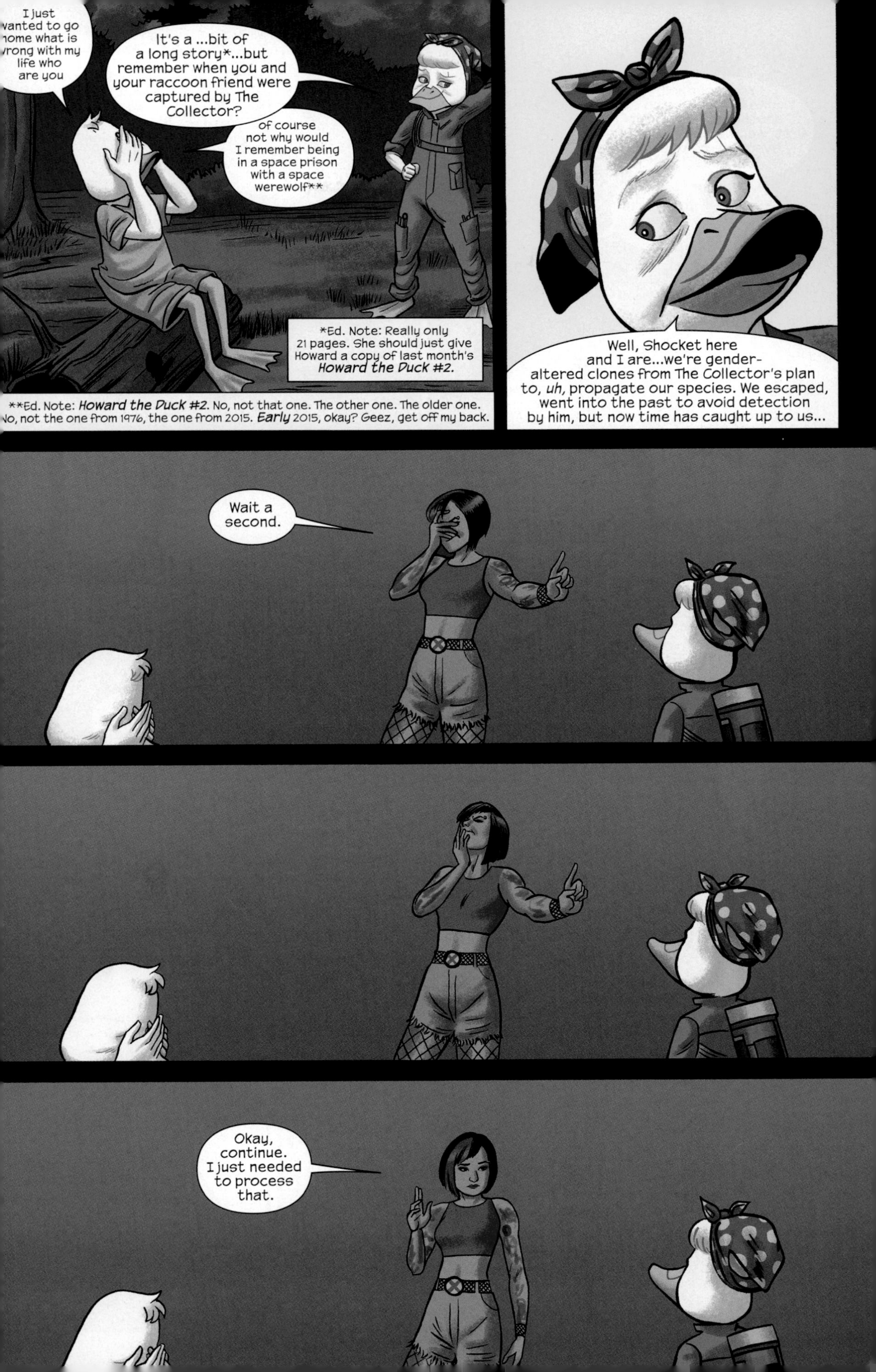
I just wanted to go home what is wrong with my life who are you
It's a ...bit of a long story*...but remember when you and your raccoon friend were captured by The Collector?
of course not why would I remember being in a space prison with a space werewolf**
*Ed. Note: Really only 21 pages. She should just give Howard a copy of last month's Howard the Duck #2.
**Ed. Note: Howard the Duck #2. No, not that one. The other one. The older one. No, not the one from 1976, the one from 2015. Early 2015, okay? Geez, get off my back.
Well, Shocket here and I are...we're gender-altered clones from The Collector's plan to, uh, propagate our species. We escaped, went into the past to avoid detection by him, but now time has caught up to us...
Wait a second.
Okay, continue. I just needed to process that.

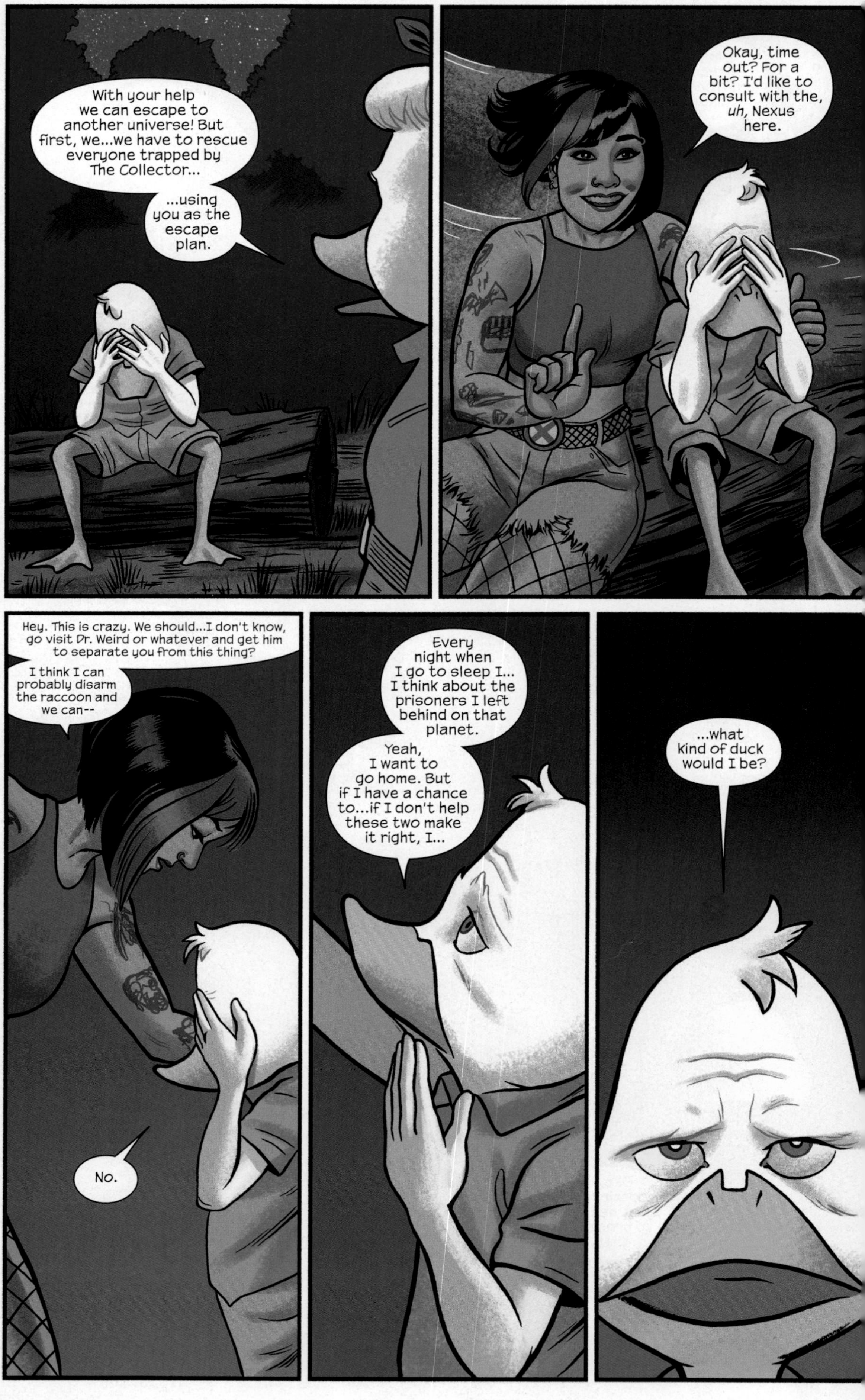
With your help we can escape to another universe! But first, we...we have to rescue everyone trapped by The Collector...
...using you as the escape plan.
Okay, time out? For a bit? I'd like to consult with the, *uh,* Nexus here.
Hey. This is crazy. We should...I don't know, go visit Dr. Weird or whatever and get him to separate you from this thing?
I think I can probably disarm the raccoon and we can--
No.
Every night when I go to sleep I... I think about the prisoners I left behind on that planet.
Yeah, I want to go home. But if I have a chance to...if I don't help these two make it right, I...
...what kind of duck would I be?

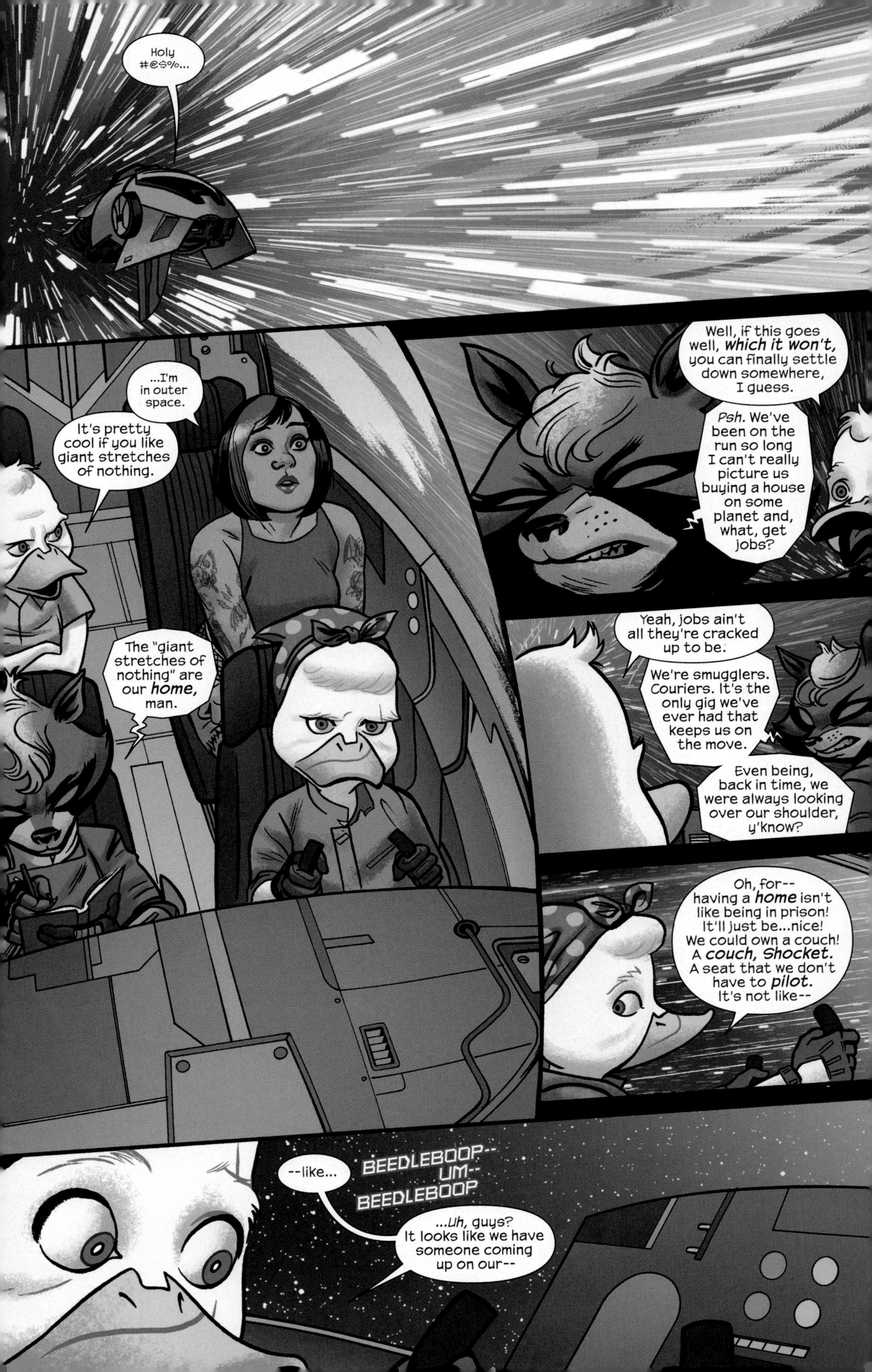
Holy #@$%...
...I'm in outer space.
It's pretty cool if you like giant stretches of nothing.
The "giant stretches of nothing" are our *home,* man.
Well, if this goes well, ***which it won't,*** you can finally settle down somewhere, I guess.
Psh. We've been on the run so long I can't really picture us buying a house on some planet and, what, get jobs?
Yeah, jobs ain't all they're cracked up to be.
We're smugglers. Couriers. It's the only gig we've ever had that keeps us on the move.
Even being, back in time, we were always looking over our shoulder, y'know?
Oh, for-- having a ***home*** isn't like being in prison! It'll just be...nice! We could own a couch! A ***couch, Shocket.*** A seat that we don't have to ***pilot.*** It's not like--
--like...
BEEDLEBOOP-- UM-- BEEDLEBOOP
...*Uh,* guys? It looks like we have someone coming up on our--

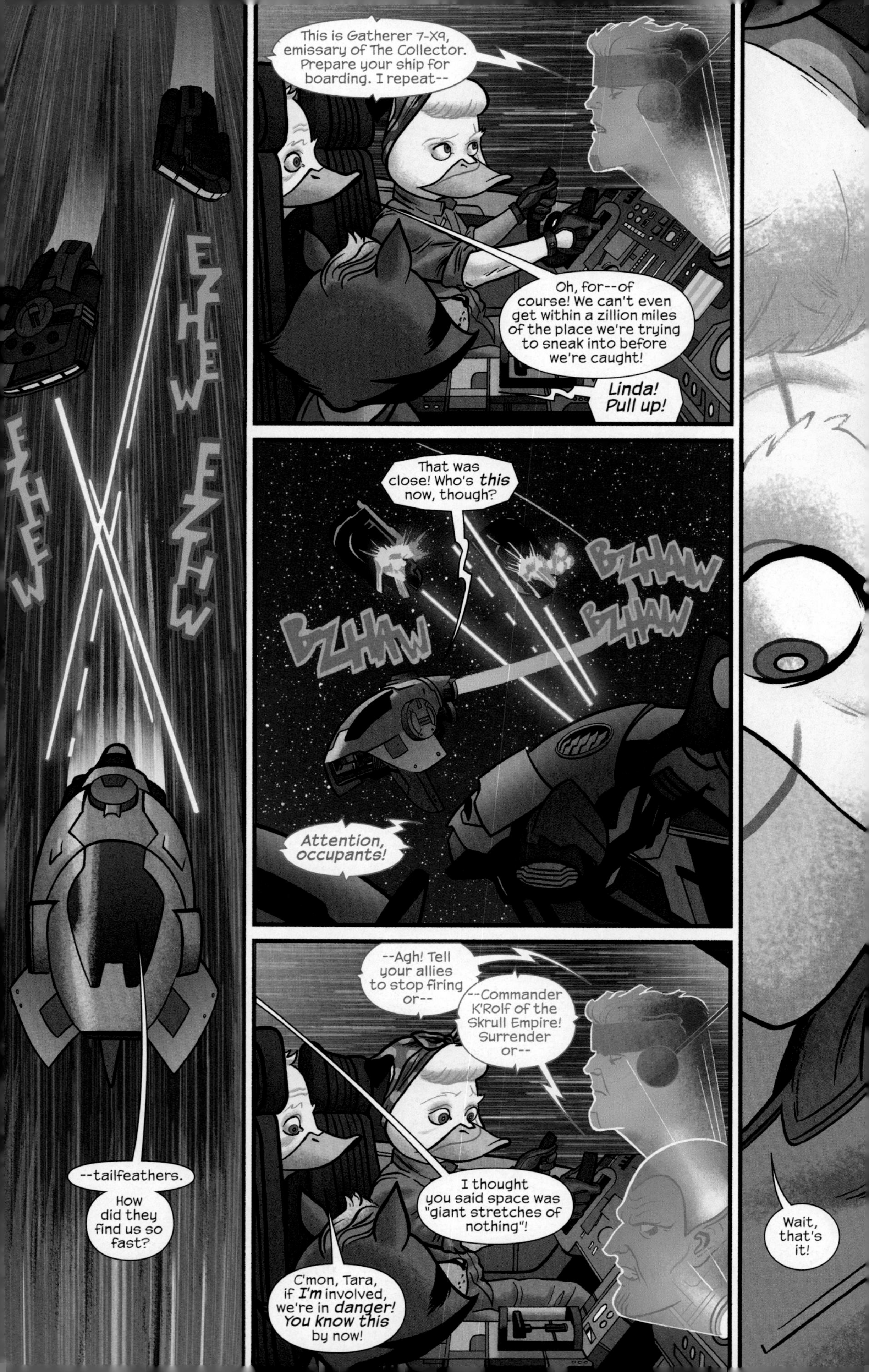

This is Gatherer 7-X9, emissary of The Collector. Prepare your ship for boarding. I repeat--
Oh, for--of course! We can't even get within a zillion miles of the place we're trying to sneak into before we're caught!
Linda! Pull up!
EZHEW EZHEW
EZHEW
--tailfeathers.
How did they find us so fast?
That was close! Who's *this* now, though?
BZHAW
BZHAW
BZHAW
Attention, occupants!
--Agh! Tell your allies to stop firing or--
--Commander K'Rolf of the Skrull Empire! Surrender or--
I thought you said space was "giant stretches of nothing"!
C'mon, Tara, if *I'm* involved, we're in *danger!* *You know this* by now!
Wait, that's it!

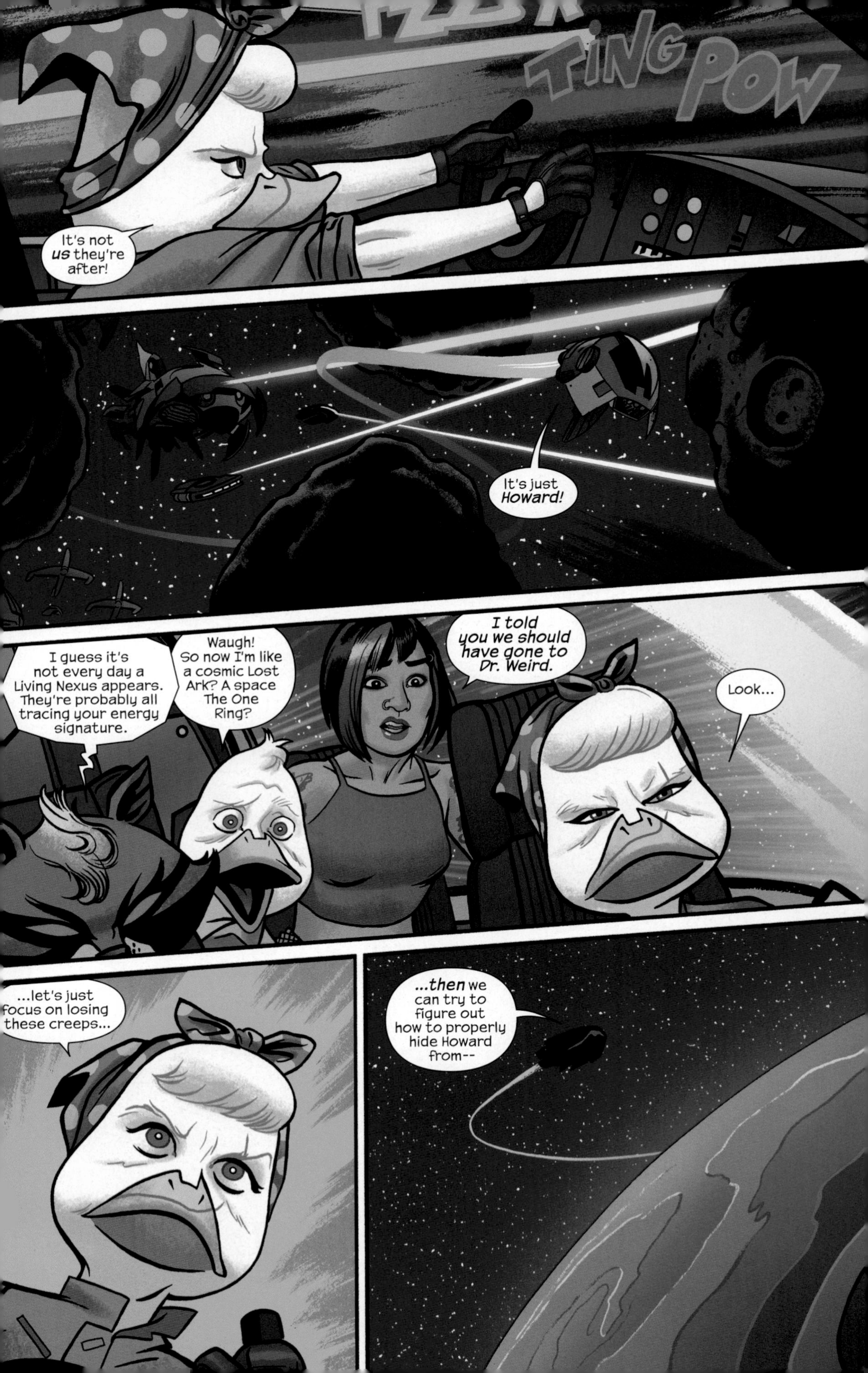
TING POW
It's not us they're after!
It's just Howard!
I guess it's not every day a Living Nexus appears. They're probably all tracing your energy signature.
Waugh! So now I'm like a cosmic Lost Ark? A space The One Ring?
I told you we should have gone to Dr. Weird.
Look...
...let's just focus on losing these creeps...
...then we can try to figure out how to properly hide Howard from--

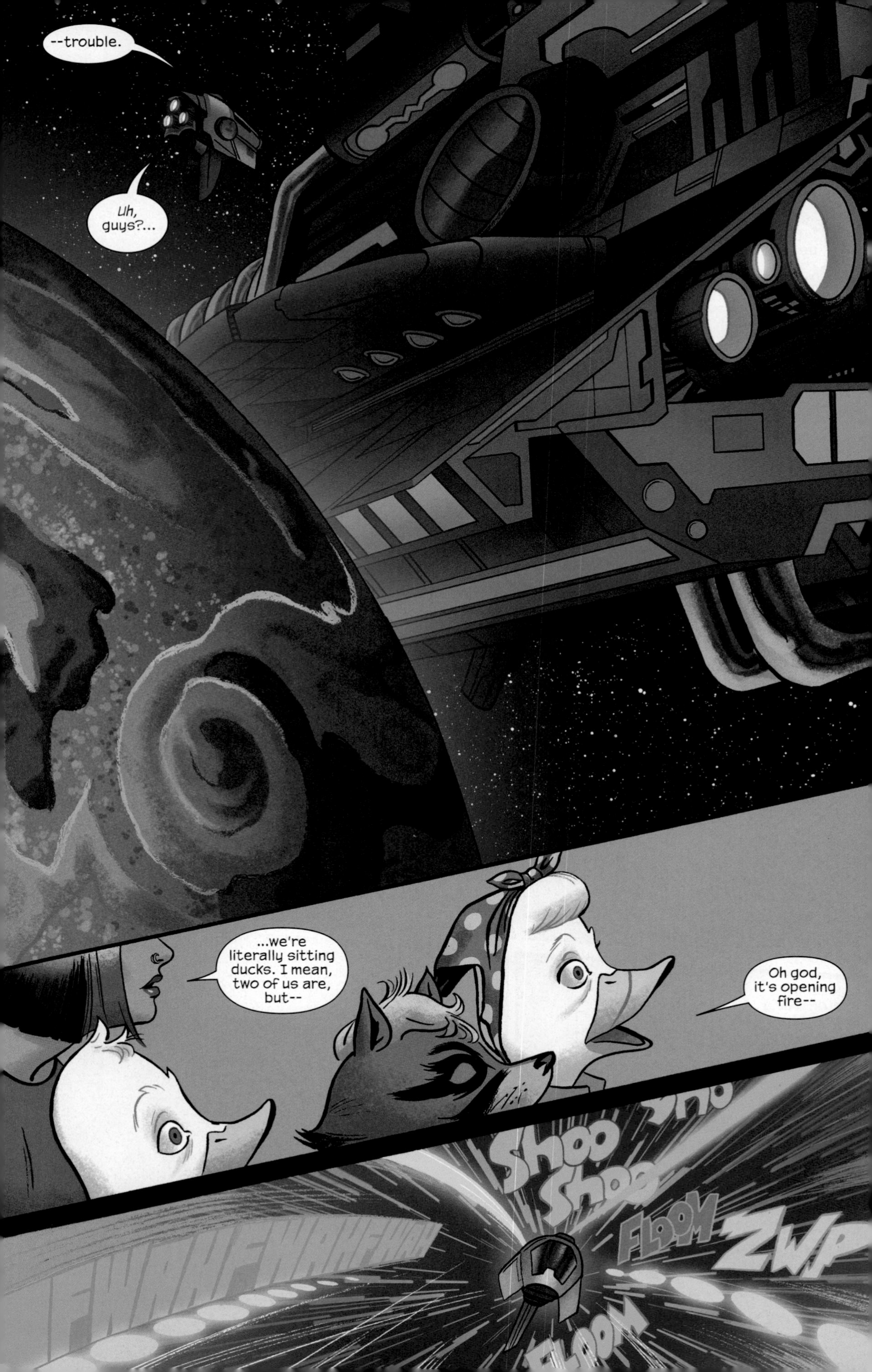
--trouble.
Uh, guys?...
...we're literally sitting ducks. I mean, two of us are, but--
Oh god, it's opening fire--
SHOO SHOO SHOO
FLOOM
ZWP
FWAH FWAH FWAH FWAH
FLOOM

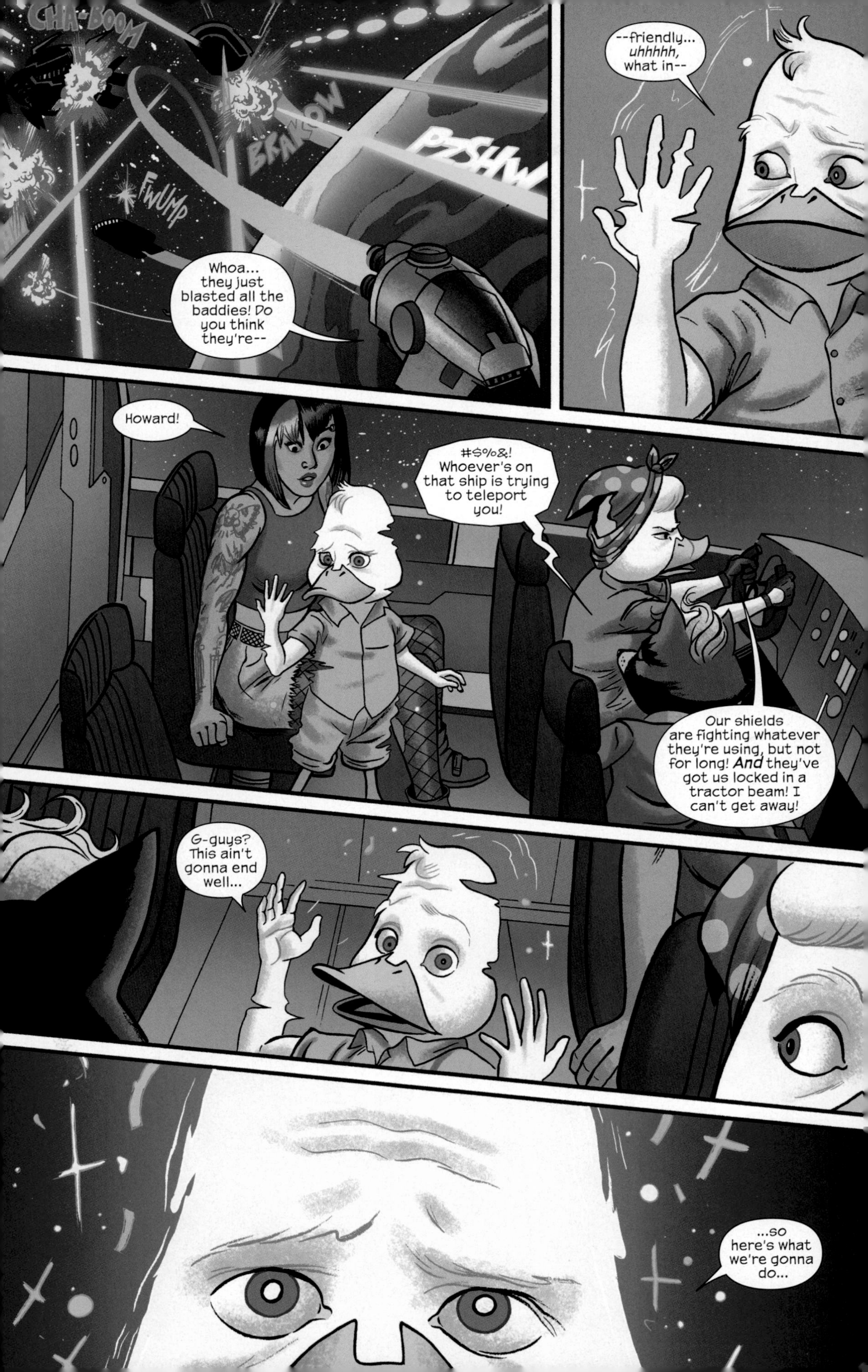
CHA-BOOM
BRAKOW
PSHW
FWUMP
Whoa... they just blasted all the baddies! Do you think they're--
--friendly... uhhhhh, what in--
Howard!
#$%&! Whoever's on that ship is trying to teleport you!
Our shields are fighting whatever they're using, but not for long! And they've got us locked in a tractor beam! I can't get away!
G-guys? This ain't gonna end well...
...so here's what we're gonna do...

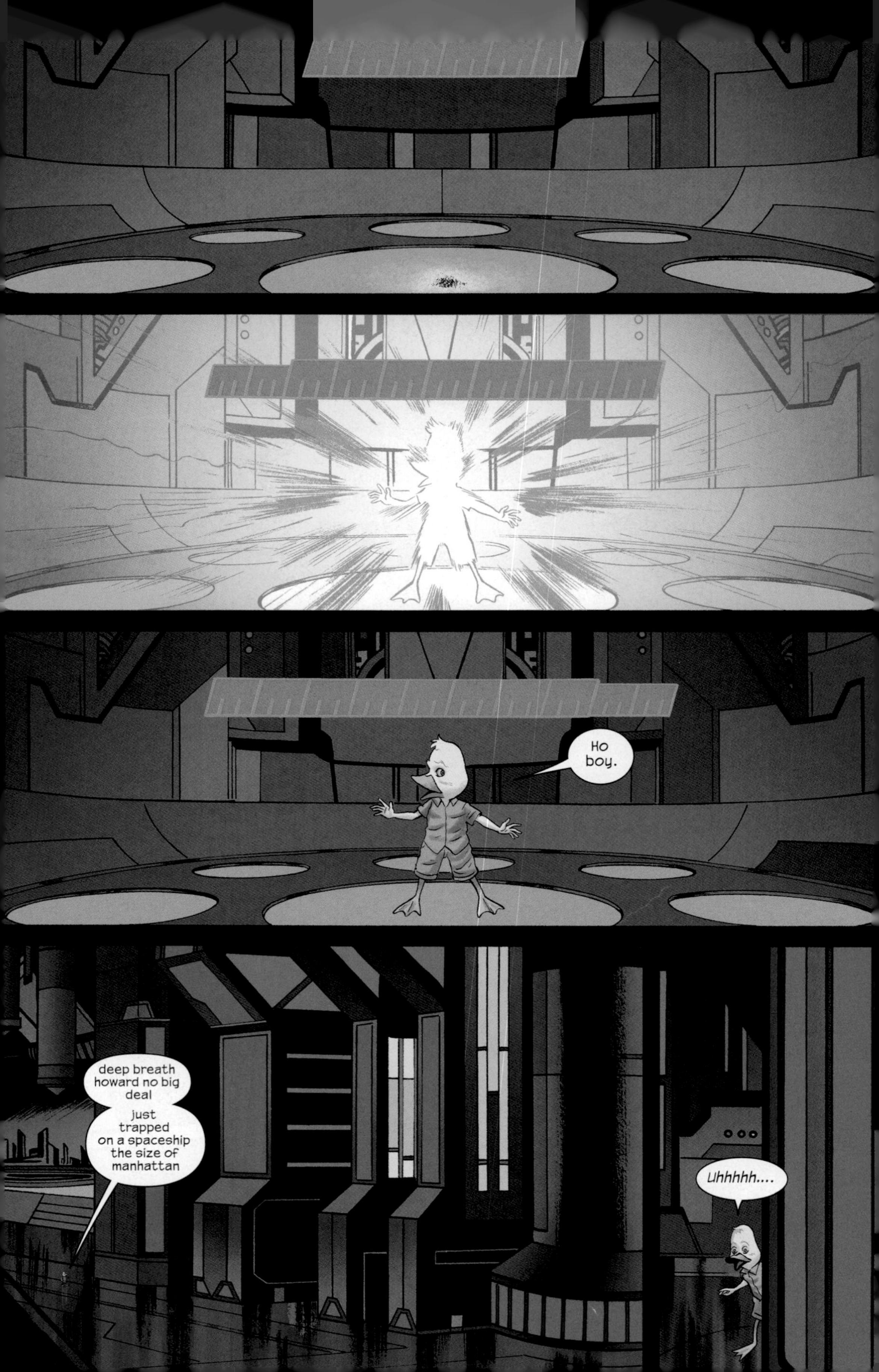
Ho boy.
deep breath howard no big deal
just trapped on a spaceship the size of manhattan
Uhhhhh....

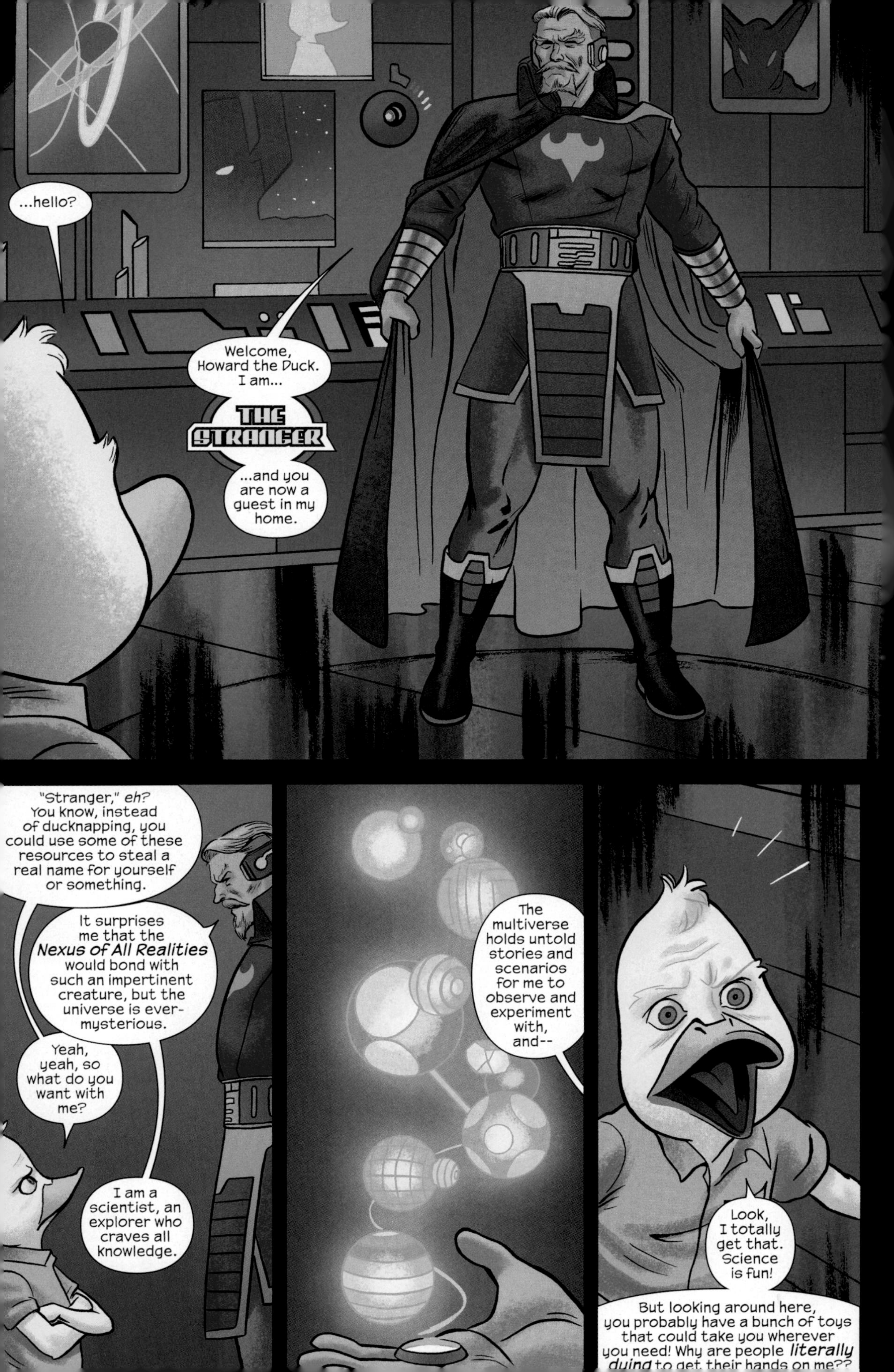
...hello?
Welcome, Howard the Duck. I am...
THE STRANGER
...and you are now a guest in my home.
"Stranger," eh? You know, instead of ducknapping, you could use some of these resources to steal a real name for yourself or something.
It surprises me that the Nexus of All Realities would bond with such an impertinent creature, but the universe is ever-mysterious.
Yeah, yeah, so what do you want with me?
I am a scientist, an explorer who craves all knowledge.
The multiverse holds untold stories and scenarios for me to observe and experiment with, and--
Look, I totally get that. Science is fun!
But looking around here, you probably have a bunch of toys that could take you wherever you need! Why are people literally dying to get their hands on me??

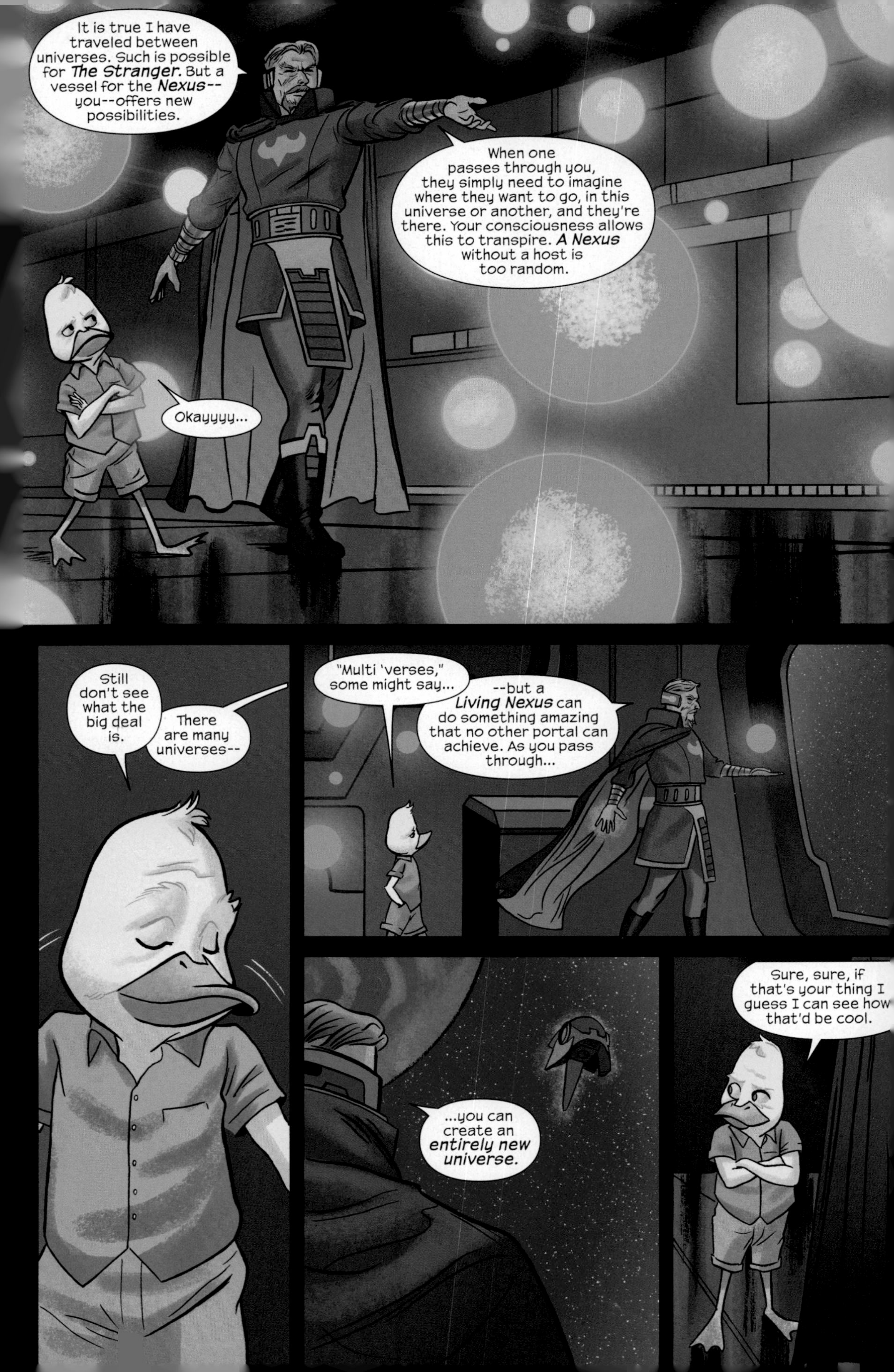
It is true I have traveled between universes. Such is possible for *The Stranger.* But a vessel for the *Nexus*--you--offers new possibilities.
When one passes through you, they simply need to imagine where they want to go, in this universe or another, and they're there. Your consciousness allows this to transpire. *A Nexus* without a host is too random.
Okayyyy...
Still don't see what the big deal is.
There are many universes--
"Multi 'verses," some might say...
--but a *Living Nexus* can do something amazing that no other portal can achieve. As you pass through...
...you can create an *entirely new universe.*
Sure, sure, if that's your thing I guess I can see how that'd be cool.

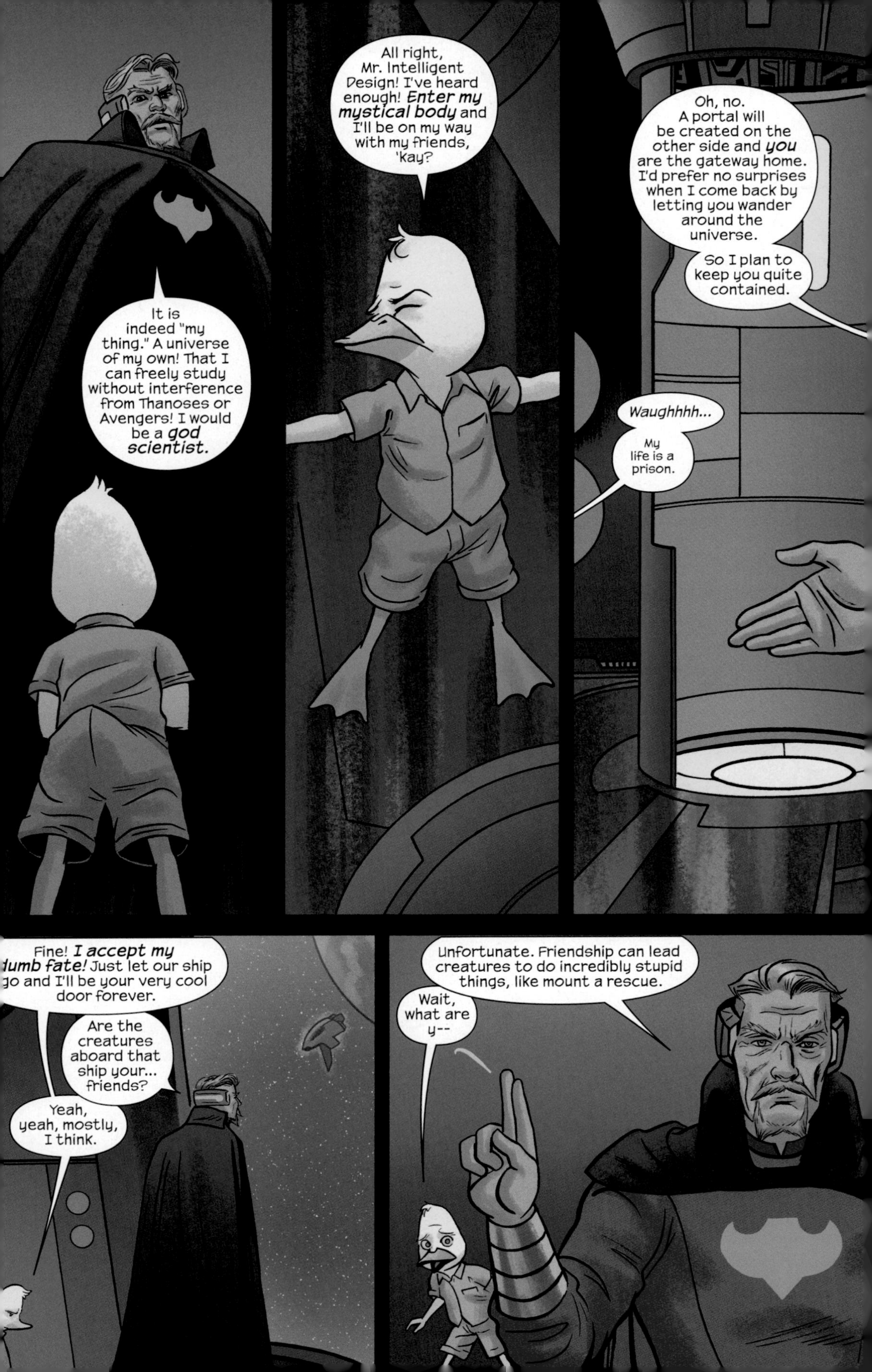
It is indeed "my thing." A universe of my own! That I can freely study without interference from Thanoses or Avengers! I would be a *god scientist*.
All right, Mr. Intelligent Design! I've heard enough! *Enter my mystical body* and I'll be on my way with my friends, 'kay?
Oh, no. A portal will be created on the other side and *you* are the gateway home. I'd prefer no surprises when I come back by letting you wander around the universe.
So I plan to keep you quite contained.
Waughhhh...
My life is a prison.
Fine! *I accept my* dumb fate! Just let our ship go and I'll be your very cool door forever.
Are the creatures aboard that ship your... friends?
Yeah, yeah, mostly, I think.
Unfortunate. Friendship can lead creatures to do incredibly stupid things, like mount a rescue.
Wait, what are y--

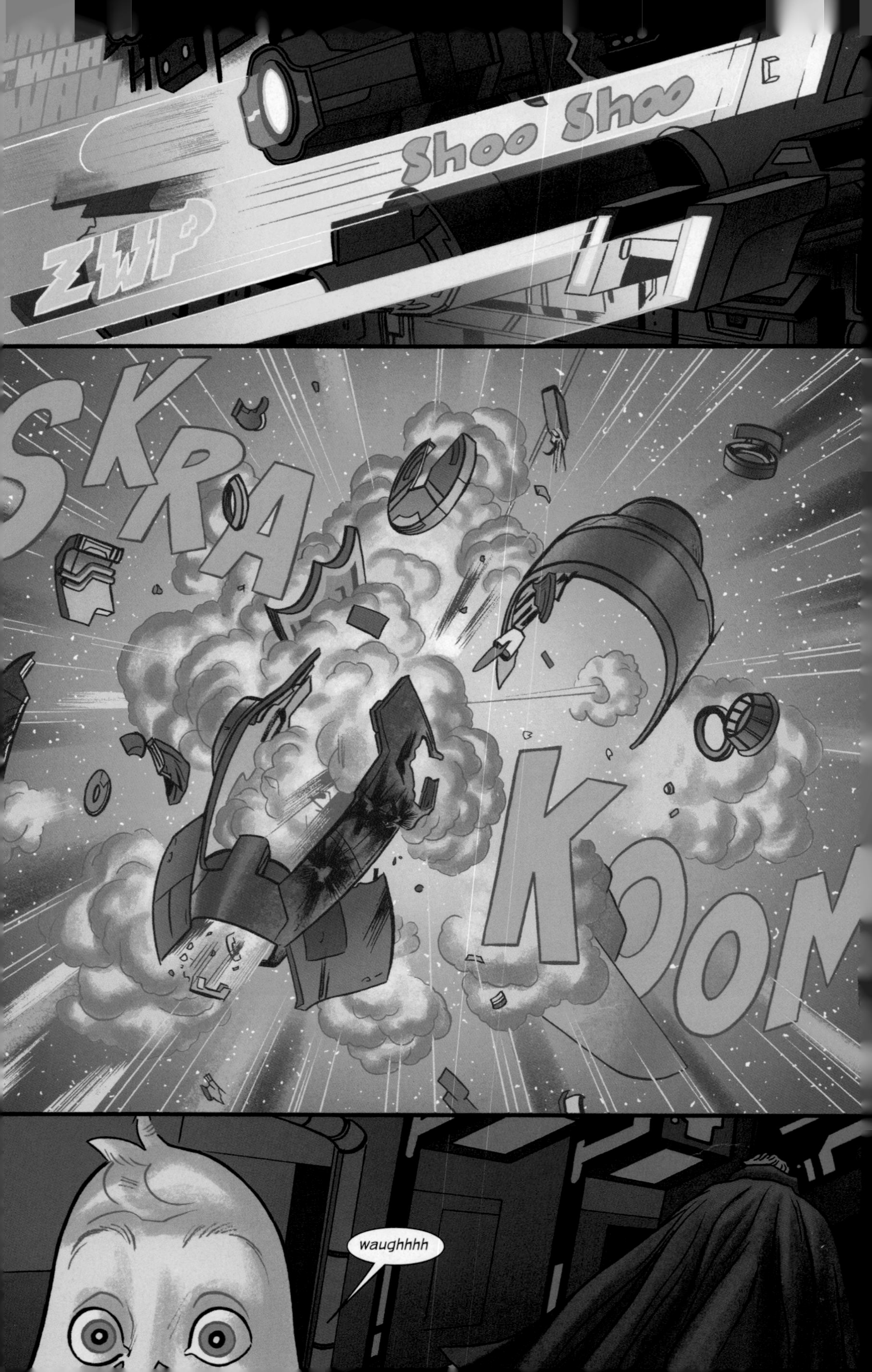
WAH
WAH
Shoo Shoo
ZWP
SKRA
KOOM
waughhhh

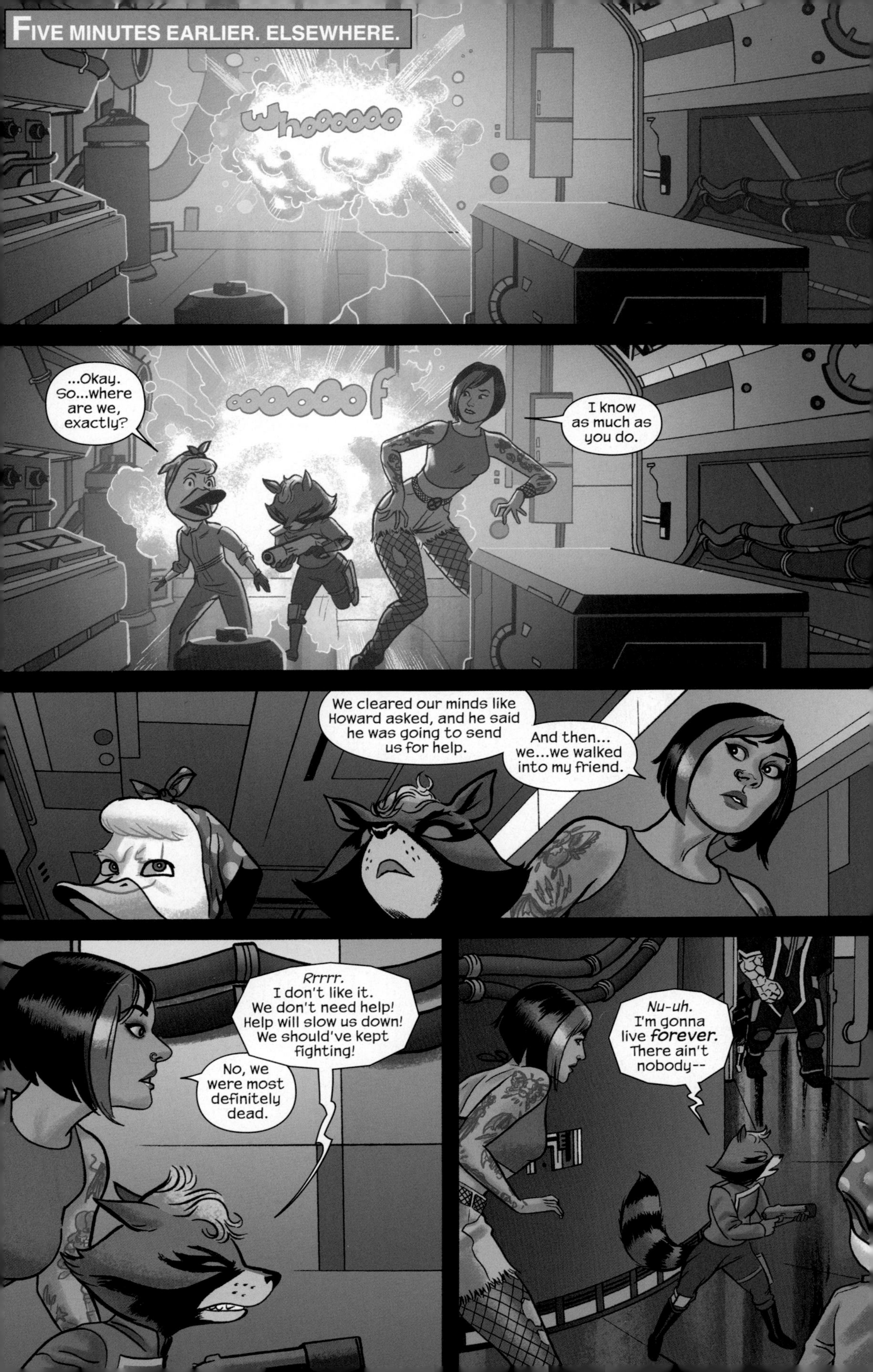
FIVE MINUTES EARLIER. ELSEWHERE.
Whooooooo
oooooof
...Okay. So...where are we, exactly?
I know as much as you do.
We cleared our minds like Howard asked, and he said he was going to send us for help.
And then... we...we walked into my friend.
Rrrrr. I don't like it. We don't need help! Help will slow us down! We should've kept fighting!
No, we were most definitely dead.
Nu-uh. I'm gonna live forever. There ain't nobody--

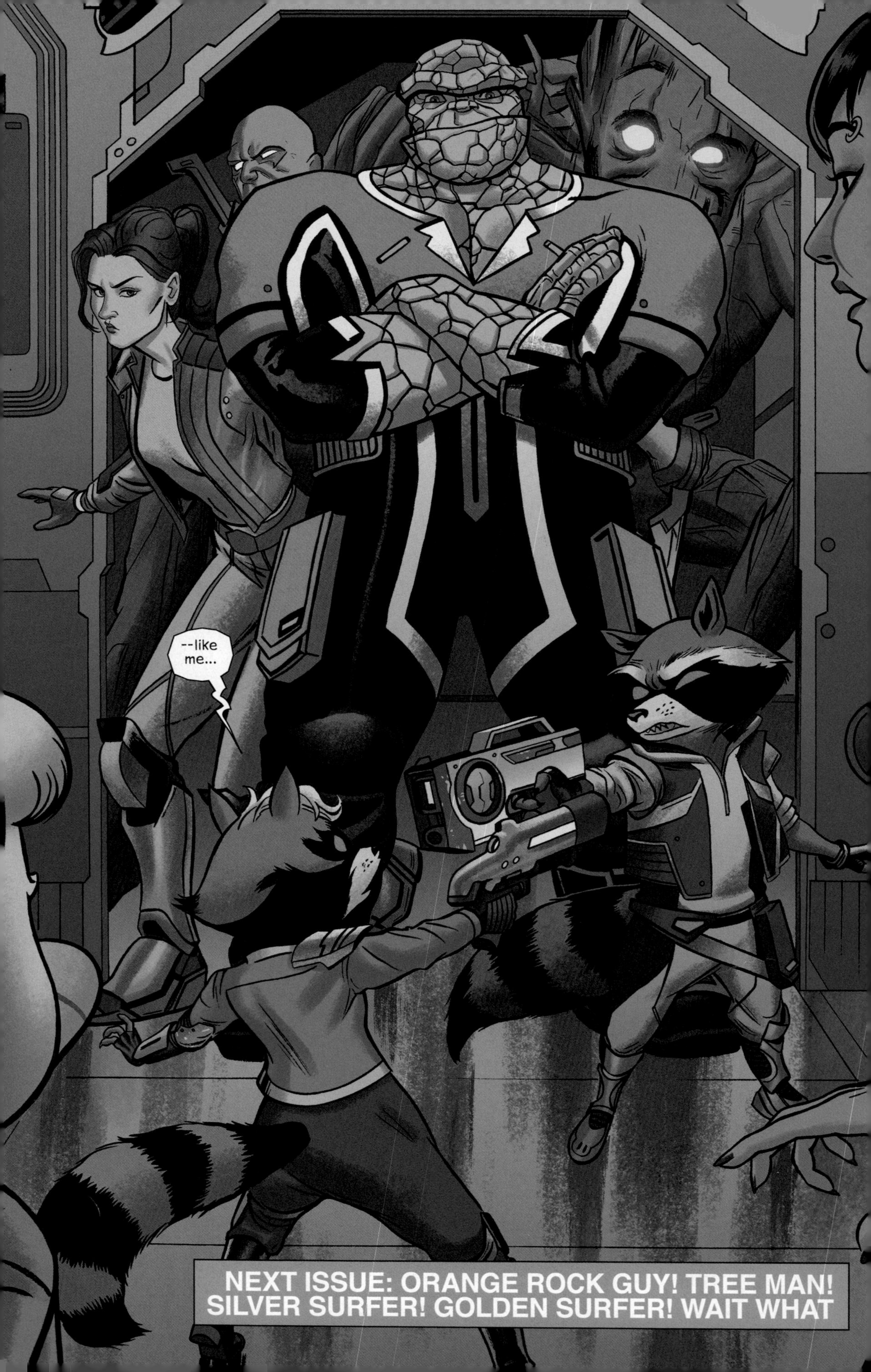
--like me...
NEXT ISSUE: ORANGE ROCK GUY! TREE MAN! SILVER SURFER! GOLDEN SURFER! WAIT WHAT

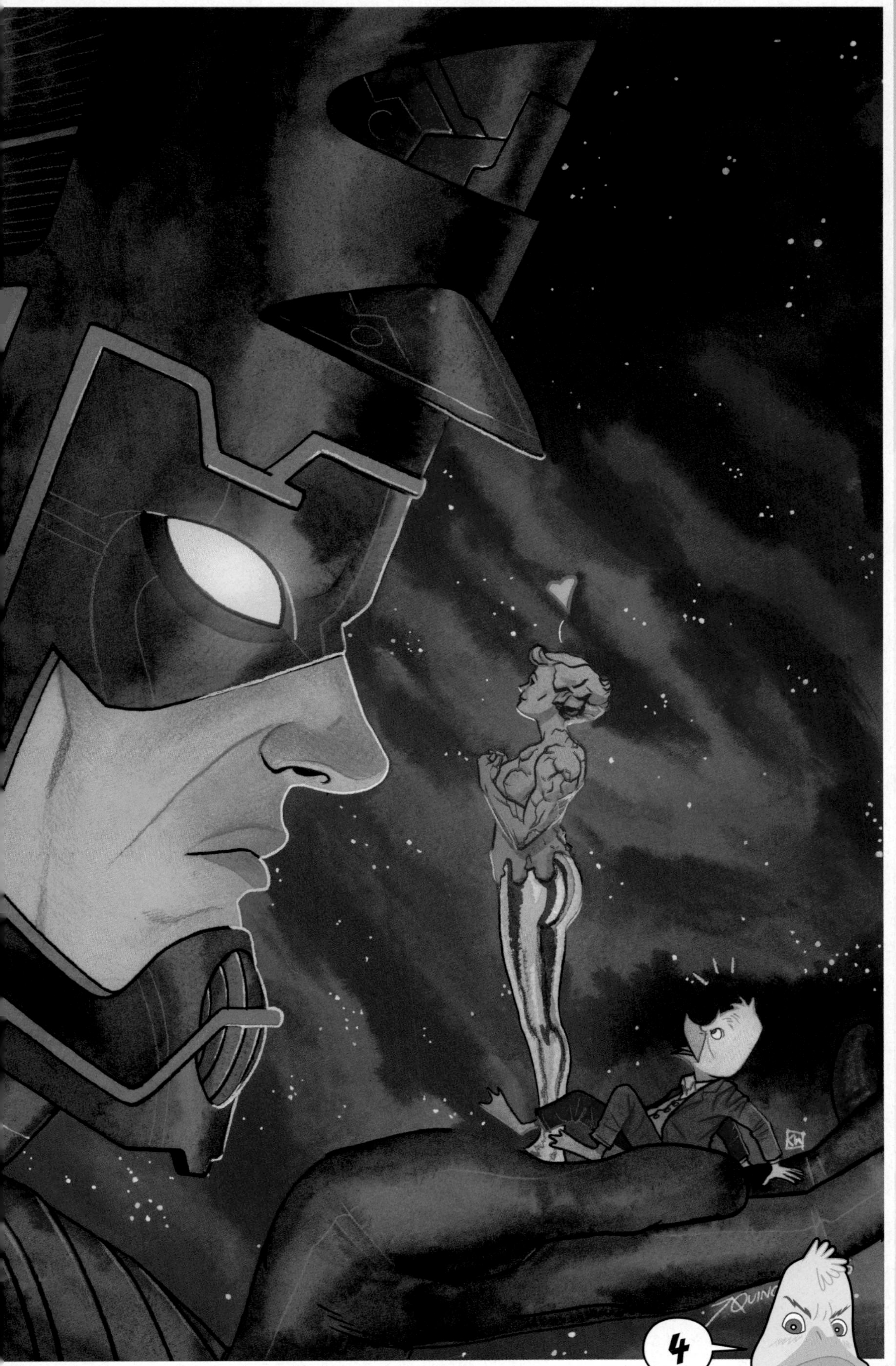

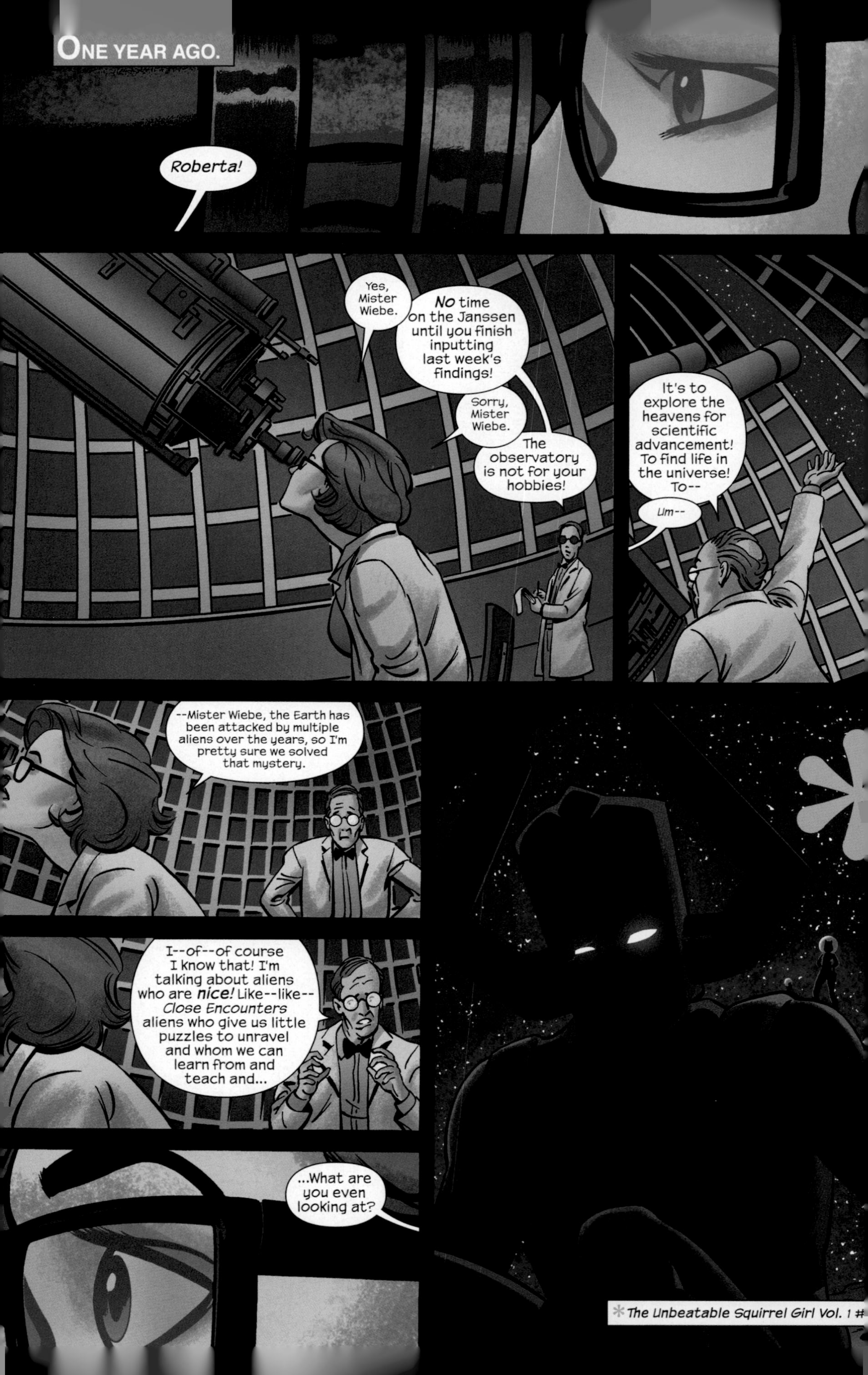
ONE YEAR AGO.
Roberta!
Yes, Mister Wiebe.
NO time on the Janssen until you finish inputting last week's findings!
Sorry, Mister Wiebe.
The observatory is not for your hobbies!
It's to explore the heavens for scientific advancement! To find life in the universe! To--
Um--
--Mister Wiebe, the Earth has been attacked by multiple aliens over the years, so I'm pretty sure we solved that mystery.
I--of--of course I know that! I'm talking about aliens who are *nice!* Like--like--*Close Encounters* aliens who give us little puzzles to unravel and whom we can learn from and teach and...
...What are you even looking at?
*The Unbeatable Squirrel Girl Vol. 1 #

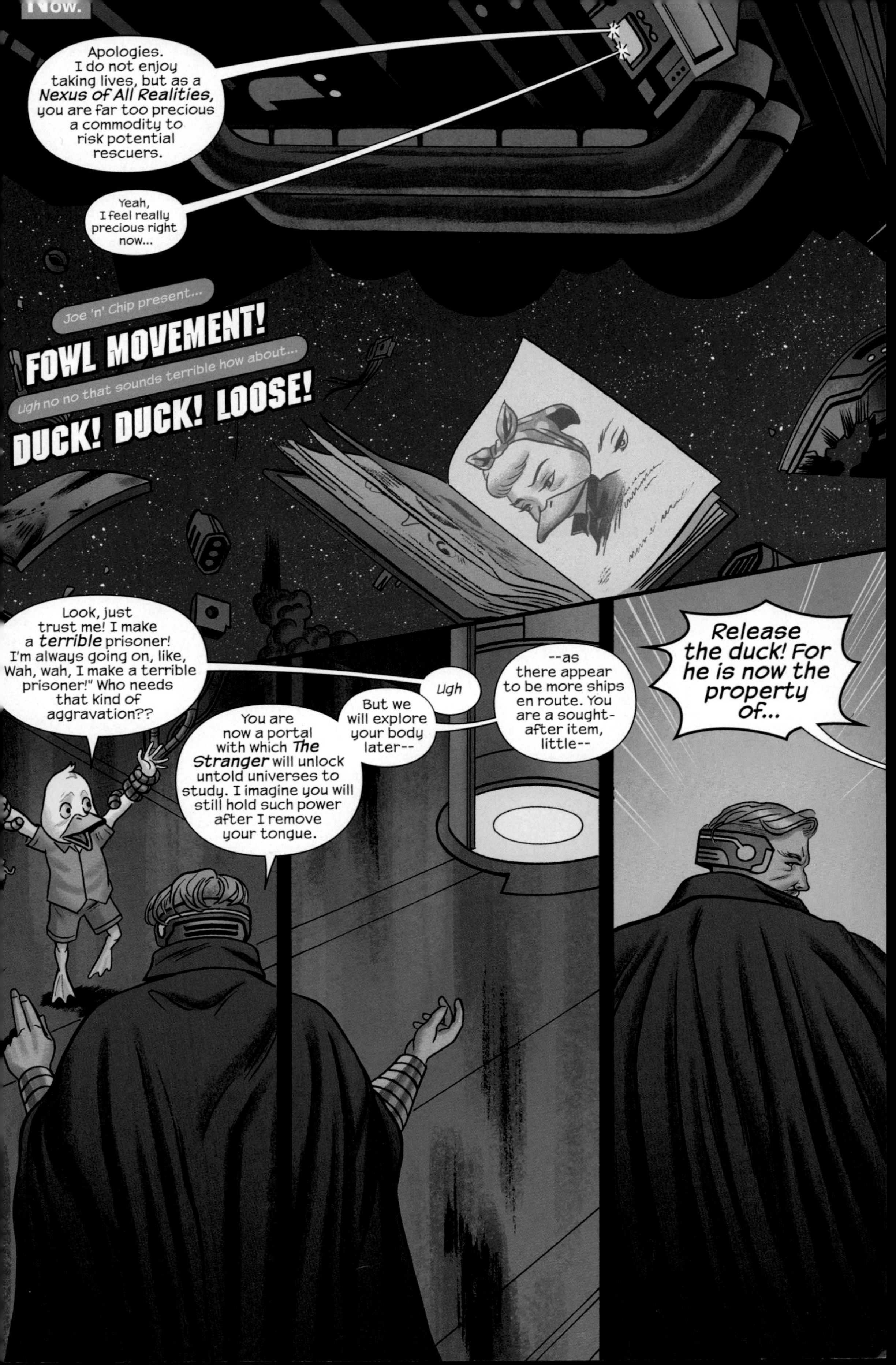
Now.
Apologies. I do not enjoy taking lives, but as a Nexus of All Realities, you are far too precious a commodity to risk potential rescuers.
Yeah, I feel really precious right now...
Joe 'n' Chip present...
FOWL MOVEMENT!
Ugh no no that sounds terrible how about...
DUCK! DUCK! LOOSE!
Look, just trust me! I make a terrible prisoner! I'm always going on, like, Wah, wah, I make a terrible prisoner!" Who needs that kind of aggravation??
Ugh
You are now a portal with which The Stranger will unlock untold universes to study. I imagine you will still hold such power after I remove your tongue.
But we will explore your body later--
--as there appear to be more ships en route. You are a sought-after item, little--
Release the duck! For he is now the property of...

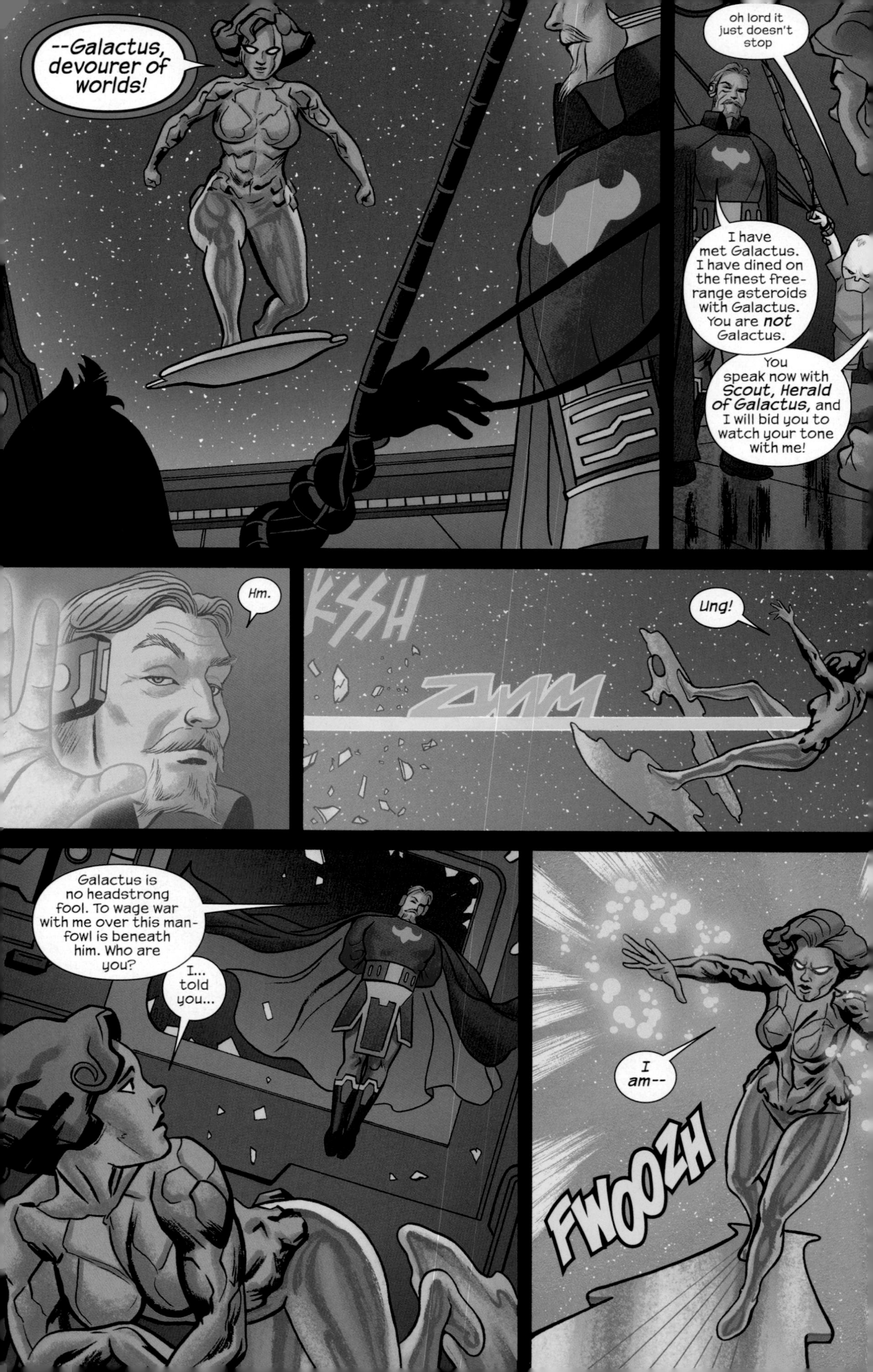
--Galactus, devourer of worlds!
oh lord it just doesn't stop
I have met Galactus. I have dined on the finest free-range asteroids with Galactus. You are not Galactus.
You speak now with Scout, Herald of Galactus, and I will bid you to watch your tone with me!
Hm.
KSSH
ZWM
Ung!
Galactus is no headstrong fool. To wage war with me over this man-fowl is beneath him. Who are you?
I... told you...
I am--
FWOOZH

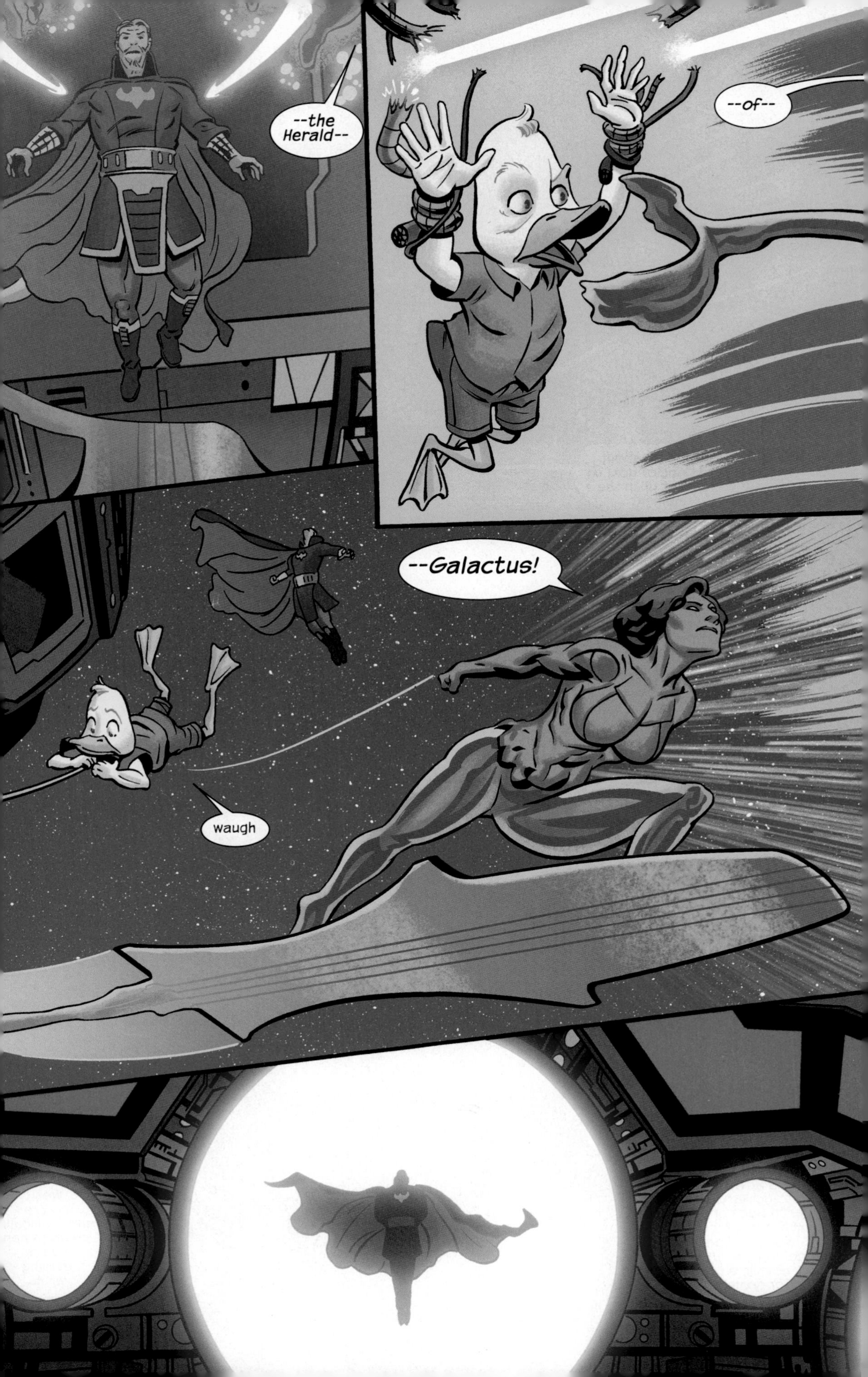
--the Herald--
--of--
--Galactus!
waugh

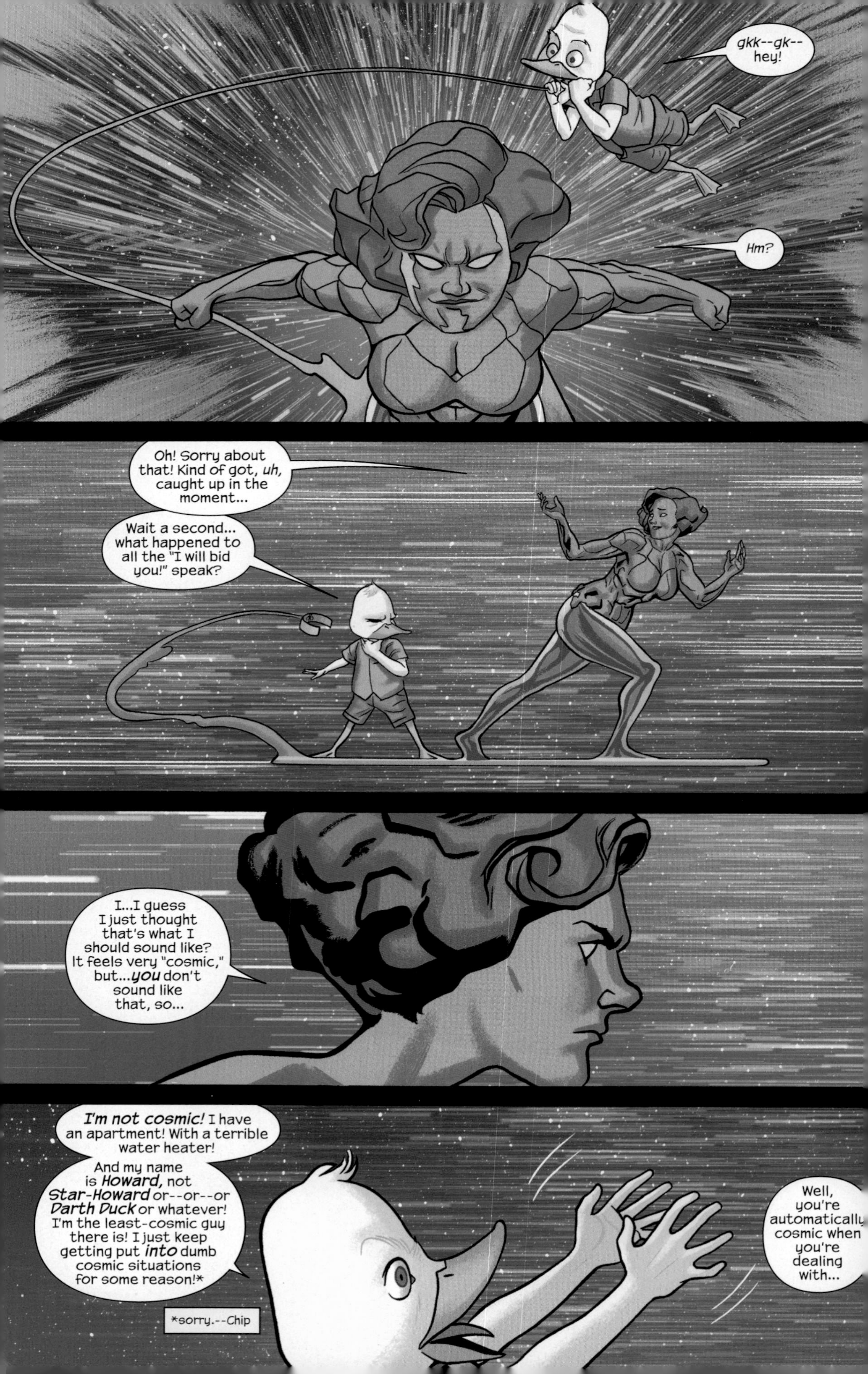
gkk--gk--
hey!
Hm?
Oh! Sorry about that! Kind of got, *uh*, caught up in the moment...
Wait a second... what happened to all the "I will bid you!" speak?
I...I guess I just thought that's what I should sound like? It feels very "cosmic," but...*you* don't sound like that, so...
I'm not cosmic! I have an apartment! With a terrible water heater!
And my name is *Howard,* not *Star-Howard* or--or--or *Darth Duck* or whatever! I'm the least-cosmic guy there is! I just keep getting put *into* dumb cosmic situations for some reason!*
*sorry.--Chip
Well, you're automatically cosmic when you're dealing with...

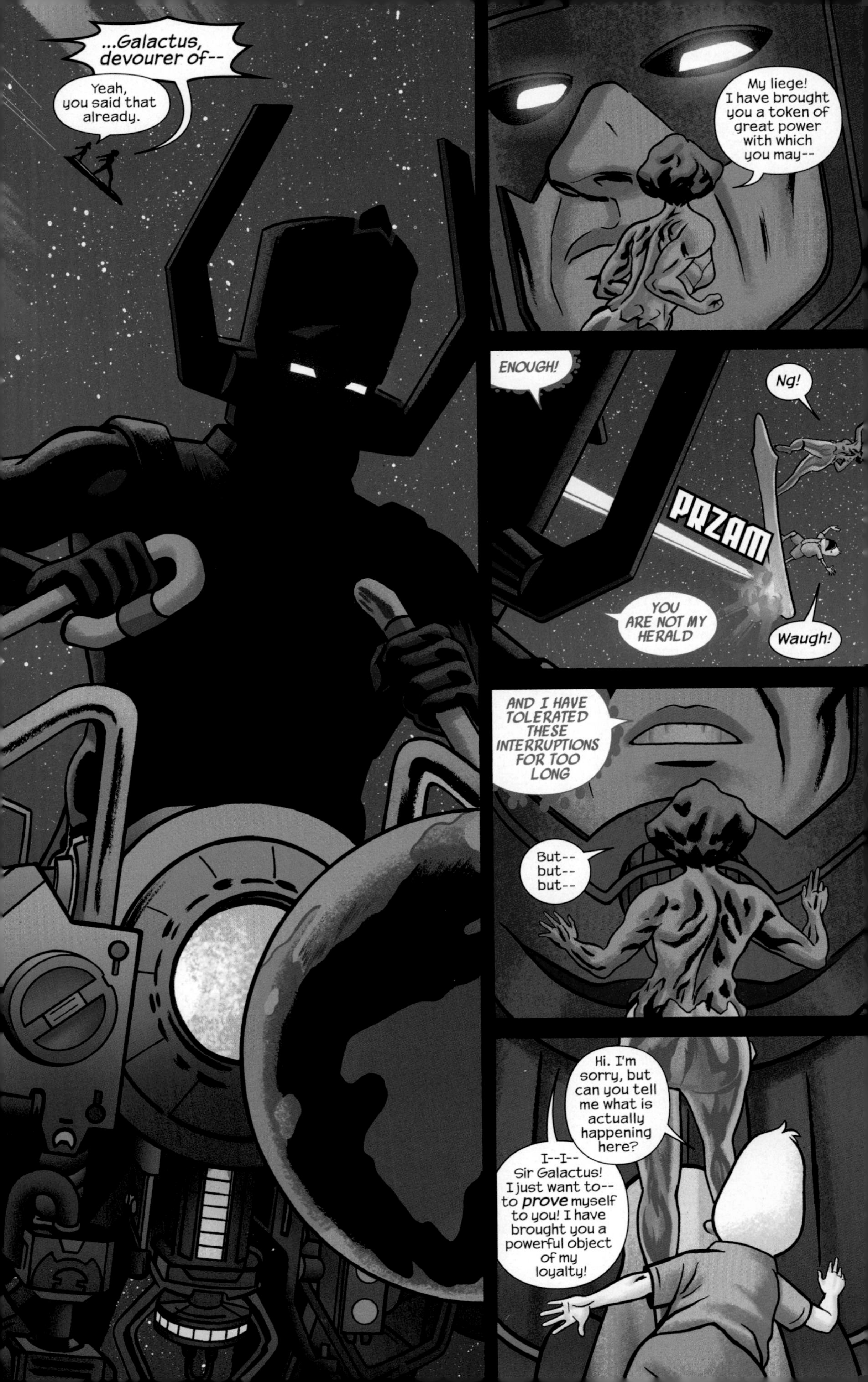
...Galactus, devourer of--
Yeah, you said that already.
My liege! I have brought you a token of great power with which you may--
ENOUGH!
Ng!
PRZAM
YOU ARE NOT MY HERALD
Waugh!
AND I HAVE TOLERATED THESE INTERRUPTIONS FOR TOO LONG
But-- but-- but--
Hi. I'm sorry, but can you tell me what is actually happening here?
I--I-- Sir Galactus! I just want to-- to *prove* myself to you! I have brought you a powerful object of my loyalty!

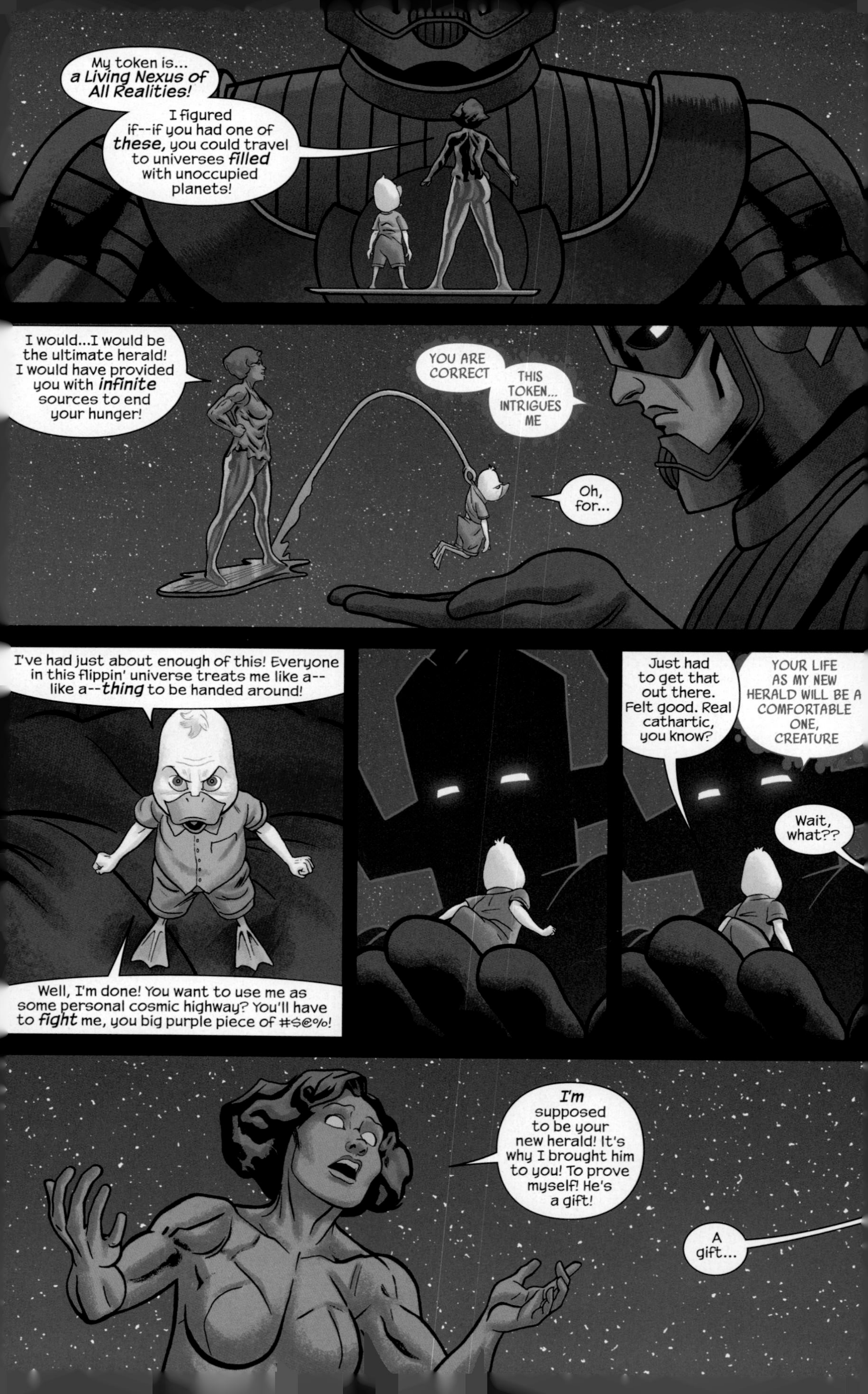
My token is... a Living Nexus of All Realities!
I figured if--if you had one of these, you could travel to universes filled with unoccupied planets!
I would...I would be the ultimate herald! I would have provided you with infinite sources to end your hunger!
YOU ARE CORRECT
THIS TOKEN... INTRIGUES ME
Oh, for...
I've had just about enough of this! Everyone in this flippin' universe treats me like a--like a--thing to be handed around!
Well, I'm done! You want to use me as some personal cosmic highway? You'll have to fight me, you big purple piece of #$@%!
Just had to get that out there. Felt good. Real cathartic, you know?
YOUR LIFE AS MY NEW HERALD WILL BE A COMFORTABLE ONE, CREATURE
Wait, what??
I'm supposed to be your new herald! It's why I brought him to you! To prove myself! He's a gift!
A gift...

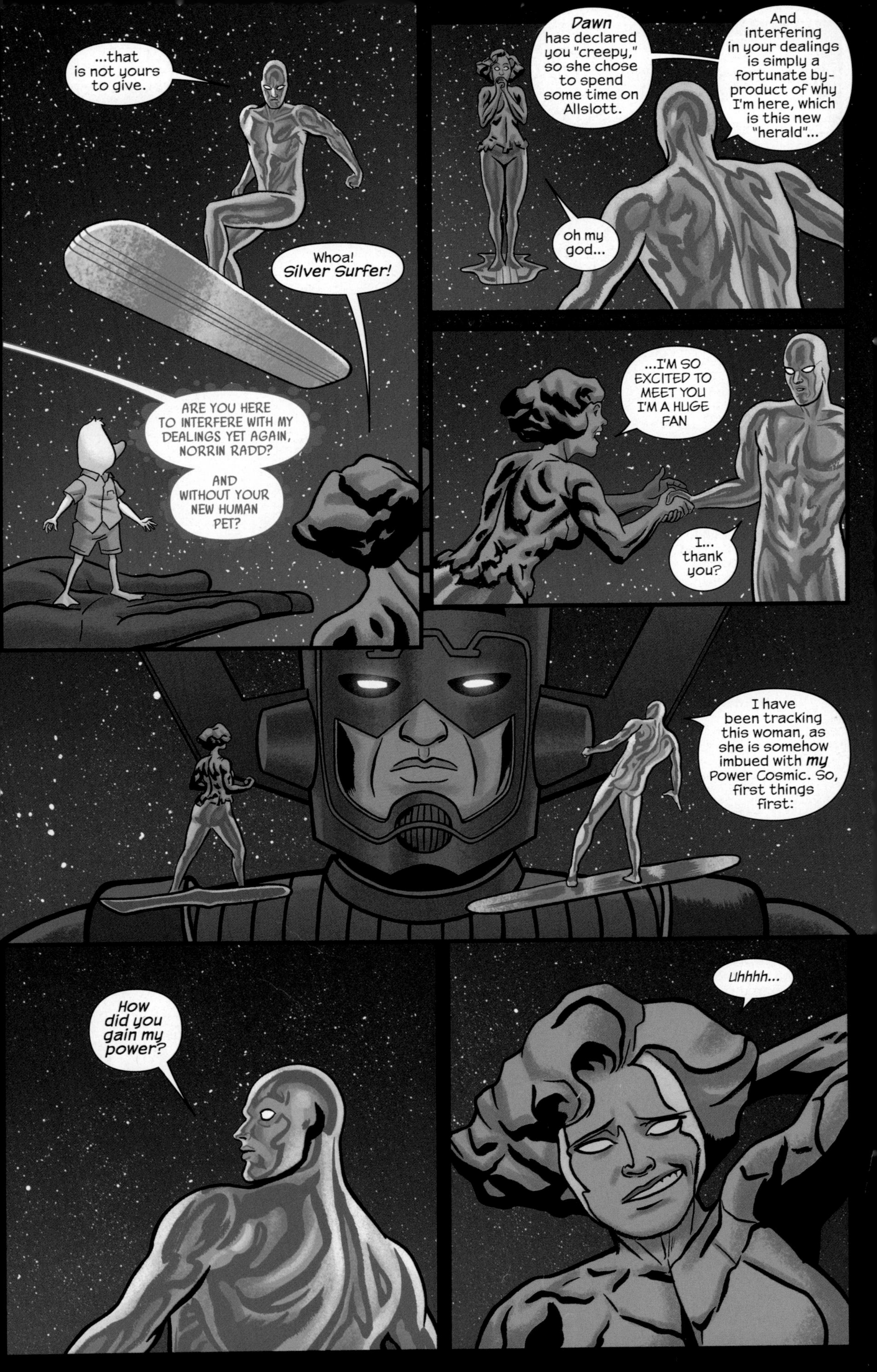

...that is not yours to give.
Whoa! Silver Surfer!
ARE YOU HERE TO INTERFERE WITH MY DEALINGS YET AGAIN, NORRIN RADD?
AND WITHOUT YOUR NEW HUMAN PET?
Dawn has declared you "creepy," so she chose to spend some time on Allslott.
And interfering in your dealings is simply a fortunate by-product of why I'm here, which is this new "herald"...
oh my god...
...I'M SO EXCITED TO MEET YOU I'M A HUGE FAN
I... thank you?
I have been tracking this woman, as she is somehow imbued with my Power Cosmic. So, first things first:
How did you gain my power?
Uhhhh...

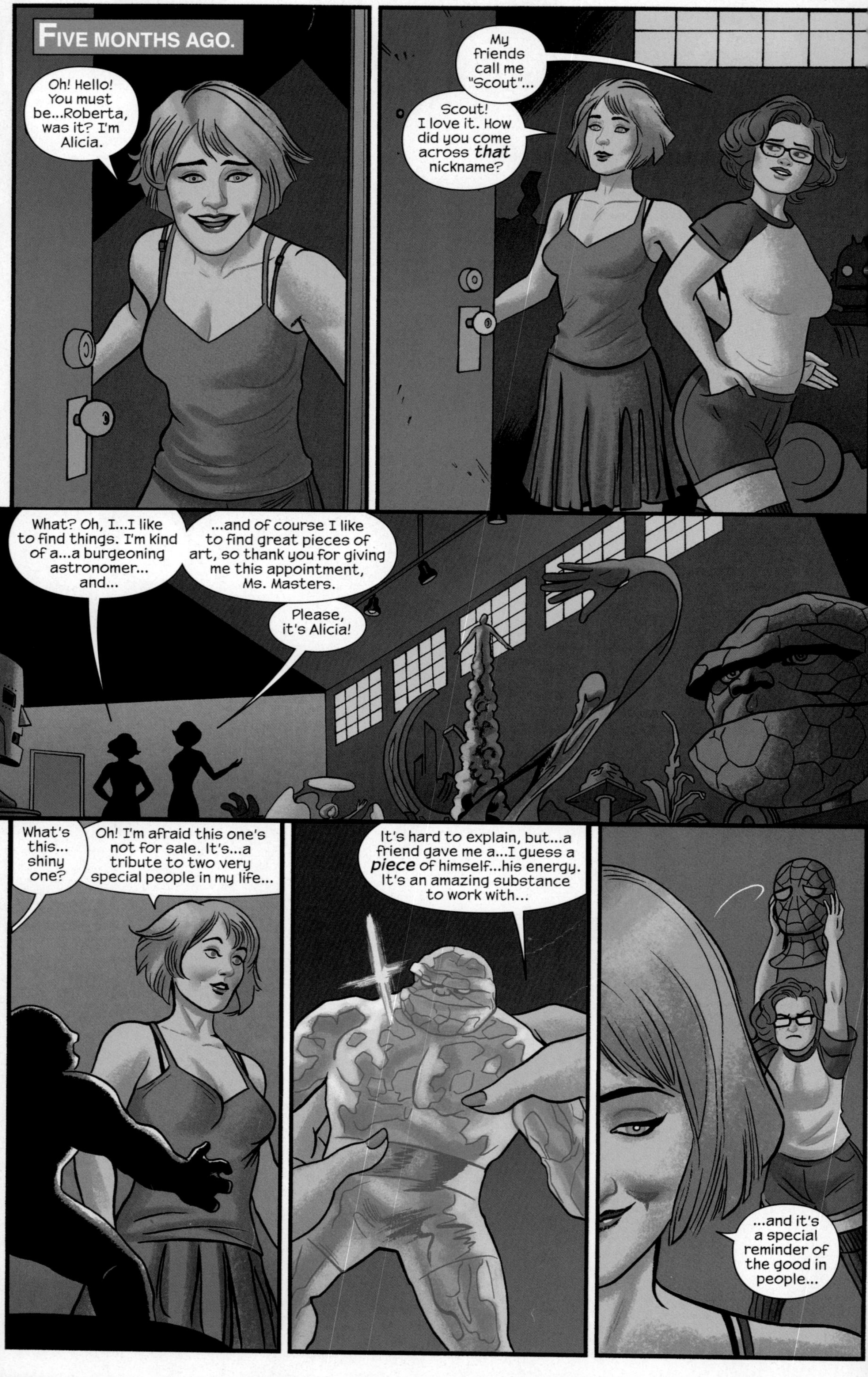
FIVE MONTHS AGO.
Oh! Hello! You must be...Roberta, was it? I'm Alicia.
My friends call me "Scout"...
Scout! I love it. How did you come across *that* nickname?
What? Oh, I...I like to find things. I'm kind of a...a burgeoning astronomer... and...
...and of course I like to find great pieces of art, so thank you for giving me this appointment, Ms. Masters.
Please, it's Alicia!
What's this... shiny one?
Oh! I'm afraid this one's not for sale. It's...a tribute to two very special people in my life...
It's hard to explain, but...a friend gave me a...I guess a *piece* of himself...his energy. It's an amazing substance to work with...
...and it's a special reminder of the good in people...

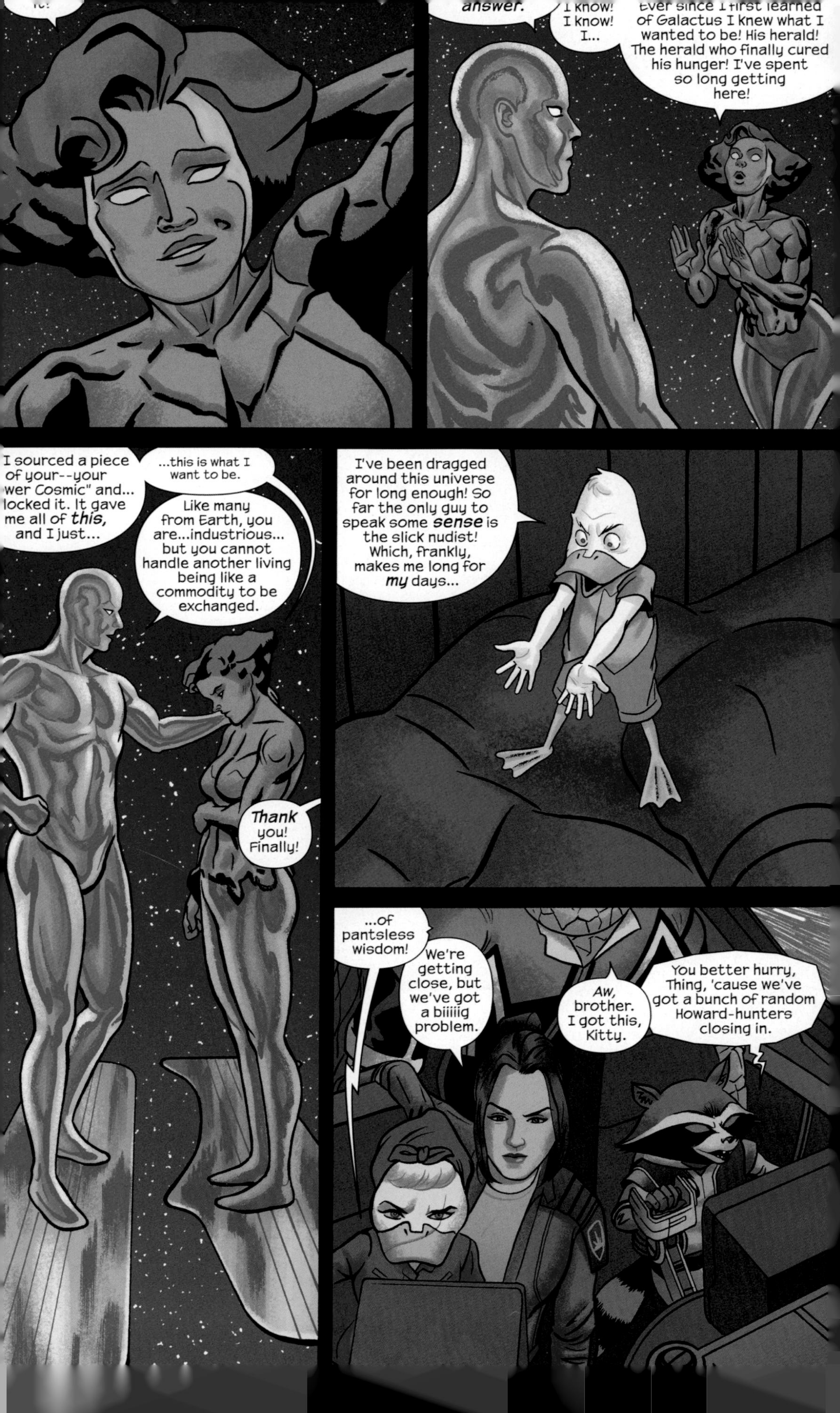
answer.
I know! I know! I...
Ever since I first learned of Galactus I knew what I wanted to be! His herald! The herald who finally cured his hunger! I've spent so long getting here!
I sourced a piece of your--your wer Cosmic" and... locked it. It gave me all of this, and I just...
...this is what I want to be.
Like many from Earth, you are...industrious... but you cannot handle another living being like a commodity to be exchanged.
Thank you! Finally!
I've been dragged around this universe for long enough! So far the only guy to speak some sense is the slick nudist! Which, frankly, makes me long for my days...
...of pantsless wisdom!
We're getting close, but we've got a biiiiig problem.
Aw, brother. I got this, Kitty.
You better hurry, Thing, 'cause we've got a bunch of random Howard-hunters closing in.

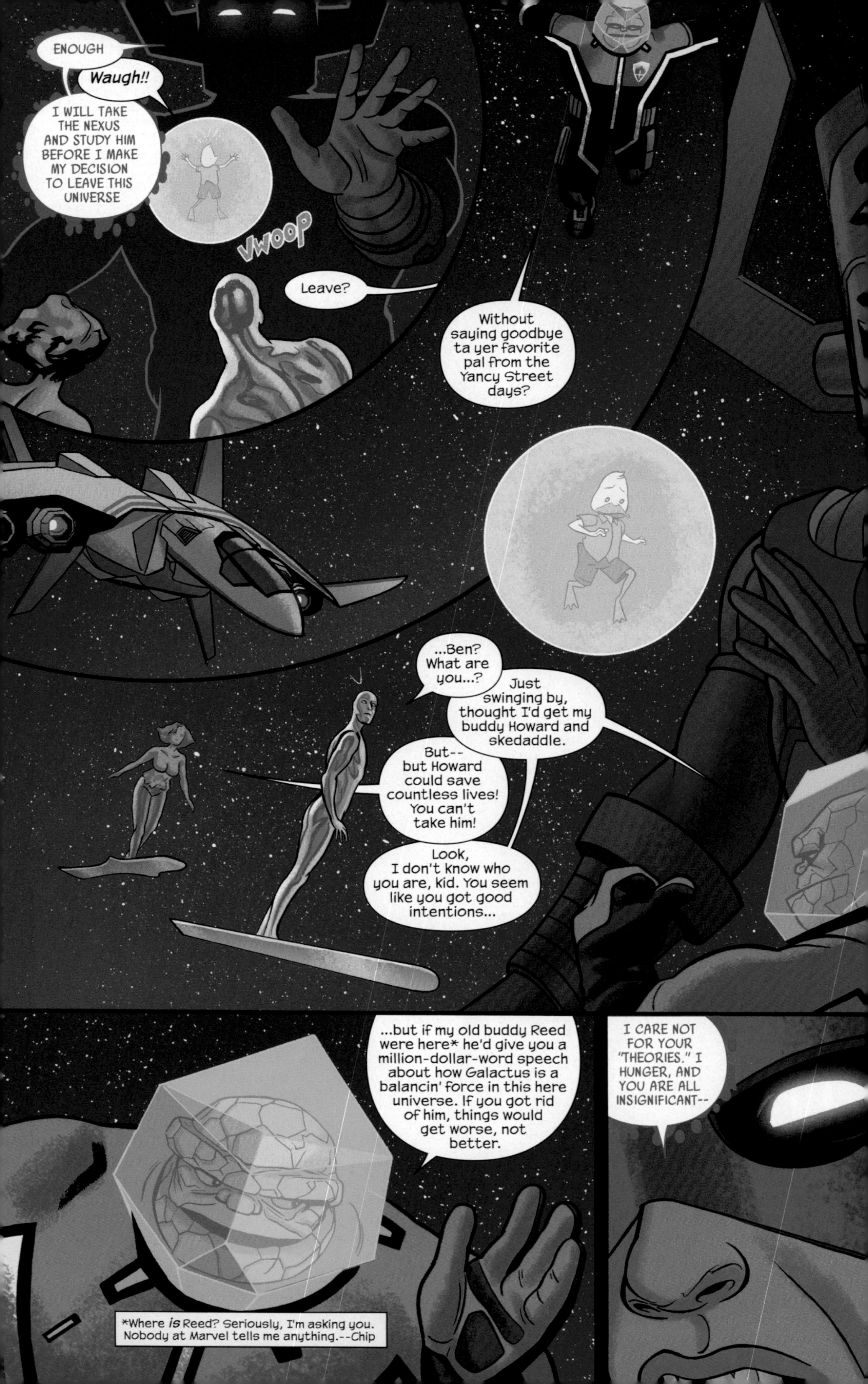
ENOUGH
Waugh!!
I WILL TAKE THE NEXUS AND STUDY HIM BEFORE I MAKE MY DECISION TO LEAVE THIS UNIVERSE
VWOOP
Leave?
Without saying goodbye ta yer favorite pal from the Yancy Street days?
...Ben? What are you...?
Just swinging by, thought I'd get my buddy Howard and skedaddle.
But--but Howard could save countless lives! You can't take him!
Look, I don't know who you are, kid. You seem like you got good intentions...
...but if my old buddy Reed were here* he'd give you a million-dollar-word speech about how Galactus is a balancin' force in this here universe. If you got rid of him, things would get worse, not better.
*Where is Reed? Seriously, I'm asking you. Nobody at Marvel tells me anything.--Chip
I CARE NOT FOR YOUR "THEORIES." I HUNGER, AND YOU ARE ALL INSIGNIFICANT--

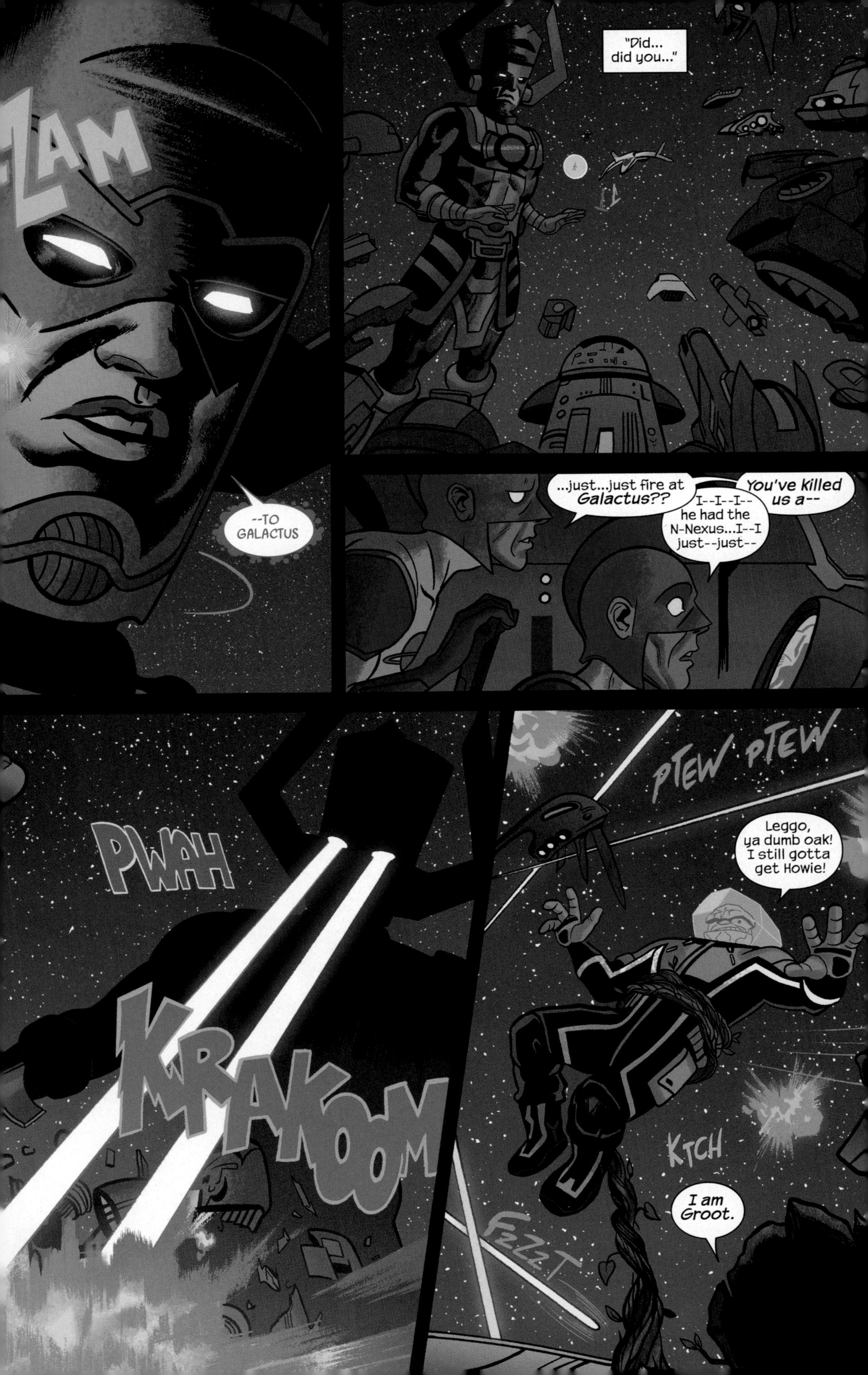
FZAM
--TO GALACTUS
"Did... did you..."
...just...just fire at Galactus??
I--I--I-- he had the N-Nexus...I--I just--just--
You've killed us a--
PWAH
KRAKOOM
PTEW PTEW
Leggo, ya dumb oak! I still gotta get Howie!
KTCH
FZZZT
I am Groot.

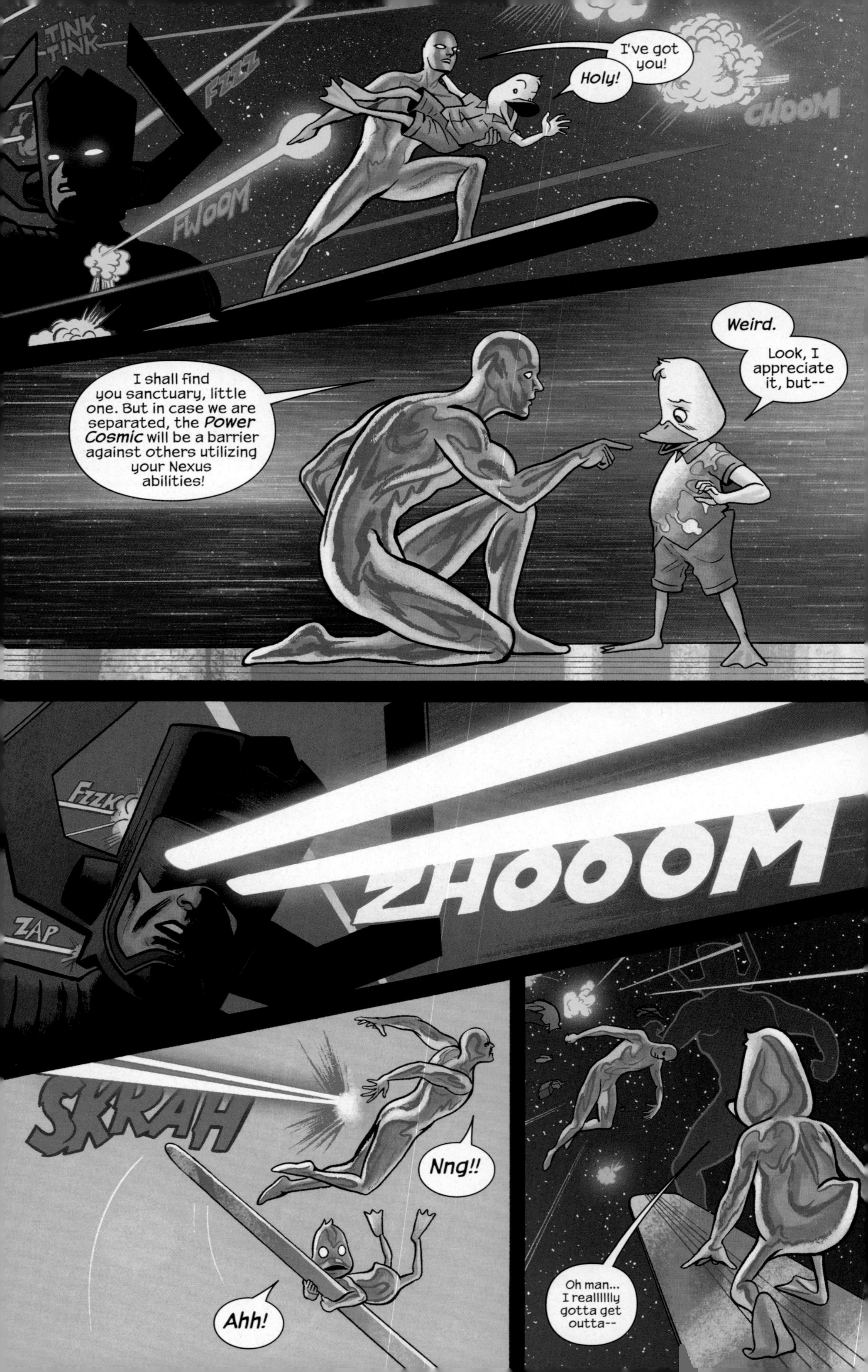
TINK TINK
FZZZ
I've got you!
Holy!
CHOOM
FWOOM
I shall find you sanctuary, little one. But in case we are separated, the *Power Cosmic* will be a barrier against others utilizing your Nexus abilities!
Weird.
Look, I appreciate it, but--
FZZK
ZHOOOM
ZAP
SKRAH
Nng!!
Ahh!
Oh man... I reallllly gotta get outta--

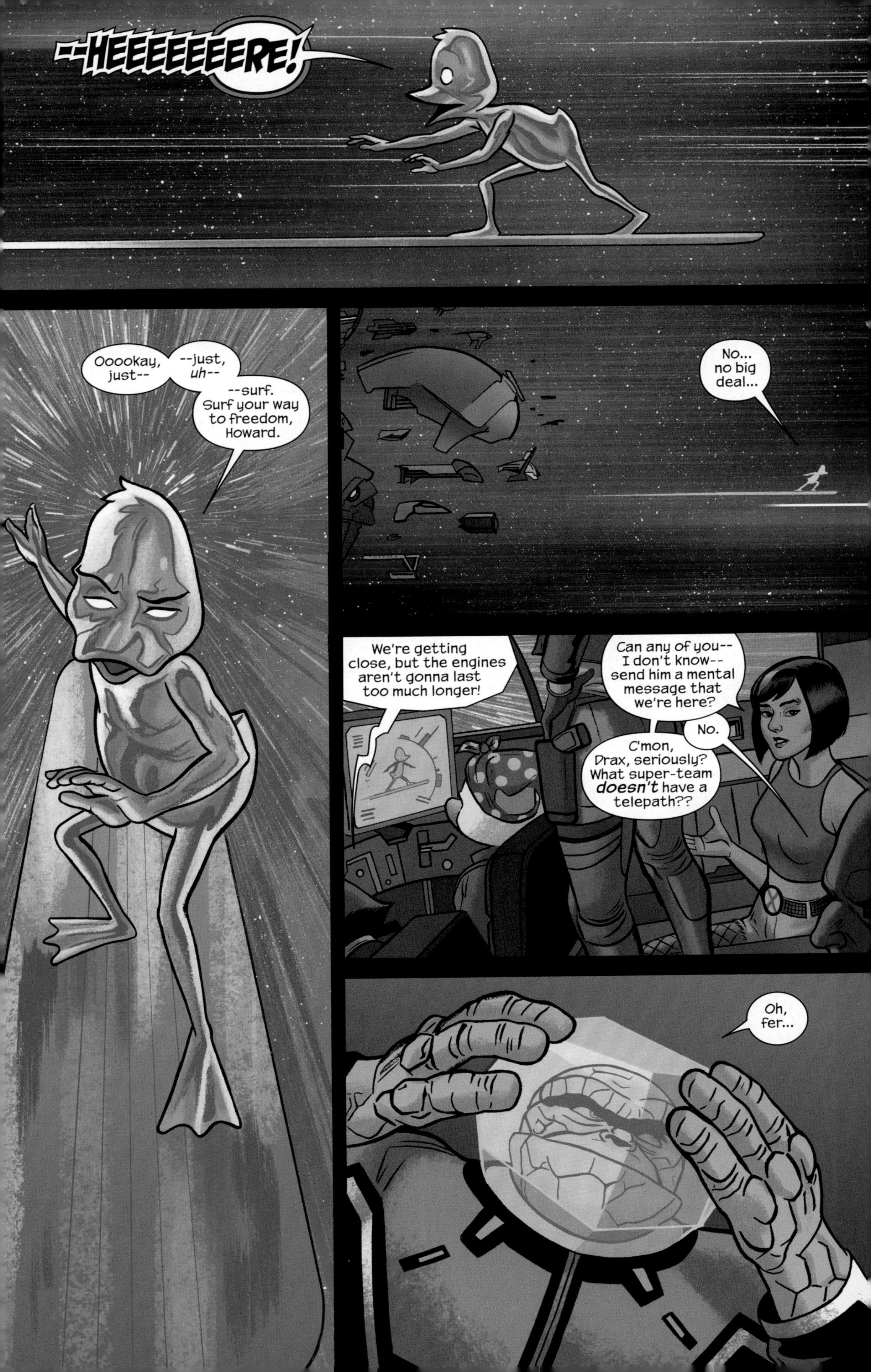
--HEEEEEEEERE!
Oooookay, just--
--just, uh--
--surf. Surf your way to freedom, Howard.
No... no big deal...
We're getting close, but the engines aren't gonna last too much longer!
Can any of you-- I don't know-- send him a mental message that we're here?
No.
C'mon, Drax, seriously? What super-team doesn't have a telepath??
Oh, fer...

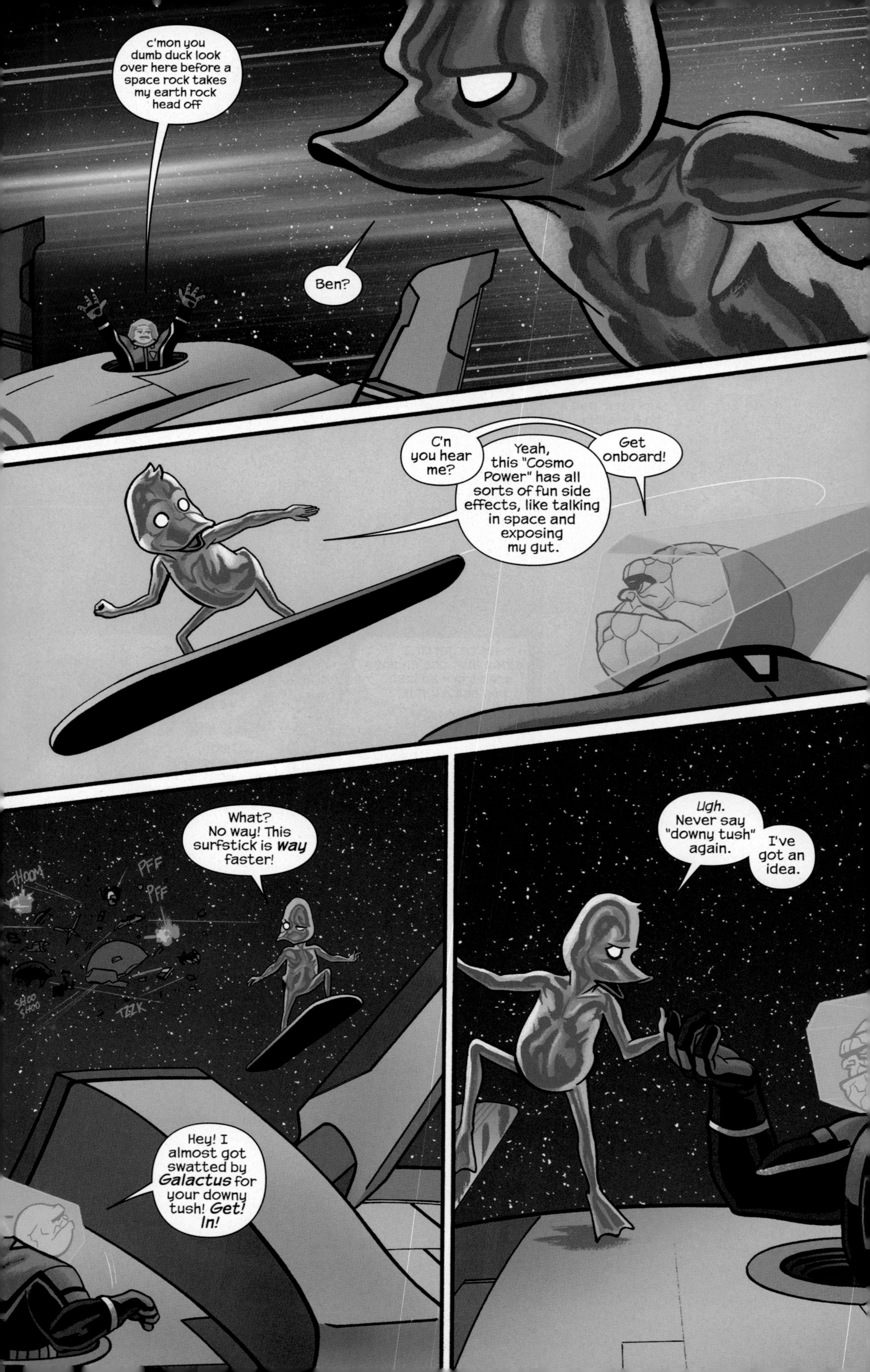
c'mon you dumb duck look over here before a space rock takes my earth rock head off
Ben?
C'n you hear me?
Yeah, this "Cosmo Power" has all sorts of fun side effects, like talking in space and exposing my gut.
Get onboard!
What? No way! This surfstick is *way* faster!
THOOM
PFF
PFF
SHOO SHOO
TZZK
Hey! I almost got swatted by *Galactus* for your downy tush! *Get! In!*
Ugh. Never say "downy tush" again.
I've got an idea.

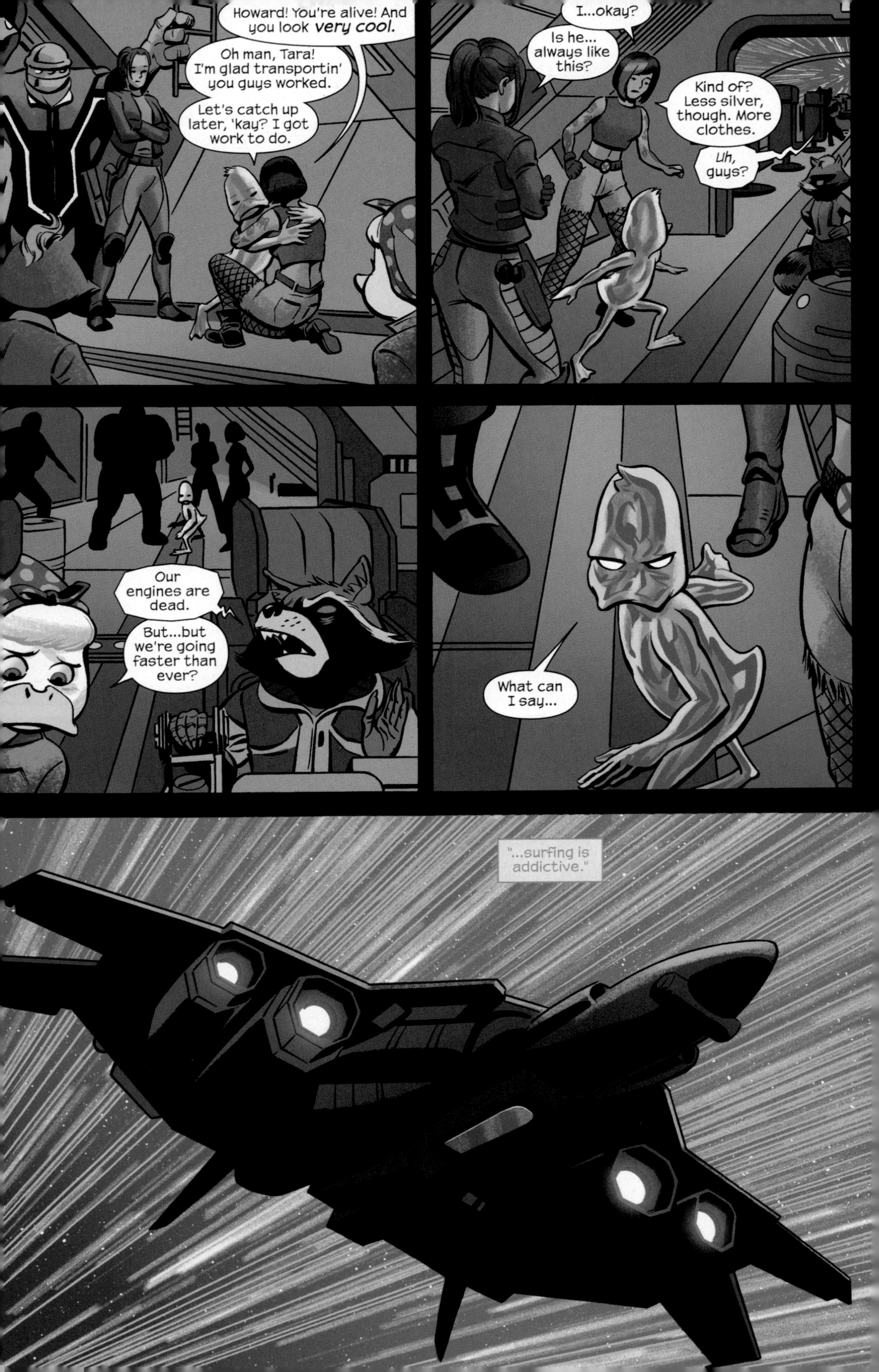
Howard! You're alive! And you look very cool.
Oh man, Tara! I'm glad transportin' you guys worked.
Let's catch up later, 'kay? I got work to do.
I...okay?
Is he... always like this?
Kind of? Less silver, though. More clothes.
Uh, guys?
Our engines are dead.
But...but we're going faster than ever?
What can I say...
"...surfing is addictive."

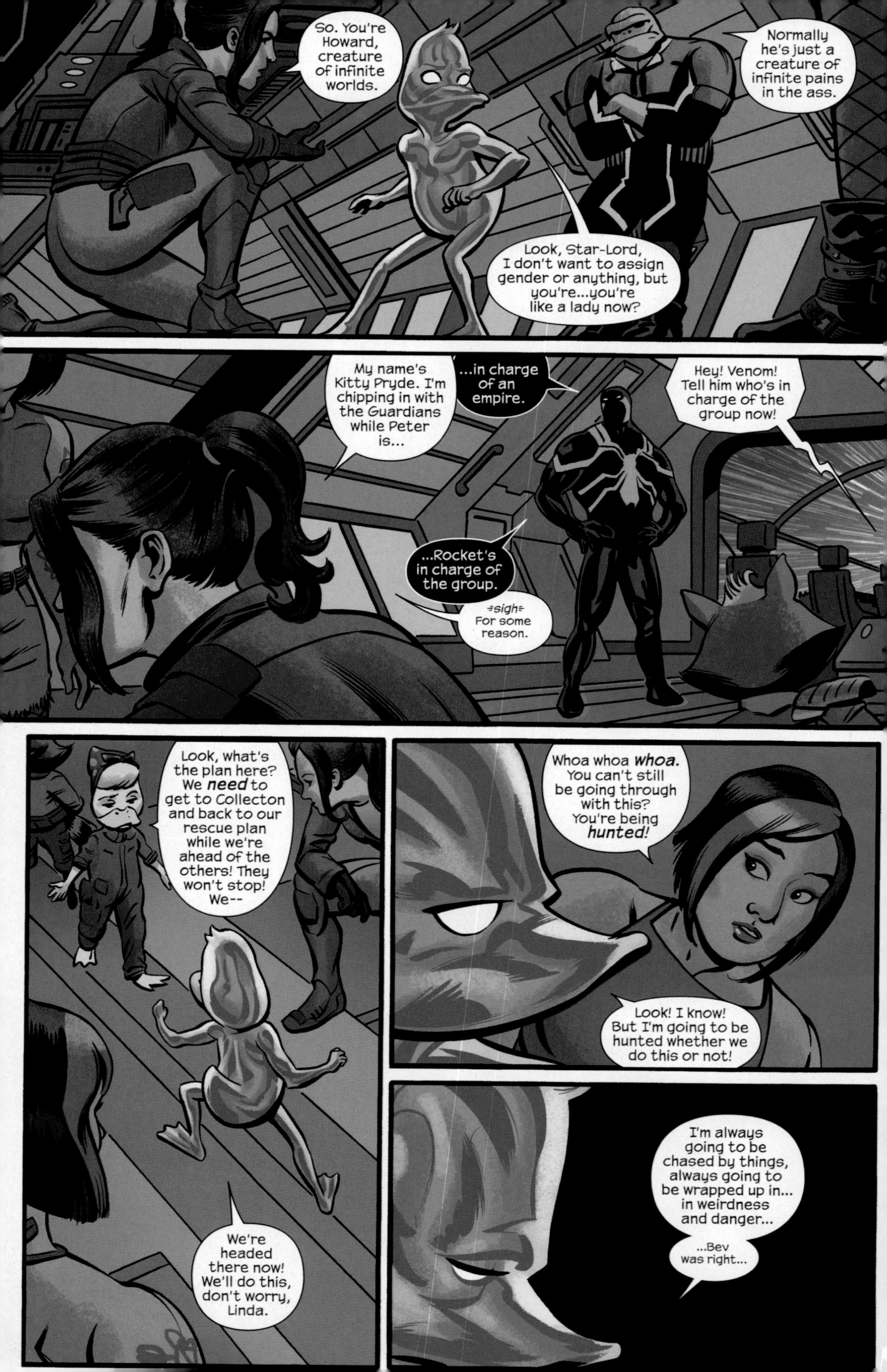

So. You're Howard, creature of infinite worlds.
Normally he's just a creature of infinite pains in the ass.
Look, Star-Lord, I don't want to assign gender or anything, but you're...you're like a lady now?
My name's Kitty Pryde. I'm chipping in with the Guardians while Peter is...
...in charge of an empire.
Hey! Venom! Tell him who's in charge of the group now!
...Rocket's in charge of the group.
=sigh= For some reason.
Look, what's the plan here? We *need* to get to Collecton and back to our rescue plan while we're ahead of the others! They won't stop! We--
We're headed there now! We'll do this, don't worry, Linda.
Whoa whoa *whoa.* You can't still be going through with this? You're being *hunted!*
Look! I know! But I'm going to be hunted whether we do this or not!
I'm always going to be chased by things, always going to be wrapped up in... in weirdness and danger...
...Bev was right...

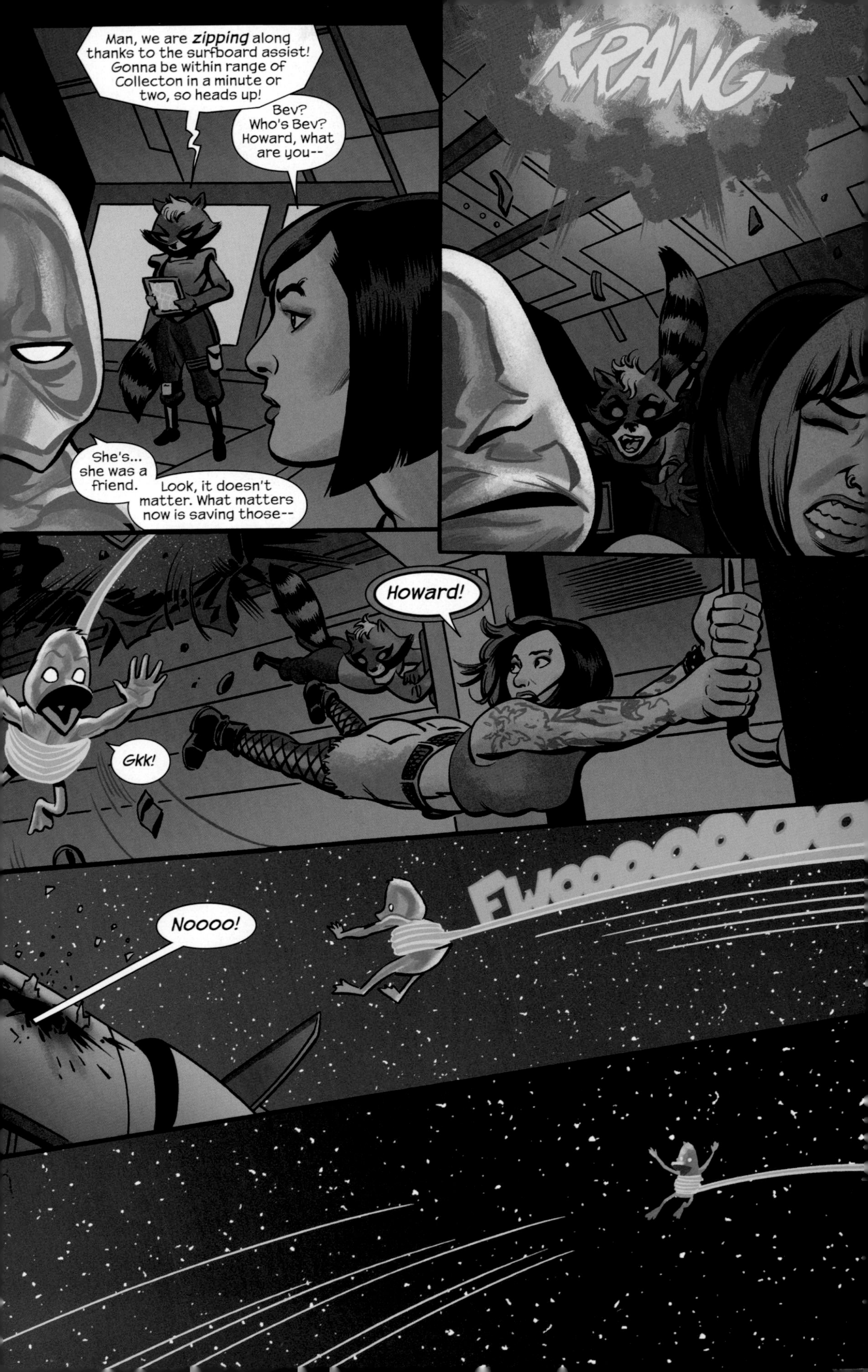
Man, we are *zipping* along thanks to the surfboard assist! Gonna be within range of Collecton in a minute or two, so heads up!
Bev? Who's Bev? Howard, what are you--
She's... she was a friend.
Look, it doesn't matter. What matters now is saving those--
KRANG
Howard!
Gkk!
FWOOOOOOOOO
Noooo!

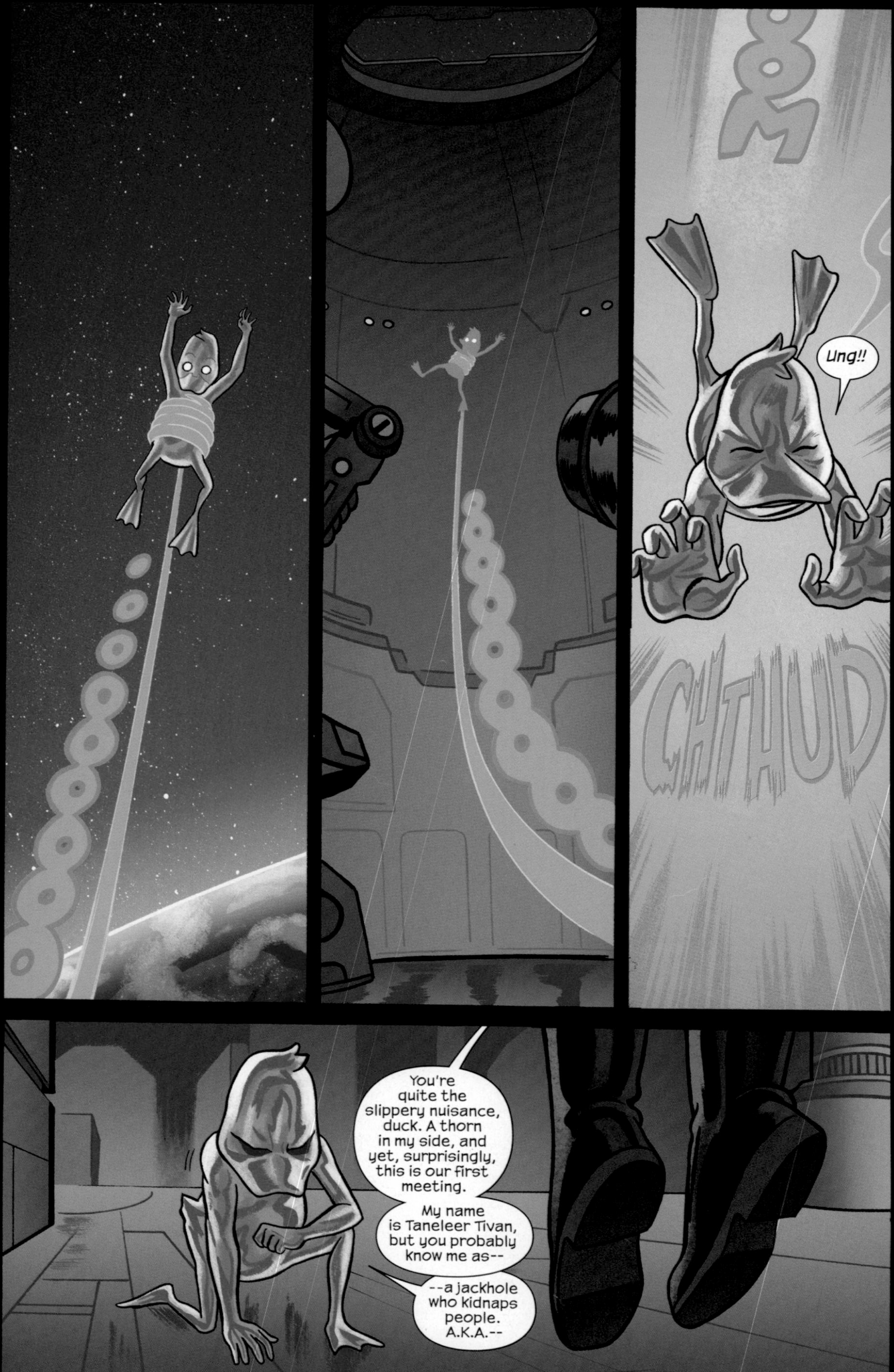
Ung!!
CHTHUD
You're quite the slippery nuisance, duck. A thorn in my side, and yet, surprisingly, this is our first meeting.
My name is Taneleer Tivan, but you probably know me as--
--a jackhole who kidnaps people. A.K.A.--

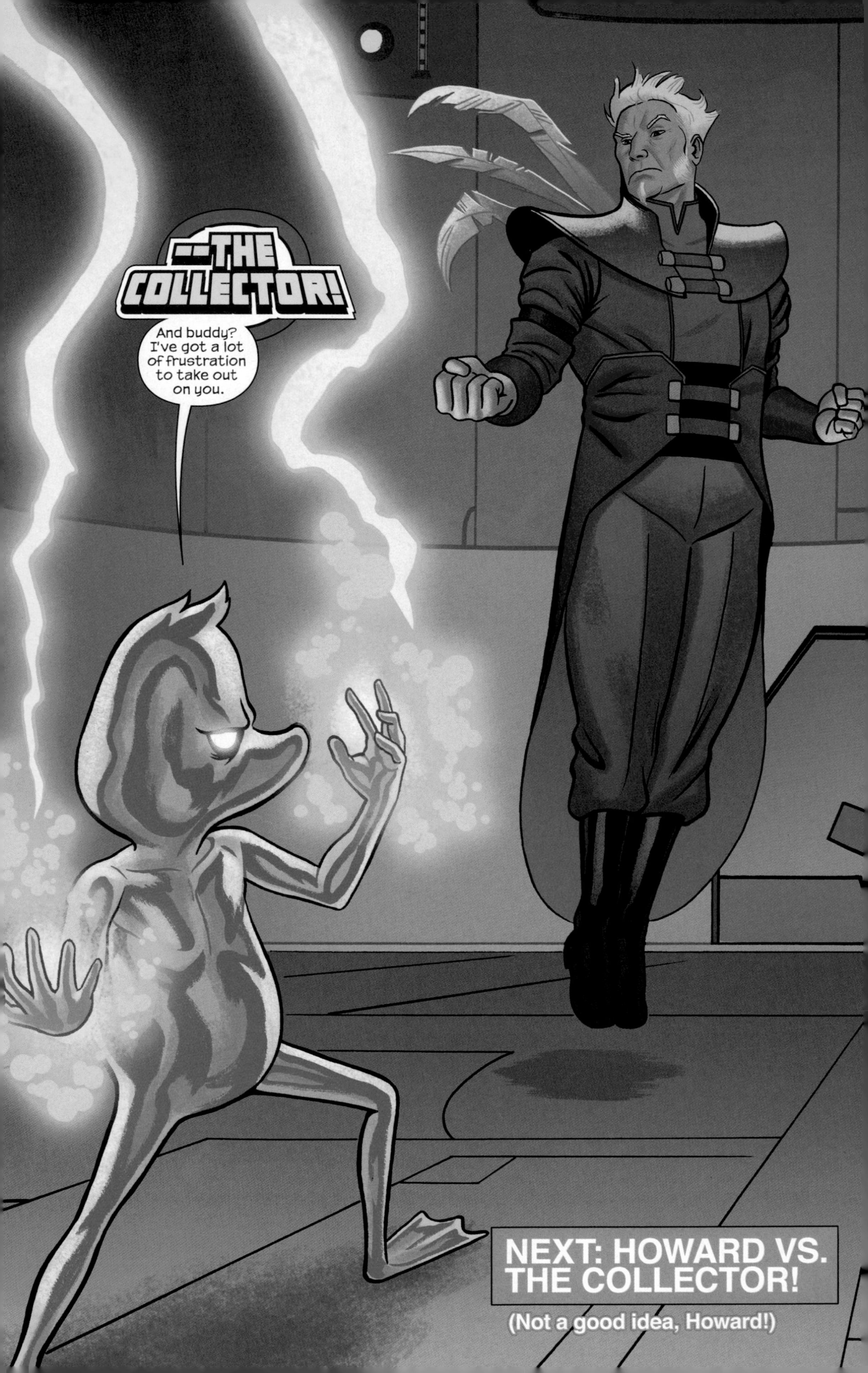
--THE COLLECTOR!
And buddy? I've got a lot of frustration to take out on you.
NEXT: HOWARD VS. THE COLLECTOR!
(Not a good idea, Howard!)

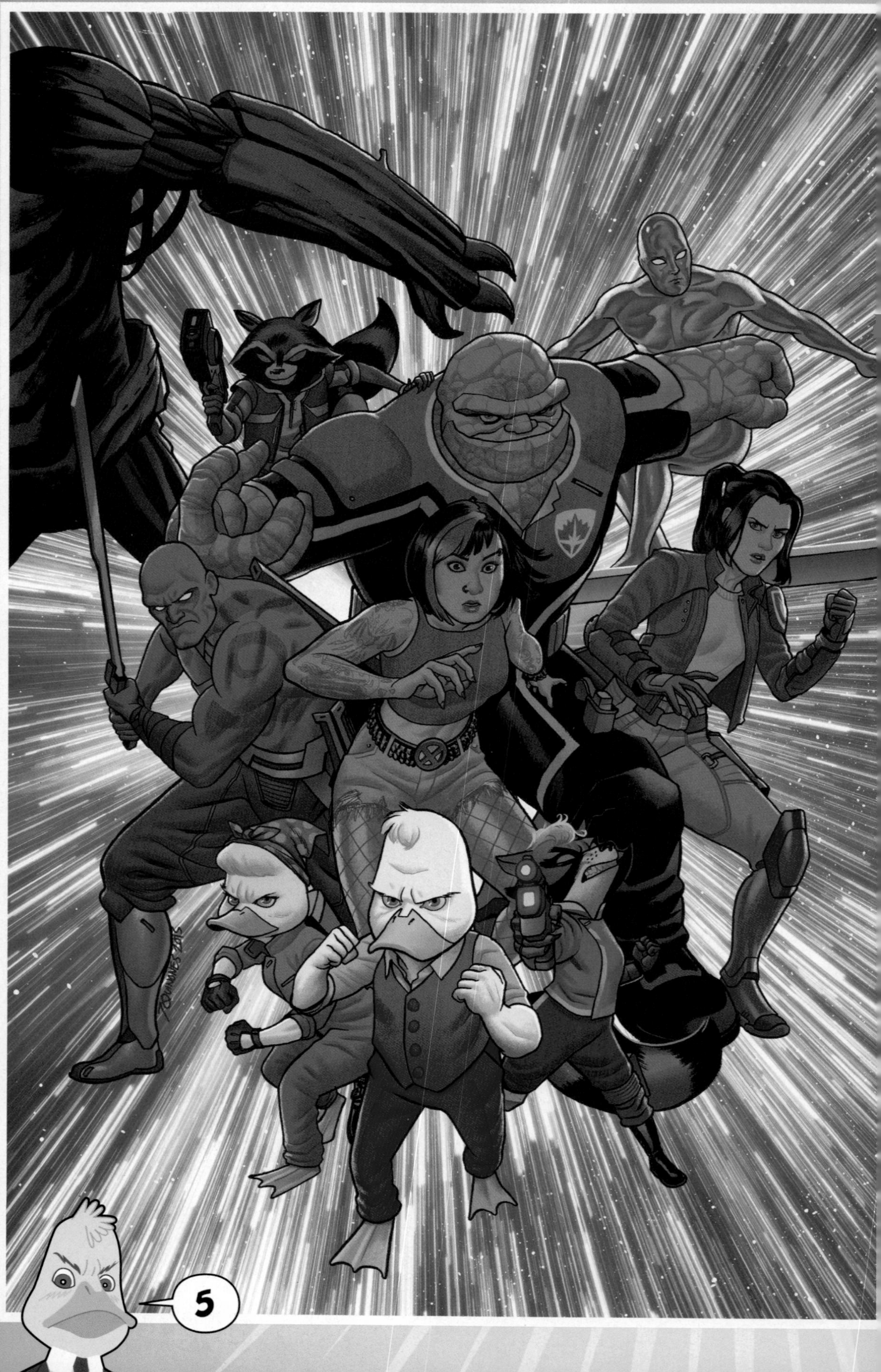

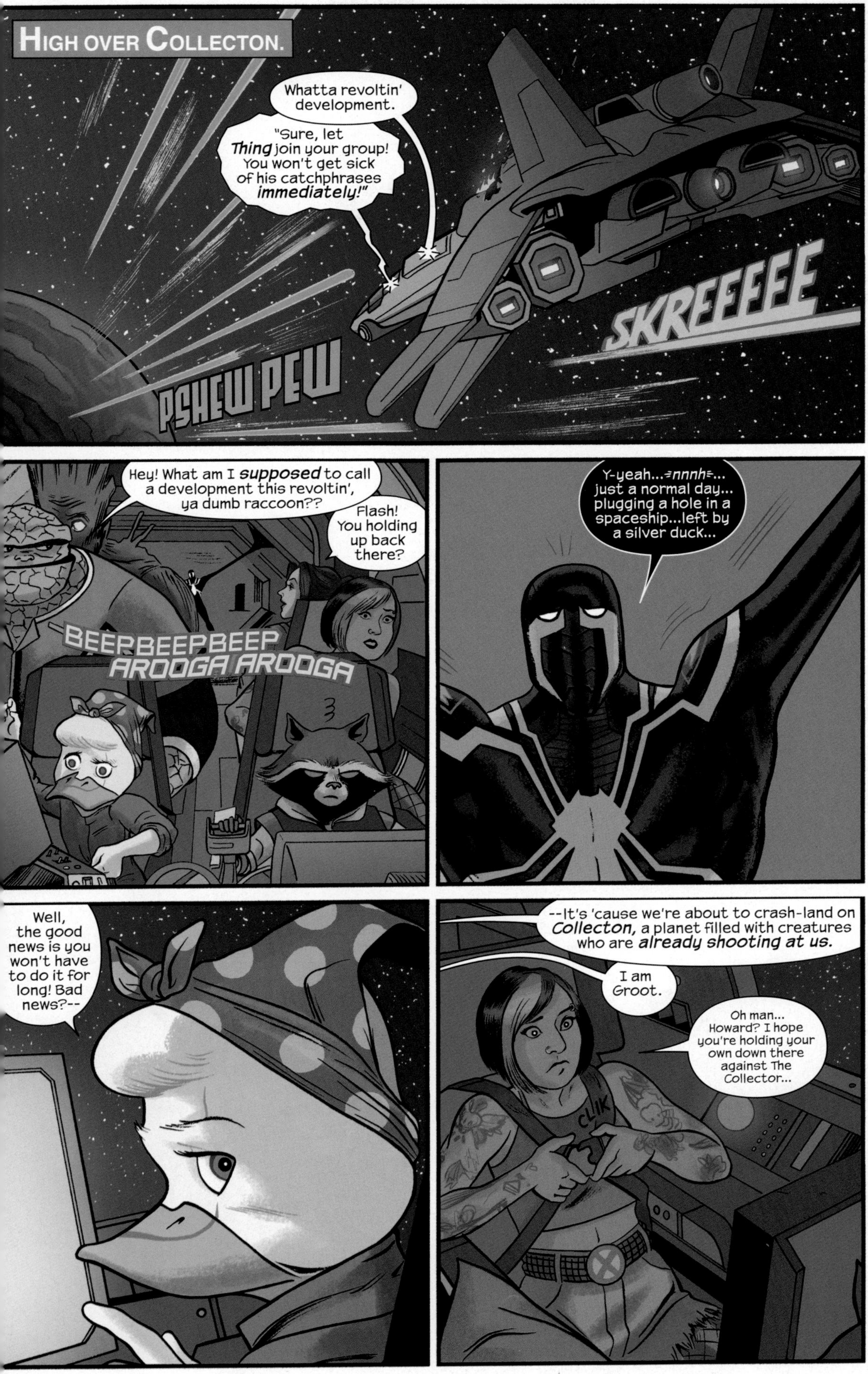

HIGH OVER COLLECTON.
Whatta revoltin' development.
"Sure, let *Thing* join your group! You won't get sick of his catchphrases *immediately!*"
SKREEEEE
PSHEW PEW
Hey! What am I *supposed* to call a development this revoltin', ya dumb raccoon??
Flash! You holding up back there?
BEEPBEEPBEEP
AROOGA AROOGA
Y-yeah...=nnnh=... just a normal day... plugging a hole in a spaceship...left by a silver duck...
Well, the good news is you won't have to do it for long! Bad news?--
--It's 'cause we're about to crash-land on *Collecton,* a planet filled with creatures who are *already shooting at us.*
I am Groot.
Oh man... Howard? I hope you're holding your own down there against The Collector...
CLIK

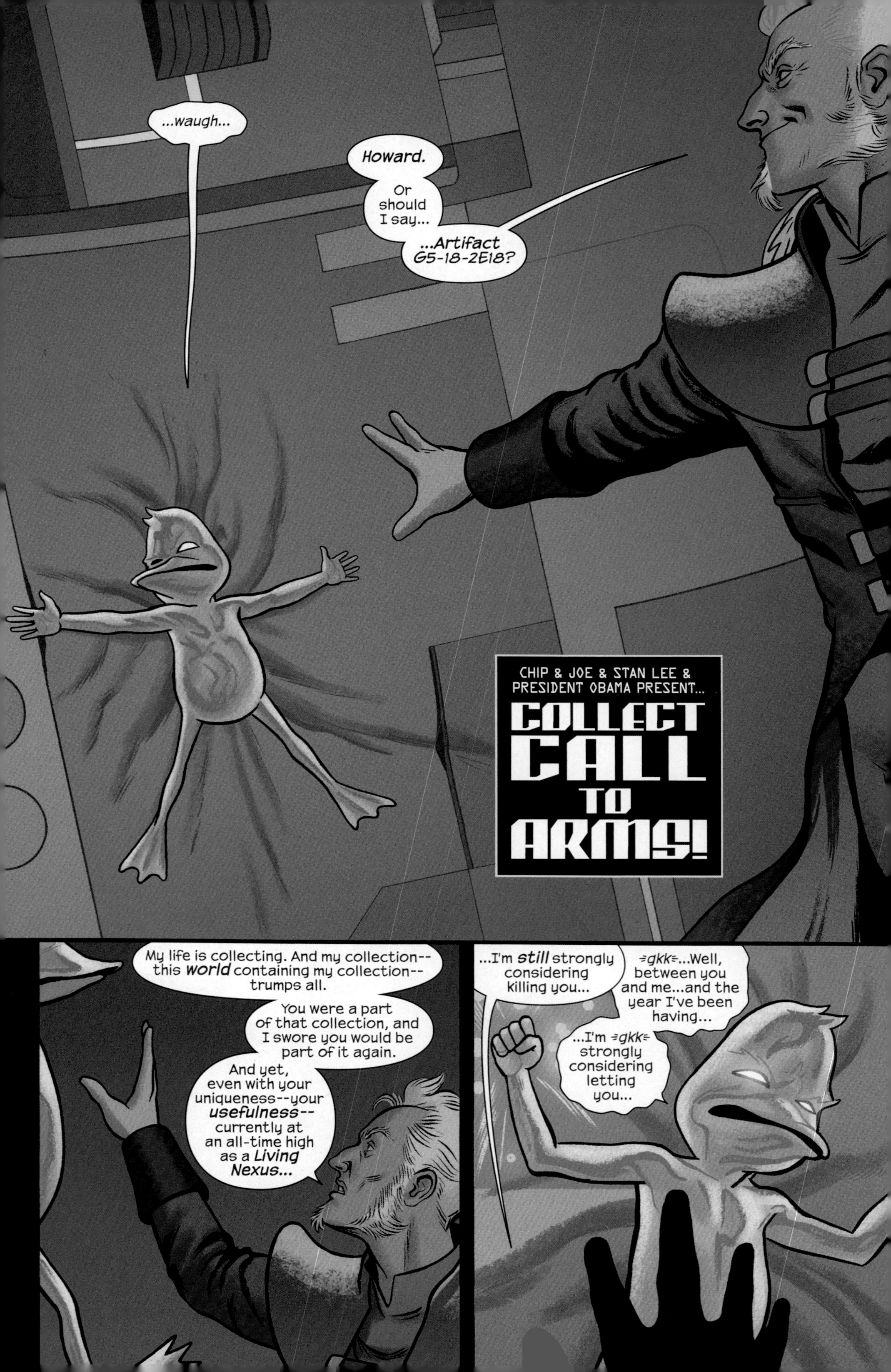

...waugh...
Howard.
Or should I say...
...Artifact G5-18-2E18?
CHIP & JOE & STAN LEE & PRESIDENT OBAMA PRESENT...
COLLECT CALL TO ARMS!
My life is collecting. And my collection--this world containing my collection--trumps all.
You were a part of that collection, and I swore you would be part of it again.
And yet, even with your uniqueness--your usefulness--currently at an all-time high as a Living Nexus...
...I'm still strongly considering killing you...
=gkk=...Well, between you and me...and the year I've been having...
...I'm =gkk= strongly considering letting you...

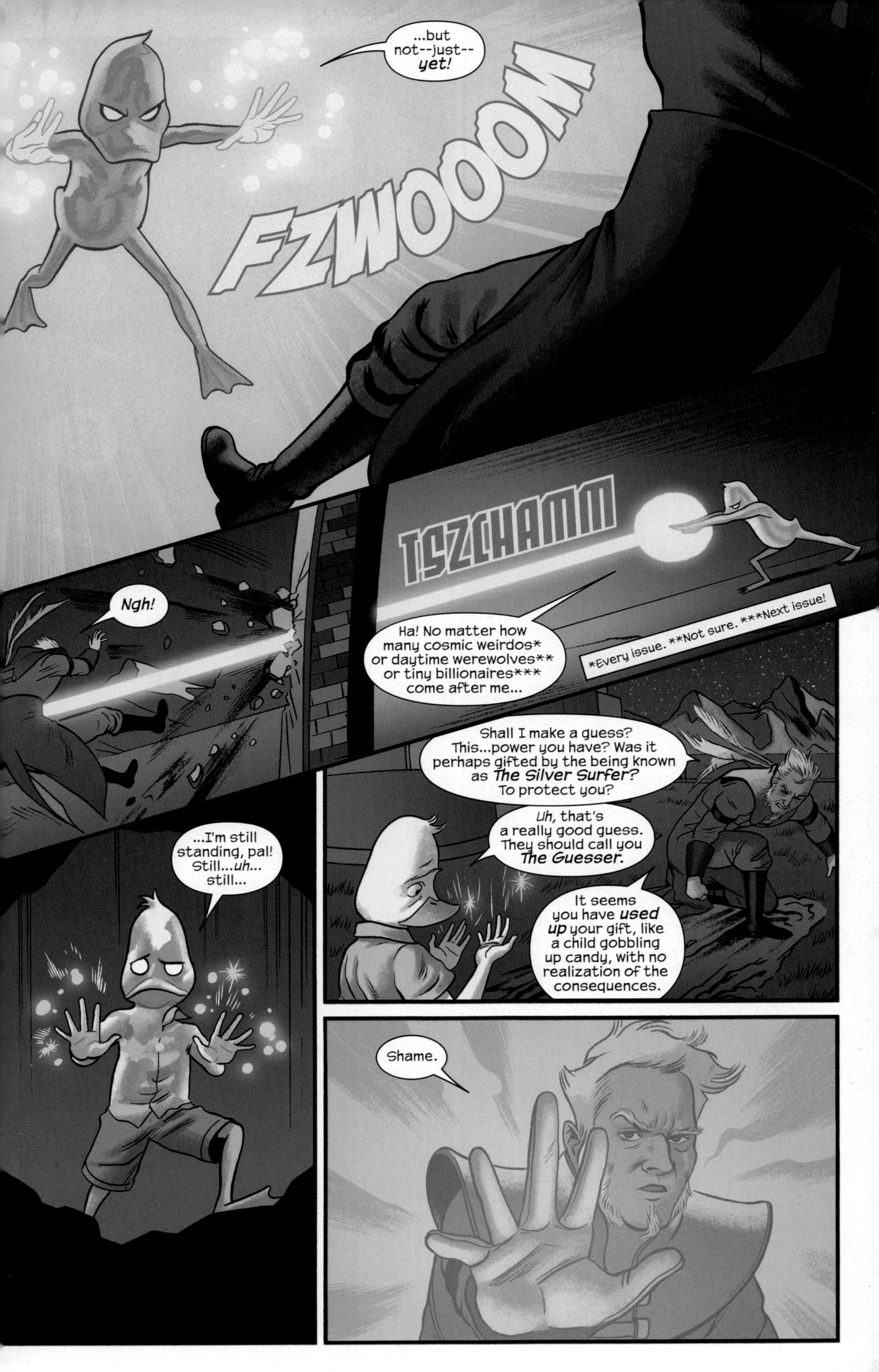
...but not--just-- yet!
FZWOOOOM
TSZCHAMM
Ngh!
Ha! No matter how many cosmic weirdos* or daytime werewolves** or tiny billionaires*** come after me...
*Every issue. **Not sure. ***Next issue!
Shall I make a guess? This...power you have? Was it perhaps gifted by the being known as The Silver Surfer? To protect you?
Uh, that's a really good guess. They should call you The Guesser.
It seems you have used up your gift, like a child gobbling up candy, with no realization of the consequences.
...I'm still standing, pal! Still...uh... still...
Shame.

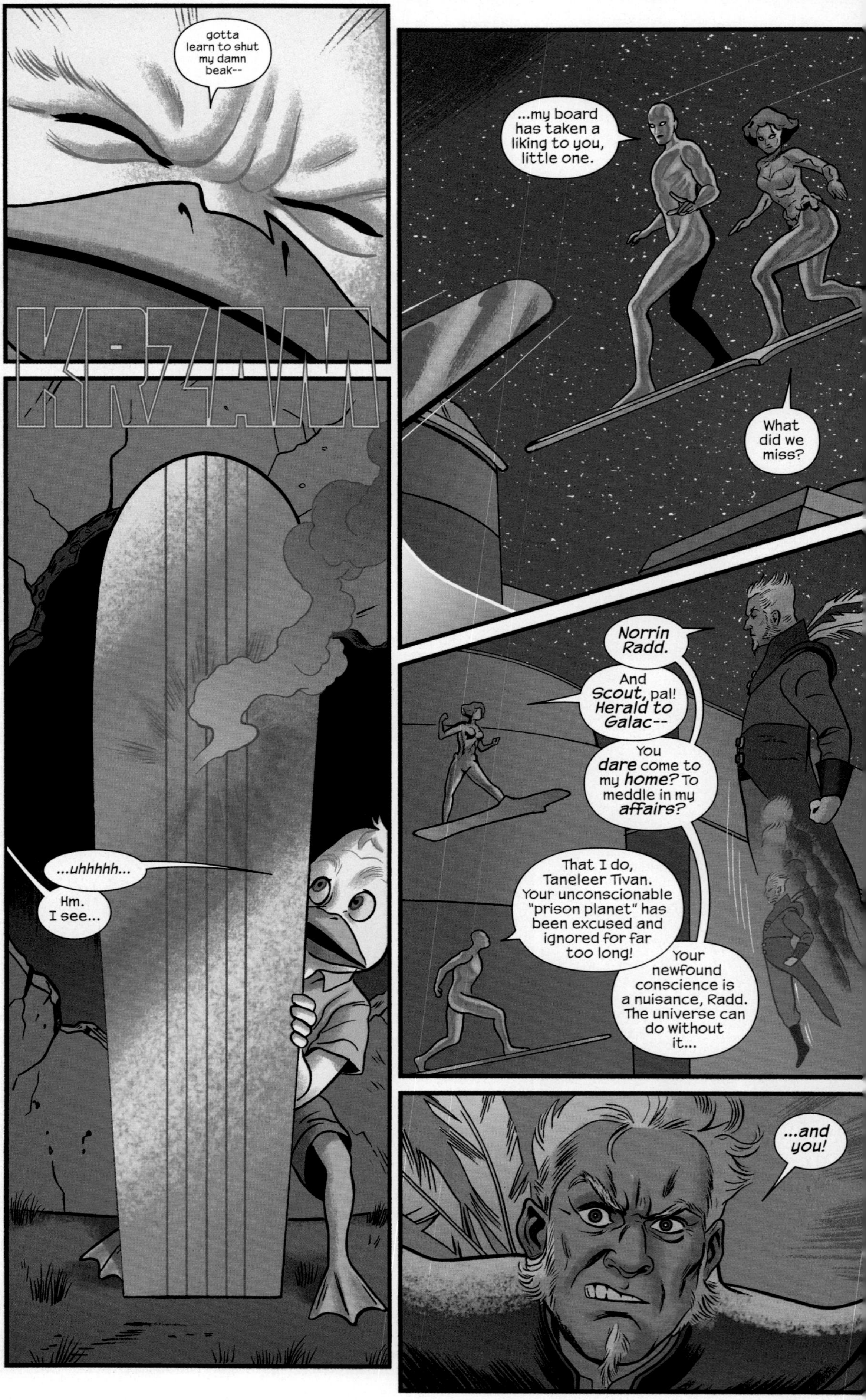
gotta learn to shut my damn beak--
KRZAAM
...uhhhhh...
Hm. I see...
...my board has taken a liking to you, little one.
What did we miss?
Norrin Radd.
And Scout, pal! Herald to Galac--
You dare come to my home? To meddle in my affairs?
That I do, Taneleer Tivan. Your unconscionable "prison planet" has been excused and ignored for far too long!
Your newfound conscience is a nuisance, Radd. The universe can do without it...
...and you!

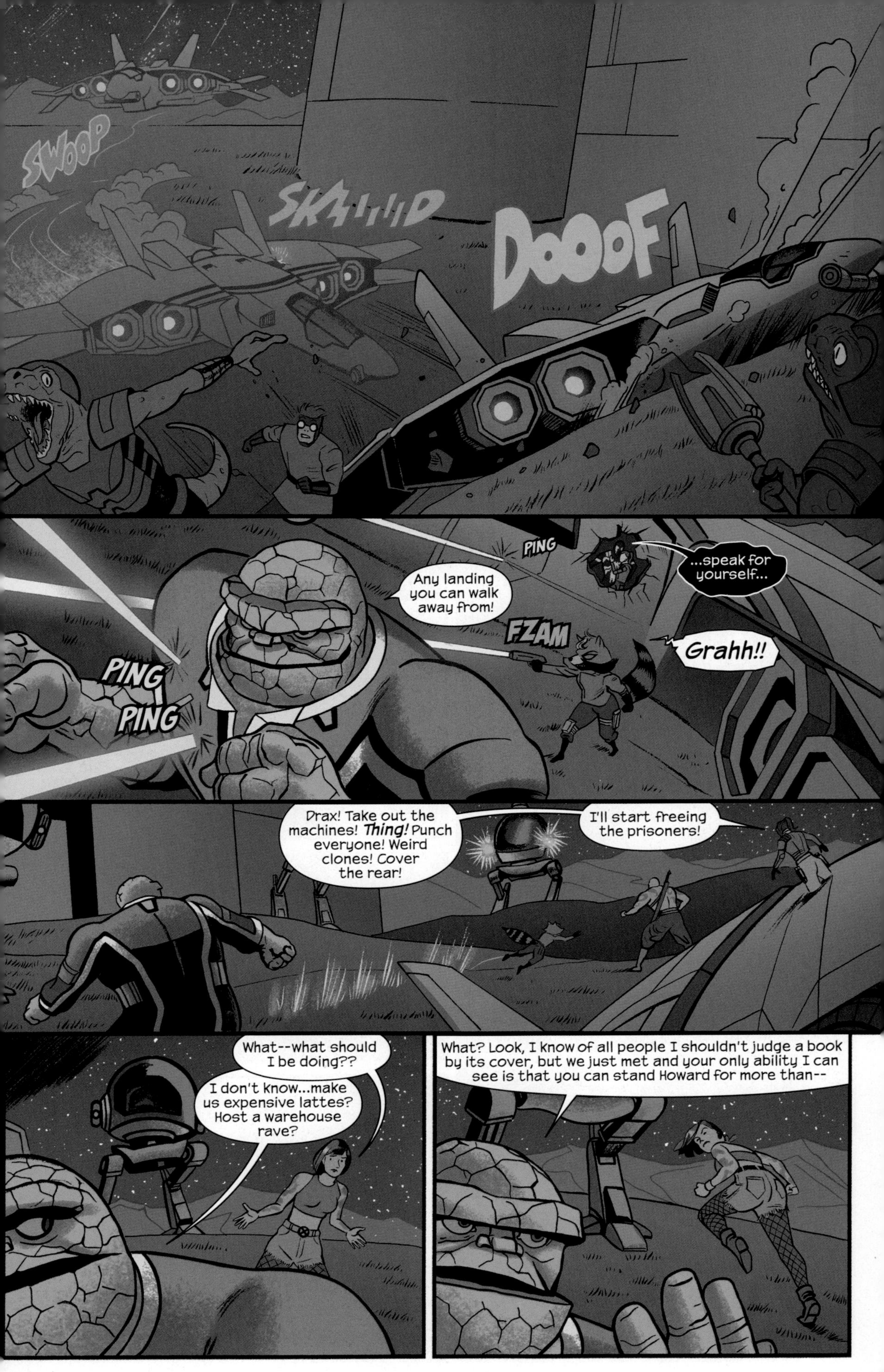
SWOOP
SKRIIID
DOOOF
PING
Any landing you can walk away from!
...speak for yourself...
FZAM
Grahh!!
PING
PING
Drax! Take out the machines! *Thing!* Punch everyone! Weird clones! Cover the rear!
I'll start freeing the prisoners!
What--what should I be doing??
I don't know...make us expensive lattes? Host a warehouse rave?
What? Look, I know of all people I shouldn't judge a book by its cover, but we just met and your only ability I can see is that you can stand Howard for more than--

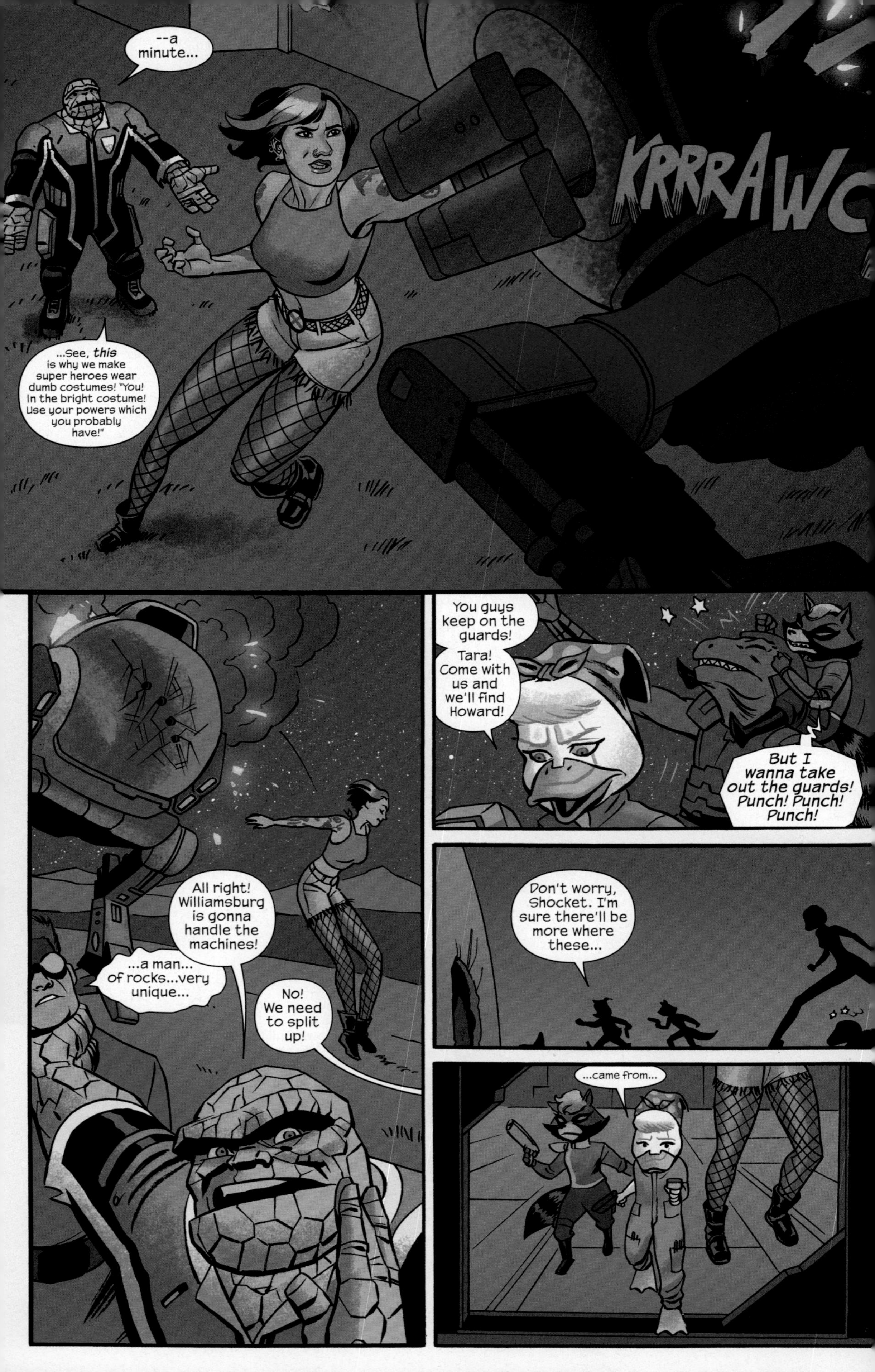
--a minute...
...See, this is why we make super heroes wear dumb costumes! "You! In the bright costume! Use your powers which you probably have!"
KRRRAWC
All right! Williamsburg is gonna handle the machines!
...a man... of rocks...very unique...
No! We need to split up!
You guys keep on the guards!
Tara! Come with us and we'll find Howard!
But I wanna take out the guards! Punch! Punch! Punch!
Don't worry, Shocket. I'm sure there'll be more where these...
...came from...

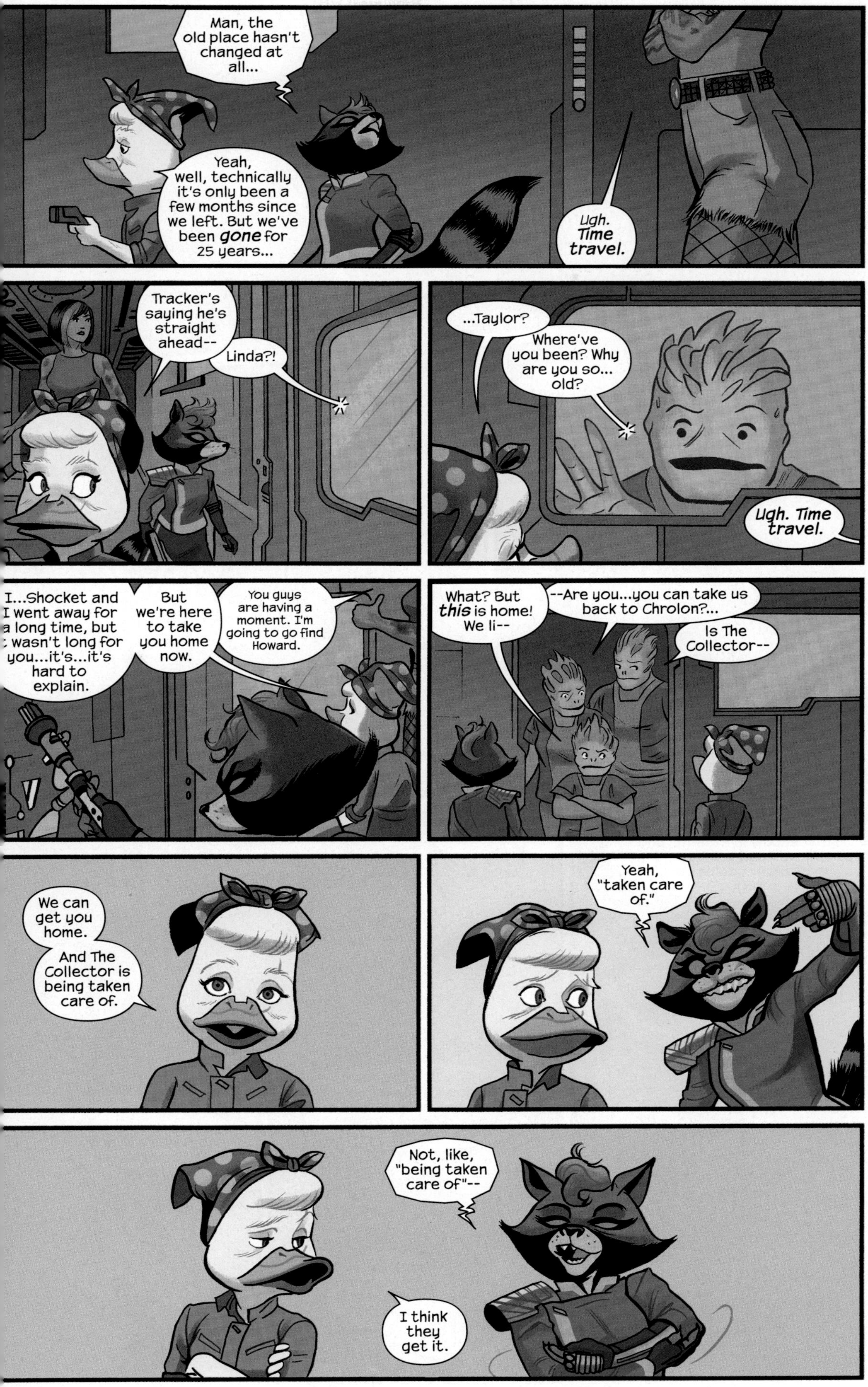
Man, the old place hasn't changed at all...
Yeah, well, technically it's only been a few months since we left. But we've been *gone* for 25 years...
Ugh. Time travel.
Tracker's saying he's straight ahead--
Linda?!
...Taylor?
Where've you been? Why are you so... old?
Ugh. Time travel.
I...Shocket and I went away for a long time, but it wasn't long for you...it's...it's hard to explain.
But we're here to take you home now.
You guys are having a moment. I'm going to go find Howard.
What? But *this* is home! We li--
--Are you...you can take us back to Chrolon?...
Is The Collector--
We can get you home.
And The Collector is being taken care of.
Yeah, "taken care of."
Not, like, "being taken care of"--
I think they get it.

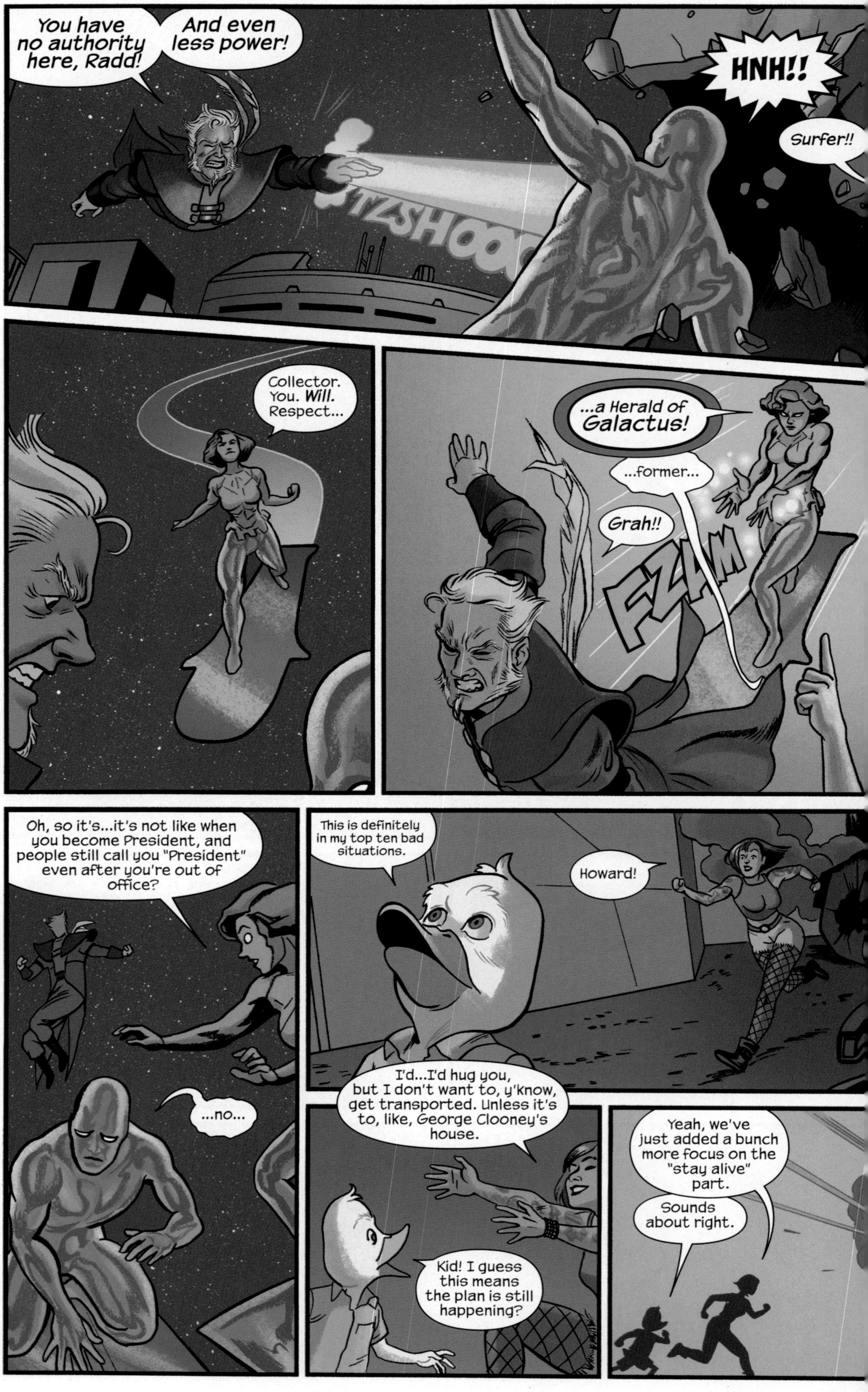
You have no authority here, Radd!
And even less power!
HNH!!
Surfer!!
TZSHOOO
Collector. You. Will. Respect...
...a Herald of Galactus!
...former...
Grah!!
FZAM
Oh, so it's...it's not like when you become President, and people still call you "President" even after you're out of office?
...no...
This is definitely in my top ten bad situations.
Howard!
I'd...I'd hug you, but I don't want to, y'know, get transported. Unless it's to, like, George Clooney's house.
Kid! I guess this means the plan is still happening?
Yeah, we've just added a bunch more focus on the "stay alive" part.
Sounds about right.

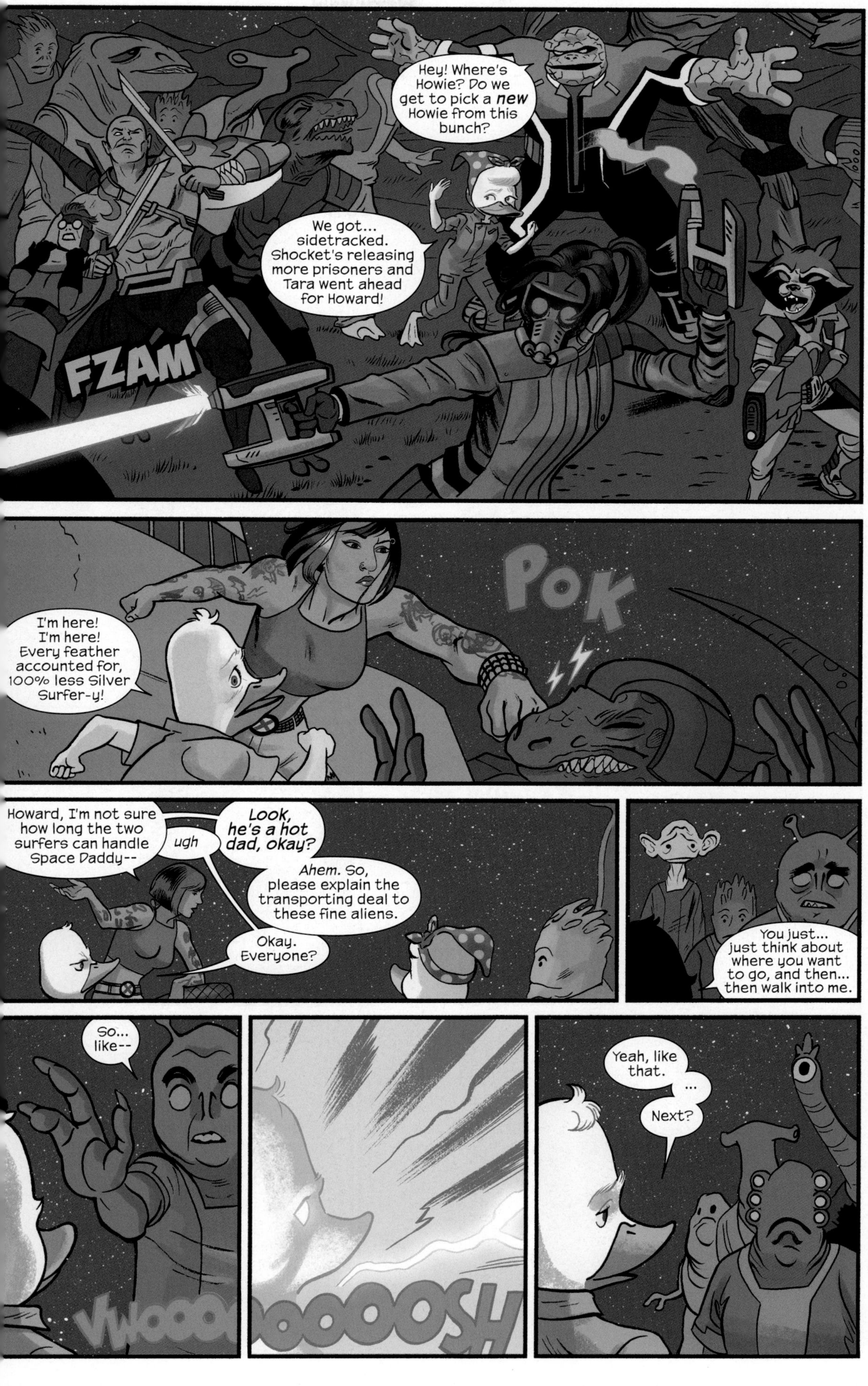
Hey! Where's Howie? Do we get to pick a *new* Howie from this bunch?
We got... sidetracked. Shocket's releasing more prisoners and Tara went ahead for Howard!
FZAM
POK
I'm here! I'm here! Every feather accounted for, 100% less Silver Surfer-y!
Howard, I'm not sure how long the two surfers can handle Space Daddy--
ugh
Look, he's a hot dad, okay?
Ahem. So, please explain the transporting deal to these fine aliens.
Okay. Everyone?
You just... just think about where you want to go, and then... then walk into me.
So... like--
VWOOOOOOOOOSH
Yeah, like that.
...
Next?

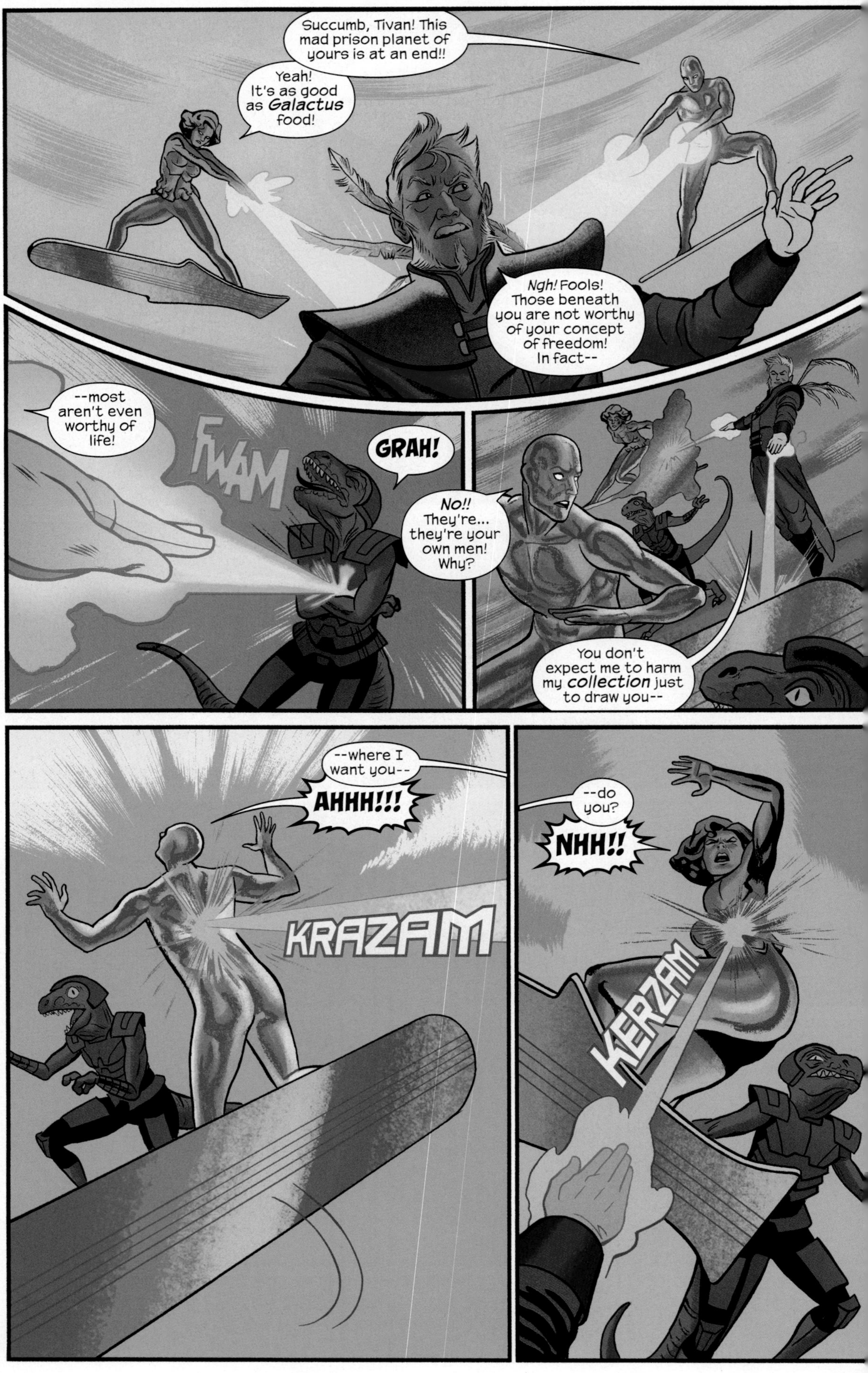
Succumb, Tivan! This mad prison planet of yours is at an end!!
Yeah! It's as good as *Galactus* food!
Ngh! Fools! Those beneath you are not worthy of your concept of freedom! In fact--
--most aren't even worthy of life!
FWAM
GRAH!
No!! They're... they're your own men! Why?
You don't expect me to harm my *collection* just to draw you--
--where I want you--
AHHH!!!
KRAZAM
--do you?
NHH!!
KERZAM

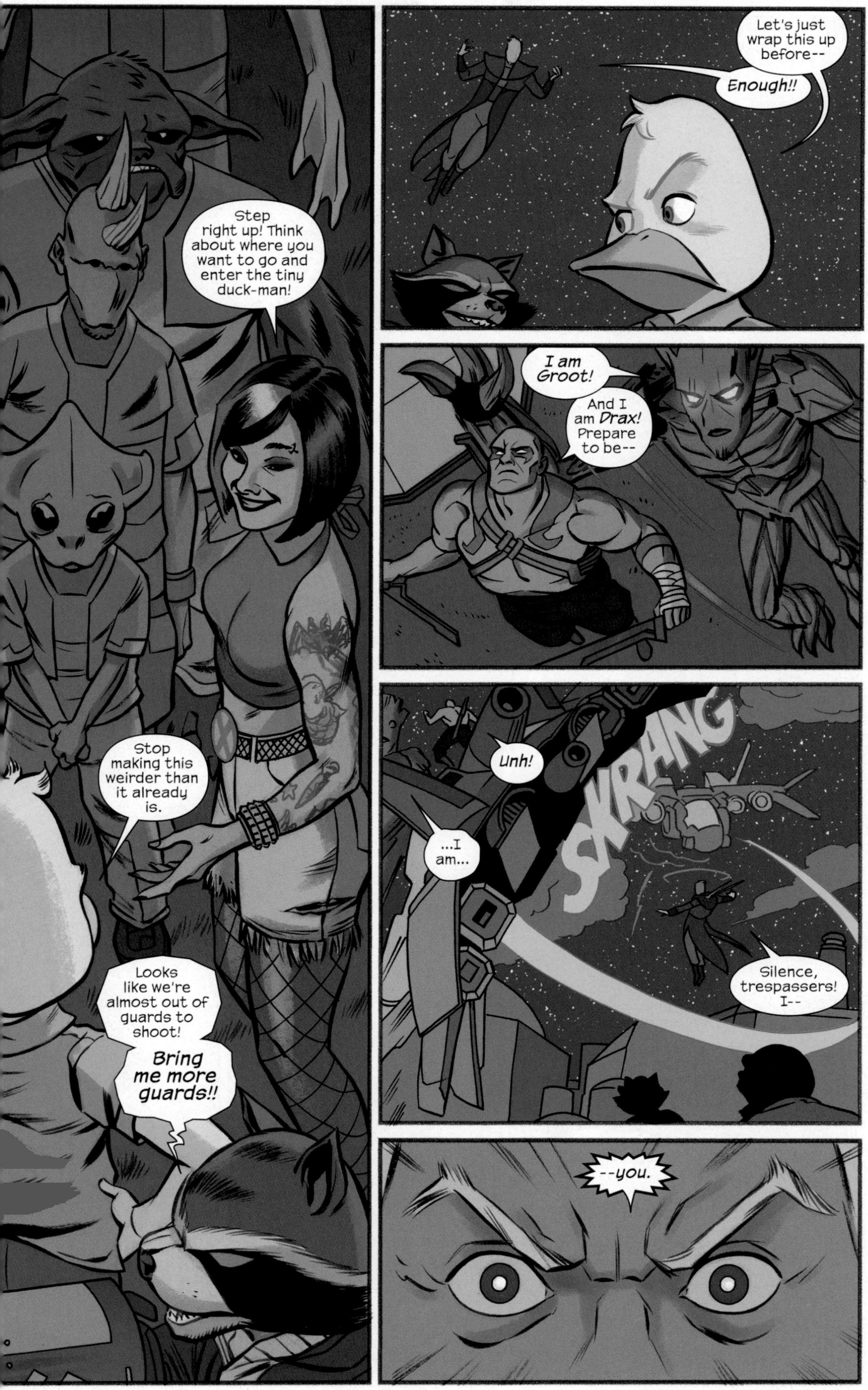
Step right up! Think about where you want to go and enter the tiny duck-man!
Stop making this weirder than it already is.
Looks like we're almost out of guards to shoot!
Bring me more guards!!
Let's just wrap this up before--
Enough!!
I am Groot!
And I am Drax! Prepare to be--
Unh!
...I am...
SKRANG
Silence, trespassers! I--
--you.

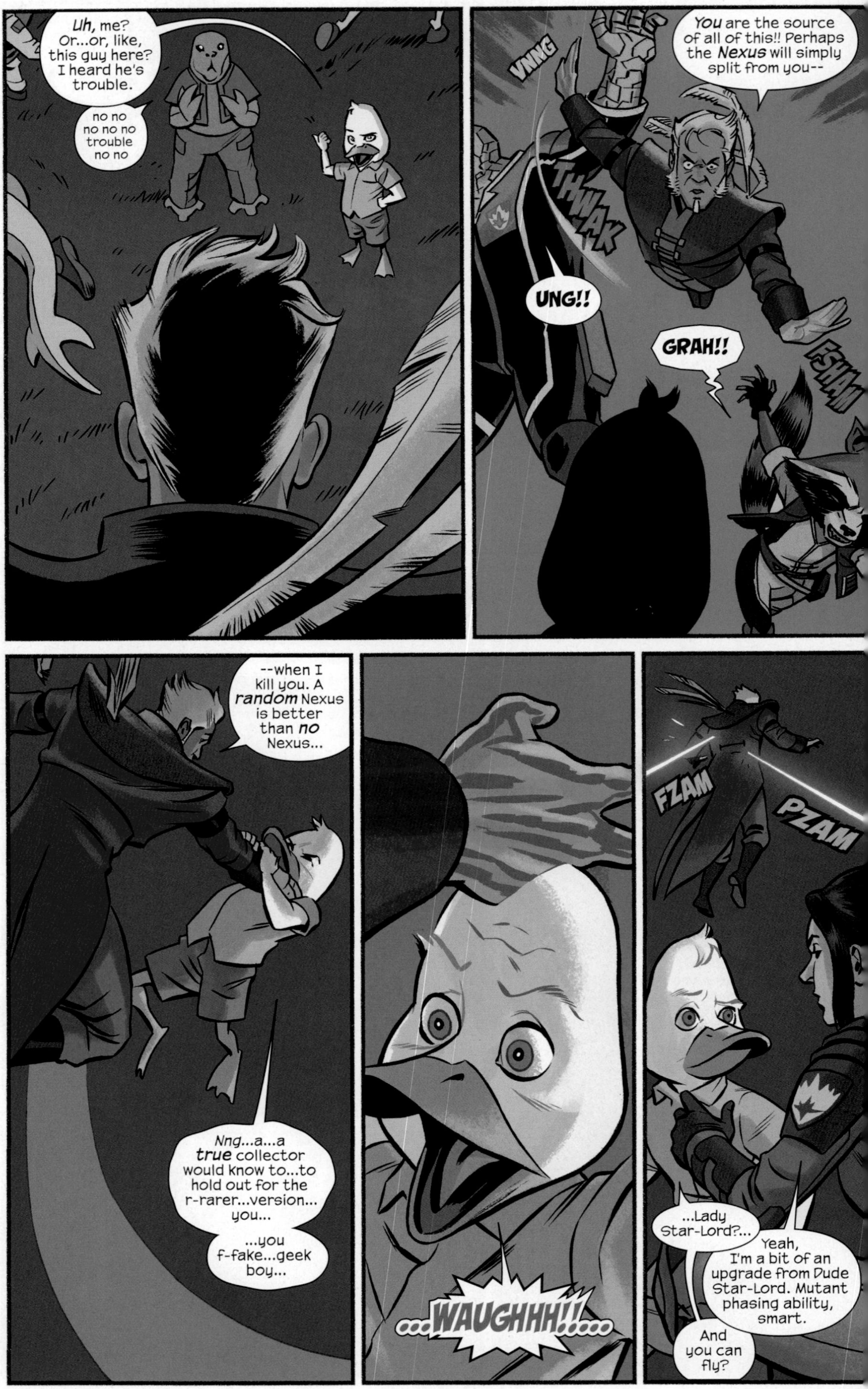
Uh, me? Or...or, like, this guy here? I heard he's trouble.
no no no no no trouble no no
VNNG
You are the source of all of this!! Perhaps the Nexus will simply split from you--
THWAK
UNG!!
GRAH!!
FSHAM
--when I kill you. A random Nexus is better than no Nexus...
Nng...a...a true collector would know to...to hold out for the r-rarer...version... you...
...you f-fake...geek boy...
...WAUGHHH!!...
FZAM
PZAM
...Lady Star-Lord?...
Yeah, I'm a bit of an upgrade from Dude Star-Lord. Mutant phasing ability, smart.
And you can fly?

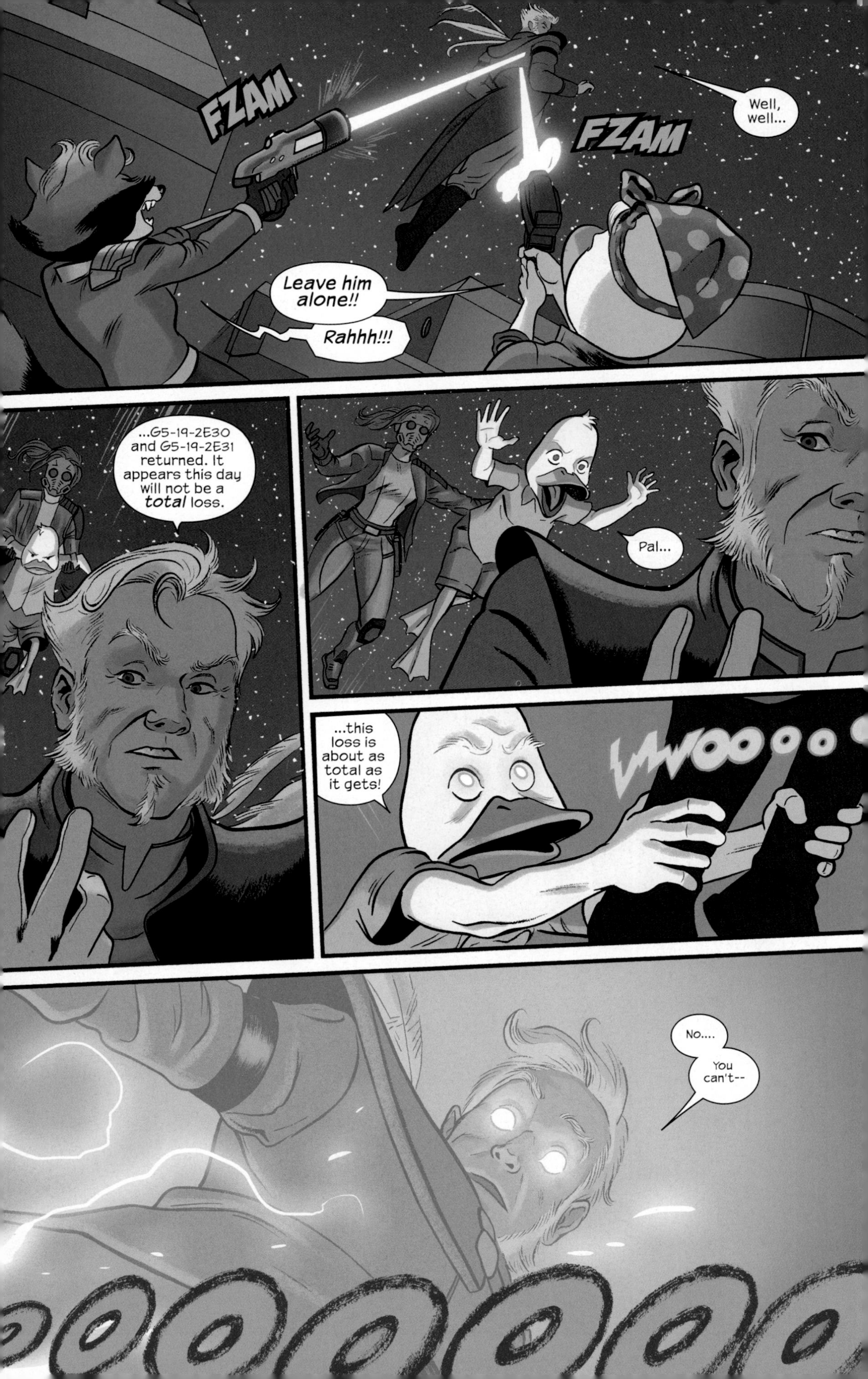
FZAM
Well, well...
FZAM
Leave him alone!!
Rahhh!!!
...G5-19-2E30 and G5-19-2E31 returned. It appears this day will not be a *total* loss.
Pal...
...this loss is about as total as it gets!
WOOOOO
No....
You can't--

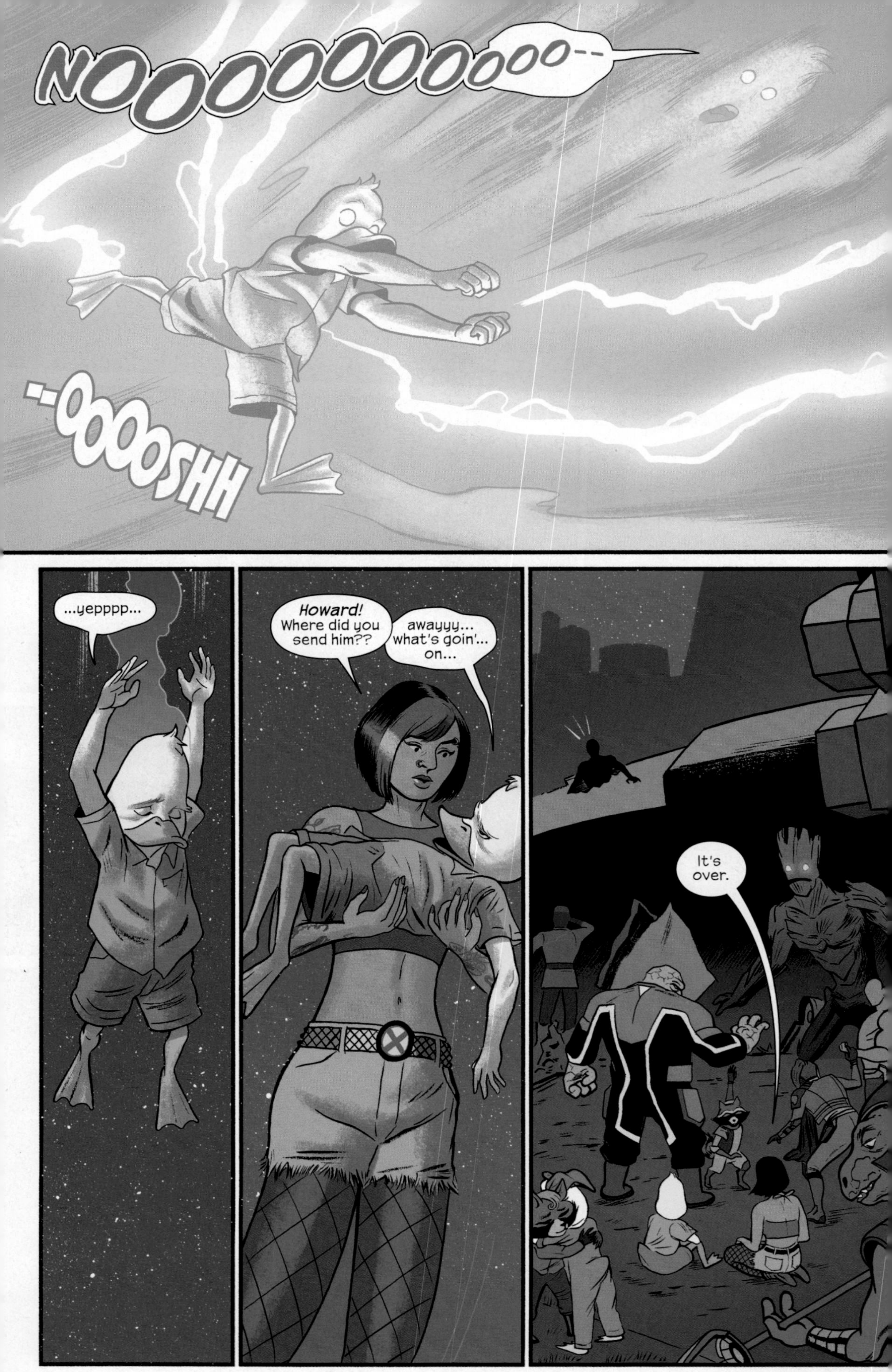
NOOOOOOOOooo--
--OOOOSHH
...yepppp...
Howard! Where did you send him??
awayyy... what's goin'... on...
It's over.

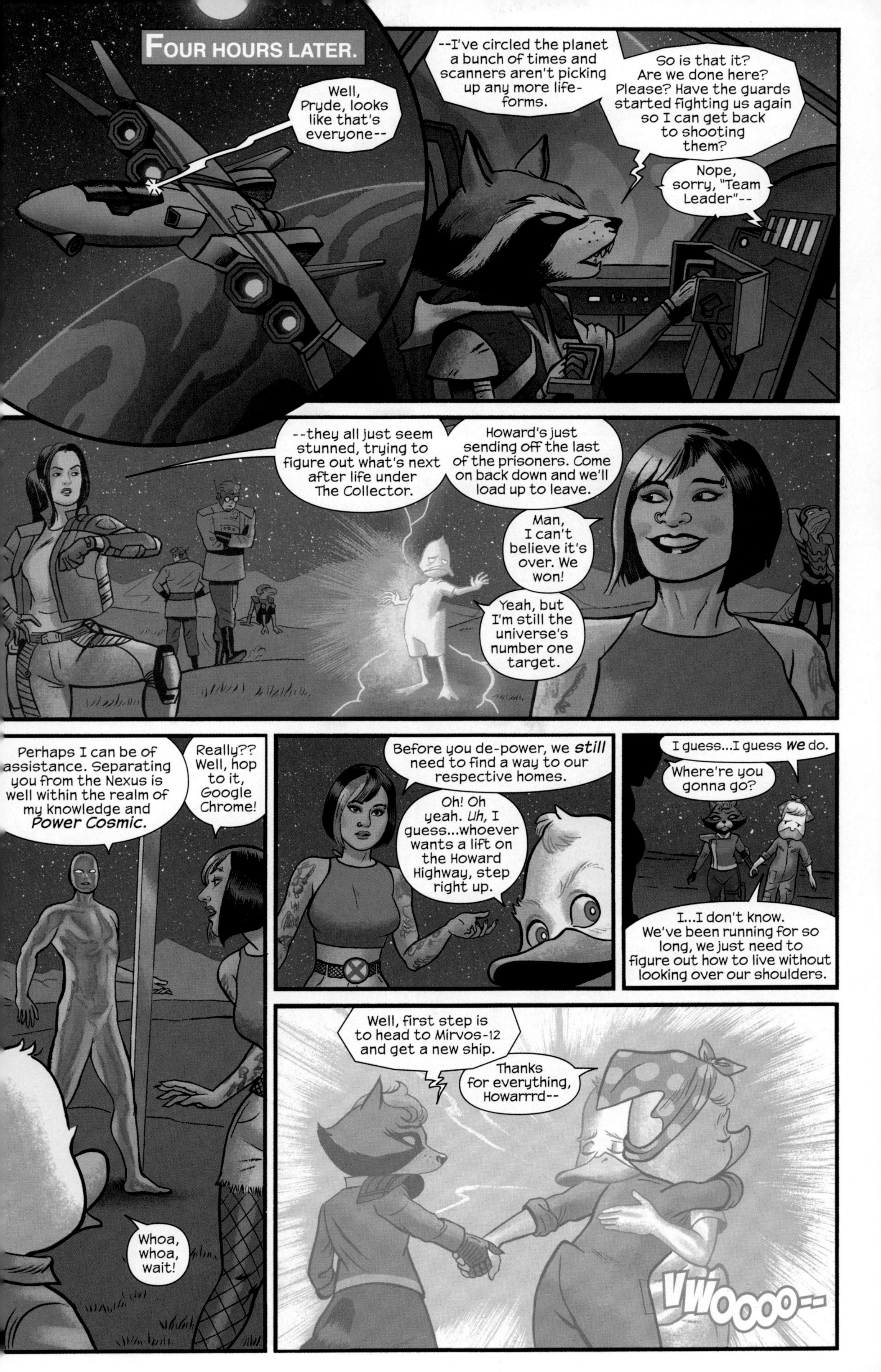
FOUR HOURS LATER.
Well, Pryde, looks like that's everyone--
--I've circled the planet a bunch of times and scanners aren't picking up any more life-forms.
So is that it? Are we done here? Please? Have the guards started fighting us again so I can get back to shooting them?
Nope, sorry, "Team Leader"--
--they all just seem stunned, trying to figure out what's next after life under The Collector.
Howard's just sending off the last of the prisoners. Come on back down and we'll load up to leave.
Man, I can't believe it's over. We won!
Yeah, but I'm still the universe's number one target.
Perhaps I can be of assistance. Separating you from the Nexus is well within the realm of my knowledge and *Power Cosmic.*
Really?? Well, hop to it, Google Chrome!
Whoa, whoa, wait!
Before you de-power, we *still* need to find a way to our respective homes.
Oh! Oh yeah. *Uh,* I guess...whoever wants a lift on the Howard Highway, step right up.
I guess...I guess *we* do.
Where're you gonna go?
I...I don't know. We've been running for so long, we just need to figure out how to live without looking over our shoulders.
Well, first step is to head to Mirvos-12 and get a new ship.
Thanks for everything, Howarrrd--
VWOOOO--

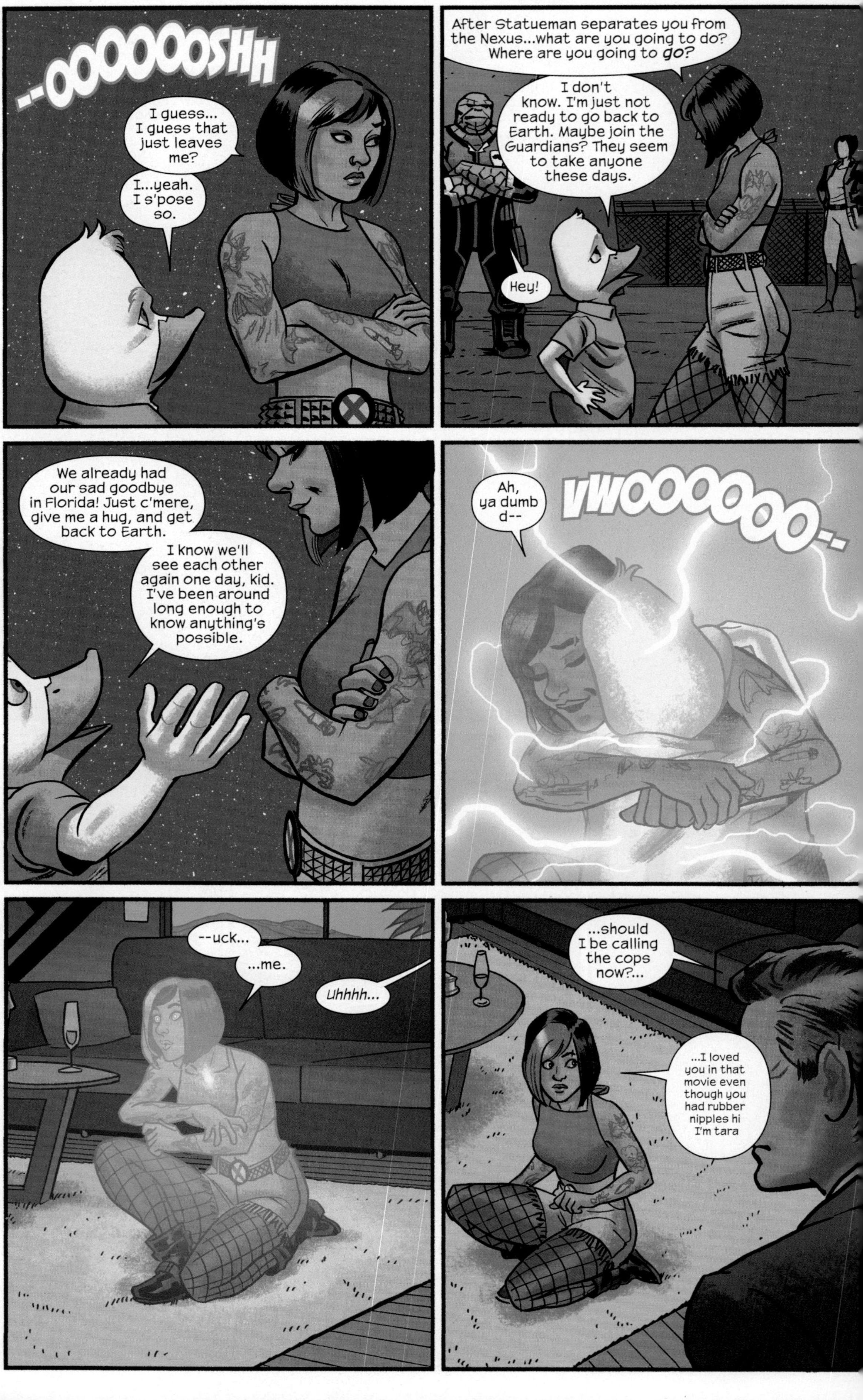

--OOOOOOSHH
I guess... I guess that just leaves me?
I...yeah. I s'pose so.
After Statueman separates you from the Nexus...what are you going to do? Where are you going to *go*?
I don't know. I'm just not ready to go back to Earth. Maybe join the Guardians? They seem to take anyone these days.
Hey!
We already had our sad goodbye in Florida! Just c'mere, give me a hug, and get back to Earth.
I know we'll see each other again one day, kid. I've been around long enough to know anything's possible.
Ah, ya dumb d--
VWOOOOOO--
--uck...
...me.
Uhhhh...
...should I be calling the cops now?...
...I loved you in that movie even though you had rubber nipples hi I'm tara

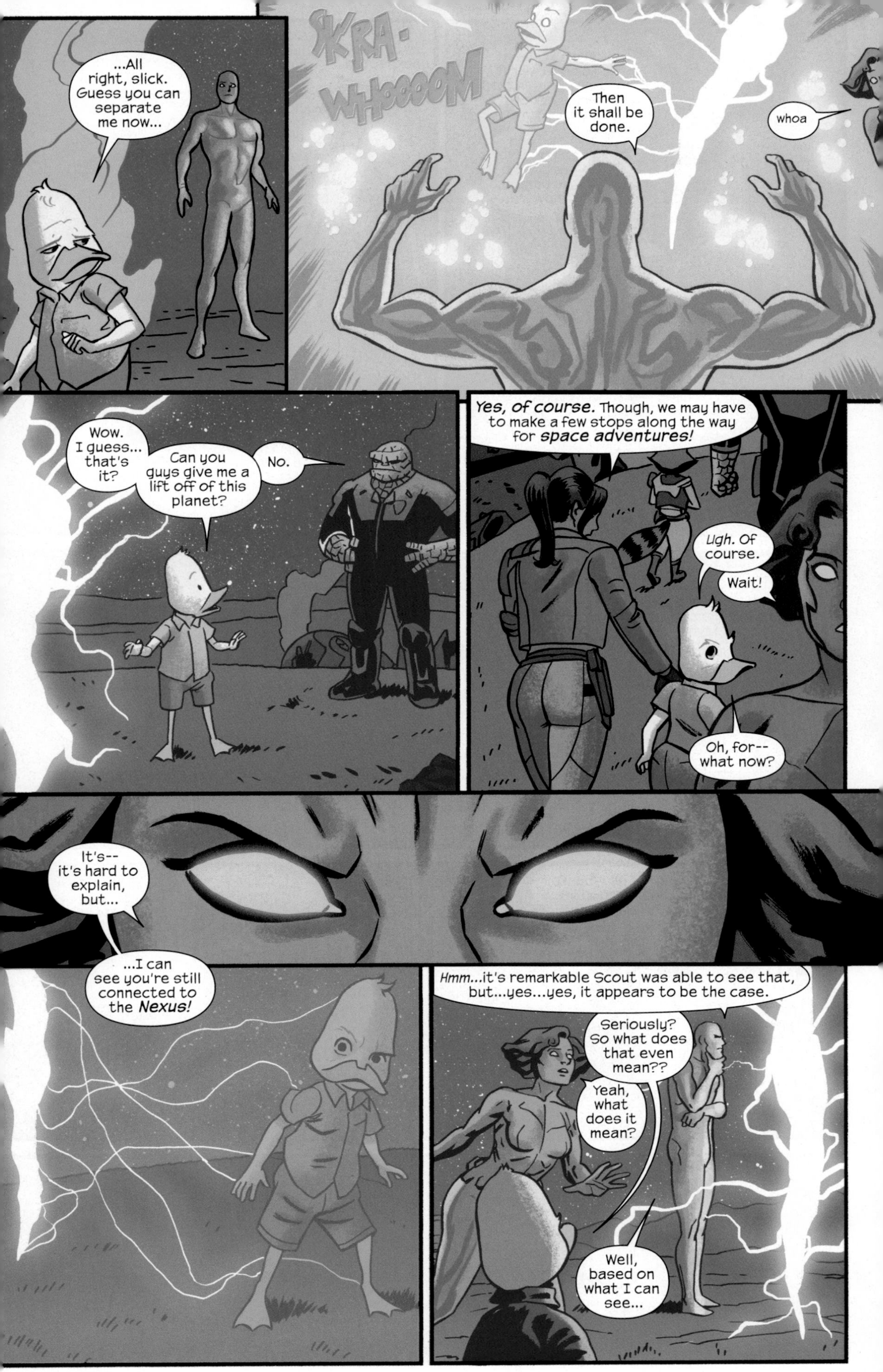
...All right, slick. Guess you can separate me now...
SKRA-WHOOOOOM
Then it shall be done.
whoa
Wow. I guess... that's it?
Can you guys give me a lift off of this planet?
No.
Yes, of course. Though, we may have to make a few stops along the way for space adventures!
Ugh. Of course.
Wait!
Oh, for--what now?
It's--it's hard to explain, but...
...I can see you're still connected to the Nexus!
Hmm...it's remarkable Scout was able to see that, but...yes...yes, it appears to be the case.
Seriously? So what does that even mean??
Yeah, what does it mean?
Well, based on what I can see...

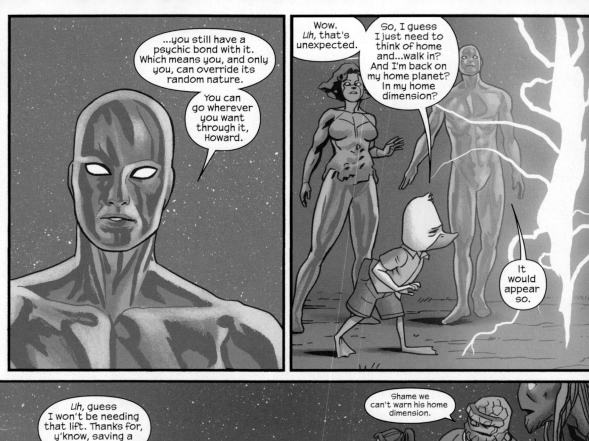

...you still have a psychic bond with it. Which means you, and only you, can override its random nature.

You can go wherever you want through it, Howard.

Wow. *Uh,* that's unexpected.

So, I guess I just need to think of home and...walk in? And I'm back on my home planet? In my home dimension?

It would appear so.

Uh, guess I won't be needing that lift. Thanks for, y'know, saving a planet with me.

Shame we can't warn his home dimension.

I am Groot.

Okay. Off I go. Thanks, guys. Have a good life... *uh...*surfing.

Will do!

Hmm.

Time to go ho--

VWOOOOOOO

OOOOOOSH

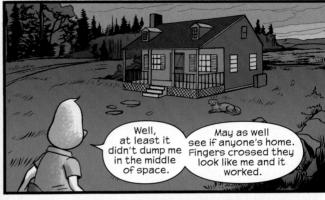

Well, at least it didn't dump me in the middle of space.

May as well see if anyone's home. Fingers crossed they look like me and it worked.

WOOF WOOF WOOF

Ah! Get away, ya mutt!

Lester? What is it, boy? You chasing ducks again?

Wh--

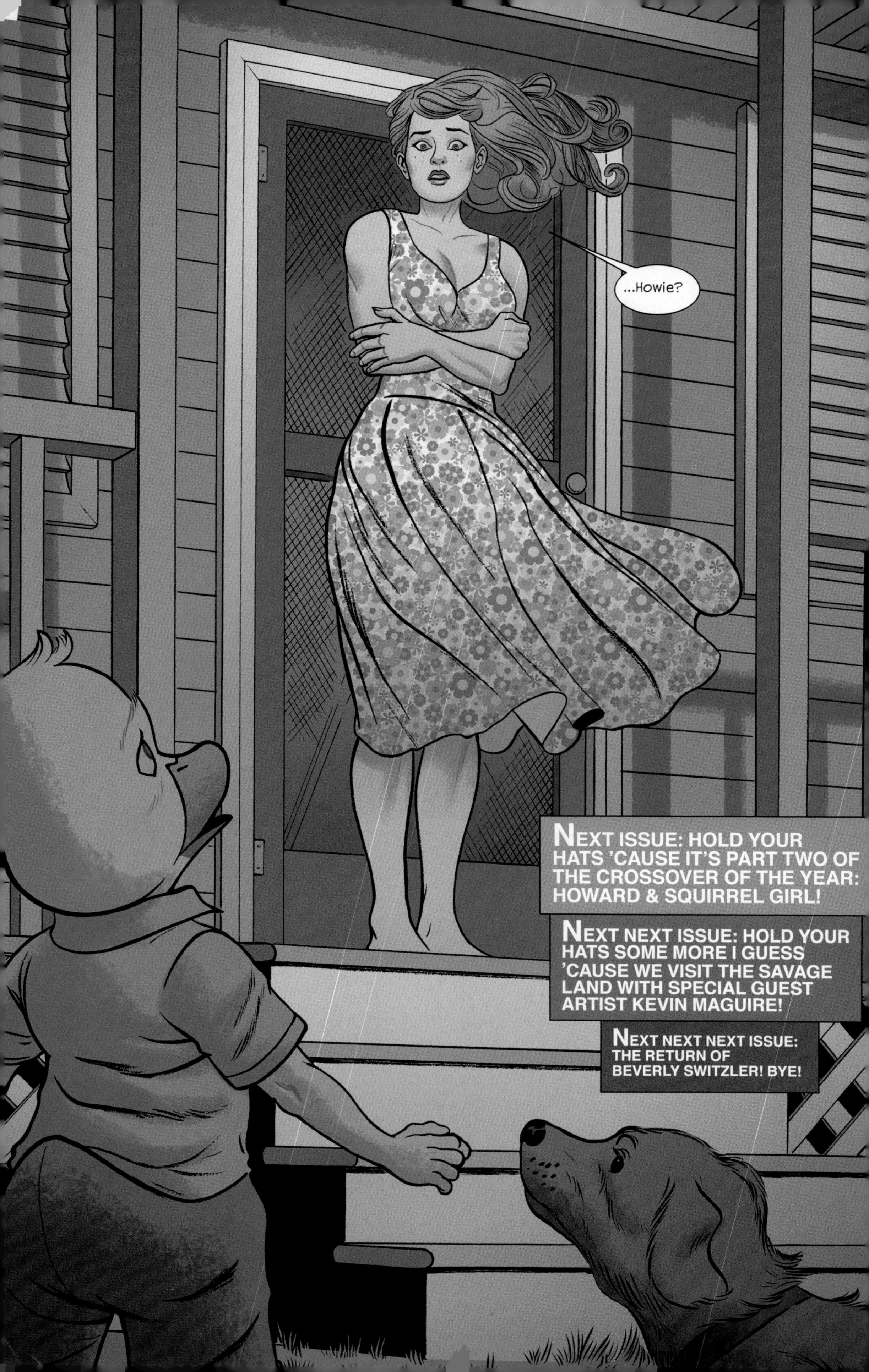
...Howie?
NEXT ISSUE: HOLD YOUR HATS 'CAUSE IT'S PART TWO OF THE CROSSOVER OF THE YEAR: HOWARD & SQUIRREL GIRL!
NEXT NEXT ISSUE: HOLD YOUR HATS SOME MORE I GUESS 'CAUSE WE VISIT THE SAVAGE LAND WITH SPECIAL GUEST ARTIST KEVIN MAGUIRE!
NEXT NEXT NEXT ISSUE: THE RETURN OF BEVERLY SWITZLER! BYE!

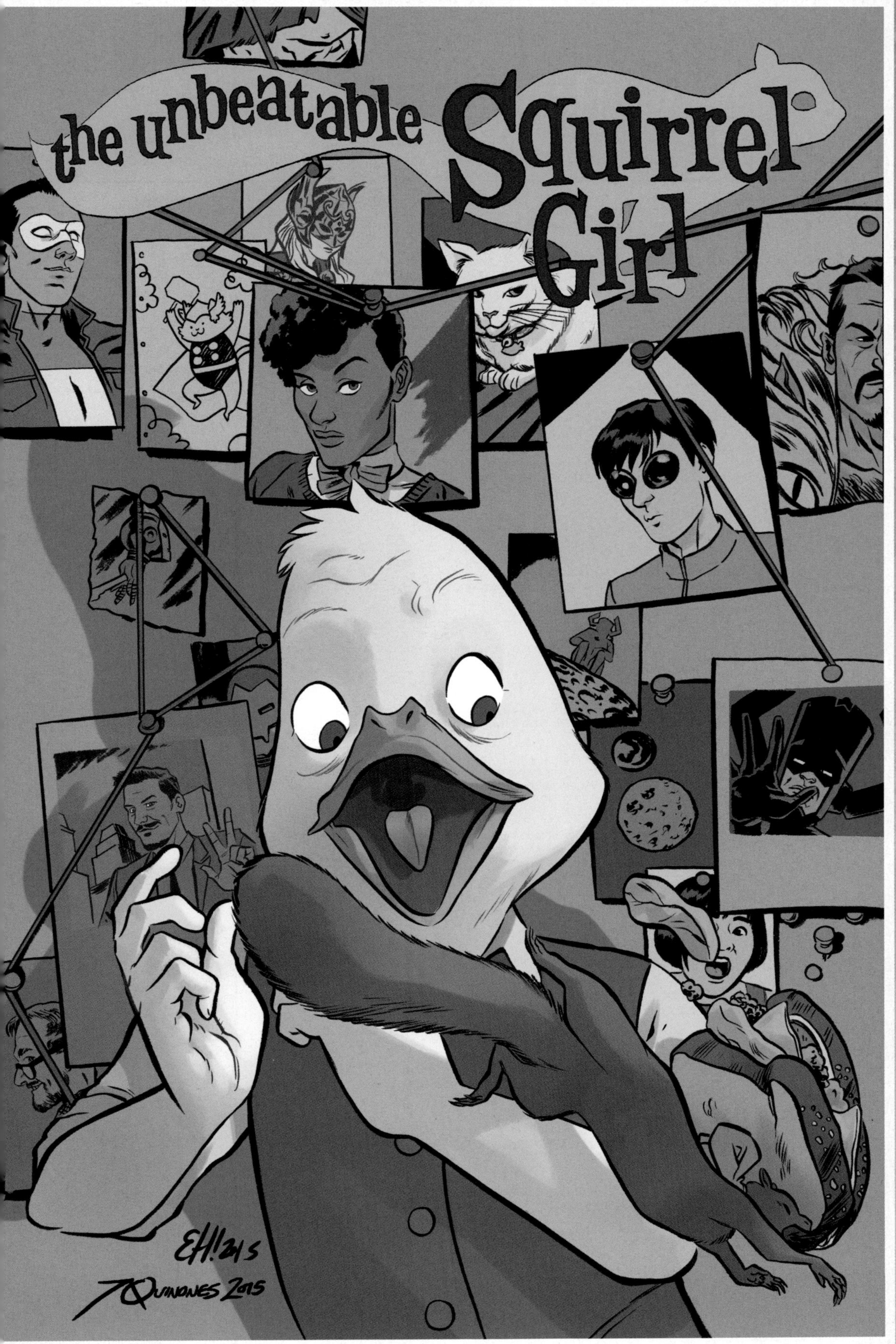
the unbeatable Squirrel Girl
EH! 2015
JQuinones 2015

UNBEATABLE SQUIRREL GIRL #6 BY ERICA HENDERSON & CHIP ZDARSKY

Doreen Green isn't just a first-year computer science student: she secretly also has all the powers of both squirrel and gir
*She uses her amazing abilities to fight crime **and** be as awesome as possible. You know her as...**The Unbeatable Squirrel Gir***
Let's catch up with what she's been up to until now, with...

Squirrel Girl *in a nutshell*

Nancy W. @sewwiththeflo
That's right. You are reading the tweets of a first-year computer science GRADUATE, friends and neighbors. 2nd year, here I come.

Nancy W. @sewwiththeflo
But first: a summer break filled with knitting, Mew, knitting, Mew, movies, knitting, and Mew.

Squirrel Girl @unbeatablesg
@sewwiththeflo OMG Nancy that sounds super great!! make it a double

Nancy W. @sewwiththeflo
@unbeatablesg Yes! It sure does! Thank you for taking an INEXPLICABLE INTEREST IN ME, RANDOM SUPER HERO!!

Squirrel Girl @unbeatablesg
@starkmantony Hey Tony!! You don't have a secret identity--do you think that's something other super heroes should try? Seems easier tbh

Tony Stark @starkmantony
@unbeatablesg Who says I don't have a secret identity? ;P

Squirrel Girl @unbeatablesg
@starkmantony omg did you just type out a winky smiley with its tongue hanging out

Squirrel Girl @unbeatablesg
@starkmantony did a founding member of the avengers and platinum-elite ceo just send me a ;P

Tony Stark @starkmantony
@unbeatablesg No. Obviously I am too important a person to have done that. It must have been my secretary, who sent it by accident.

Squirrel Girl @unbeatablesg
@starkmantony your secretary. who handles chatting online for you. who reads your messages and then takes your dictated responses.

Tony Stark @starkmantony
@unbeatablesg Tell her yes, Jarvis, and let's leave it there. Stop typing, Jarvis. There's no reason for you to be typing. Jarvis.

Squirrel Girl @unbeatablesg
@starkmantony hahaha NICE TRY ;P ;P ;P

Howard The Duck @imhowatrd
thids siote is badf!!@ how comr thisd wax the onhyl namr lefy

Howard The Duck @imhowatrd
anf its hardf top tyhpe wi8tghy feqaythers anbyewayh!1 whyt wolujd anyon e ujse thyis stu[id sitew

Squirrel Girl @unbeatablesg
@imhowatrd You should talk to the Hulk! The fact that @HULKYSMASHY was the only name left for HIM just serves to increase his anger too!!

HULK @HULKYSMASHY
@unbeatablesg @imhowatrd HULK ALSO GET ANGRY THAT WE CAN SEND MAN TO MOON BUT SOMEHOW CAN'T FILTER OUT PEOPLE SASSING HULK ON THIS SITE??

HULK @HULKYSMASHY
@unbeatablesg @imhowatrd HULK DOESN'T NEED RANDOS TELLING HIM OFF!!!! HULK SMASH ENOUGH KEYBOARDS ALREADY!!!

HULK @HULKYSMASHY
@unbeatablesg @imhowatrd ARGH!! HJGIHBDA,N'K',KNGDS'HJRWPO98Y43POUEQ IU'

Squirrel Girl @unbeatablesg
@HULKYSMASHY @imhowatrd It's okay big guy! They don't know the REAL you, remember!!

Howard The Duck @imhowatrd
@unbeatablesg @HULKYSMASHY i donlt kmow anyt of youi perople

search!

#kraVAN

#kraVAN

#kraVAN

#kraVAN

#kraVAN

#kraVAN4life

Ryan North with
Chip Zdarsky - writers
Erica Henderson - artist
Chip again - trading card artist
Joe Quinones - van art, *uh,* artist
Rico Renzi - color artist
Travis Lanham - letterer & production
Erica Henderson with
Joe Quinones - cover artists
Erica Henderson with
Chip Zdarsky; Tradd Moore
& Matthew Wilson;
Kamome Shirahama -
variant cover artists
Chris Robinson - ex-asst. editor
Charles Beacham - new asst. editor
Wil Moss - editor
Tom Brevoort - executive editor
Axel Alonso - editor in chief
Joe Quesada - chief creative officer
Dan Buckley - publisher
Alan Fine - exec. producer

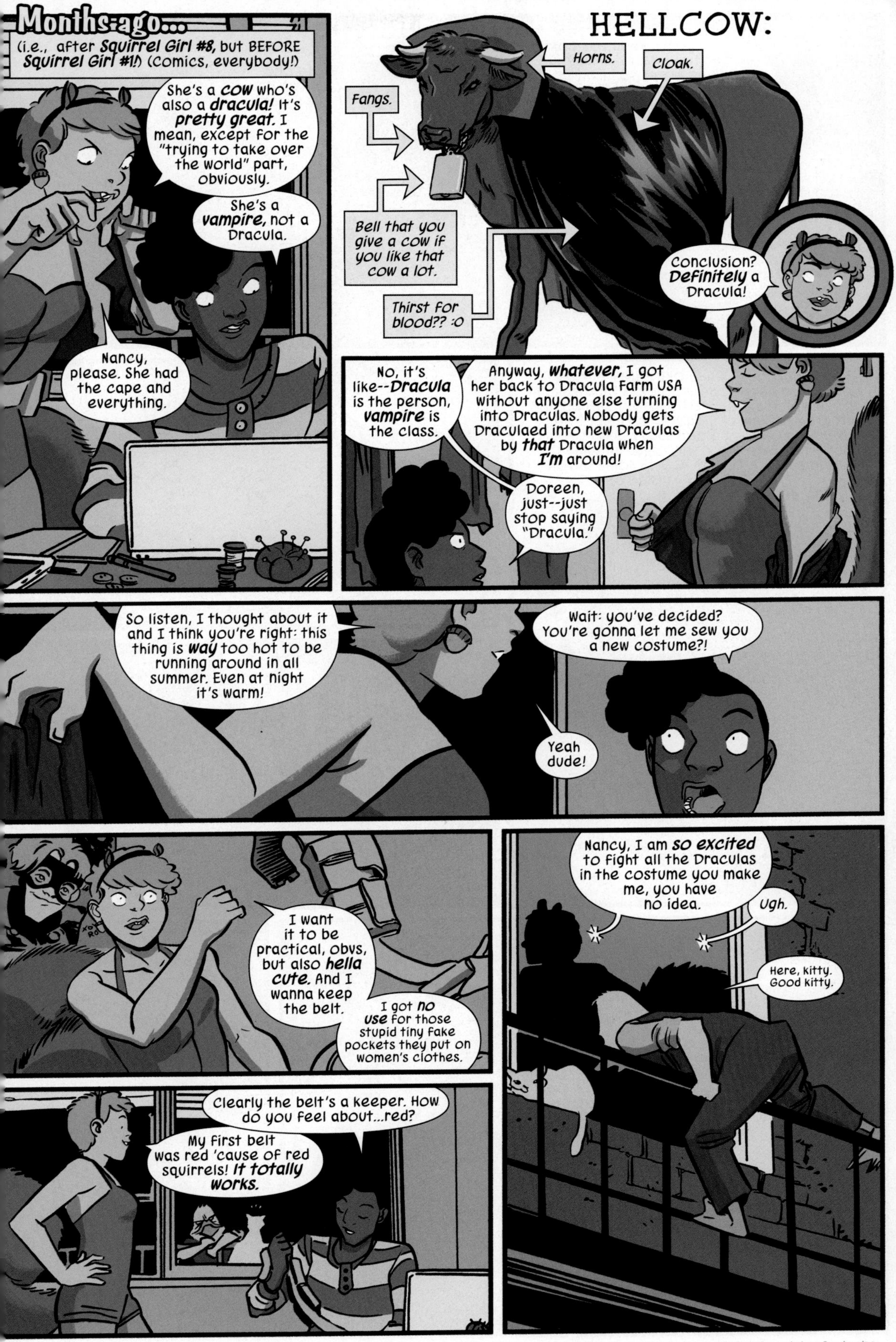
Months ago...
(i.e., after Squirrel Girl #8, but BEFORE Squirrel Girl #1!) (Comics, everybody!)
HELLCOW:
She's a COW who's also a dracula! It's pretty great. I mean, except for the "trying to take over the world" part, obviously.
She's a vampire, not a Dracula.
Nancy, please. She had the cape and everything.
Horns.
Cloak.
Fangs.
Bell that you give a cow if you like that cow a lot.
Thirst for blood?? :o
Conclusion? Definitely a Dracula!
No, it's like--Dracula is the person, vampire is the class.
Anyway, whatever, I got her back to Dracula Farm USA without anyone else turning into Draculas. Nobody gets Draculaed into new Draculas by that Dracula when I'm around!
Doreen, just--just stop saying "Dracula."
So listen, I thought about it and I think you're right: this thing is way too hot to be running around in all summer. Even at night it's warm!
Wait: you've decided? You're gonna let me sew you a new costume?!
Yeah dude!
I want it to be practical, obvs, but also hella cute. And I wanna keep the belt.
I got no use for those stupid tiny fake pockets they put on women's clothes.
Nancy, I am so excited to fight all the Draculas in the costume you make me, you have no idea.
Ugh.
Here, kitty. Good kitty.
Clearly the belt's a keeper. How do you feel about...red?
My first belt was red 'cause of red squirrels! It totally works.

Oh, and if it strikes terror into the cowardly and superstitious hearts of criminals, all the better! So to summarize: practical, cute, reduces criminals to a state of quivering and abject terror, useful pockets and/or belt. Got it, Chip?

Is this...do you do this in every issue? Does Marvel pay more for these?

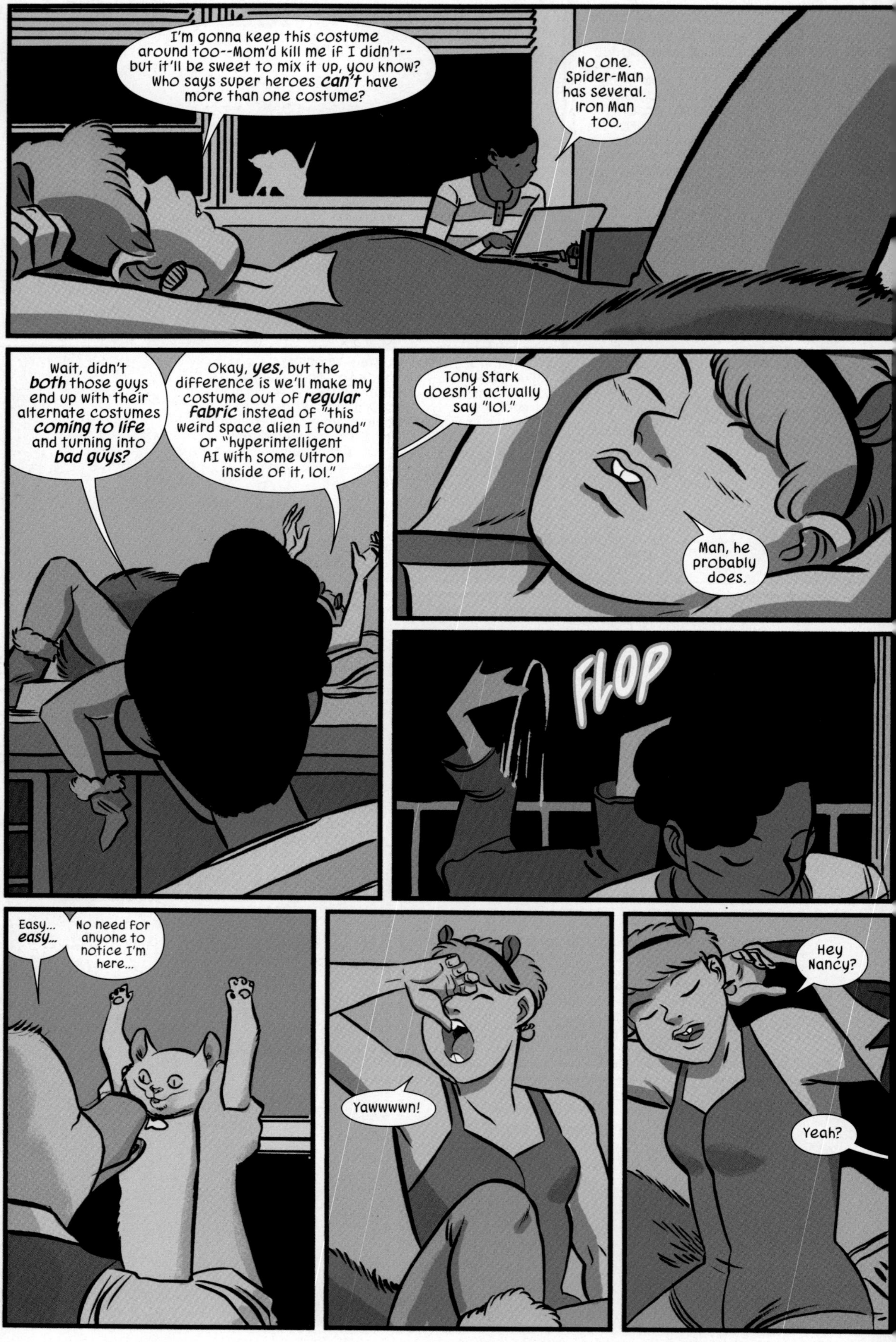
I'm gonna keep this costume around too--Mom'd kill me if I didn't--but it'll be sweet to mix it up, you know? Who says super heroes can't have more than one costume?
No one. Spider-Man has several. Iron Man too.
Wait, didn't both those guys end up with their alternate costumes coming to life and turning into bad guys?
Okay, yes, but the difference is we'll make my costume out of regular fabric instead of "this weird space alien I found" or "hyperintelligent AI with some Ultron inside of it, lol."
Tony Stark doesn't actually say "lol."
Man, he probably does.
FLOP
Easy... easy...
No need for anyone to notice I'm here...
Yawwwwn!
Hey Nancy?
Yeah?

DUCK!!

the unbeatable SQUIRREL Girl

in "ANIMAL HOUSE" Part One

WAAUGH!

Starring:

Squirrel Girl	Nancy Whitehead	Howard the Duck	Tippy-Toe	Bad Guy Whose Name We Haven't Revealed Yet
a.k.a. Doreen Green a.k.a. "The Woman Jumping Through The Window"	a.k.a. @sewwiththeflo a.k.a. "The Woman Whose Cat Was About To Be Stolen If You Were Paying Attention These Past Two Pages"	a.k.a. "Howard" a.k.a. "Hey, Is That A Talking Duck?? Hey Look, It's A Talking Duck! Hey, Talking Duck! Say Something Funny!! Hey!"	a.k.a. "The Most Electrifying Squirrel In Comics Entertainment" a.k.a. "She's Actually On Vacation During This Story But We All Wanted To Mention Her So We Could See Her In Her Vacation Garb"	a.k.a. "Keep Reading And You'll Find Out More" a.k.a. "Seriously, Who Stops Reading A Comic Only Three Pages In? Seriously." a.k.a. "Fine, It's 'Shannon'"

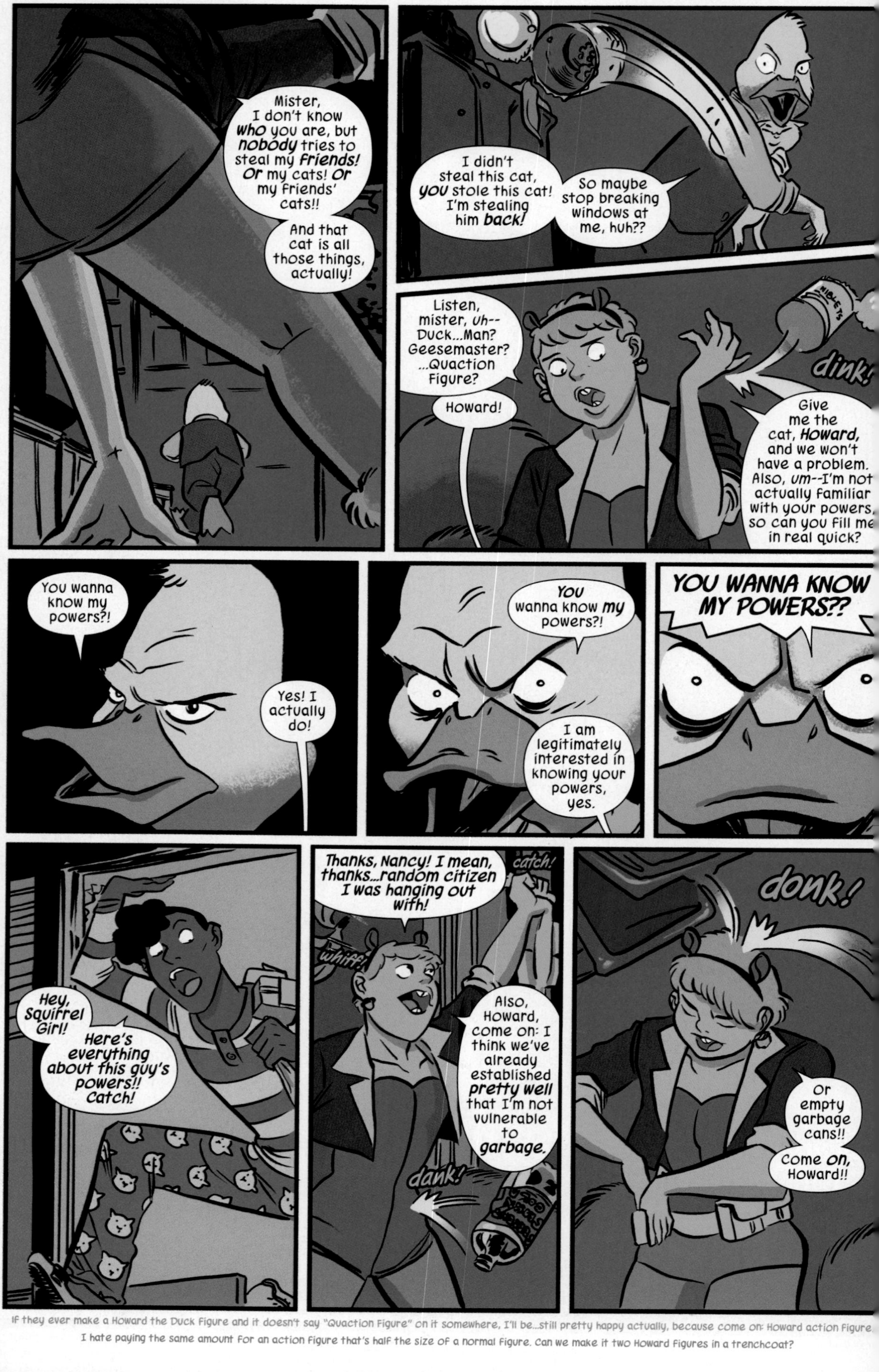
Mister, I don't know who you are, but nobody tries to steal my friends! Or my cats! Or my friends' cats!!
And that cat is all those things, actually!
I didn't steal this cat, you stole this cat! I'm stealing him back!
So maybe stop breaking windows at me, huh??
Listen, mister, uh-- Duck...Man? Geesemaster? ...Quaction Figure?
Howard!
NIBLETS
dink!
Give me the cat, Howard, and we won't have a problem. Also, um--I'm not actually familiar with your powers, so can you fill me in real quick?
You wanna know my powers?!
Yes! I actually do!
You wanna know my powers?!
I am legitimately interested in knowing your powers, yes.
YOU WANNA KNOW MY POWERS??
Hey, Squirrel Girl!
Here's everything about this guy's powers!! Catch!
Thanks, Nancy! I mean, thanks...random citizen I was hanging out with!
catch!
whiff!
Also, Howard, come on: I think we've already established pretty well that I'm not vulnerable to garbage.
dank!
donk!
Or empty garbage cans!!
Come on, Howard!!

If they ever make a Howard the Duck figure and it doesn't say "Quaction Figure" on it somewhere, I'll be...still pretty happy actually, because come on: Howard action figure.
I hate paying the same amount for an action figure that's half the size of a normal figure. Can we make it two Howard figures in a trenchcoat?

quack!

HOWARD THE DUCK

-LOOK AT THIS GUY! I GUESS HE'S A WEIRD...DUCK...MAN?
-DOES HE HAVE HANDS OR FEATHERS? IT'S FEATHERS, RIGHT? DOES HE DO THAT THING WHERE EACH FEATHER IS, LIKE, A FINGER??
-HOW WOULD THAT EVEN WORK THOUGH?? THEY'D GET ALL BENT
-ANYWAY I'M **PRETTY SURE** HIS POWERS INCLUDE A) TALKING TO DUCKS B) CONTROLLING DUCKS C) TEAMING UP WITH 100 REGULAR-SIZED DUCKS TO FORM ONE GIANT DUCK
-THAT'S ALL I KNOW (**AND ALL I CARE** TO KNOW) ABOUT THIS GUY, SO HERE'S A JOKE TO FILL UP THE REST OF THIS CARD: HOW DO YOU GET DOWN OFF A HORSE? YOU DON'T! YOU GET DOWN OFF A DUCK!! [IT TOOK ME A LONG TIME TO FIGURE THAT JOKE OUT, BUT LATER I FOUND OUT IT'S REFERRING TO "DOWN" AS IN "DUCK FEATHERS"]

YOU CAN REARRANGE THE LETTERS IN "HOWARD" TO SPELL "WHO RAD"! ANSWER: NOT THIS GUY!

Seriously? You can team up with 100 regular-sized ducks to form one giant-sized duck, and instead you're stealing Mew?

What? No! Who's Mew? And who says I can team up with ducks to form bigger ducks?!

Give me that.

Hey!

SNATCH

I'm not a *villain*. I'm a *private detective*.

Oh my *gosh*. A private *Ducktective*.

Heard 'em all before, lady. Here.

SCRIBBLE SCRIBBLE

DEADPOOL'S GUIDE TO SUPER VILLAINS

CARD 135 OF 4522

SOME JERK'S GUIDE TO SUPER ~~GREAT~~ DETECTIVES

quack!

HOWARD THE DUCK

GREAT PRIVATE DETECTIVE!

-LOOK AT THIS GUY! I GUESS HE'S A WEIRD...DUCK...MAN? GREAT PRIVATE DETECTIVE!
-DOES HE HAVE HANDS OR FEATHERS? IT'S FEATHERS, RIGHT? DOES HE DO THAT THING WHERE EACH FEATHER IS, LIKE, A FINGER?? HE HAS HANDS, OBVIOUSLY HE HAS HANDS
-HOW WOULD THAT EVEN WORK THOUGH?? THEY'D GET ALL BENT CALL HIM TO SOLVE YOUR CRIMES
-ANYWAY I'M **PRETTY SURE** HIS POWERS INCLUDE A) TALKING TO DUCKS B) CONTROLLING DUCKS C) TEAMING UP WITH 100 REGULAR-SIZED DUCKS TO FORM ONE GIANT DUCK
-THAT'S ALL I KNOW (AND ALL I CARE TO KNOW) ABOUT THIS GUY, SO HERE'S A JOKE TO FILL UP THE REST OF THIS CARD: HOW DO YOU GET DOWN OFF A HORSE? YOU DON'T! YOU GET DOWN OFF A DUCK!! [IT TOOK ME A LONG TIME TO FIGURE THAT JOKE OUT, BUT LATER I FOUND OUT IT'S REFERRING TO "DOWN" AS IN "DUCK FEATHERS"]
HE IS GOOD AT MYSTERIES AND HAS A COOL FRIEND WITH TATTOOS AND KNOWS AN OLD LADY WHO WORKS FOR HIM AS AN OFFICE ADMINISTRATOR

YOU CAN REARRANGE THE LETTERS IN "HOWARD" TO SPELL "WHO RAD"! ANSWER: NOT THIS GUY! UNLESS THERE'S OTHER HOWARDS AROUND, THERE'S NO NEED TO ALWAYS ADD "THE DUCK" AFTER HIS NAME, THANKS!!

f you're wondering why Howard's card is number 135, 135 is the sum of 40 plus 34 plus 61, and those numbers make up an ASCII-art duck. *OBSERVE:* ("=

("= ((ha ha see what i did there ha ha

I got hired to find a missing cat by the name of "Biggs," with assurances the cat had *zero* super-powers. No *Infinity Gauntlets* or *Abundant Gloves* or *whatever other baloney* that has made every other case I've taken such a *hassle.*

Except guess what? *All cats look alike.*

I should've realized a bunch of *indistinguishable hairless apes* would keep *hairy pet proto-apes* that are even harder to figure out!

Hey!

Nevermind. Hey, Fun Fact: Did you know *rodents* are among the closest living relatives to primates? So squirrels are *more similar* to humans, genetically, than just about any other non-primate animal!

Oh, no, see--cats aren't proto-apes. Humans and cats are both vertebrates, true, but they're about as closely related as humans and ducks are, which--

I mean, I say "just about" because you need to account for tree shrews and flying lemurs, which aren't *actually* lemurs, but--

I'm working on a program for class that goes through genomes. You put in two animals and it tells you which is closer to humans.

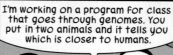

...it's not important.

SCIENCE CORNER: Actually, humans and ducks diverged when mammals and birds did (pre-dinosaurs), but humans and cats diverged later as mammals diversified. So humans actually share *MORE* genes with cats than they do with ducks. Sorry, Howard.

Um, actually, humans are *very* different from cats and ducks. Citation: my own eyes.

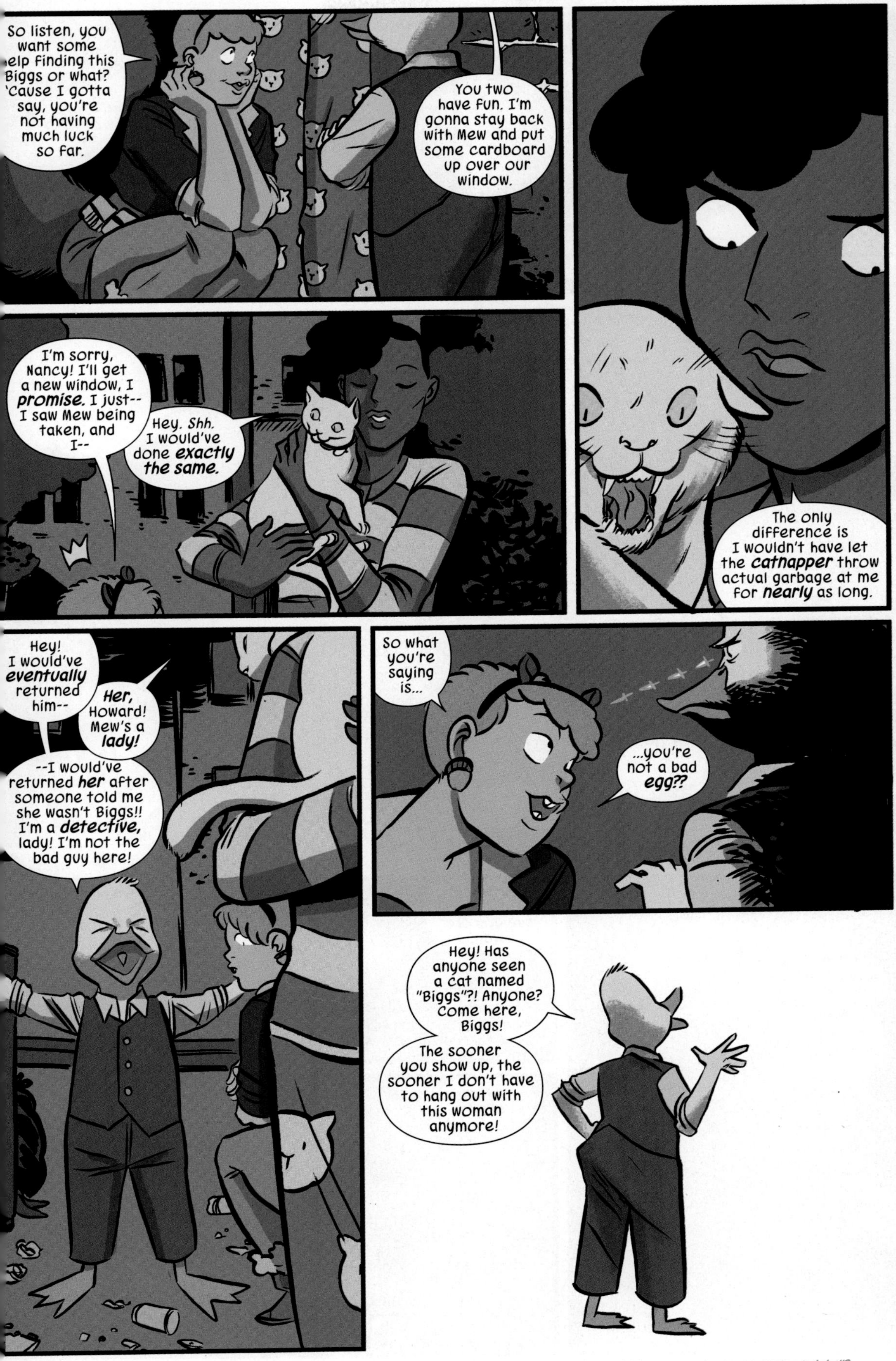

So listen, you want some elp finding this Biggs or what? 'Cause I gotta say, you're not having much luck so far.
You two have fun. I'm gonna stay back with Mew and put some cardboard up over our window.
I'm sorry, Nancy! I'll get a new window, I promise. I just-- I saw Mew being taken, and I--
Hey. Shh. I would've done exactly the same.
The only difference is I wouldn't have let the catnapper throw actual garbage at me for nearly as long.
Hey! I would've eventually returned him--
Her, Howard! Mew's a lady!
--I would've returned her after someone told me she wasn't Biggs!! I'm a detective, lady! I'm not the bad guy here!
So what you're saying is...
...you're not a bad egg??
Hey! Has anyone seen a cat named "Biggs"?! Anyone? Come here, Biggs!
The sooner you show up, the sooner I don't have to hang out with this woman anymore!

I'm sorry, Howard, I thought you'd like the duck puns! I'm big into the nut puns myself, so I just assumed. You might even say nut puns are...me in a *nutshell?* *Ugh* I didn't realize this was a crossover with the *PUN*isher.

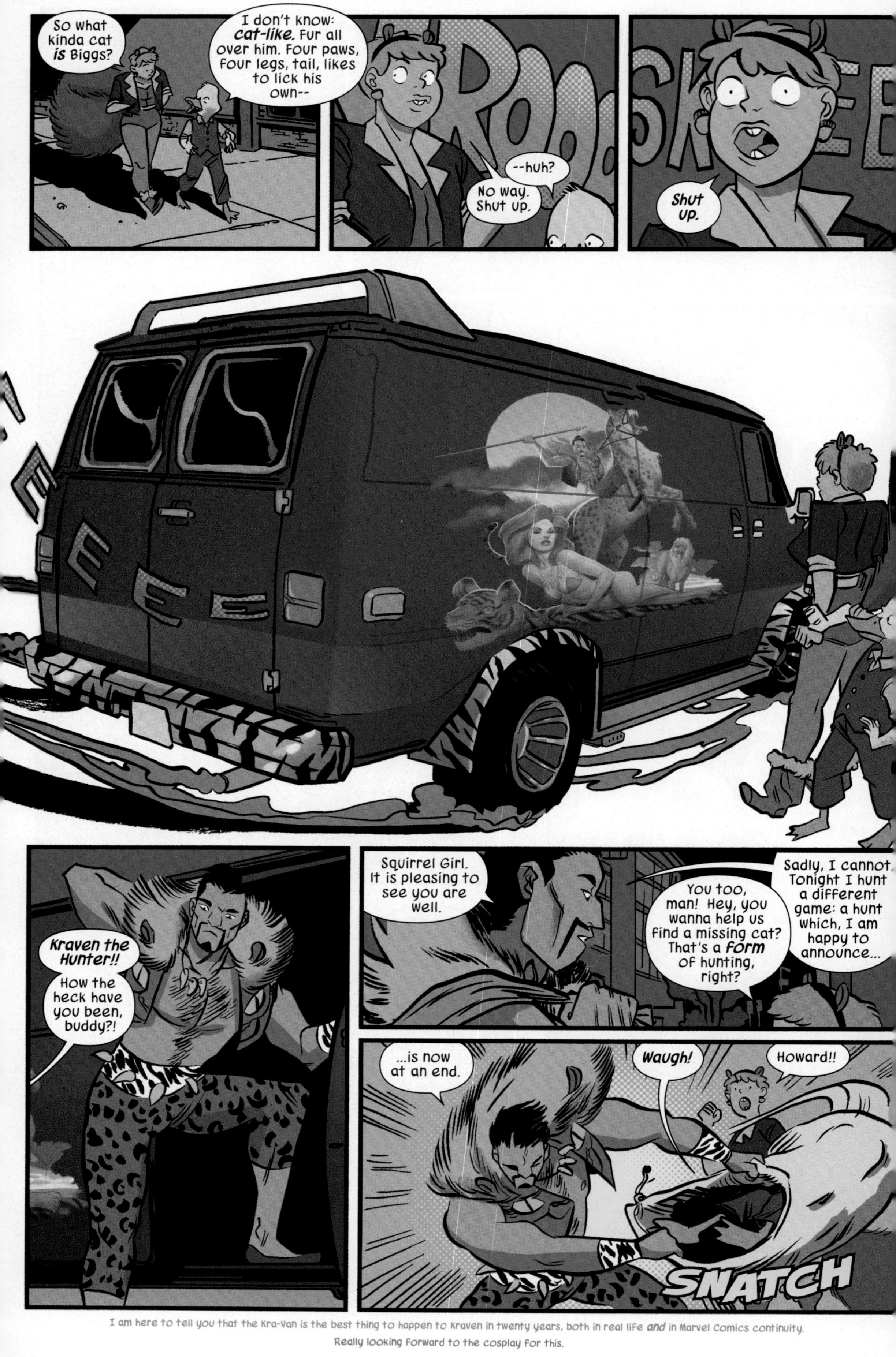
So what kinda cat *is* Biggs?
I don't know: **cat-like.** Fur all over him. Four paws, four legs, tail, likes to lick his own--
--huh?
No way. Shut up.
Shut up.
Kraven the Hunter!!
How the heck have you been, buddy?!
Squirrel Girl. It is pleasing to see you are well.
You too, man! Hey, you wanna help us find a missing cat? That's a *form* of hunting, right?
Sadly, I cannot. Tonight I hunt a different game: a hunt which, I am happy to announce...
...is now at an end.
Waugh!
Howard!!
SNATCH

I am here to tell you that the Kra-Van is the best thing to happen to Kraven in twenty years, both in real life *and* in Marvel Comics continuity. Really looking forward to the cosplay for this.

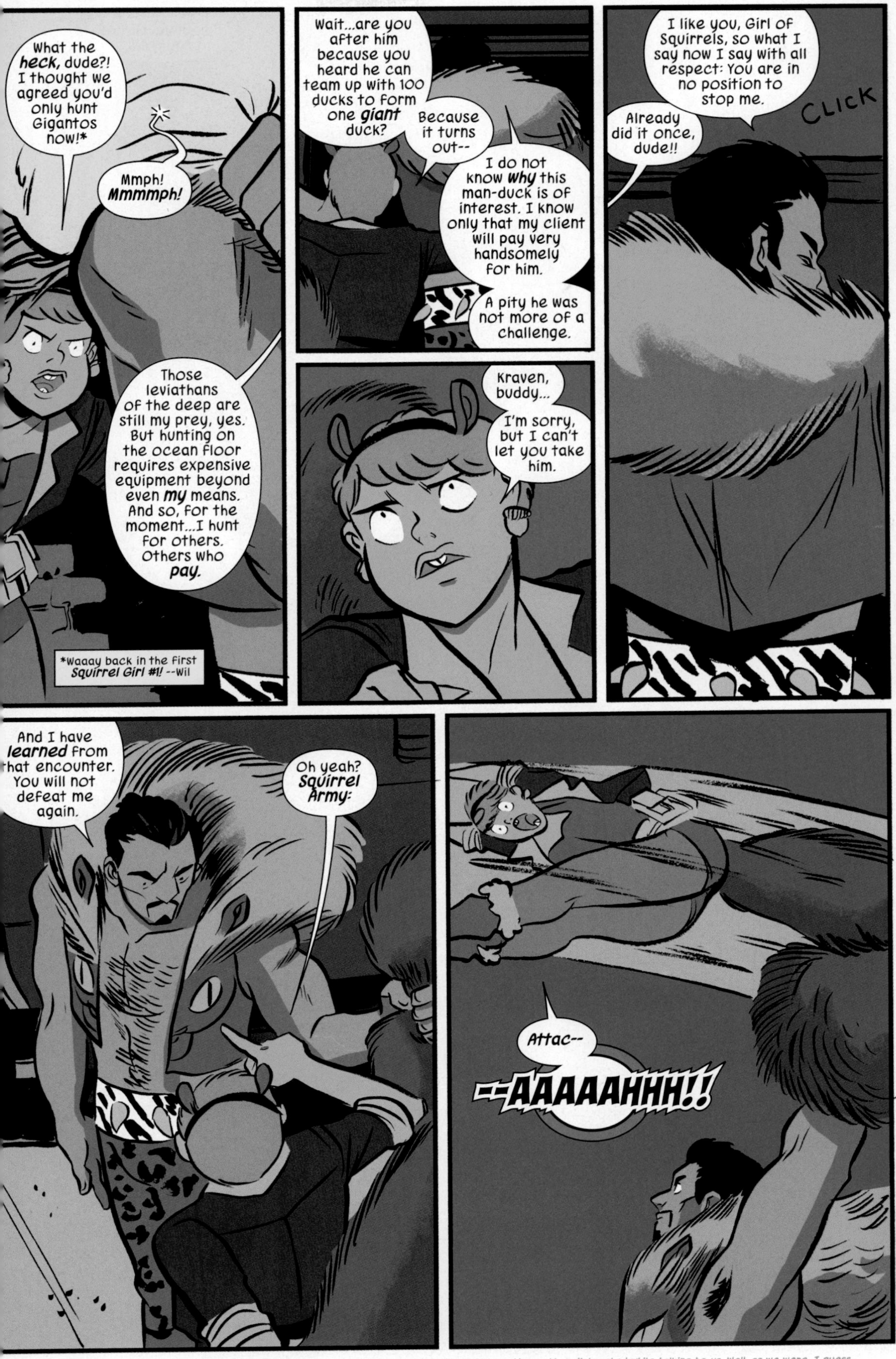
What the **heck,** dude?! I thought we agreed you'd only hunt Gigantos now!*
Mmph! **Mmmmph!**
Those leviathans of the deep are still my prey, yes. But hunting on the ocean floor requires expensive equipment beyond even **my** means. And so, for the moment...I hunt for others. Others who **pay.**
*Waaay back in the first *Squirrel Girl #1!* --Wil
Wait...are you after him because you heard he can team up with 100 ducks to form one **giant** duck?
Because it turns out--
I do not know **why** this man-duck is of interest. I know only that my client will pay very handsomely for him.
A pity he was not more of a challenge.
Kraven, buddy...
I'm sorry, but I can't let you take him.
I like you, Girl of Squirrels, so what I say now I say with all respect: You are in no position to stop me.
CLICK
Already did it once, dude!!
And I have **learned** from that encounter. You will not defeat me again.
Oh yeah? **Squirrel Army:**
Attac--
--AAAAAHHH!!

The nearby squirrels are all: ***"attacaaaaahhhh"?*** That's not an actual command! Squirrel Girl must've gotten distracted while talking to us. Well, as we were, I guess.

OK.

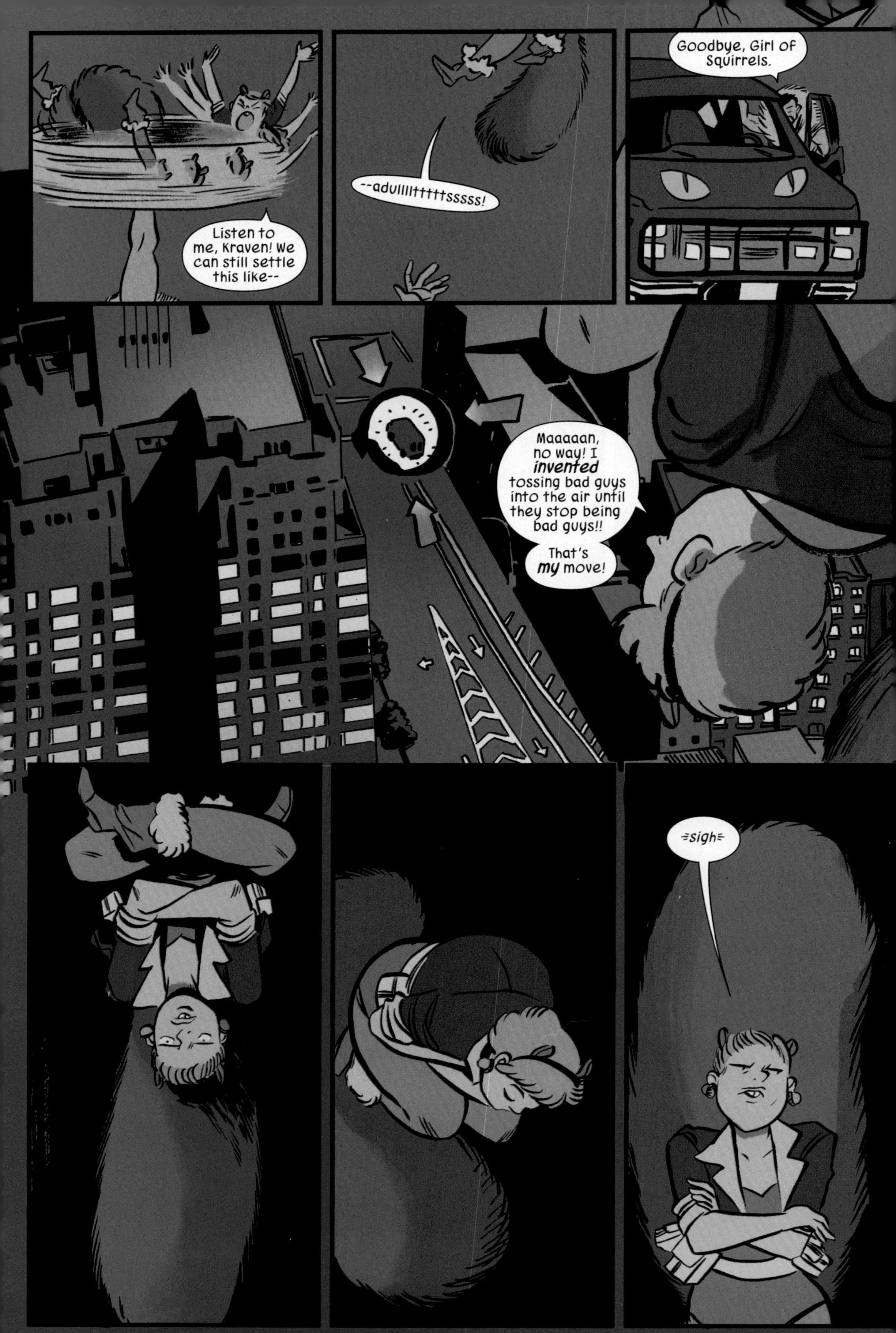
Listen to me, Kraven! We can still settle this like--
--adullllltttttsssss!
Goodbye, Girl of Squirrels.
Maaaaan, no way! I *invented* tossing bad guys into the air until they stop being bad guys!!
That's *my* move!
=sigh=

Huh! So ***that's*** what that feels like!

I would be so conflicted, 'cause I'm in a battle, but being tossed into the air would be so much fun!

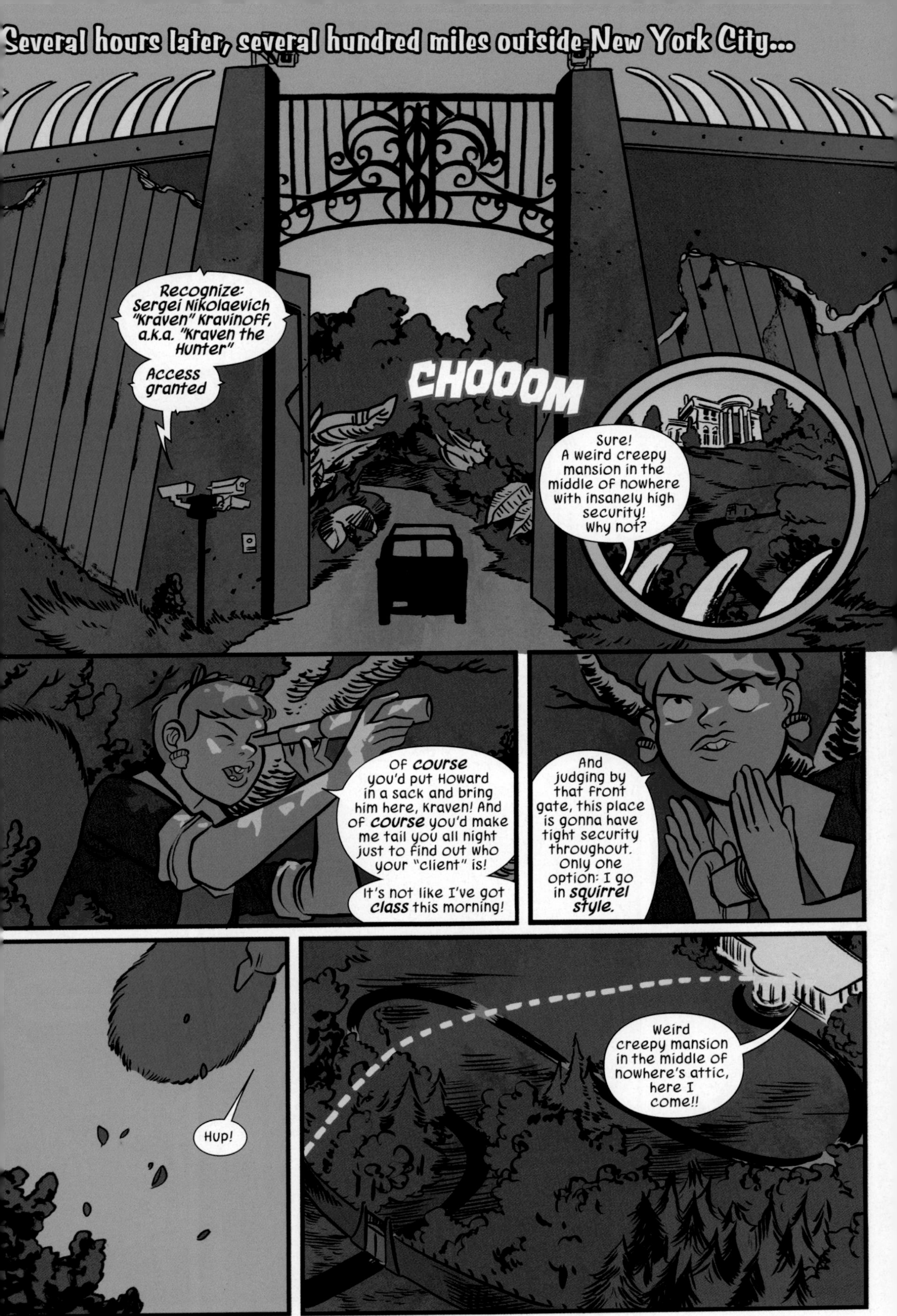
Several hours later, several hundred miles outside New York City...
Recognize: Sergei Nikolaevich "Kraven" Kravinoff, a.k.a. "Kraven the Hunter"
Access granted
CHOOOM
Sure! A weird creepy mansion in the middle of nowhere with insanely high security! Why not?
Of course you'd put Howard in a sack and bring him here, Kraven! And of course you'd make me tail you all night just to find out who your "client" is!
It's not like I've got class this morning!
And judging by that front gate, this place is gonna have tight security throughout. Only one option: I go in squirrel style.
Hup!
Weird creepy mansion in the middle of nowhere's attic, here I come!!

I'm worried about Doreen Green missing class too, but don't worry: she reads ahead, so when she has to miss class like this, she doesn't fall too far behind. Thanks, Doreen! Now we can all enjoy the rest of this comic without worrying.

Hm. I heard she just skims.

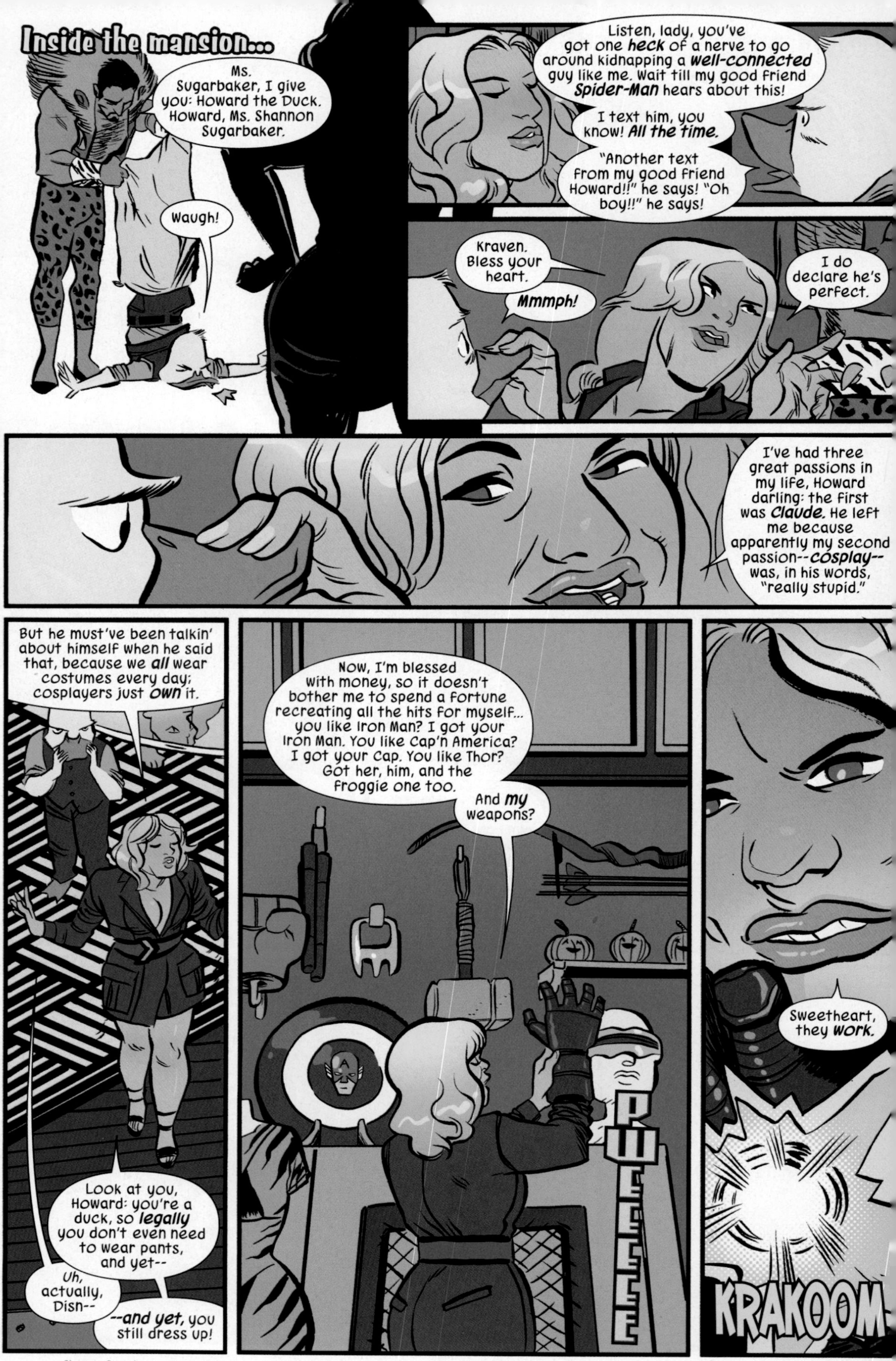
Inside the mansion...
Ms. Sugarbaker, I give you: Howard the Duck. Howard, Ms. Shannon Sugarbaker.
Waugh!
Listen, lady, you've got one heck of a nerve to go around kidnapping a well-connected guy like me. Wait till my good friend Spider-Man hears about this!
I text him, you know! All the time.
"Another text from my good friend Howard!!" he says! "Oh boy!!" he says!
Kraven. Bless your heart.
Mmmph!
I do declare he's perfect.
I've had three great passions in my life, Howard darling: the first was Claude. He left me because apparently my second passion--cosplay--was, in his words, "really stupid."
But he must've been talkin' about himself when he said that, because we all wear costumes every day; cosplayers just OWN it.
Look at you, Howard: you're a duck, so legally you don't even need to wear pants, and yet--
Uh, actually, Disn--
--and yet, you still dress up!
Now, I'm blessed with money, so it doesn't bother me to spend a fortune recreating all the hits for myself... you like Iron Man? I got your Iron Man. You like Cap'n America? I got your Cap. You like Thor? Got her, him, and the froggie one too.
And my weapons?
PWEEEEE
Sweetheart, they work.
KRAKOOM

Shannon Sugarbaker will not tolerate anyone in the room being more of a Southern Belle than her and that is all you need to know about Shannon Sugarbaker. It's why I *cannot* be in the same room with Shannon Sugarbaker.

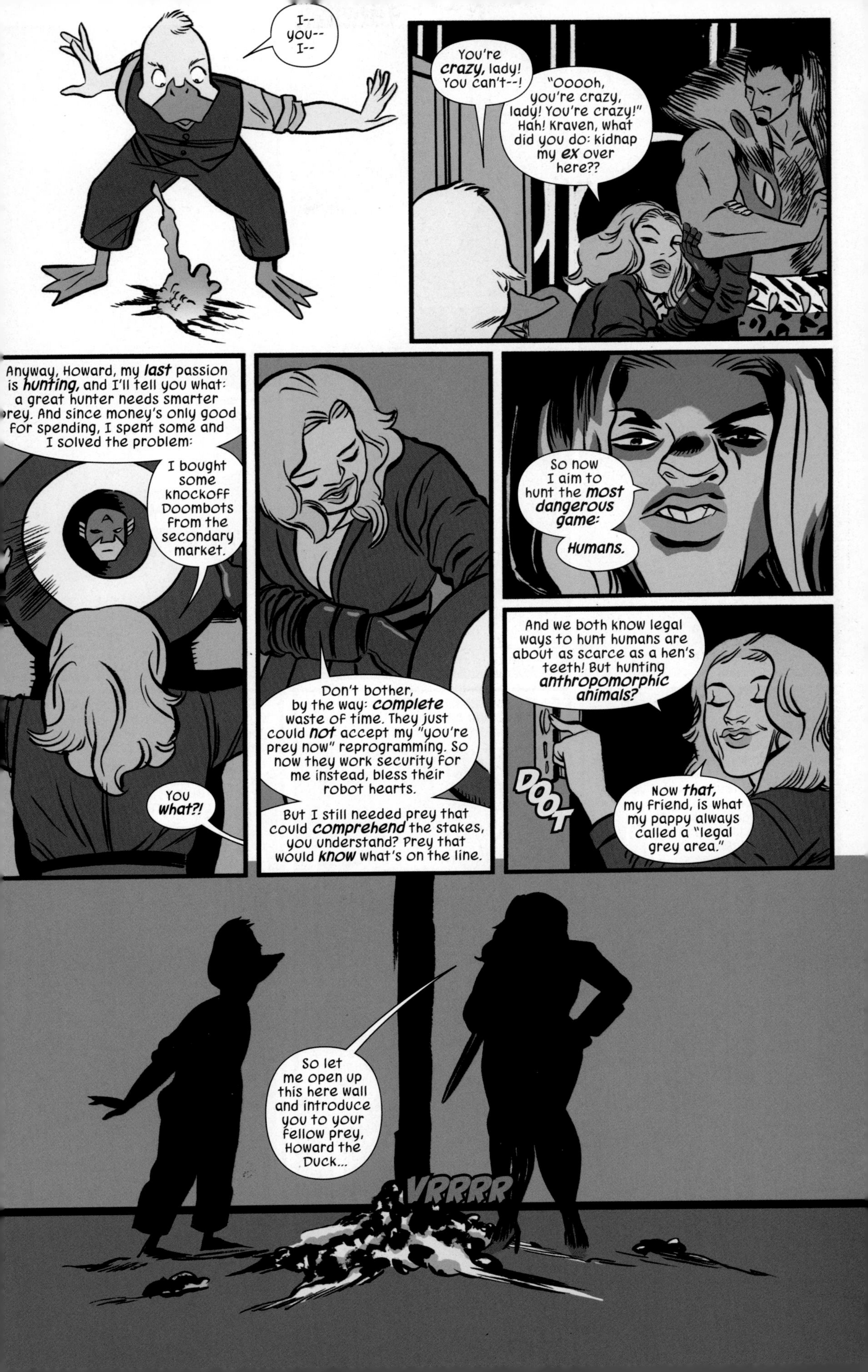

I-- you-- I--
You're crazy, lady! You can't--!
"Ooooh, you're crazy, lady! You're crazy!" Hah! Kraven, what did you do: kidnap my ex over here??
Anyway, Howard, my last passion is hunting, and I'll tell you what: a great hunter needs smarter prey. And since money's only good for spending, I spent some and I solved the problem:
I bought some knockoff Doombots from the secondary market.
You what?!
Don't bother, by the way: complete waste of time. They just could not accept my "you're prey now" reprogramming. So now they work security for me instead, bless their robot hearts.
But I still needed prey that could comprehend the stakes, you understand? Prey that would know what's on the line.
So now I aim to hunt the most dangerous game:
Humans.
And we both know legal ways to hunt humans are about as scarce as a hen's teeth! But hunting anthropomorphic animals?
DOOT
Now that, my friend, is what my pappy always called a "legal grey area."
So let me open up this here wall and introduce you to your fellow prey, Howard the Duck...
VRRRR

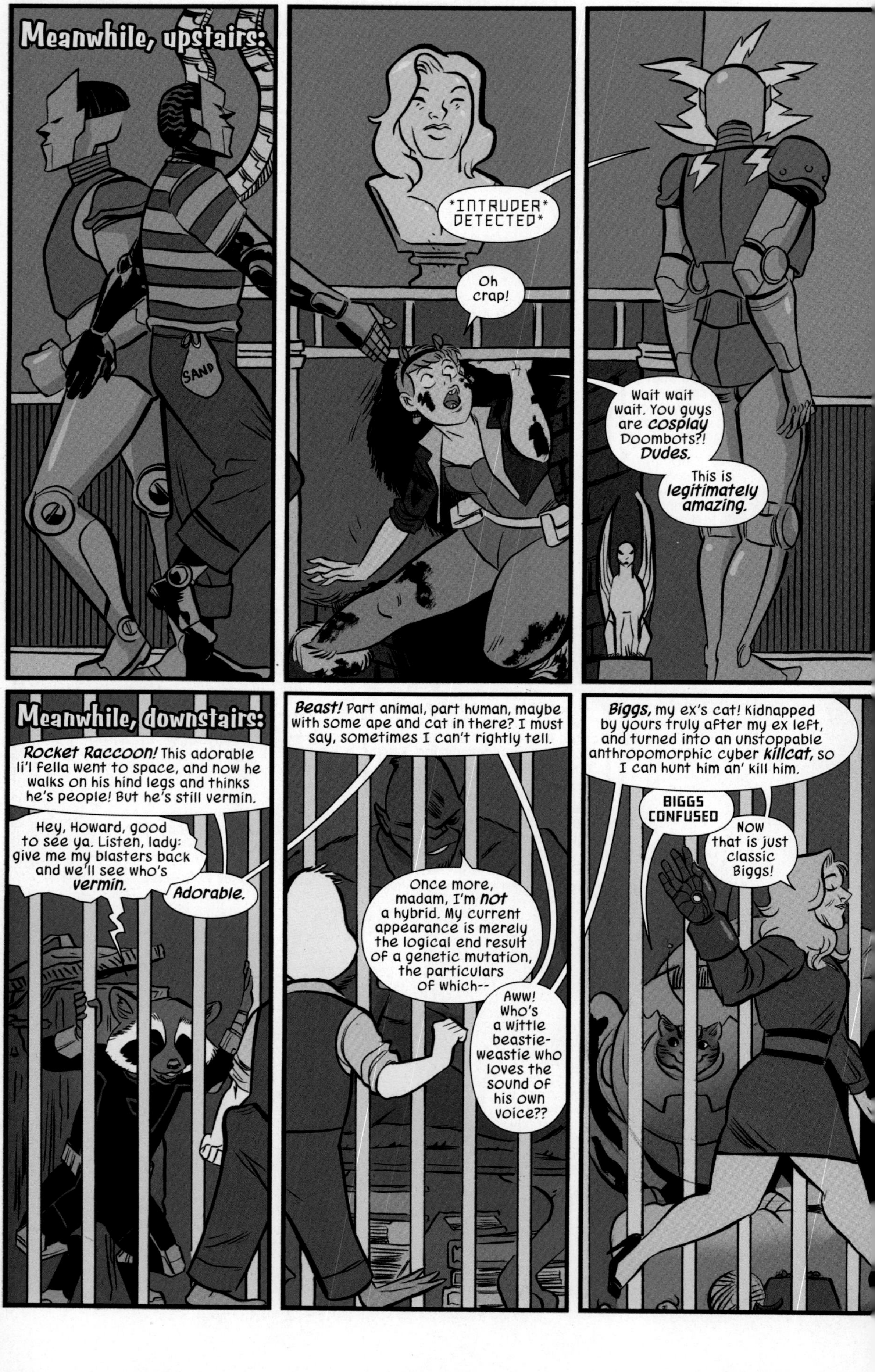
Meanwhile, upstairs:
INTRUDER DETECTED*
Oh crap!
Wait wait wait. You guys are cosplay Doombots?! Dudes.
This is legitimately amazing.
Meanwhile, downstairs:
Rocket Raccoon! This adorable li'l fella went to space, and now he walks on his hind legs and thinks he's people! But he's still vermin.
Hey, Howard, good to see ya. Listen, lady: give me my blasters back and we'll see who's vermin.
Adorable.
Beast! Part animal, part human, maybe with some ape and cat in there? I must say, sometimes I can't rightly tell.
Once more, madam, I'm not a hybrid. My current appearance is merely the logical end result of a genetic mutation, the particulars of which--
Aww! Who's a wittle beastie-weastie who loves the sound of his own voice??
Biggs, my ex's cat! Kidnapped by yours truly after my ex left, and turned into an unstoppable anthropomorphic cyber killcat, so I can hunt him an' kill him.
BIGGS CONFUSED
Now that is just classic Biggs!

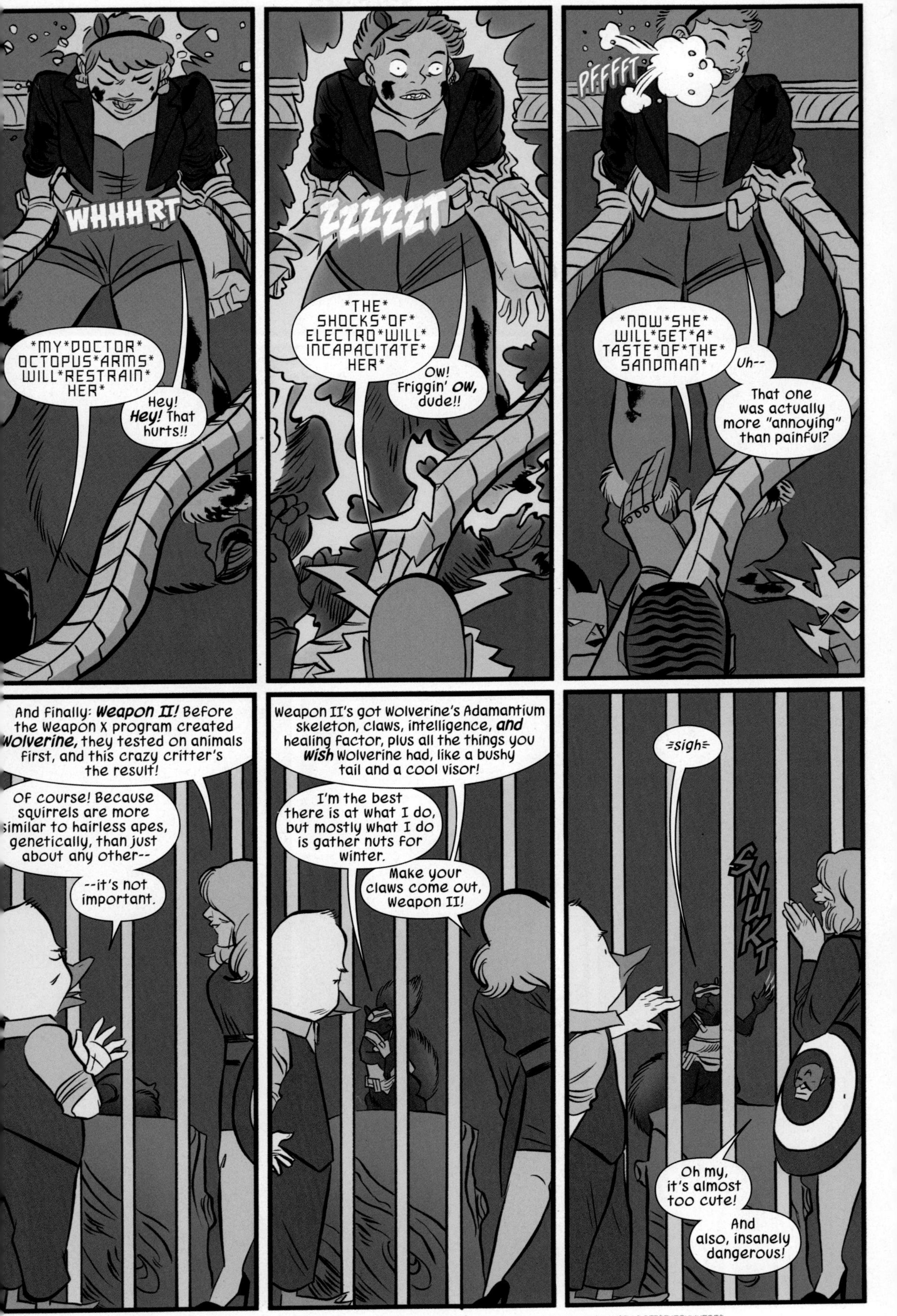
WHHHRT
*MY*DOCTOR*OCTOPUS*ARMS*WILL*RESTRAIN*HER*
Hey! *Hey!* That hurts!!
ZZZZZT
*THE*SHOCKS*OF*ELECTRO*WILL*INCAPACITATE*HER*
Ow! Friggin' *OW,* dude!!
PFFFFT
*NOW*SHE*WILL*GET*A*TASTE*OF*THE*SANDMAN*
Uh--
That one was actually more "annoying" than painful?
And finally: *Weapon II!* Before the Weapon X program created *Wolverine,* they tested on animals first, and this crazy critter's the result!
Of course! Because squirrels are more similar to hairless apes, genetically, than just about any other--
--it's not important.
Weapon II's got Wolverine's Adamantium skeleton, claws, intelligence, *and* healing factor, plus all the things you *wish* Wolverine had, like a bushy tail and a cool visor!
I'm the best there is at what I do, but mostly what I do is gather nuts for winter.
Make your claws come out, Weapon II!
=sigh=
SNIKT
Oh my, it's almost too cute!
And also, insanely dangerous!

*THERE*CAN*BE*NO*ESCAPE*/*MY*SAND*WAS*PROGRAMMED*TO*BE*COARSE*AND*ROUGH*AND*IRRITATING*AND*TO*GET*EVERYWHERE*

SCIENCE CORNER: Interesting sand fact: sand is actually just dirt but different I guess!

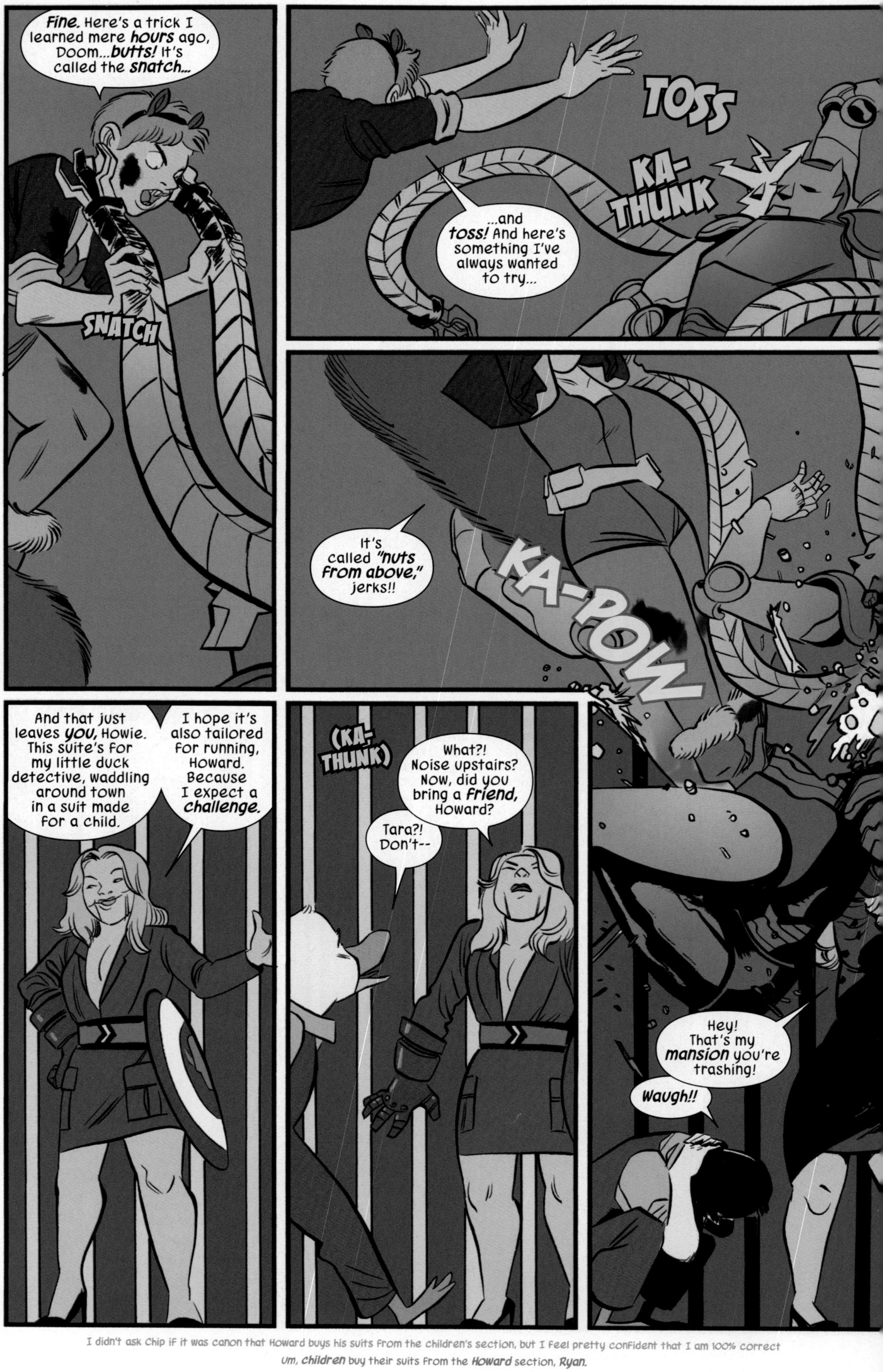
Fine. Here's a trick I learned mere hours ago, Doom...butts! It's called the snatch...
SNATCH
TOSS
KA-THUNK
...and toss! And here's something I've always wanted to try...
It's called "nuts from above," jerks!!
KA-POW
And that just leaves you, Howie. This suite's for my little duck detective, waddling around town in a suit made for a child.
I hope it's also tailored for running, Howard. Because I expect a challenge.
(KA-THUNK)
What?! Noise upstairs? Now, did you bring a friend, Howard?
Tara?! Don't--
Hey! That's my mansion you're trashing!
Waugh!!

I didn't ask Chip if it was canon that Howard buys his suits from the children's section, but I feel pretty confident that I am 100% correct

Um, *children* buy their suits from the *Howard* section, *Ryan*.

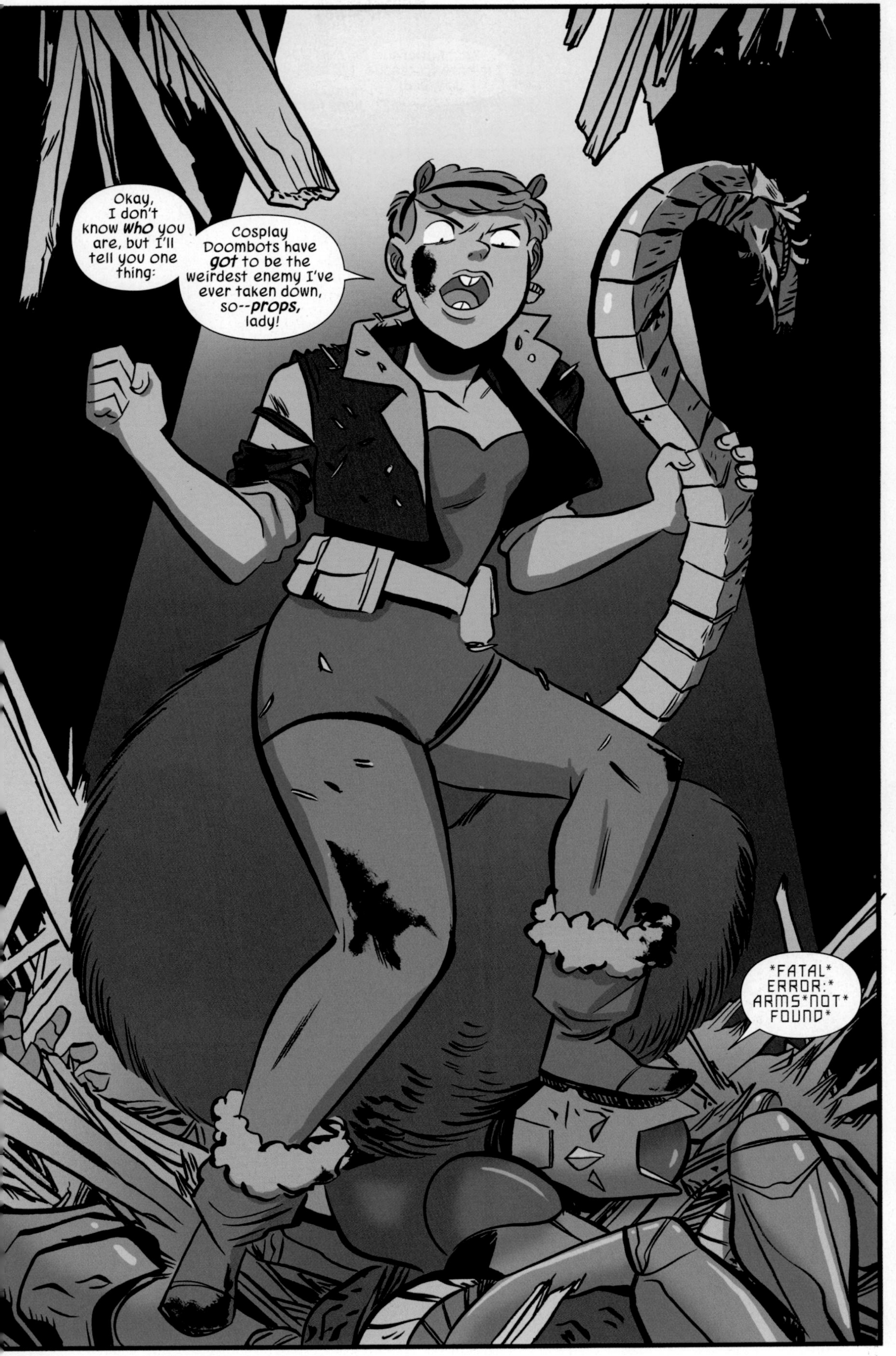
Okay, I don't know who you are, but I'll tell you one thing:
Cosplay Doombots have got to be the weirdest enemy I've ever taken down, so--props, lady!
FATAL ERROR:* ARMS*NOT* FOUND*

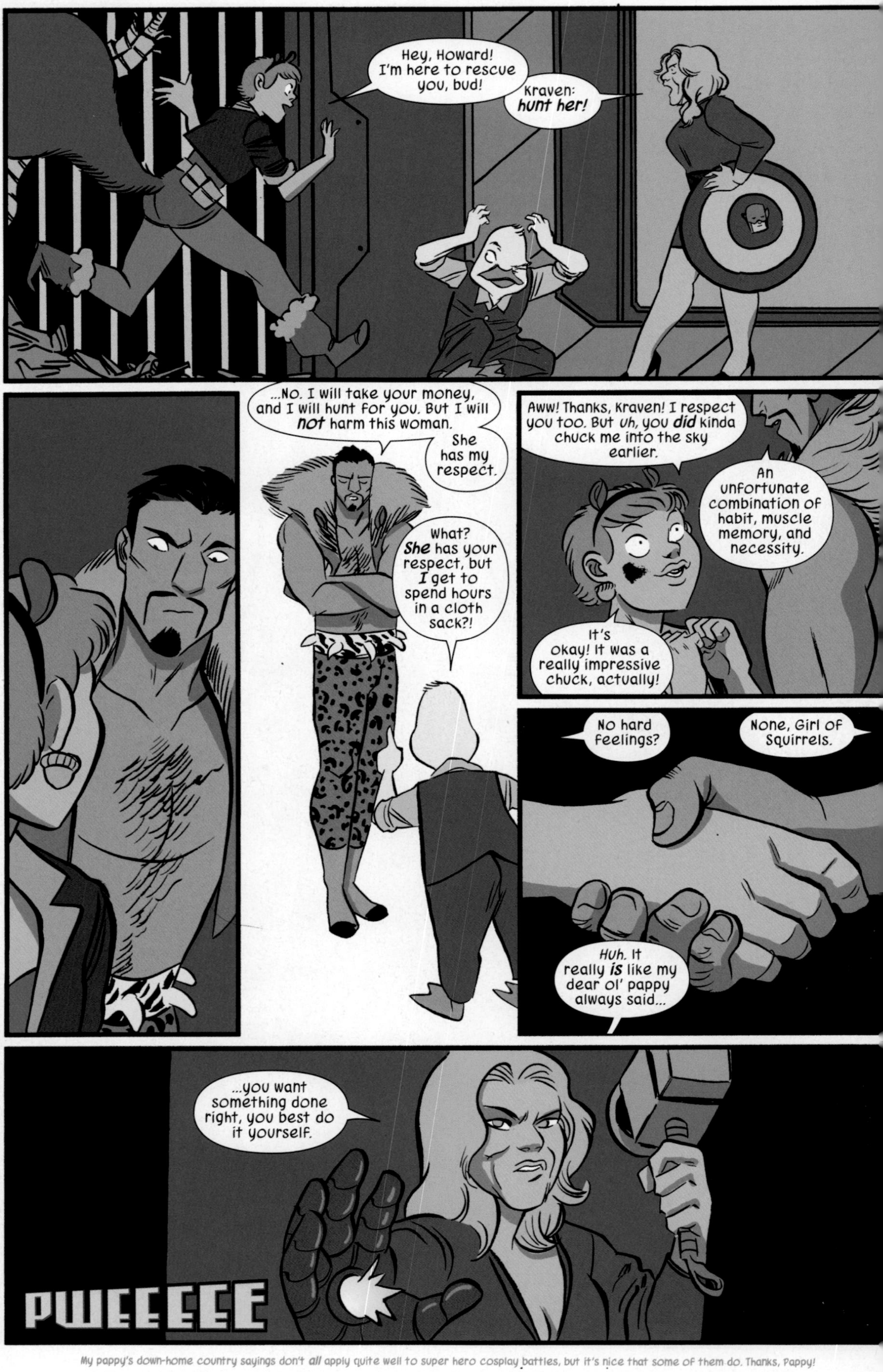
Hey, Howard! I'm here to rescue you, bud!
Kraven: *hunt her!*
...No. I will take your money, and I will hunt for you. But I will ***not*** harm this woman.
She has my respect.
What? ***She*** has your respect, but ***I*** get to spend hours in a cloth sack?!
Aww! Thanks, Kraven! I respect you too. But *uh*, you ***did*** kinda chuck me into the sky earlier.
An unfortunate combination of habit, muscle memory, and necessity.
It's okay! It was a really impressive chuck, actually!
No hard feelings?
None, Girl of Squirrels.
Huh. It really ***is*** like my dear ol' pappy always said...
...you want something done right, you best do it yourself.
PWEEEEE

*My pappy's down-home country sayings don't **all** apply quite well to super hero cosplay battles, but it's nice that some of them do. Thanks, Pappy!*
Um, if you want something done right, you hire a person who specializes in the task that needs completing. Your pappy needs to be corrected.

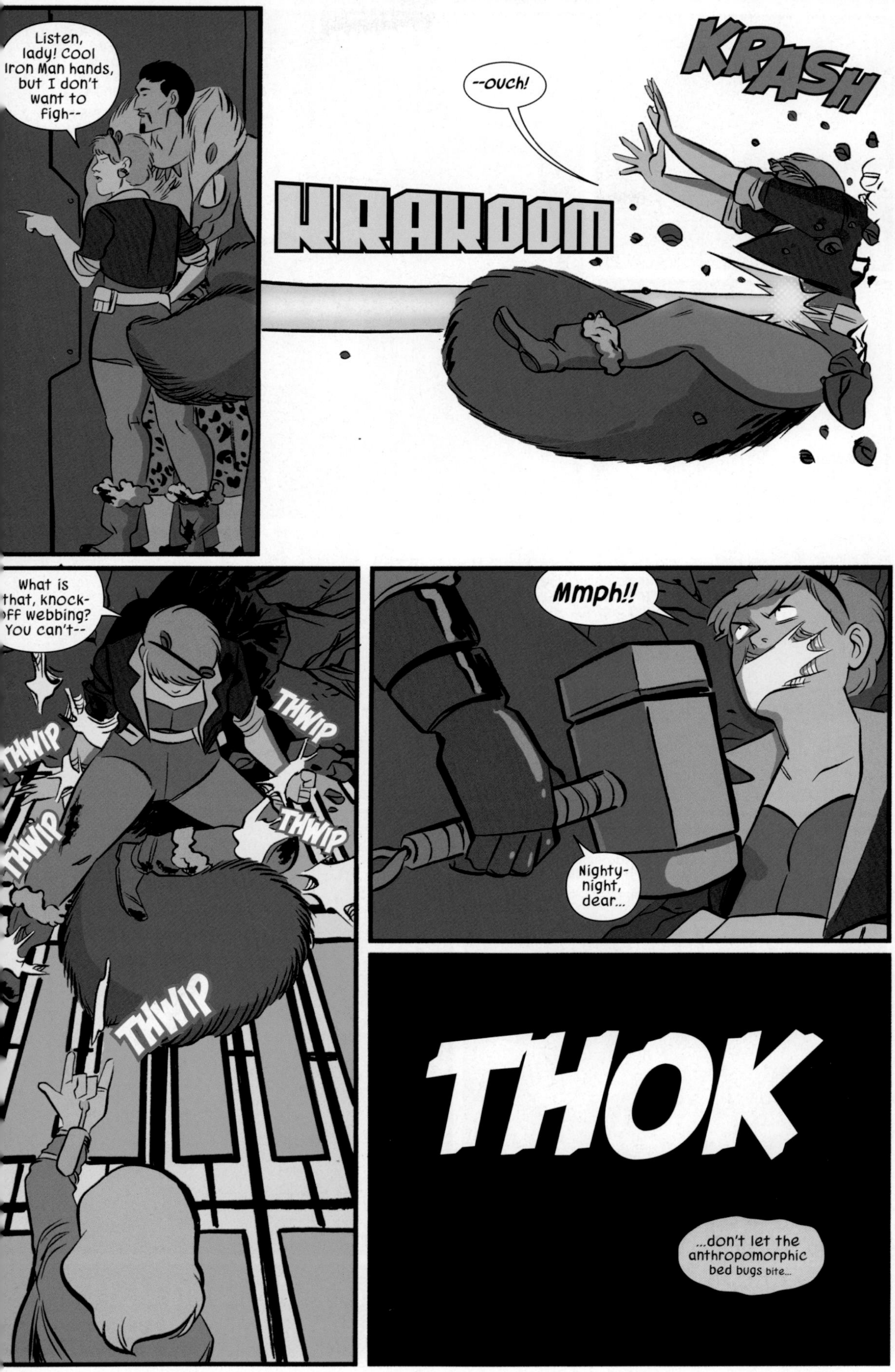
Listen, lady! Cool Iron Man hands, but I don't want to figh--
--ouch!
KRAKOOM
KRASH
What is that, knock-off webbing? You can't--
THWIP
THWIP
THWIP
THWIP
THWIP
Mmph!!
Nighty-night, dear...
THOK
...don't let the anthropomorphic bed bugs bite...

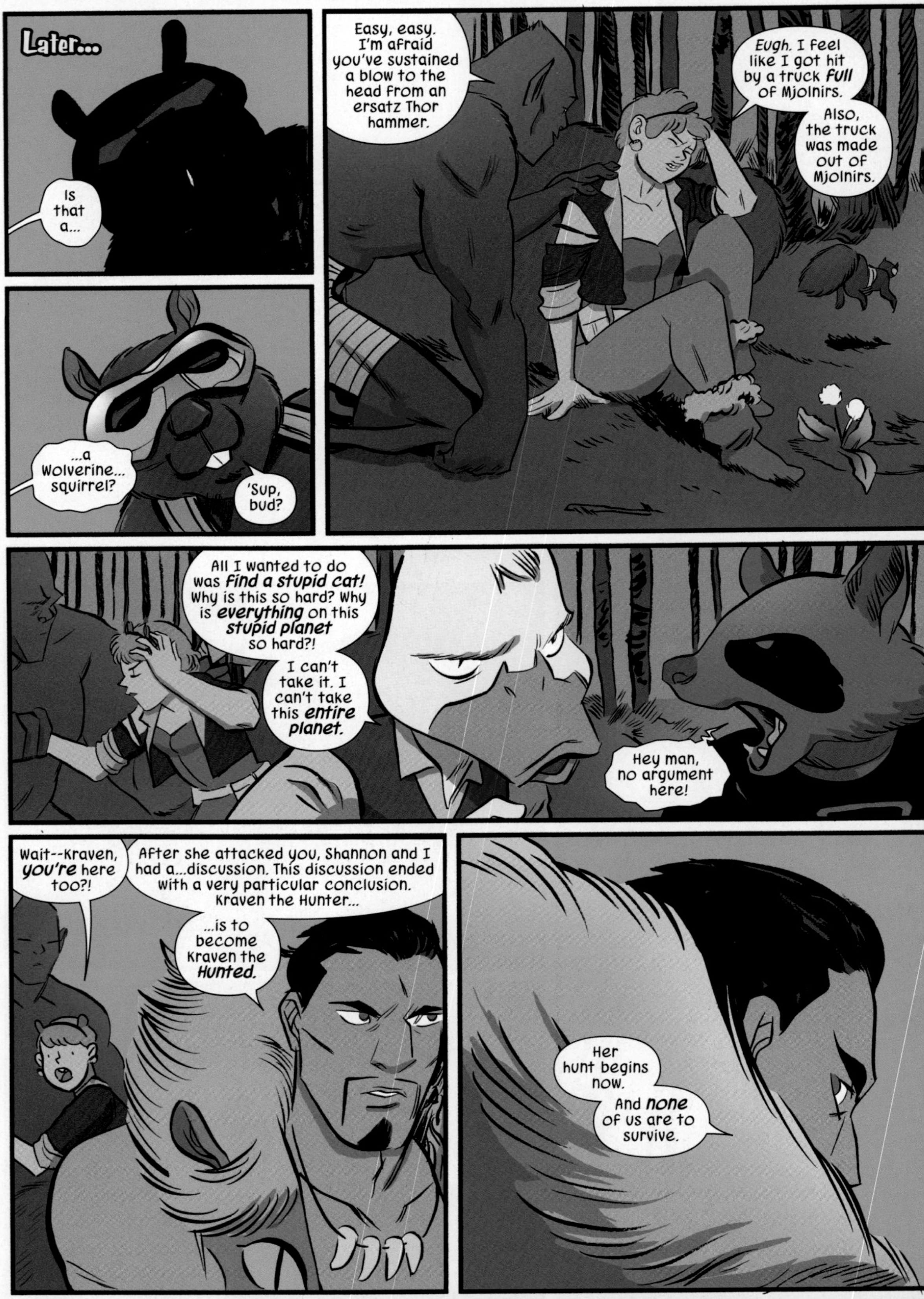
Later...
Is that a...
...a Wolverine... squirrel?
'Sup, bud?
Easy, easy. I'm afraid you've sustained a blow to the head from an ersatz Thor hammer.
Eugh. I feel like I got hit by a truck FULL of Mjolnirs.
Also, the truck was made out of Mjolnirs.
All I wanted to do was find a stupid cat! Why is this so hard? Why is everything on this stupid planet so hard?!
I can't take it. I can't take this entire planet.
Hey man, no argument here!
Wait--Kraven, you're here too?!
After she attacked you, Shannon and I had a...discussion. This discussion ended with a very particular conclusion. Kraven the Hunter...
...is to become Kraven the Hunted.
Her hunt begins now.
And none of us are to survive.

Continued in HOWARD THE DUCK #6, out next month!

But I'll give you a hint: basically what happens in it is (spoiler alert) ADVENTURE??

Also: cosplay. Lots of cosplay.
I'm cosplaying right now! It's as a guy who forgot that he now has to write a whole *Howard the Duck* comic!!

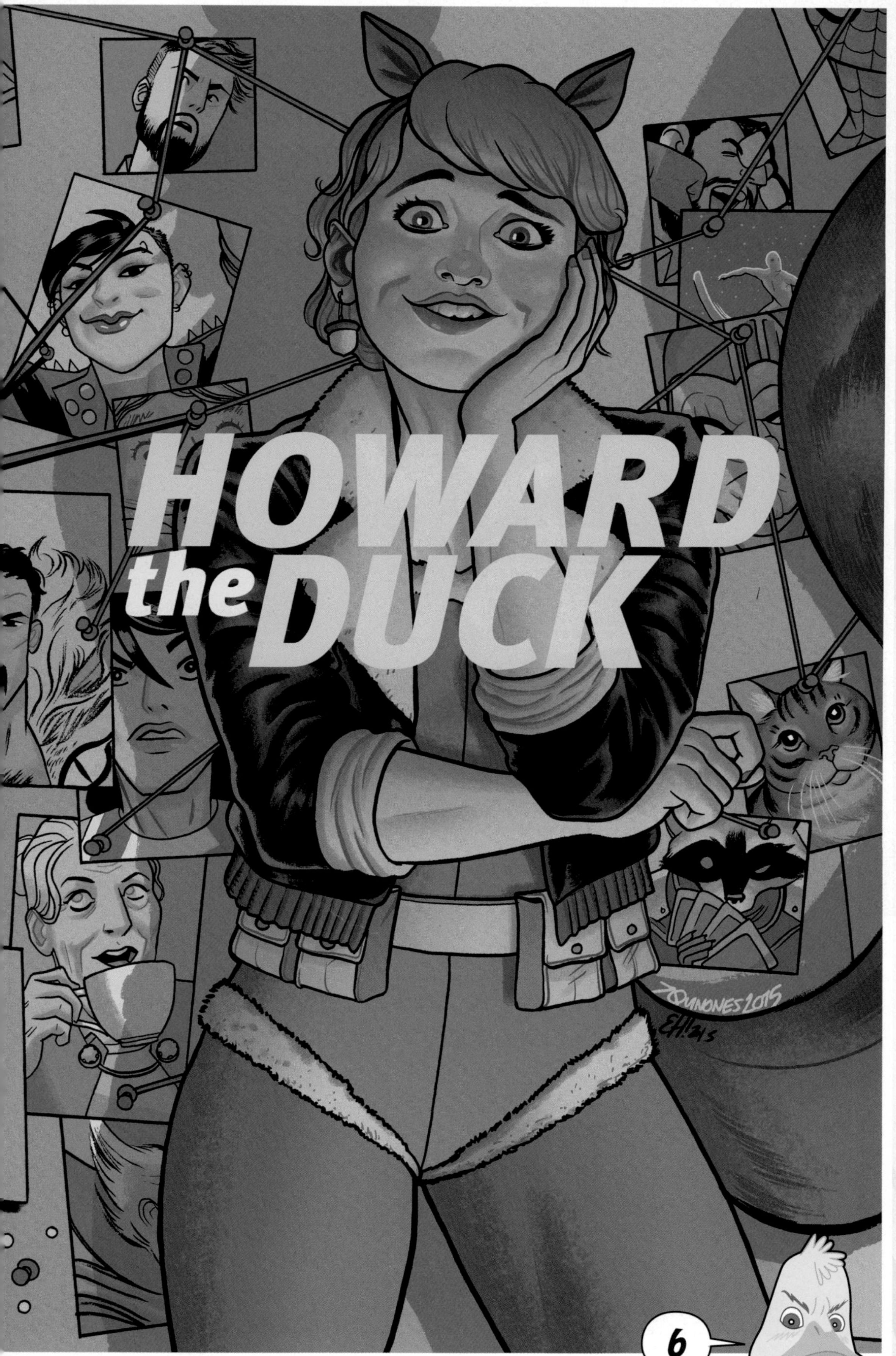
HOWARD the DUCK
QUINONES 2015
EH! 2015

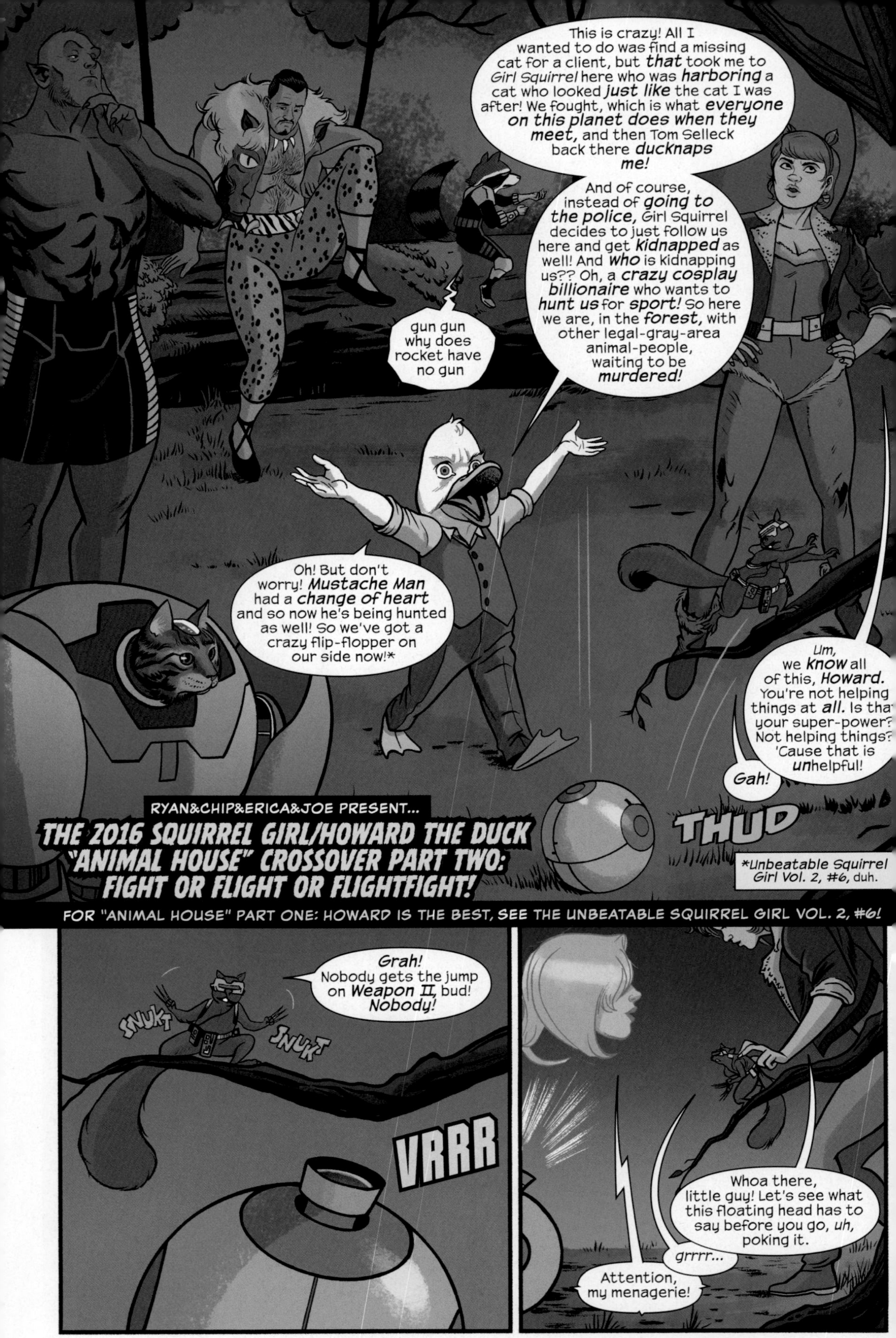
This is crazy! All I wanted to do was find a missing cat for a client, but *that* took me to *Girl Squirrel* here who was *harboring* a cat who looked *just like* the cat I was after! We fought, which is what *everyone on this planet does when they meet*, and then Tom Selleck back there *ducknaps me!*
And of course, instead of *going to the police*, Girl Squirrel decides to just follow us here and get *kidnapped* as well! And *who* is kidnapping us?? Oh, a *crazy cosplay billionaire* who wants to *hunt us* for *sport!* So here we are, in the *forest*, with other legal-gray-area animal-people, waiting to be *murdered!*
gun gun why does rocket have no gun
Oh! But don't worry! *Mustache Man* had a *change of heart* and so now he's being hunted as well! So we've got a crazy flip-flopper on our side now!*
Um, we *know* all of this, *Howard*. You're not helping things at *all*. Is that your super-power? Not helping things? 'Cause that is *un*helpful!
Gah!
THUD
RYAN&CHIP&ERICA&JOE PRESENT...
THE 2016 SQUIRREL GIRL/HOWARD THE DUCK "ANIMAL HOUSE" CROSSOVER PART TWO: FIGHT OR FLIGHT OR FLIGHTFIGHT!
*Unbeatable Squirrel Girl Vol. 2, #6, duh.
FOR "ANIMAL HOUSE" PART ONE: HOWARD IS THE BEST, SEE THE UNBEATABLE SQUIRREL GIRL VOL. 2, #6!
Grah! Nobody gets the jump on *Weapon II*, bud! *Nobody!*
SNUKT
SNUKT
VRRR
Whoa there, little guy! Let's see what this floating head has to say before you go, *uh*, poking it.
grrrr...
Attention, my menagerie!

So, Ryan does these weird "alt text" things in *Squirrel Girl* to prove that they're not just about "mainstream text," I guess. Cool stuff, guys! And if you're here from *Squirrel Girl*, you should know normally Chip *doesn't* do this text at the bottom, so if you look at the other issues, you'll just be disappointed!! Okay bye

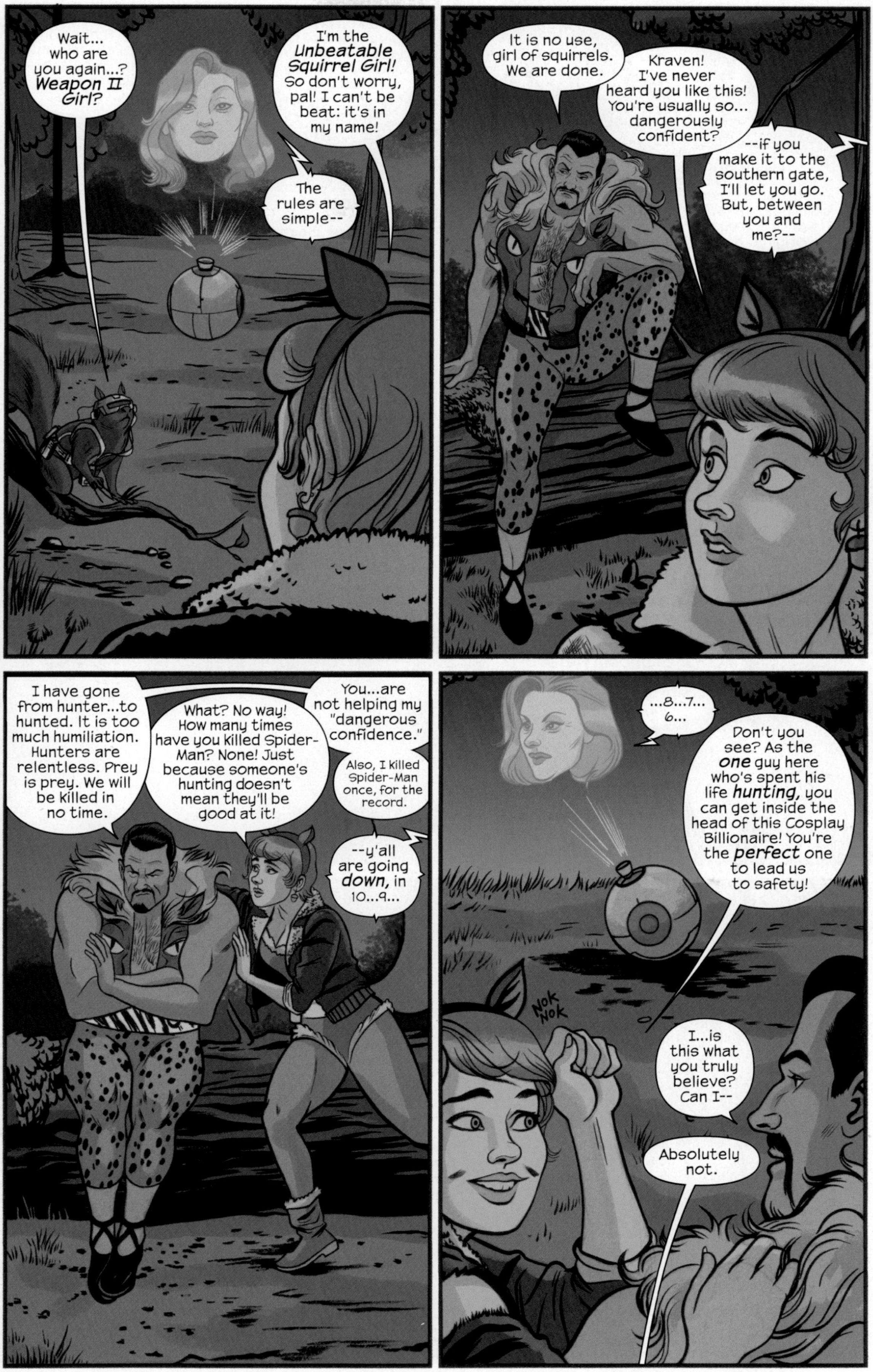
Wait... who are you again...? *Weapon II Girl?*
I'm the *Unbeatable Squirrel Girl!* So don't worry, pal! I can't be beat: it's in my name!
The rules are simple--
It is no use, girl of squirrels. We are done.
Kraven! I've never heard you like this! You're usually so... dangerously confident?
--if you make it to the southern gate, I'll let you go. But, between you and me?--
I have gone from hunter...to hunted. It is too much humiliation. Hunters are relentless. Prey is prey. We will be killed in no time.
What? No way! How many times have you killed Spider-Man? None! Just because someone's hunting doesn't mean they'll be good at it!
You...are not helping my "dangerous confidence."
Also, I killed Spider-Man once, for the record.
--y'all are going *down,* in 10...9...
...8...7... 6...
Don't you see? As the *one* guy here who's spent his life *hunting,* you can get inside the head of this Cosplay Billionaire! You're the *perfect* one to lead us to safety!
NOK NOK
I...is this what you truly believe? Can I--
Absolutely not.

Weapon II was in the same program as the old ***Wolverine,*** who was ***Weapon X!*** You probably thought that was just an "X" and not a "10"! Funny story: Professor Xavier actually named the X-Men ***"Ten-Men,"*** because he wanted ten guys on the team, but nobody got it so he just let people believe it was X-Men.

Now *that's* a tenhilarating addition to Marvel canon!

...5...4...3...

The situation is too dire to trust a--pardon the reductive terminology--*villain* to lead this group. As an original *X-Man*--

Here we go, "Beast in Show"...

--I'm clearly the best equipped to tackle our predicament.

This woman has no concept of the legality of what she's done, or *who* she's "hunting."

I can only imagine she would hate *and* fear having the full wrath of the mutant population on her head should something happen to me, an original *X-Man*.

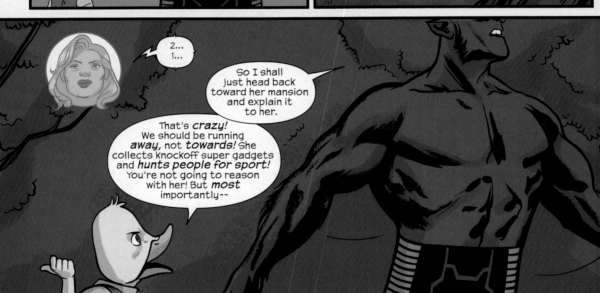

2...1...

So I shall just head back toward her mansion and explain it to her.

That's *crazy!* We should be running *away,* not *towards!* She collects knockoff super gadgets and *hunts people for sport!* You're not going to reason with her! But *most* importantly--

--we're out of time. waugh.

KRA KOOM

Don't call yourself *Beast* if you're super smart and want people to listen to you! Take a page from *Mr. Fantastic,* who wouldn't listen to a *Mr. Fantastic?* Even *Dr. Doom* knew he should let people know he's a *doctor* in his name.

Thought you could ever only have a character say "...we're out of time" in a time travel story? *Think again.*

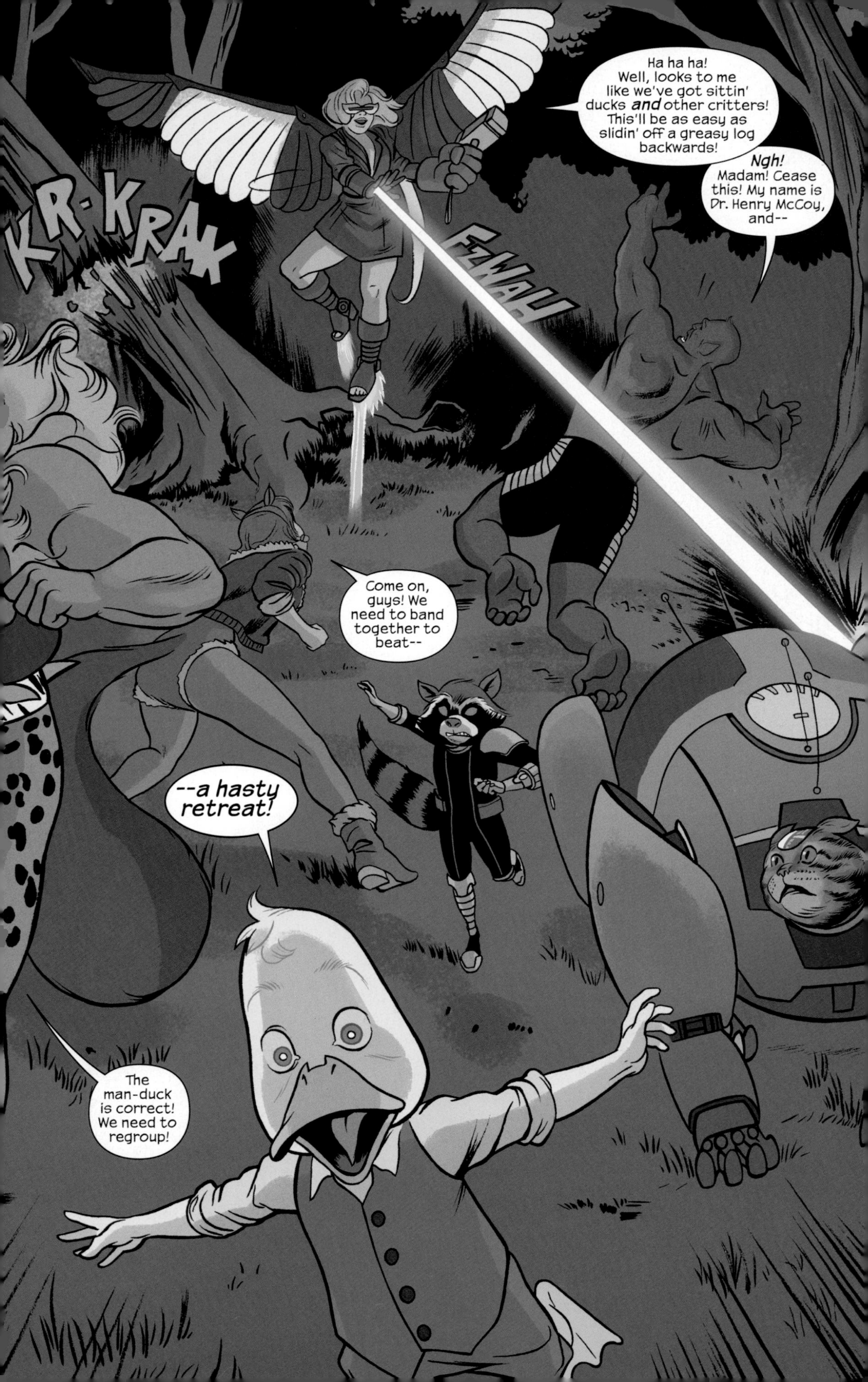
Ha ha ha! Well, looks to me like we've got sittin' ducks *and* other critters! This'll be as easy as slidin' off a greasy log backwards!
Ngh! Madam! Cease this! My name is Dr. Henry McCoy, and--
KR-KRAK
FZWAH
Come on, guys! We need to band together to beat--
--a hasty retreat!
The man-duck is correct! We need to regroup!

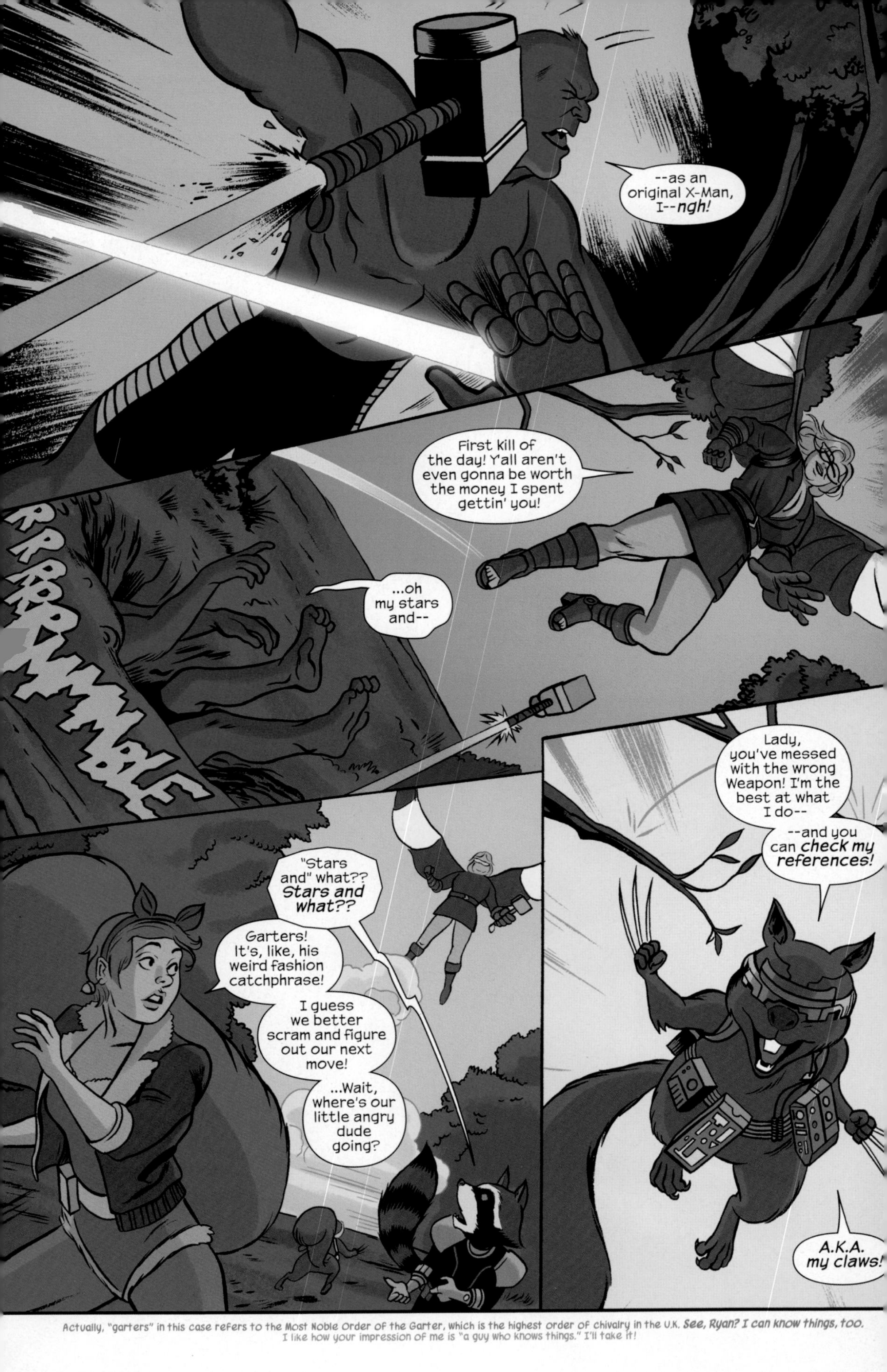
--as an original X-Man, I--*ngh!*
First kill of the day! Y'all aren't even gonna be worth the money I spent gettin' you!
RRRRRUMMBLE
...oh my stars and--
Lady, you've messed with the wrong Weapon! I'm the best at what I do--
--and you can *check my references!*
A.K.A. my claws!
"Stars and" what?? *Stars and what??*
Garters! It's, like, his weird fashion catchphrase!
I guess we better scram and figure out our next move!
...Wait, where's our little angry dude going?

Actually, "garters" in this case refers to the Most Noble Order of the Garter, which is the highest order of chivalry in the U.K. *See, Ryan? I can know things, too.*
I like how your impression of me is "a guy who knows things." I'll take it!

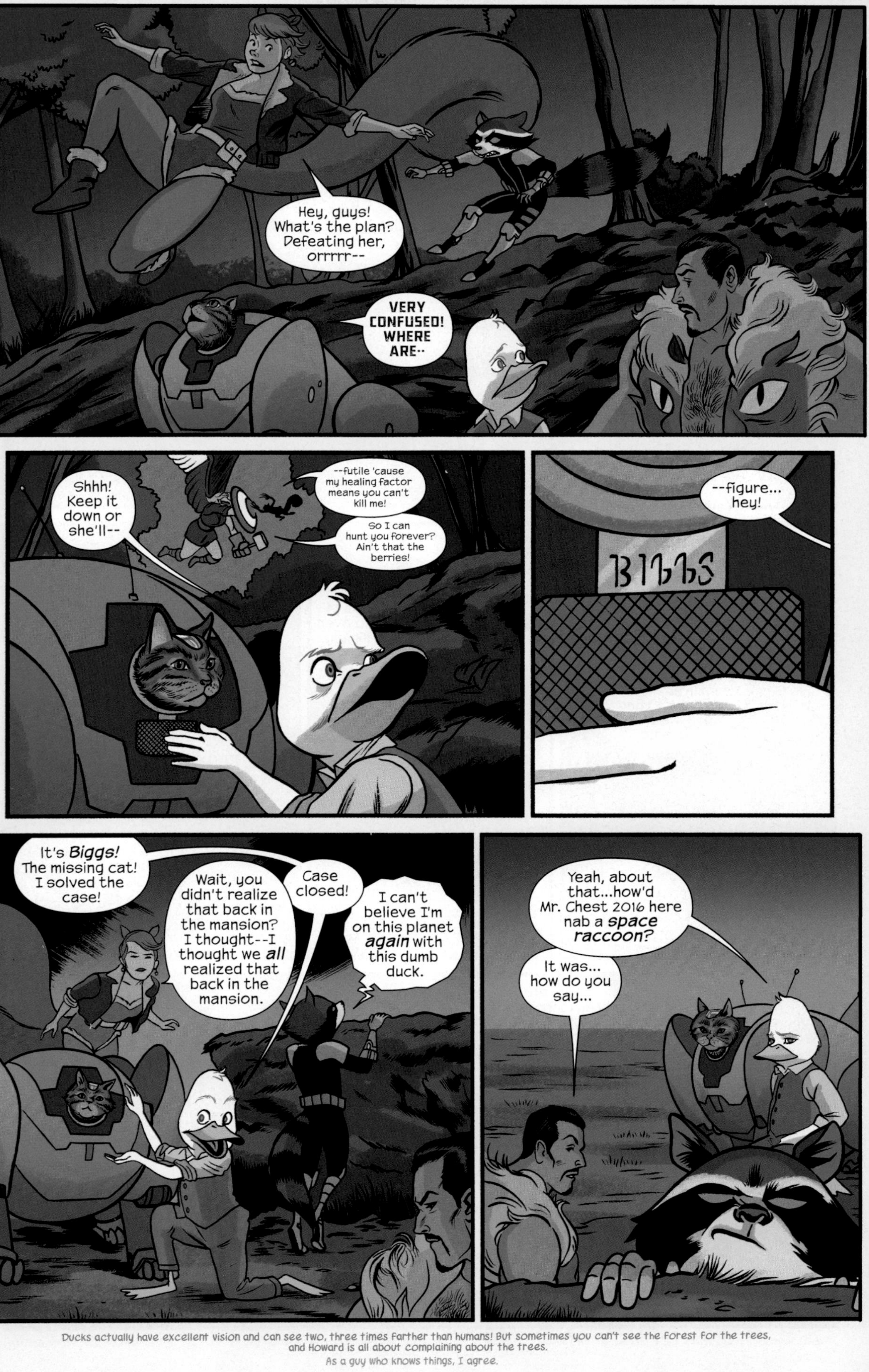
Hey, guys! What's the plan? Defeating her, orrrrr--
VERY CONFUSED! WHERE ARE--
Shhh! Keep it down or she'll--
--futile 'cause my healing factor means you can't kill me!
So I can hunt you forever? Ain't that the berries!
--figure... hey!
BIBBS
It's Biggs! The missing cat! I solved the case!
Wait, you didn't realize that back in the mansion? I thought--I thought we all realized that back in the mansion.
Case closed!
I can't believe I'm on this planet again with this dumb duck.
Yeah, about that...how'd Mr. Chest 2016 here nab a space raccoon?
It was... how do you say...

Ducks actually have excellent vision and can see two, three times farther than humans! But sometimes you can't see the forest for the trees, and Howard is all about complaining about the trees.

As a guy who knows things, I agree.

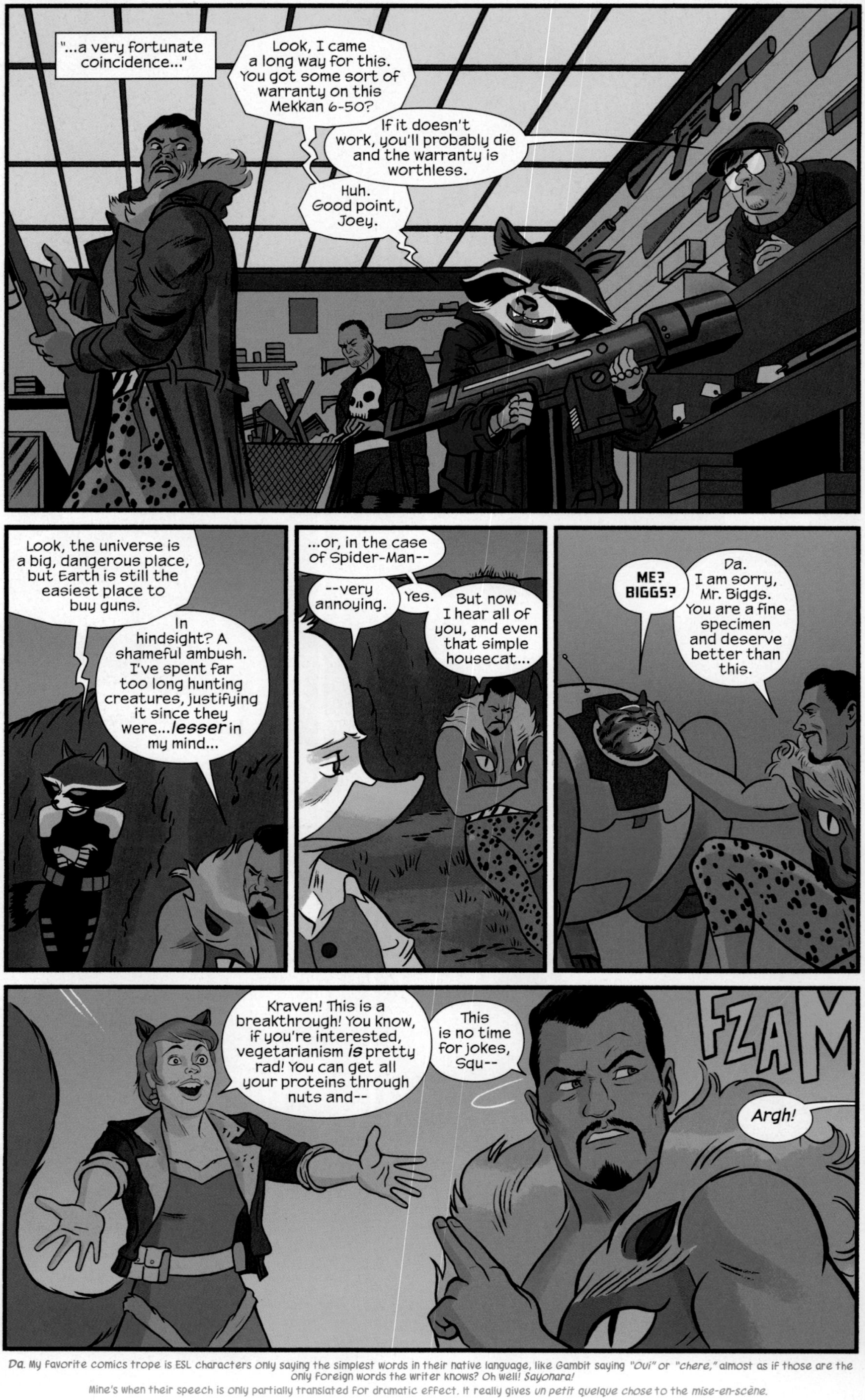
"...a very fortunate coincidence..."
Look, I came a long way for this. You got some sort of warranty on this Mekkan 6-50?
If it doesn't work, you'll probably die and the warranty is worthless.
Huh. Good point, Joey.
Look, the universe is a big, dangerous place, but Earth is still the easiest place to buy guns.
In hindsight? A shameful ambush. I've spent far too long hunting creatures, justifying it since they were...*lesser* in my mind...
...or, in the case of Spider-Man--
--very annoying.
Yes.
But now I hear all of you, and even that simple housecat...
ME? BIGGS?
Da. I am sorry, Mr. Biggs. You are a fine specimen and deserve better than this.
Kraven! This is a breakthrough! You know, if you're interested, vegetarianism *is* pretty rad! You can get all your proteins through nuts and--
This is no time for jokes, Squ--
FZAM
Argh!

Da. My favorite comics trope is ESL characters only saying the simplest words in their native language, like Gambit saying *"Oui"* or *"chere,"* almost as if those are the only foreign words the writer knows? Oh well! *Sayonara!*

Mine's when their speech is only partially translated for dramatic effect. It really gives *un petit quelque chose* to the *mise-en-scène.*

...ngh... my healing factor'll...do its job...like a little...body hospital... and then...

UGH STOP TALKING ABOUT YOUR HEALING FACTOR NOBODY CARES

This ain't over, bud... urk!

RRMMMMMMBILLE

Hooookay, so Wolverteeny is down. What now?

Even if we made it to the finish line, there's no way she'd just let us go! We'd be back with Avengers and Fantastic Fours and maybe even cops in no time!

Hmm, then our only options are to ambush her here in the woods or head to the mansion. We can then... ugh...call for help...or find something we can use against her.

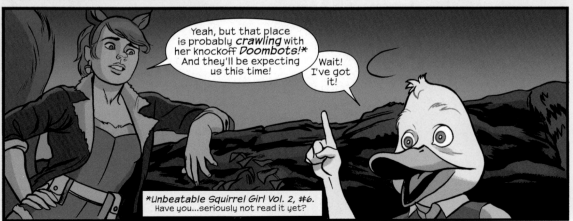

Yeah, but that place is probably crawling with her knockoff Doombots!* And they'll be expecting us this time!

Wait! I've got it!

*Unbeatable Squirrel Girl Vol. 2, #6. Have you...seriously not read it yet?

And who calls their abilities a "Factor"? That's like me saying my "writing Factor" will finish this script in no time, or Ryan saying "My tall Factor will help me get that can on the top shelf." It's weird, man.
Chip, look, do you want the can or not?

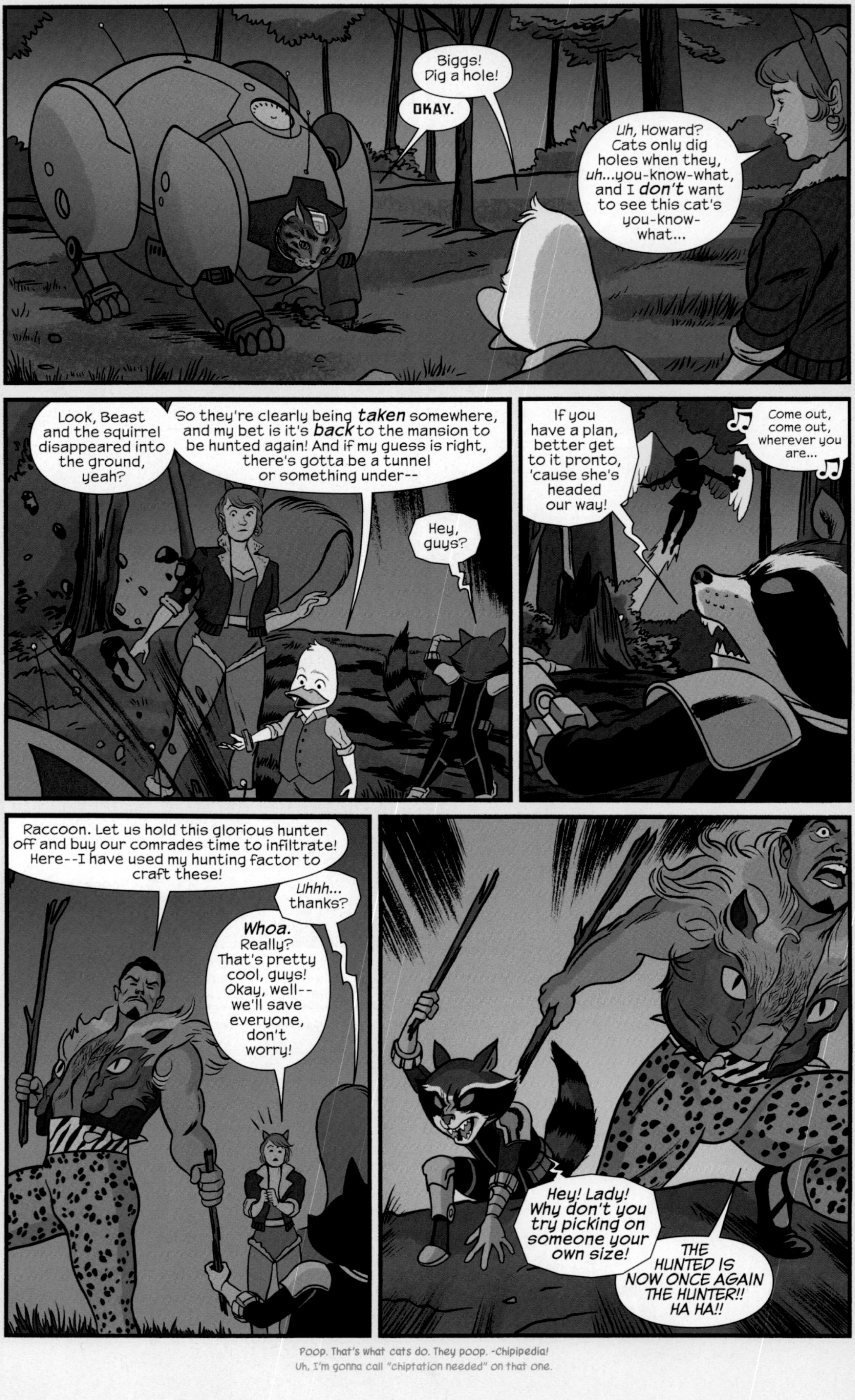
Biggs! Dig a hole!
OKAY.
Uh, Howard? Cats only dig holes when they, uh...you-know-what, and I don't want to see this cat's you-know-what...
Look, Beast and the squirrel disappeared into the ground, yeah?
So they're clearly being taken somewhere, and my bet is it's back to the mansion to be hunted again! And if my guess is right, there's gotta be a tunnel or something under--
Hey, guys?
If you have a plan, better get to it pronto, 'cause she's headed our way!
Come out, come out, wherever you are...
Raccoon. Let us hold this glorious hunter off and buy our comrades time to infiltrate! Here--I have used my hunting factor to craft these!
Uhhh... thanks?
Whoa. Really? That's pretty cool, guys! Okay, well-- we'll save everyone, don't worry!
Hey! Lady! Why don't you try picking on someone your own size!
THE HUNTED IS NOW ONCE AGAIN THE HUNTER!! HA HA!!

Poop. That's what cats do. They poop. -Chipipedia!
Uh, I'm gonna call "chiptation needed" on that one.

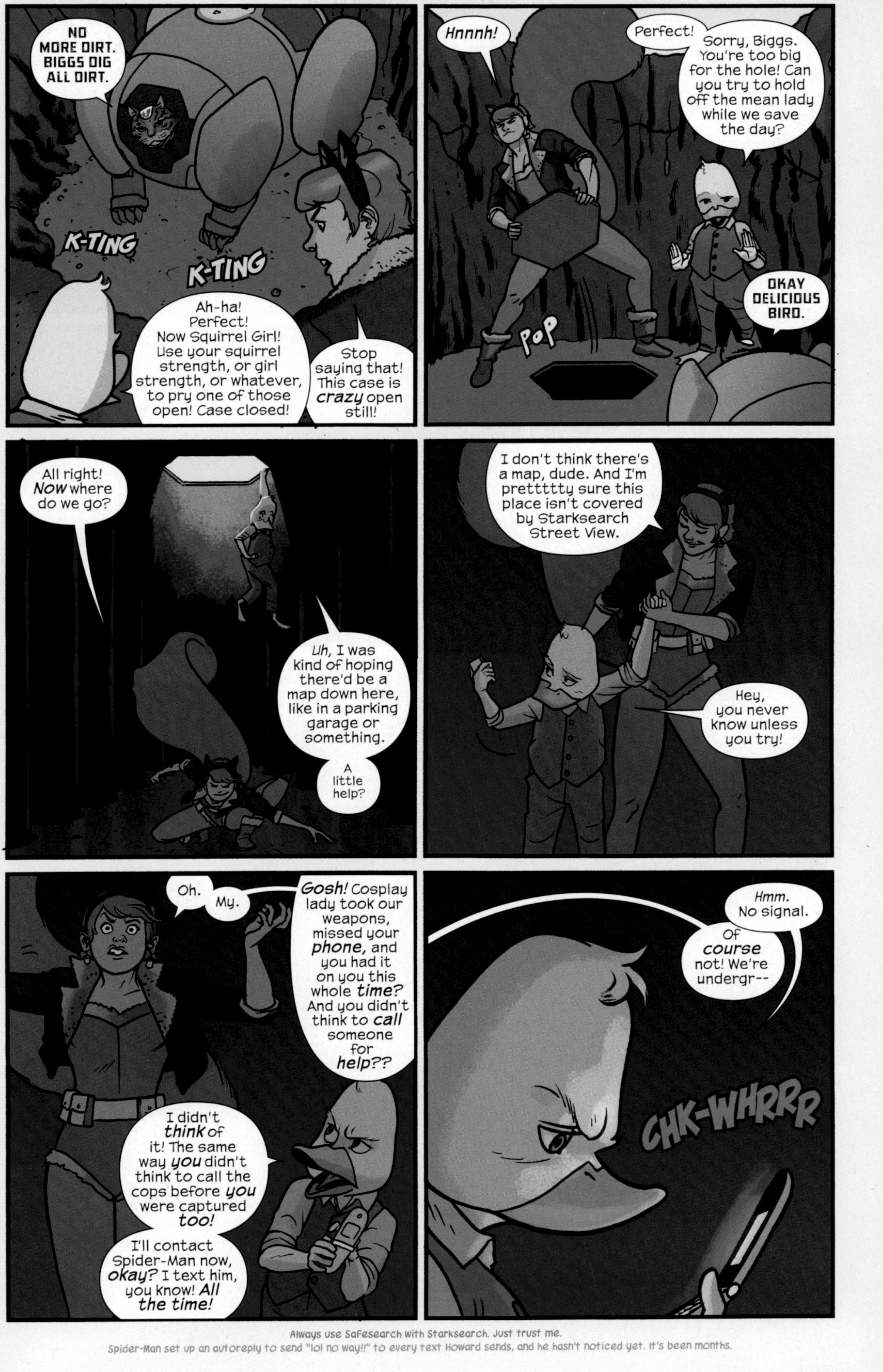
NO MORE DIRT. BIGGS DIG ALL DIRT.
K-TING
K-TING
Ah-ha! Perfect! Now Squirrel Girl! Use your squirrel strength, or girl strength, or whatever, to pry one of those open! Case closed!
Stop saying that! This case is *crazy* open still!
Hnnnh!
Perfect!
Sorry, Biggs. You're too big for the hole! Can you try to hold off the mean lady while we save the day?
OKAY DELICIOUS BIRD.
POP
All right! *Now* where do we go?
Uh, I was kind of hoping there'd be a map down here, like in a parking garage or something.
A little help?
I don't think there's a map, dude. And I'm prettttty sure this place isn't covered by Starksearch Street View.
Hey, you never know unless you try!
Oh.
My.
Gosh! Cosplay lady took our weapons, missed your *phone,* and you had it on you this whole *time?* And you didn't think to *call* someone for *help??*
I didn't *think* of it! The same way *you* didn't think to call the cops before *you* were captured *too!*
I'll contact Spider-Man now, *okay?* I text him, you know! *All the time!*
Hmm. No signal.
Of *course* not! We're undergr--
CHK-WHRRR

Always use Safesearch with Starksearch. Just trust me.
Spider-Man set up an autoreply to send "lol no way!!" to every text Howard sends, and he hasn't noticed yet. It's been months.

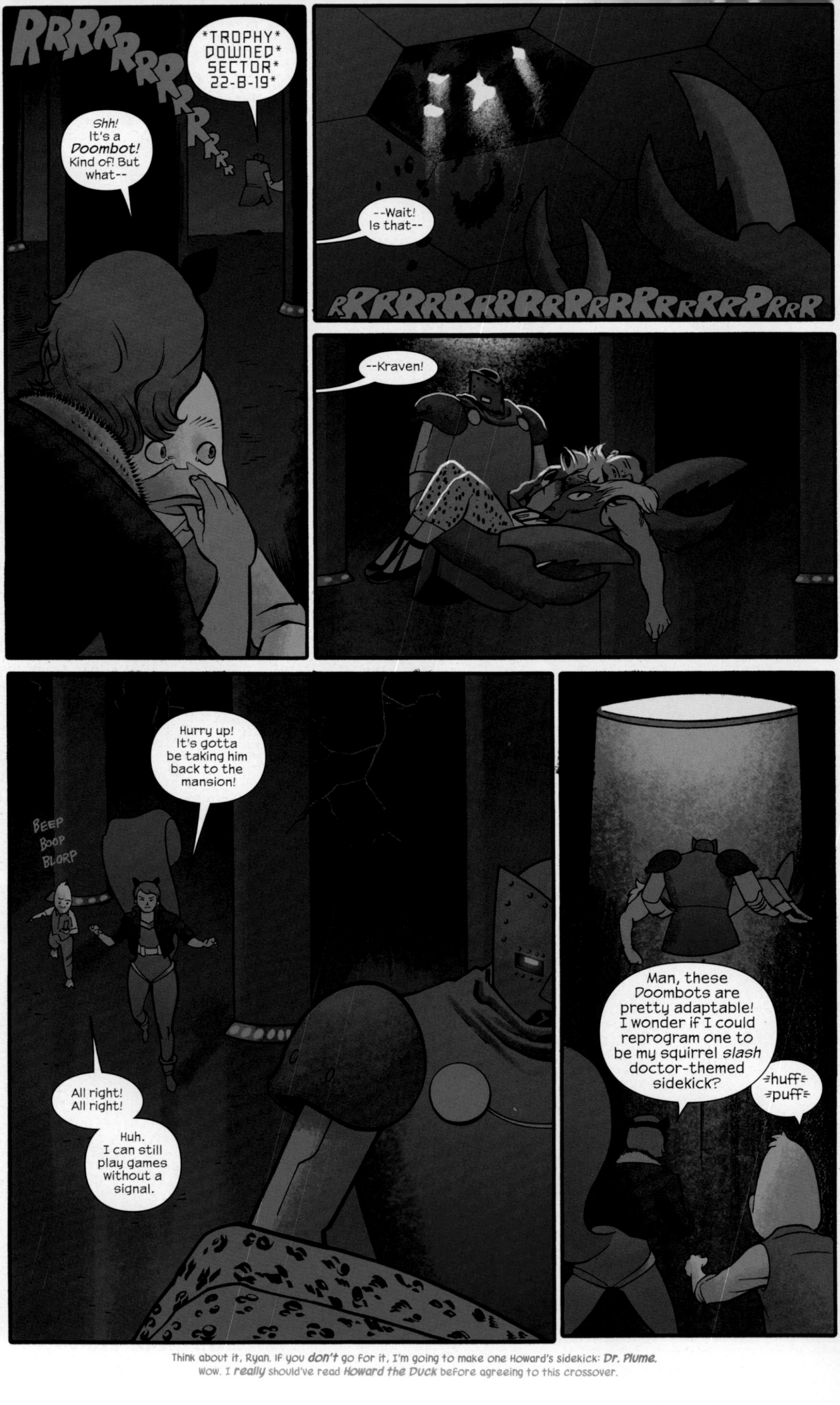
RRRRRRRRRRRRRRRRR
TROPHY DOWNED* SECTOR* 22-B-19*
Shh! It's a Doombot! Kind of! But what--
--Wait! Is that--
RRRRRRRRRRRRRRRRRRRRRRRRRRR
--Kraven!
Hurry up! It's gotta be taking him back to the mansion!
BEEP BOOP BLORP
All right! All right!
Huh. I can still play games without a signal.
Man, these Doombots are pretty adaptable! I wonder if I could reprogram one to be my squirrel slash doctor-themed sidekick?
huff puff

Think about it, Ryan. If you *don't* go for it, I'm going to make one Howard's sidekick: *Dr. Plume.*
Wow. I *really* should've read *Howard the Duck* before agreeing to this crossover.

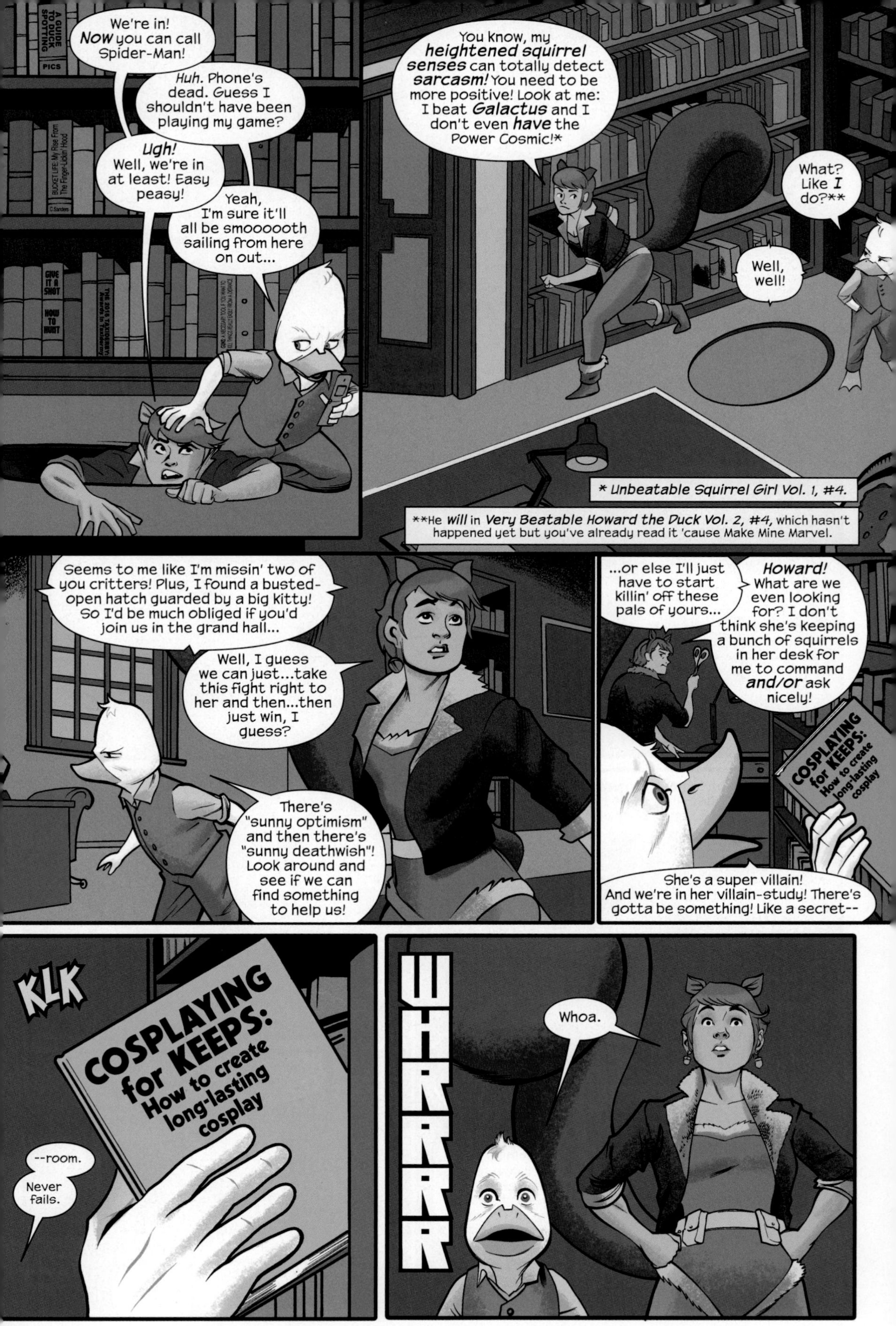
We're in! NOW you can call Spider-Man!
Huh. Phone's dead. Guess I shouldn't have been playing my game?
Ugh! Well, we're in at least! Easy peasy!
Yeah, I'm sure it'll all be smooooth sailing from here on out...
A GUIDE TO DUCK SPOTTING
PICS
BUCKET LIFE: My Rise From The Finger-Lickin' Hood
GIVE IT A SHOT
HOW TO HUNT
You know, my heightened squirrel senses can totally detect sarcasm! You need to be more positive! Look at me: I beat Galactus and I don't even have the Power Cosmic!*
What? Like I do?**
Well, well!
* Unbeatable Squirrel Girl Vol. 1, #4.
**He will in Very Beatable Howard the Duck Vol. 2, #4, which hasn't happened yet but you've already read it 'cause Make Mine Marvel.
Seems to me like I'm missin' two of you critters! Plus, I found a busted-open hatch guarded by a big kitty! So I'd be much obliged if you'd join us in the grand hall...
Well, I guess we can just...take this fight right to her and then...then just win, I guess?
There's "sunny optimism" and then there's "sunny deathwish"! Look around and see if we can find something to help us!
...or else I'll just have to start killin' off these pals of yours...
Howard! What are we even looking for? I don't think she's keeping a bunch of squirrels in her desk for me to command and/or ask nicely!
COSPLAYING for KEEPS: How to create long-lasting cosplay
She's a super villain! And we're in her villain-study! There's gotta be something! Like a secret--
KLK
COSPLAYING for KEEPS: How to create long-lasting cosplay
--room.
Never fails.
WHRRRR
Whoa.

Other cosplay books: *Be the Hero You Want to See in the World But Without Powers, House of M: Designer Mutant Cosplay, Cos and Effect: Succeed in your Job by Dressing Like Storm.*
Not to mention *Fired with Cos: How You Too Can Get Fired For Dressing like Storm 24/7, We Have a Dress Code Here*

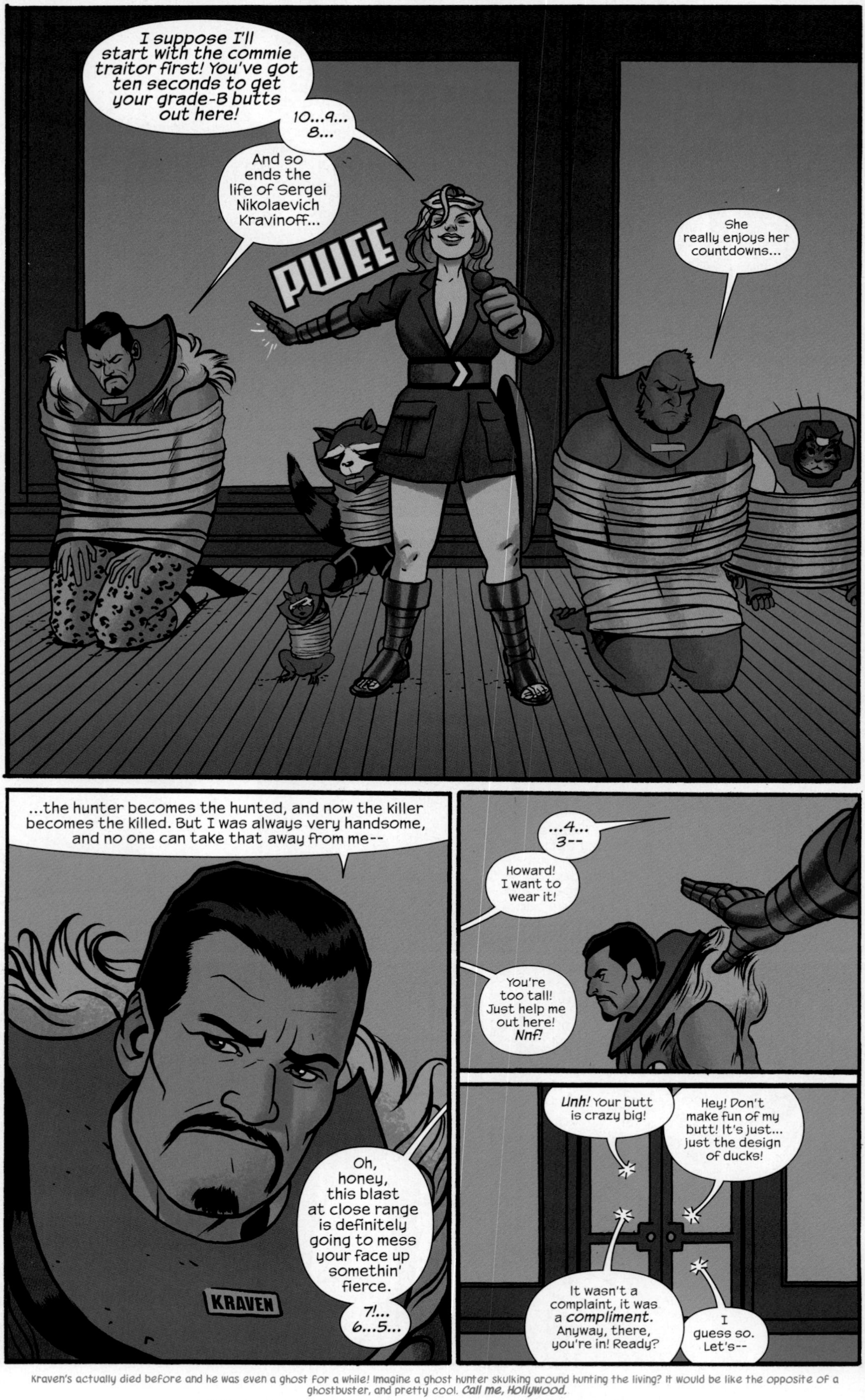
I suppose I'll start with the commie traitor first! You've got ten seconds to get your grade-B butts out here!
10...9... 8...
And so ends the life of Sergei Nikolaevich Kravinoff...
PWEE
She really enjoys her countdowns...
...the hunter becomes the hunted, and now the killer becomes the killed. But I was always very handsome, and no one can take that away from me--
Oh, honey, this blast at close range is definitely going to mess your face up somethin' fierce.
7!... 6...5...
KRAVEN
...4... 3--
Howard! I want to wear it!
You're too tall! Just help me out here! Nnf!
Unh! Your butt is crazy big!
Hey! Don't make fun of my butt! It's just... just the design of ducks!
It wasn't a complaint, it was a compliment. Anyway, there, you're in! Ready?
I guess so. Let's--

Kraven's actually died before and he was even a ghost for a while! Imagine a ghost hunter skulking around hunting the living? It would be like the opposite of a ghostbuster, and pretty cool. ***Call me, Hollywood.***

Hollywood, my idea is like Chip's, only better because it's *also* like ***Die Hard.*** Call me First.

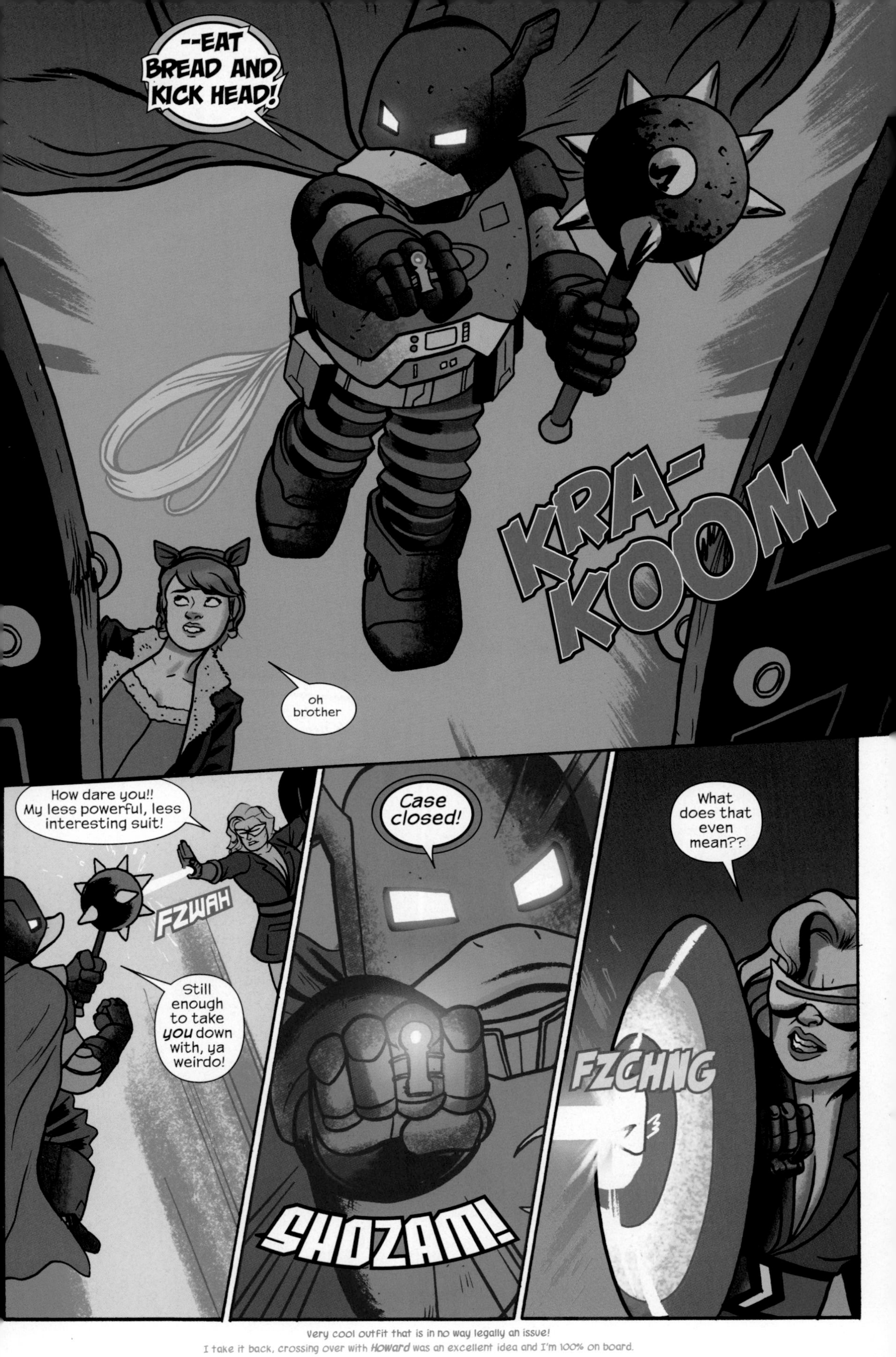
--EAT BREAD AND KICK HEAD!
KRA-KOOM
oh brother
How dare you!! My less powerful, less interesting suit!
FZWAH
Still enough to take *you* down with, ya weirdo!
Case closed!
SHOZAM!
What does that even mean??
FZCHNG

Very cool outfit that is in no way legally an issue!
I take it back, crossing over with ***Howard*** was an excellent idea and I'm 100% on board.

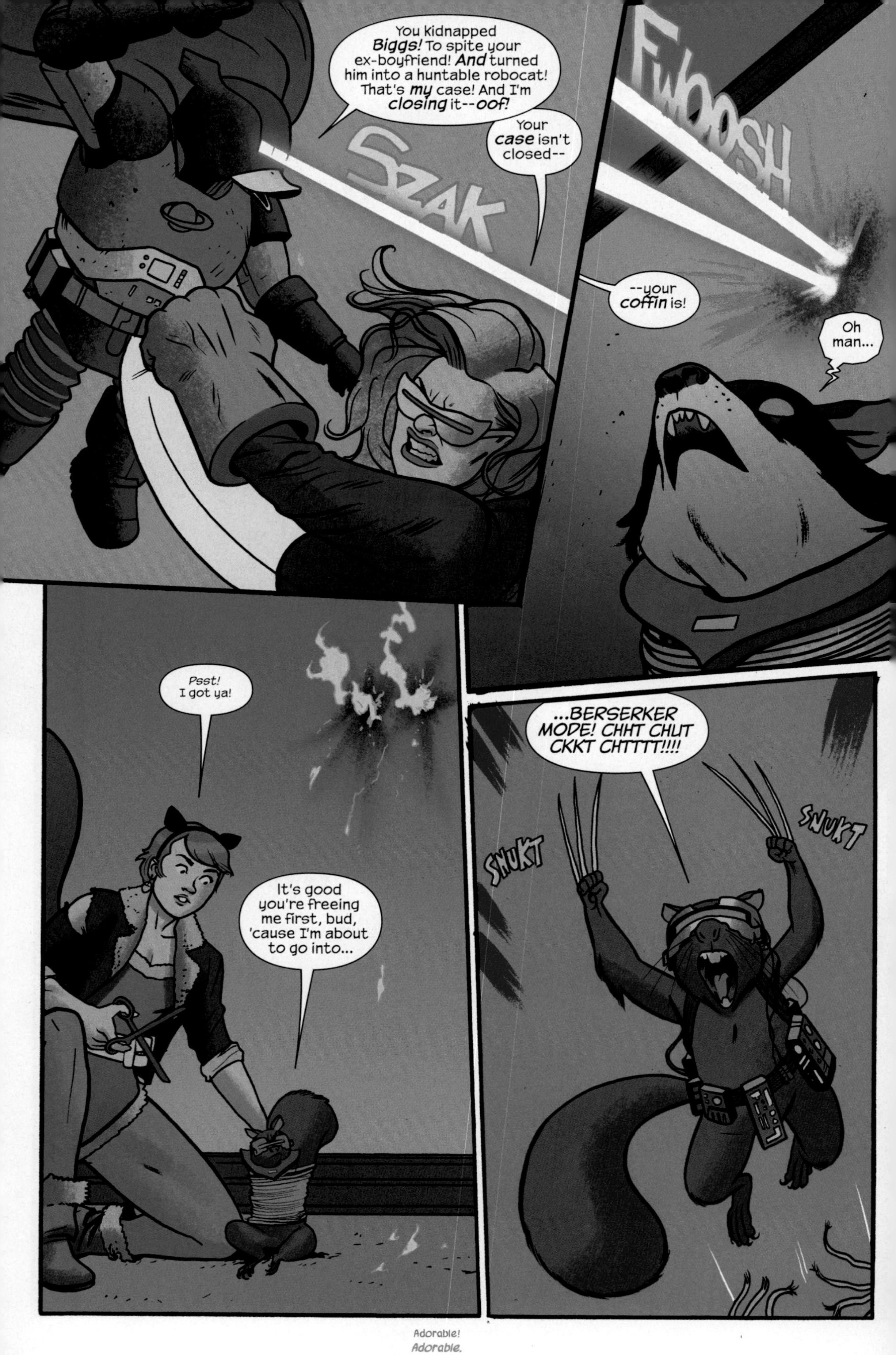
You kidnapped Biggs! To spite your ex-boyfriend! And turned him into a huntable robocat! That's my case! And I'm closing it--oof!
SZAK
Your case isn't closed--
FWOOSH
--your coffin is!
Oh man...
Psst! I got ya!
It's good you're freeing me first, bud, 'cause I'm about to go into...
...BERSERKER MODE! CHHT CHUT CKKT CHTTTT!!!!
SNUKT
SNUKT

Adorable!
Adorable.

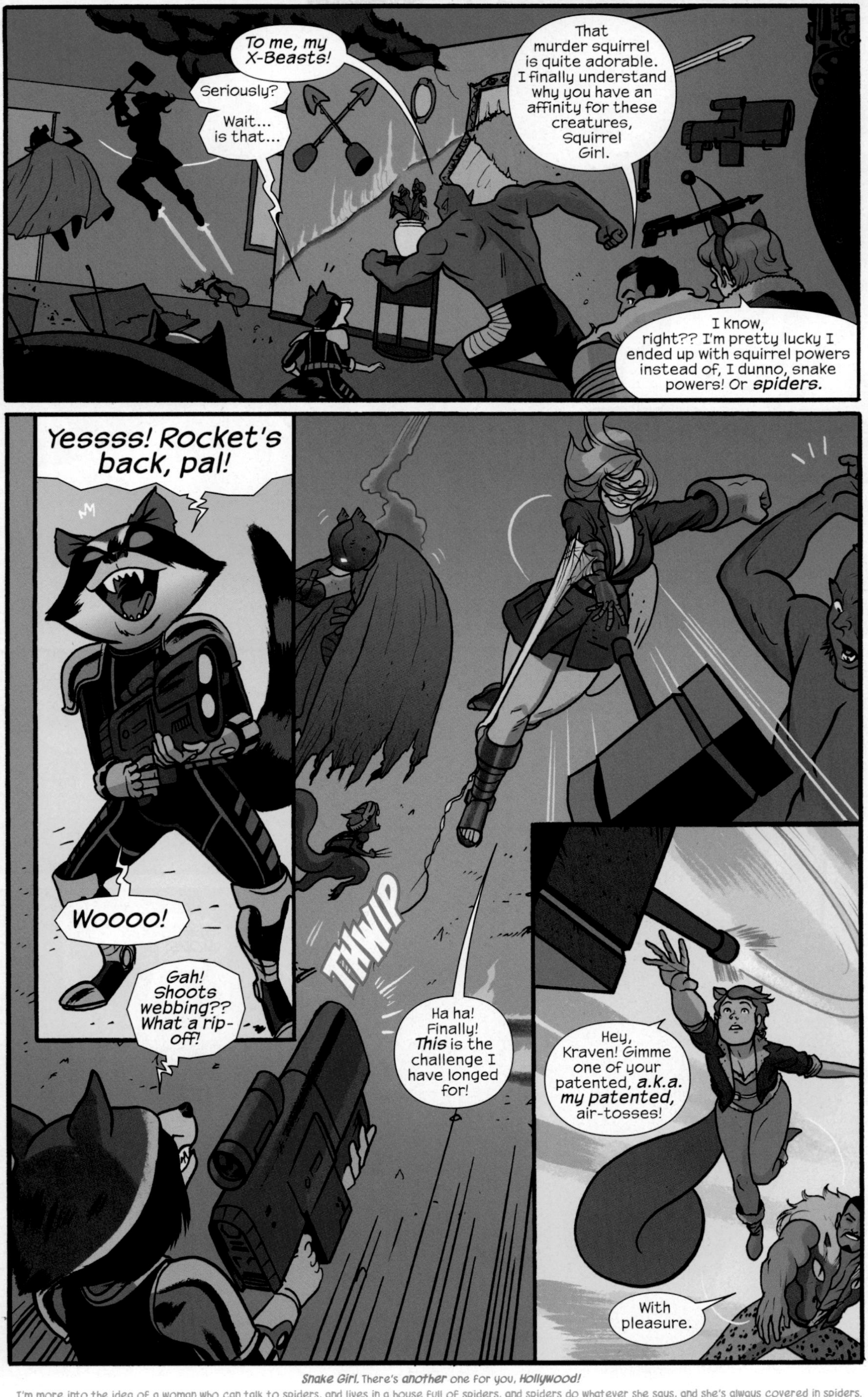
To me, my X-Beasts!
Seriously?
Wait... is that...
That murder squirrel is quite adorable. I finally understand why you have an affinity for these creatures, Squirrel Girl.
I know, right?? I'm pretty lucky I ended up with squirrel powers instead of, I dunno, snake powers! Or spiders.
Yessss! Rocket's back, pal!
Woooo!
Gah! Shoots webbing?? What a rip-off!
THWIP
Ha ha! Finally! This is the challenge I have longed for!
Hey, Kraven! Gimme one of your patented, a.k.a. my patented, air-tosses!
With pleasure.

Snake Girl. There's *another* one for you, *Hollywood!*
I'm more into the idea of a woman who can talk to spiders, and lives in a house full of spiders, and spiders do whatever she says, and she's always covered in spiders. *Nobody would ever mess with her.*

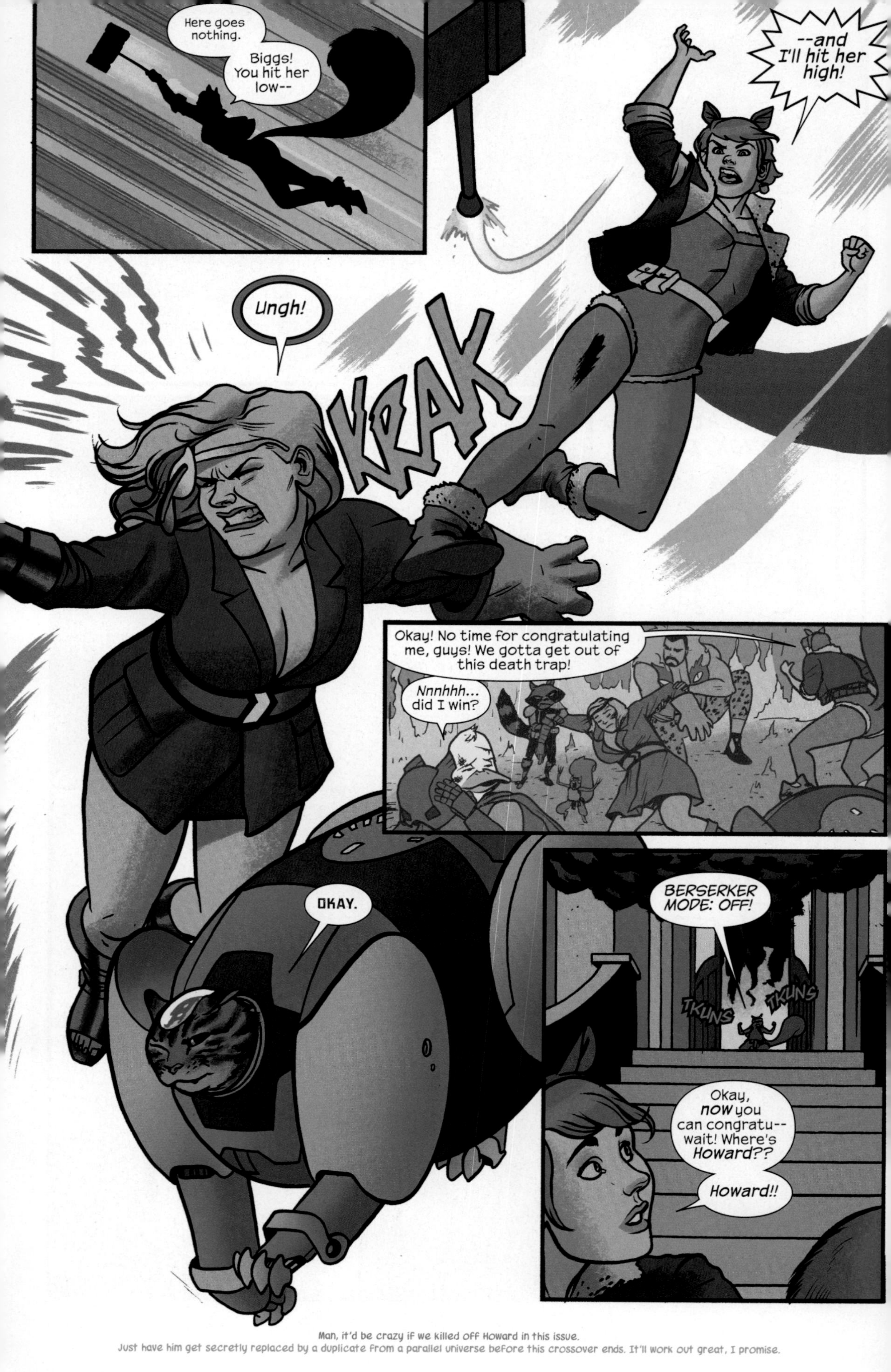
Here goes nothing.
Biggs! You hit her low--
--and I'll hit her high!
Ungh!
KRAK
Okay! No time for congratulating me, guys! We gotta get out of this death trap!
Nnnhhh... did I win?
OKAY.
BERSERKER MODE: OFF!
TKUNG
TKUNG
Okay, NOW you can congratu-- wait! Where's Howard??
Howard!!

Man, it'd be crazy if we killed off Howard in this issue.
Just have him get secretly replaced by a duplicate from a parallel universe before this crossover ends. It'll work out great, I promise.

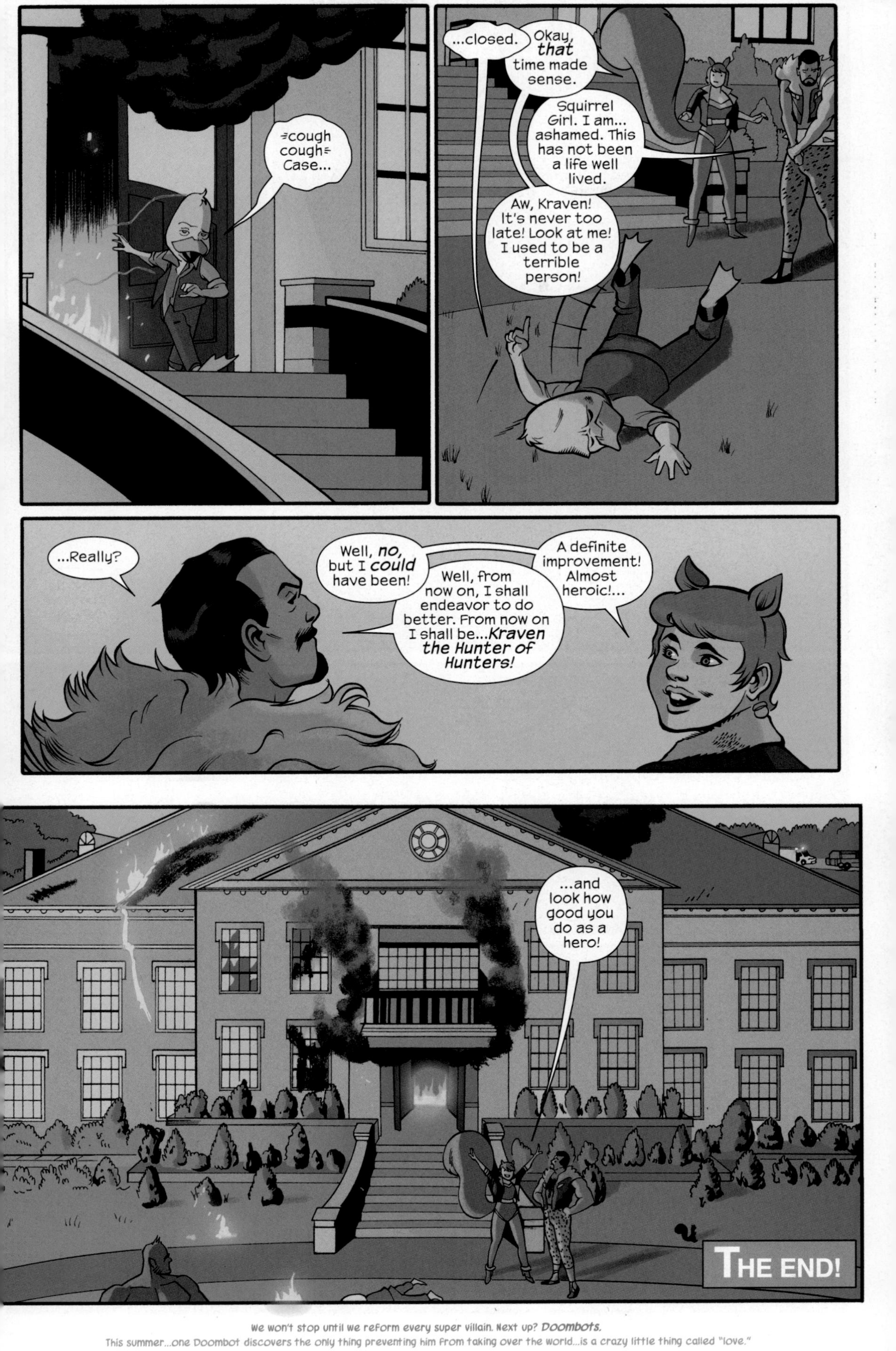

=cough cough= Case...
...closed.
Okay, that time made sense.
Squirrel Girl. I am... ashamed. This has not been a life well lived.
Aw, Kraven! It's never too late! Look at me! I used to be a terrible person!
...Really?
Well, no, but I could have been!
A definite improvement! Almost heroic!...
Well, from now on, I shall endeavor to do better. From now on I shall be...Kraven the Hunter of Hunters!
...and look how good you do as a hero!
THE END!

We won't stop until we reform every super villain. Next up? *Doombots.*
This summer...one Doombot discovers the only thing preventing him from taking over the world...is a crazy little thing called "love."

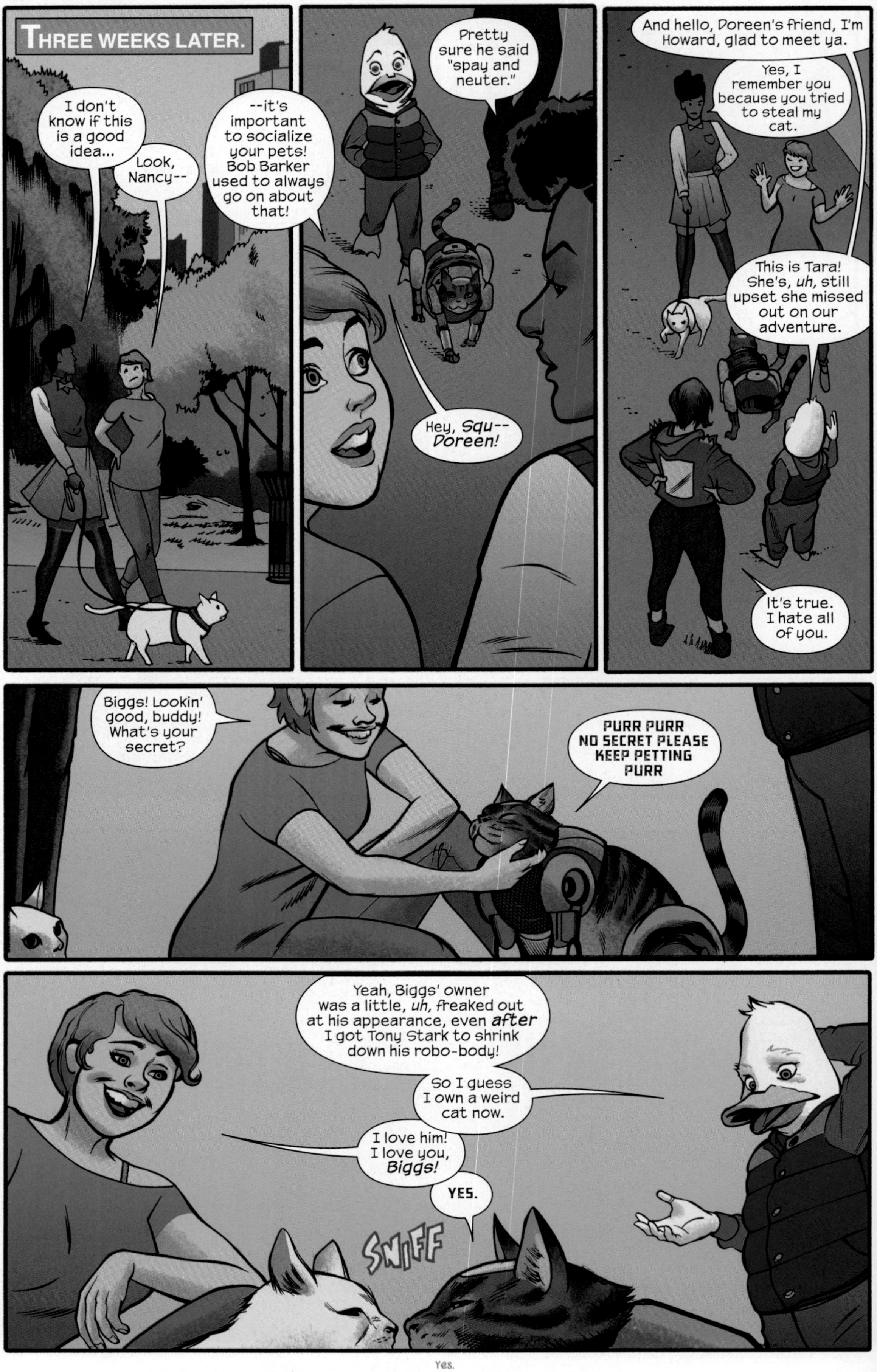
THREE WEEKS LATER.
I don't know if this is a good idea...
Look, Nancy--
--it's important to socialize your pets! Bob Barker used to always go on about that!
Pretty sure he said "spay and neuter."
Hey, Squ-- Doreen!
And hello, Doreen's friend, I'm Howard, glad to meet ya.
Yes, I remember you because you tried to steal my cat.
This is Tara! She's, uh, still upset she missed out on our adventure.
It's true. I hate all of you.
Biggs! Lookin' good, buddy! What's your secret?
PURR PURR NO SECRET PLEASE KEEP PETTING PURR
Yeah, Biggs' owner was a little, uh, freaked out at his appearance, even after I got Tony Stark to shrink down his robo-body!
So I guess I own a weird cat now.
I love him! I love you, Biggs!
YES.
SNIFF

Yes.
That other cat is named "Mew" and she appears in *several Squirrel Girl* issues. That's right. *Our* comic has cats, *too.*

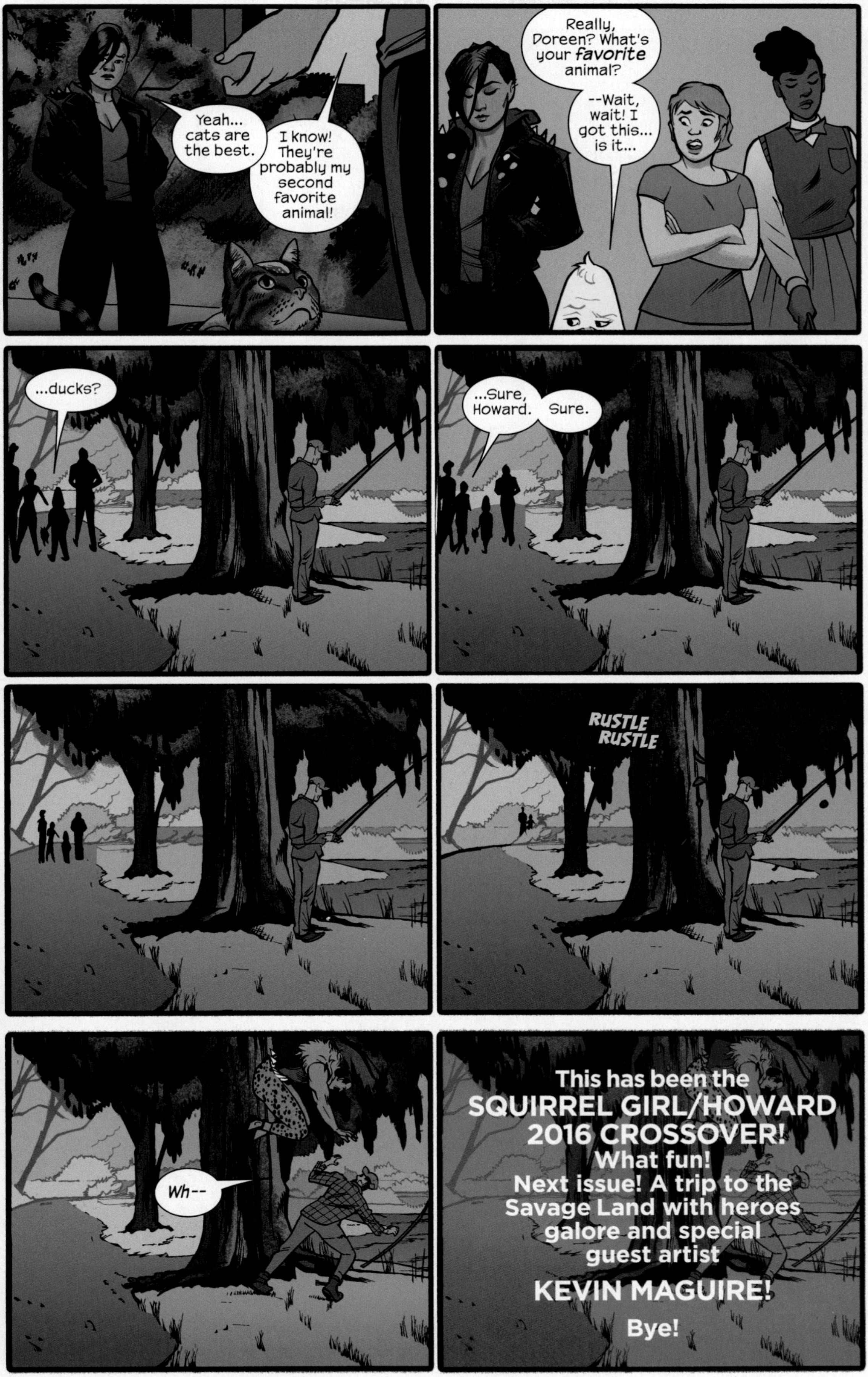
Yeah... cats are the best.
I know! They're probably my second favorite animal!
Really, Doreen? What's your *favorite* animal?
--Wait, wait! I got this... is it...
...ducks?
...Sure, Howard.
Sure.
RUSTLE RUSTLE
Wh--
This has been the SQUIRREL GIRL/HOWARD 2016 CROSSOVER! What fun!
Next issue! A trip to the Savage Land with heroes galore and special guest artist
KEVIN MAGUIRE!
Bye!

I never wanted this to end. Except I only get paid when it ends.
Chip, it was fun to help you out and write some little words beneath your comic about a talking duck who is mad at things.

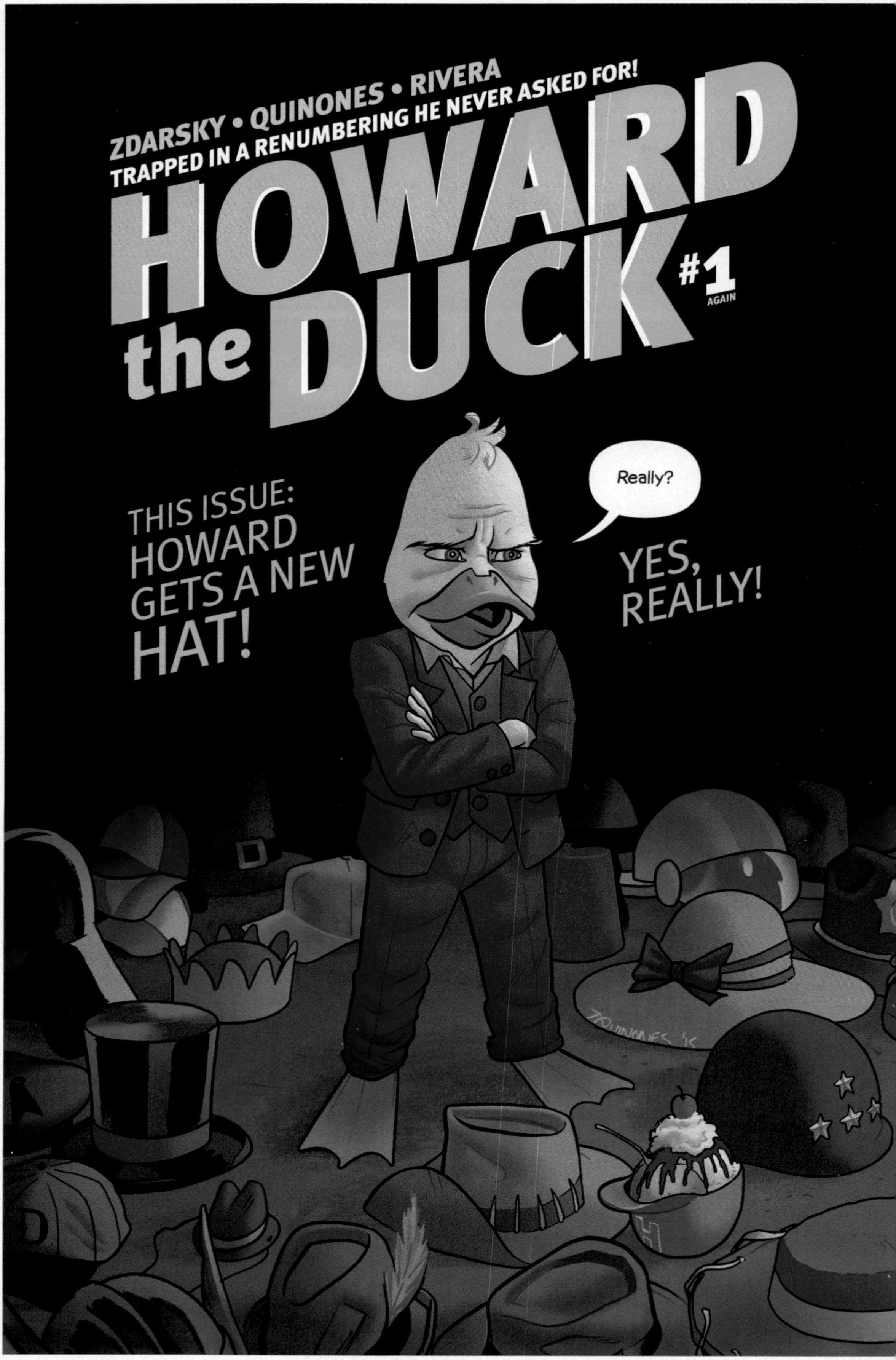
ZDARSKY • QUINONES • RIVERA
TRAPPED IN A RENUMBERING HE NEVER ASKED FOR!
HOWARD the DUCK
#1 AGAIN
THIS ISSUE: HOWARD GETS A NEW HAT!
Really?
YES, REALLY!

#1 VARIANT BY JOE QUINONES

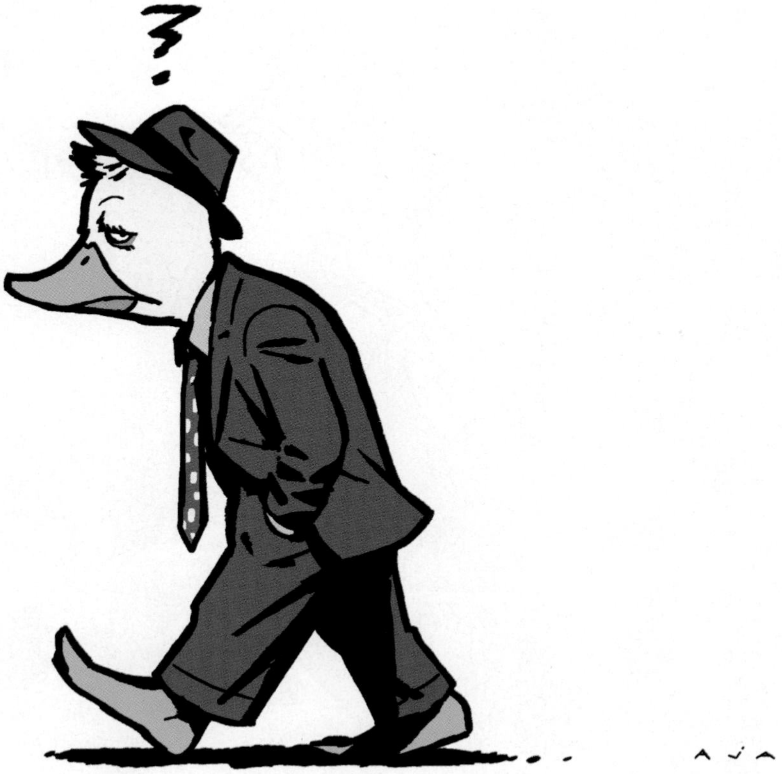
AJA

#1 VARIANT BY DAVID AJA

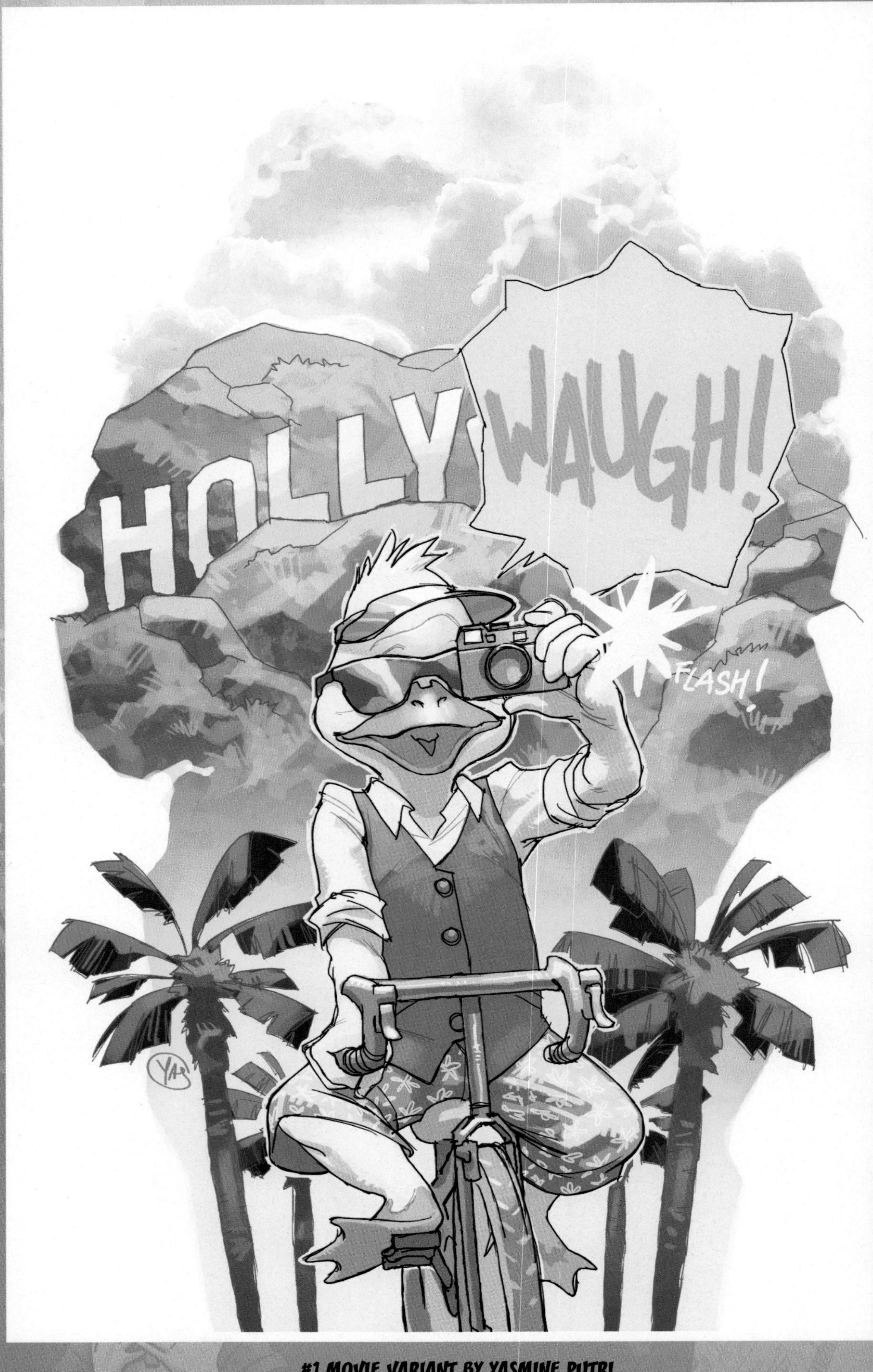
HOLLY
WAUGH!
FLASH!

#1 MOVIE VARIANT BY YASMINE PUTRI

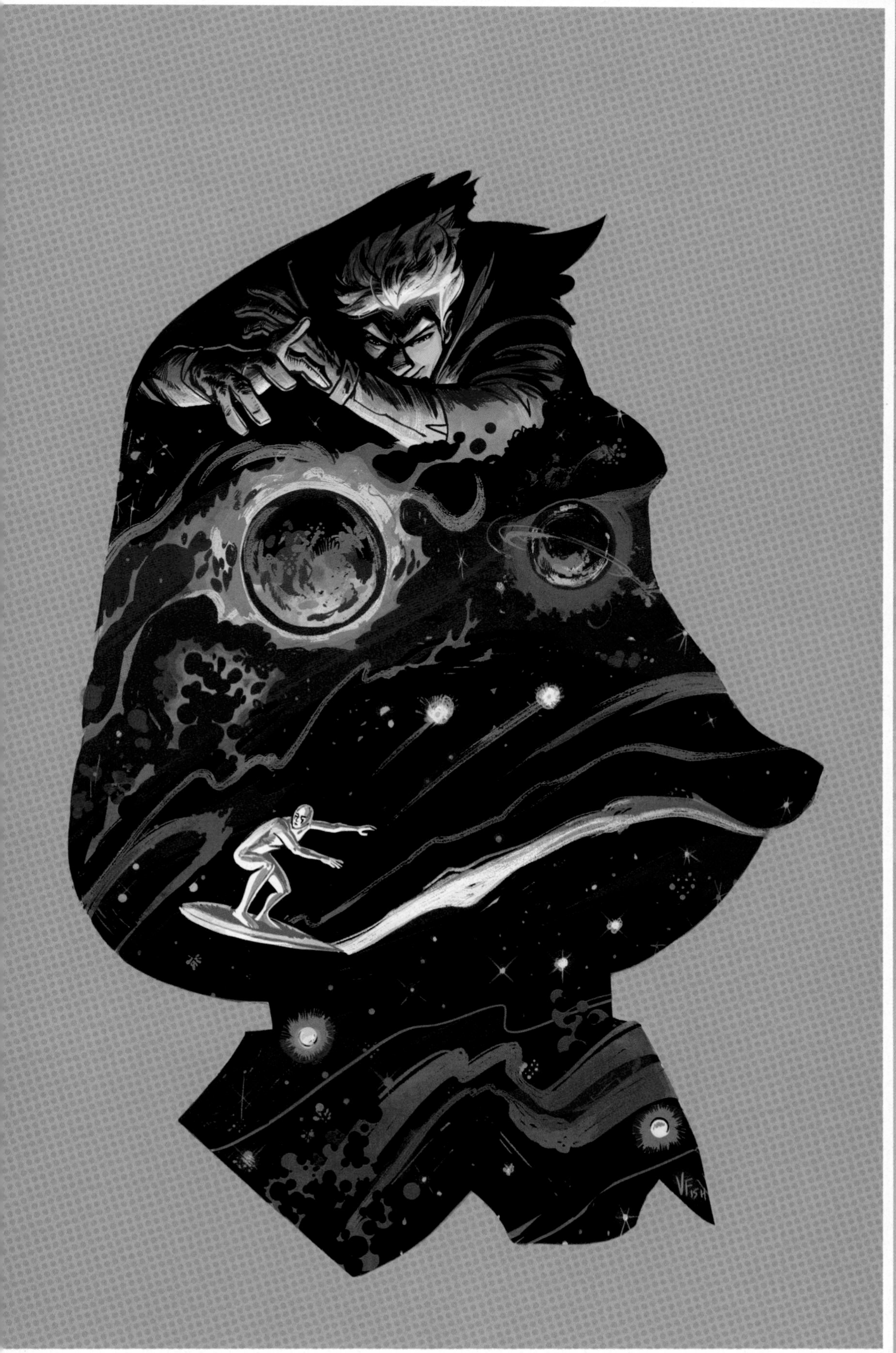

#1 VARIANT BY VERONICA FISH

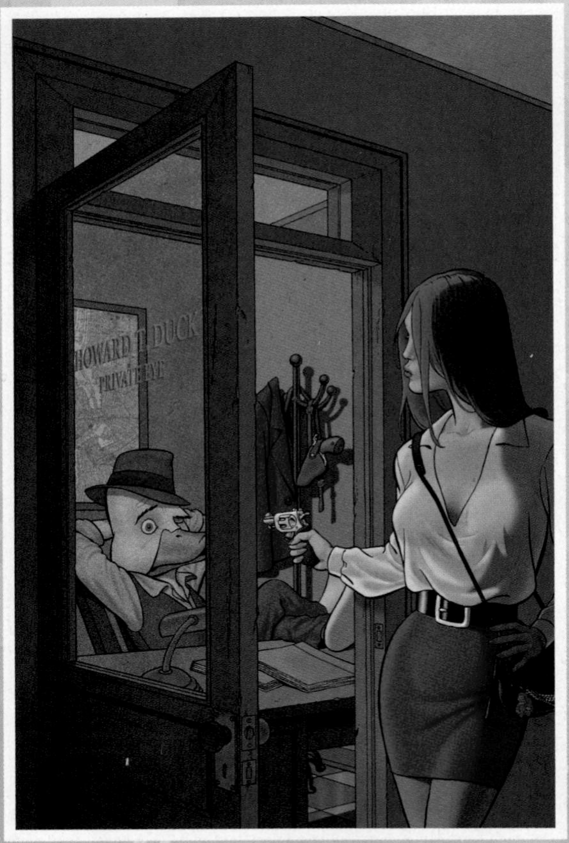
HOWARD T. DUCK
PRIVATE EYE

#1 VARIANT
BY BOB MCLOED

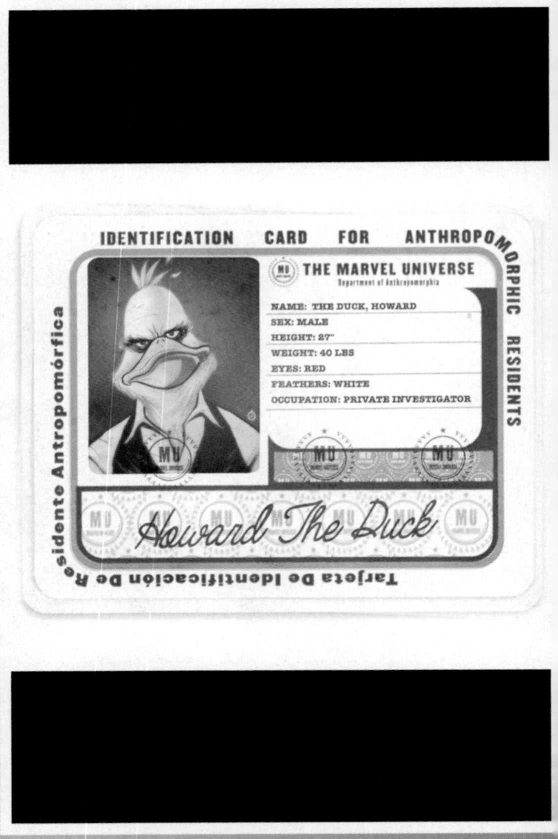
IDENTIFICATION CARD FOR ANTHROPOMORPHIC RESIDENTS
THE MARVEL UNIVERSE
Department of Anthropomorphia
NAME: THE DUCK, HOWARD
SEX: MALE
HEIGHT: 27"
WEIGHT: 40 LBS
EYES: RED
FEATHERS: WHITE
OCCUPATION: PRIVATE INVESTIGATOR
Howard The Duck
Tarjeta De Identificación De Residente Antropomórfica

#1 HIP-HOP VARIANT
BY JUAN DOE

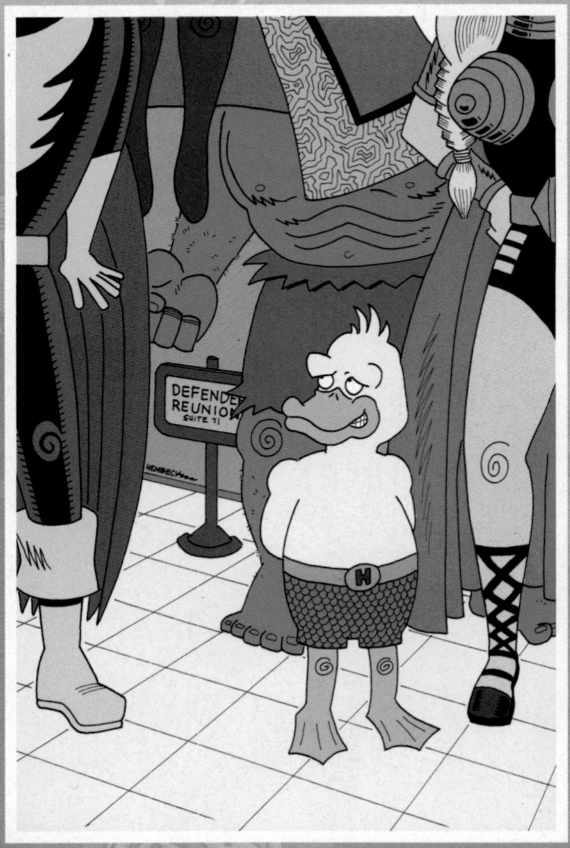
DEFENDE
REUNIO
SUITE 71
HEMBECK

#2 VARIANT
BY FRED HEMBECK & RACHELLE ROSENBERG

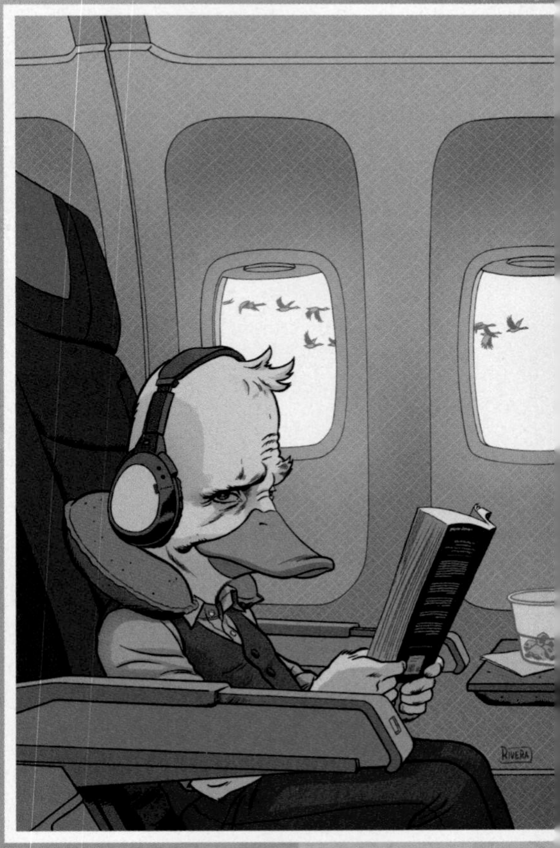
RIVERA

#3 VARIANT
BY PAOLO RIVERA

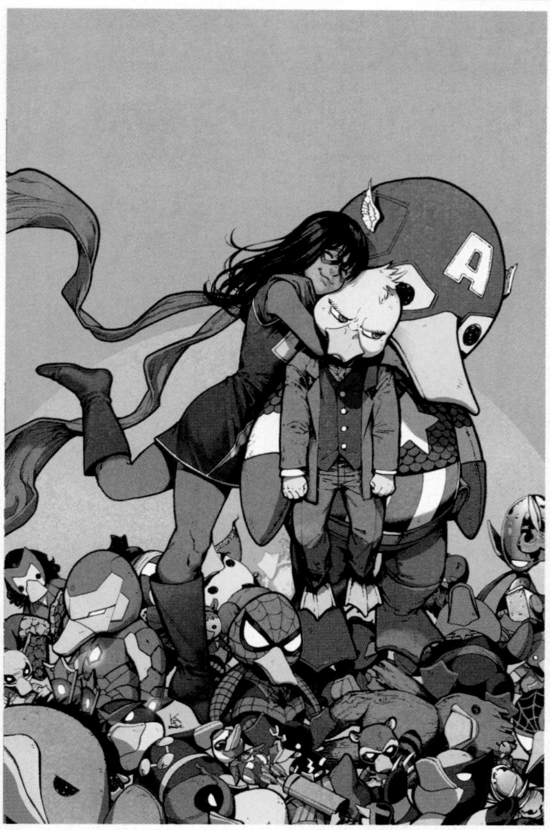

#4 VARIANT
BY KAMOME SHIRAHAMA

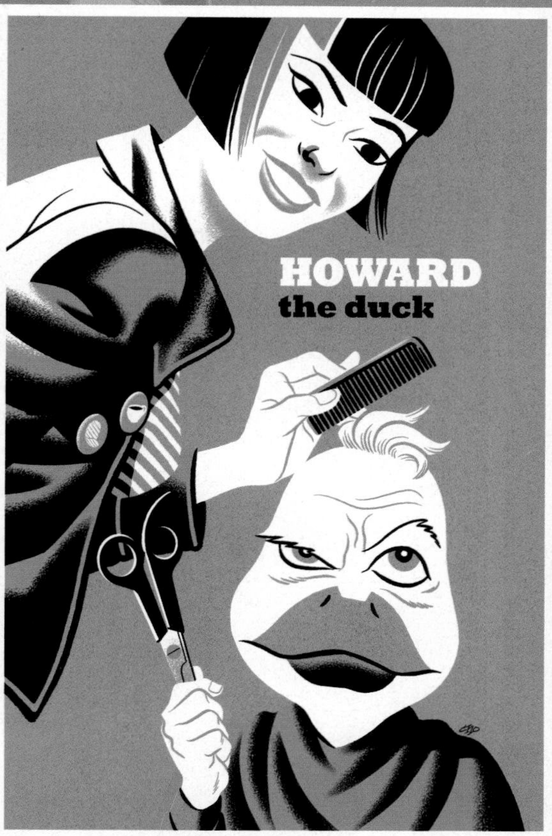
HOWARD
the duck

#4 VARIANT
BY MICHAEL CHO

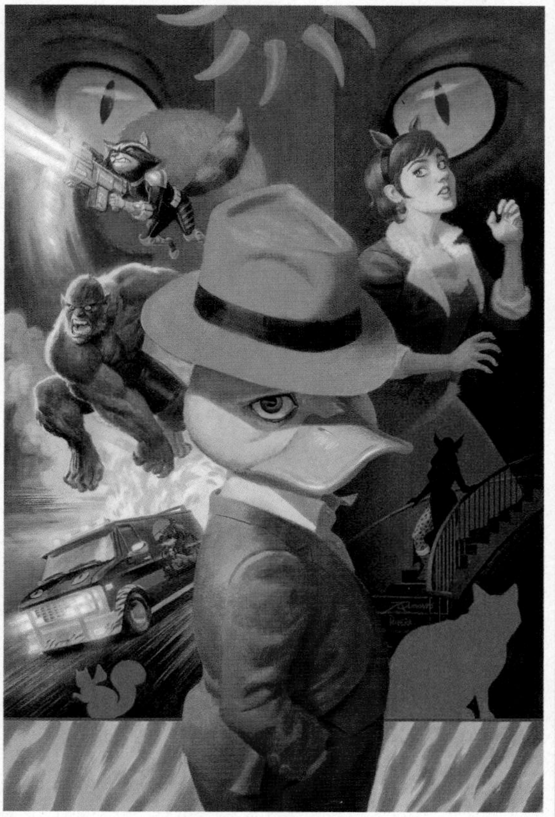

#6 VARIANT
BY JOE QUINONES & PAOLO RIVERA

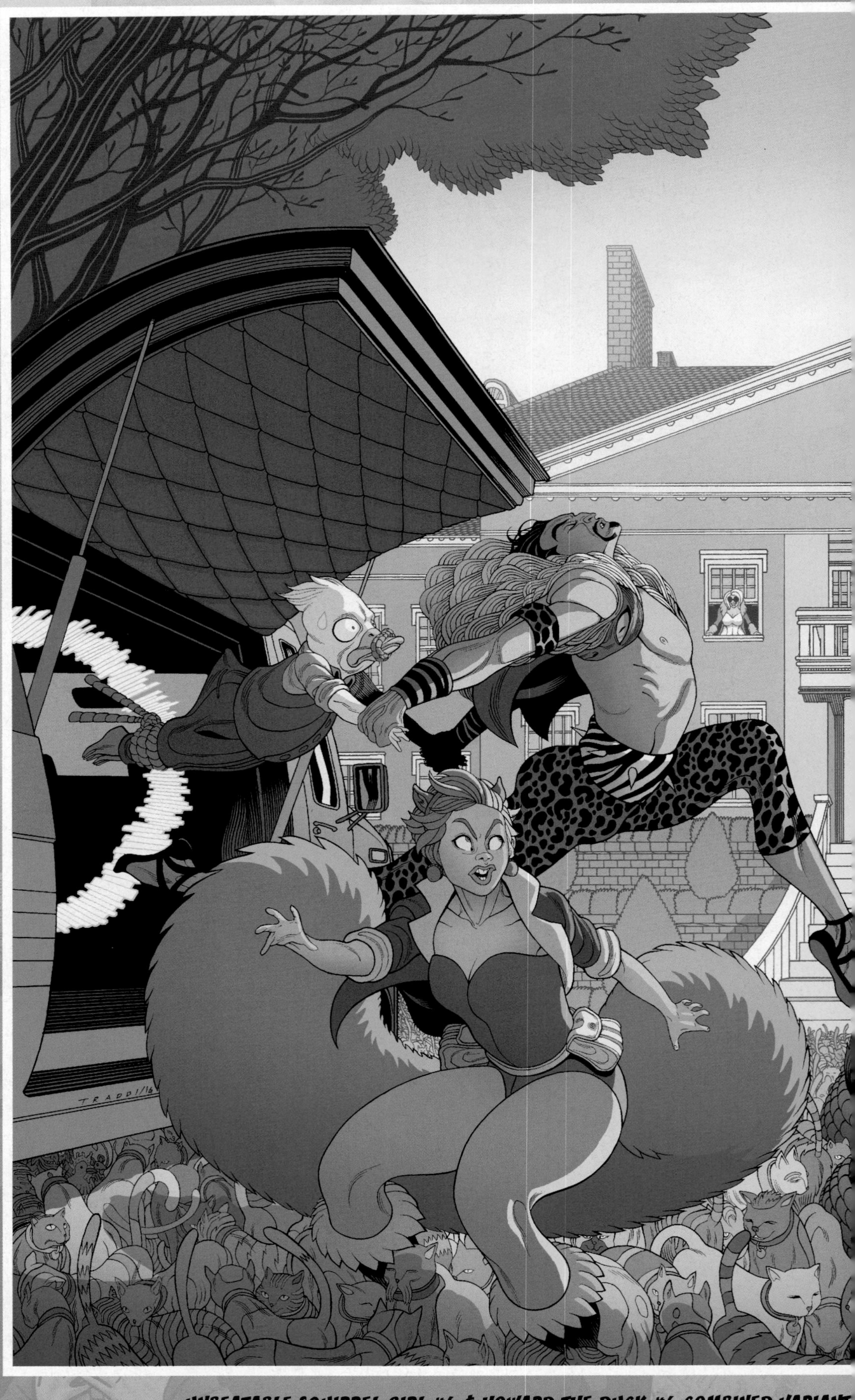

UNBEATABLE SQUIRREL GIRL #6 & HOWARD THE DUCK #6 COMBINED VARIANT

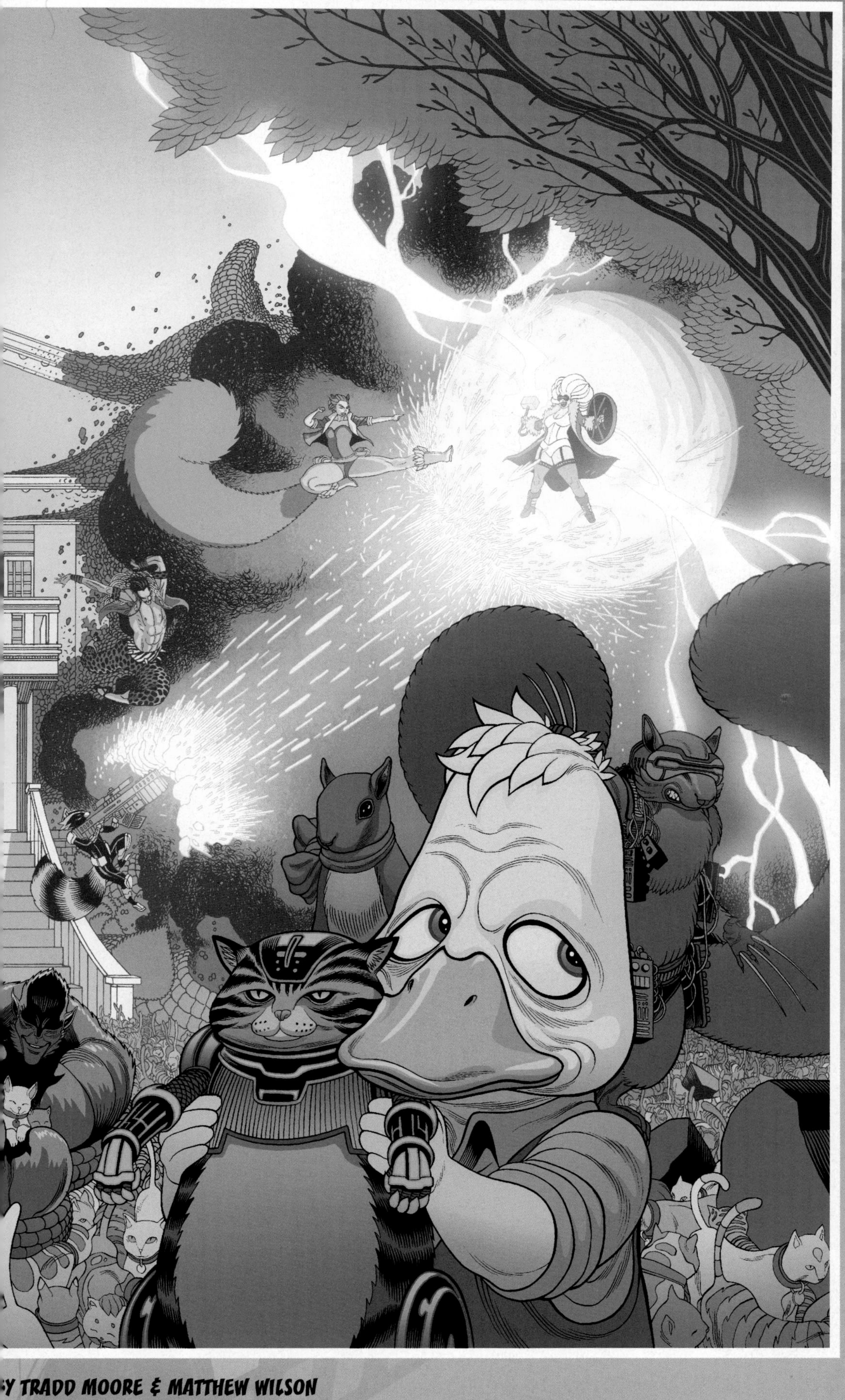

SY TRADD MOORE & MATTHEW WILSON

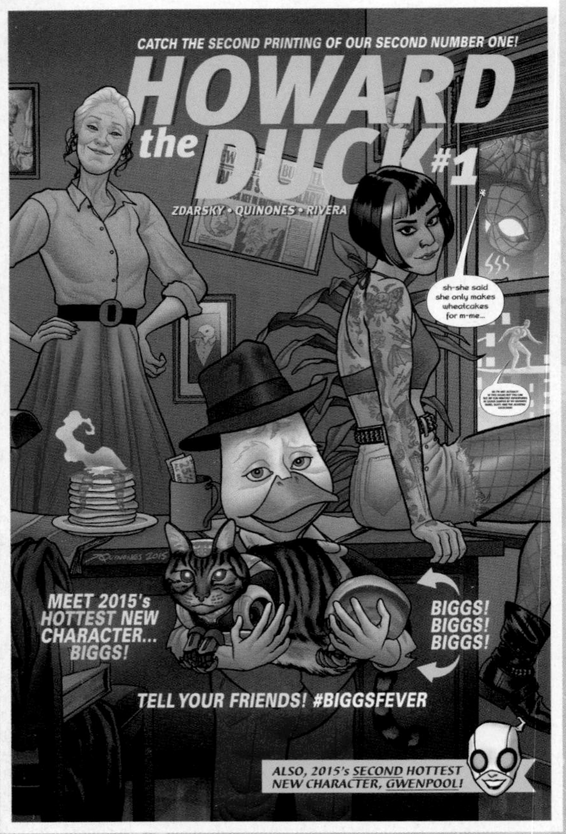
CATCH THE SECOND PRINTING OF OUR SECOND NUMBER ONE!
HOWARD the DUCK #1
ZDARSKY • QUINONES • RIVERA
sh-she said she only makes wheatcakes for m-me...
MEET 2015's HOTTEST NEW CHARACTER... BIGGS!
BIGGS! BIGGS! BIGGS!
TELL YOUR FRIENDS! #BIGGSFEVER
ALSO, 2015's SECOND HOTTEST NEW CHARACTER, GWENPOOL!

#1 2ND-PRINTING VARIANT
BY JOE QUINONES

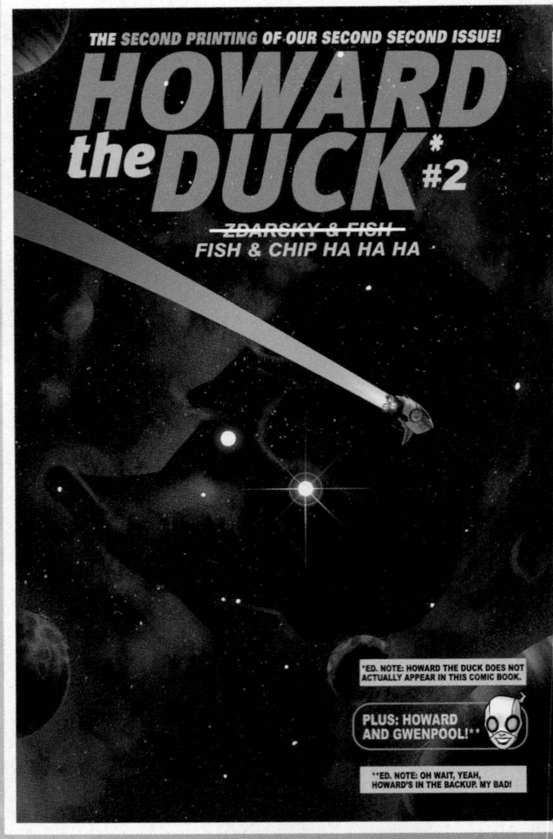
THE SECOND PRINTING OF OUR SECOND SECOND ISSUE!
HOWARD the DUCK* #2
~~ZDARSKY & FISH~~
FISH & CHIP HA HA HA
*ED. NOTE: HOWARD THE DUCK DOES NOT ACTUALLY APPEAR IN THIS COMIC BOOK.
PLUS: HOWARD AND GWENPOOL!**
**ED. NOTE: OH WAIT, YEAH, HOWARD'S IN THE BACKUP. MY BAD!

#2 2ND-PRINTING VARIANT
BY JOE QUINONES

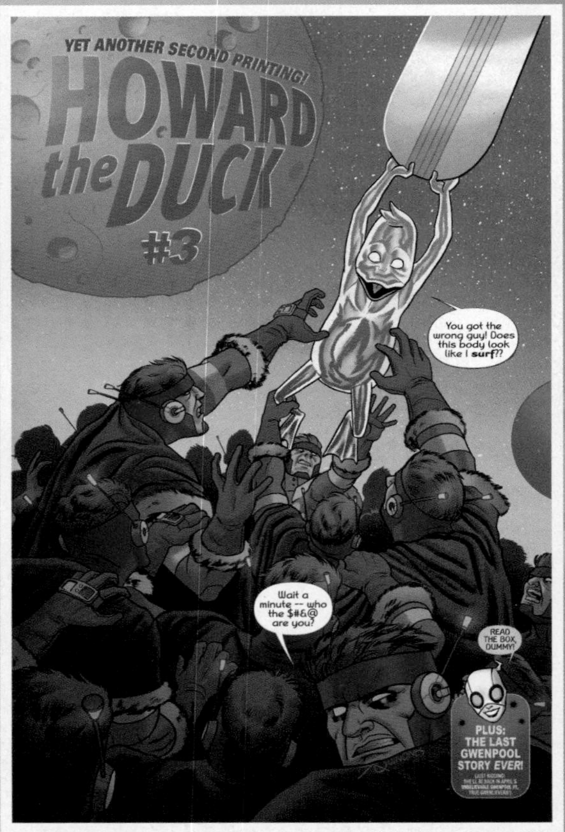
YET ANOTHER SECOND PRINTING!
HOWARD the DUCK #3
You got the wrong guy! Does this body look like I surf??
Wait a minute -- who the $#&@ are you?
READ THE BOX, DUMMY!
PLUS: THE LAST GWENPOOL STORY EVER!

#3 2ND-PRINTING VARIANT
BY JOE QUINONES